Elite Cultures

The anthropological study of elites has gained increasing prominence with the shift of the anthropological gaze toward issues of power, prestige and status in the societies of anthropologists themselves. However, our understanding of elites is often partial, obscured as it is by the theoretical weaknesses of Western models on the one hand and, on the other, by the difficulties in studying elites from the 'inside'. Drawing on a diverse, comparative ethnographic literature, this new volume examines the intimate spaces and cultural practices of those elites who occupy positions of power and authority across a variety of different settings.

Using ethnographic case studies from a wide range of geographical areas, including Mexico, Peru Amazonia, Indonesia, Sri Lanka, Europe, North America and Africa, the contributors explore the inner worlds of meaning and practice that define and sustain elite identities. They also provide insights into the cultural mechanisms that maintain elite status, and into the complex ways that elite groups relate to, and are embedded within, wider social and historical processes. The book addresses a number of fundamental questions about the nature of elites and society such as:

- How do elites in different societies maintain their position of domination?
- How do elites reproduce themselves over time?
- How do elites represent themselves?
- How can we study elites anthropologically?
- What implications does this study have for the discipline of anthropology?

In exemplifying anthropology's contribution to the study of power, this book provides a welcome and timely addition to the literature as well as to current debates about the scope and direction of the discipline itself.

Cris Shore and **Stephen Nugent** are both Readers in Anthropology at Goldsmiths College, University of London. Cris Shore is also Head of the Anthropology Department.

ASA Monographs (Vol no 38)

Elite Cultures

Anthropological perspectives

Edited by Cris Shore and Stephen Nugent

London and New York

First published 2002
by Routledge
11 New Fetter Lane, London EC4P 4EE

Simultaneously published in the USA and Canada
by Routledge
29 West 35th Street, New York, NY 10001

Routledge is an imprint of the Taylor & Francis Group

Typeset in Bembo by Taylor & Francis Books Ltd
Printed and bound in Great Britain by TJ International Ltd,
Padstow, Cornwall

British Library Cataloguing in Publication Data
A catalogue record for this book is available from the
British Library

Library of Congress Cataloging in Publication Data
Elite cultures: anthropological perspectives/edited by Cris Shore
and Stephen Nugent.
p. cm.–(ASA monographs; v. 38)
Includes bibliographical references and index.
1. Elite (Social sciences)–Cross-cultural studies. 2. Power (Social
sciences)–Cross-cultural studies. I. Shore, Cris. II. Nugent, Stephen
(Stephen L.) III. A.S.A. monographs; 38.
GN492.25 .E34 2002
305.5'2–dc21   2001058511

ISBN 0–415–27794–9 (hbk)
ISBN 0–415–27795–7 (pbk)

To the memory of Abner Cohen (1921–2001)

Contents

Plates

Contributors

John Eade is Professor of Sociology and Anthropology at the University of Surrey Roehampton. He has undertaken research on issues of identity and ethnicity first in Calcutta and then, for the last twenty years, in the East End of London. He co-edited, with Michael Sallnow, *Contesting the Sacred: The Anthropology of Christian Pilgrimage* (1991) and his other publications have focussed on the politics of Bangladeshi community representation, the Islamisation of urban space and tourism. He is currently co-editing a volume on urban studies and is a founding editor of *Journeys; The International Journal of Travel and Travel Writing*.

Grant Evans is Reader in Anthropology at the University of Hong Kong. His latest books on Laos are an edited collection, *Laos: Culture and Society* (1999), and a short history, *The Land In-between* (2002). He has also recently co-edited a regional collection, *Where China Meets Southeast Asia: Social and Cultural Change in the Border Regions* (2000).

Sandra J.T.M. Evers is Lecturer in Anthropology at the Free University of Amsterdam. She specialises in Southwest Indian Ocean studies, with a particular focus on Madagascar. Dr Evers's field work and publications examine frontier societies and inequality within the context of globalisation, poverty, urban and rural transformation and sustainable development.

Ronald Frankenberg has carried out research in Wales (1952–6), Zambia (1966–9) and Italy (1972–3). Over the course of a long career, he has had extensive experience of participant observation on elites, not only as Dean of a Medical School in Zambia and chair of an important national committee, but also as mining trade union official in Britain (1956–60). He later made use of all this experience in trying to show similarities in the practices of village, national political, and judicial and commercial elites (1972, 1990) before specialising for more than a decade in Medical Anthropology at Brunel and Keele Universities.

John Gledhill is Max Gluckman Professor of Social Anthropology at the University of Manchester and co-managing editor of *Critique of Anthropology*.

His research covers both indigenous and non-indigenous communities in Mexico, with a focus on social movements, politics, political economy and transnational migration. He is author of *Power and Its Disguises: Anthropological Perspectives on Politics* as well as more specialist monographs and papers.

Keith Hart is a research fellow in the University of Aberdeen's Arkleton Centre and lives in Paris. He has taught in a number of universities on both sides of the Atlantic, especially at Cambridge, where he was the Director of the African Studies Centre. He has carried out research in Ghana, the Caribbean and South Africa and has worked as a journalist, consultant and gambler. Keith Hart is the author of *The Memory Bank: Money in an Unequal World* (2000) and of *The Political Economy of West African Agriculture* (1982); he was co-editor of *C.L.R. James's American Civilization* (1993) and of *Why Angola Matters* (1995).

Penelope Harvey is Professor of Social Anthropology at the University of Manchester. She is author of *Hybrids of Modernity: Anthropology, the Nation State and the Universal Exhibition* (Routledge 1996) and co-edited *Sex and Violence: Issues of Representation and Experience* with Peter Gow (Routledge, 1994). She has just completed a monograph on language and power in the Peruvian Andes entitled *Categorical Disruptions: Being Bilingual in the Margins of the State.*

Monica Konrad is Visiting Fellow at the Institute of Commonwealth Studies, University of London where she has been collecting pre-symptomatic illness narratives as part of a project on genealogical ethics and predictive genetic technologies in the UK. Current research focuses further on comparative medical moralities and global genomics. She is part of an interdisciplinary advisory team developing science-art collaborations for hospital-based visual healthcare and is involved with health architects on spatial innovation for various therapeutic environments.

Stephen Nugent is Reader in Anthropology at Goldsmiths. Among his publications are *Big Mouth: the Amazon Speaks* (1990) and *Amazonian Caboclo Society: an Essay on Invisibility and Peasant Economy* (1993). In 2000 he completed an ethno-documentary film, 'Where's the Rabbi? Jewish Communities in the Lower Amazon'. With John Gledhill he co-edits *Critique of Anthropology.*

Laura Peers is a Canadian-trained historian, anthropologist, and museum curator, interested in First Nations histories and their representation. She is currently Curator of the Pitt Rivers Museum and Lecturer in the School of Anthropology, University of Oxford. Recent publications include 'Playing Ourselves: Native Peoples and Public History Sites', *The Public Historian*, 21(4).

Michael Rowlands is Professor of Anthropology at University College London. He has particular interests in material culture, cultural heritage and long term historical change. His most recent publications have included work on cultural memory and transmission and heritage politics in West Africa.

Cris Shore is Reader in Anthropology and Head of Department at Goldsmiths College, London. His major fieldwork was carried out among Communist Party activists in Italy, and EU Civil Servants in Brussels. His current research focuses on the anthropology of institutions and policies, particularly those of the European Union. Recent publications include *Building Europe: The Cultural Politics of European Integration* (2000), *Anthropology of Policy* (co-edited with Susan Wright, 1997) and *Anthropology and Cultural Studies* (co-edited with Stephen Nugent, 1997).

Jonathan Spencer is Professor of the Anthropology of South Asia at the University of Edinburgh. He is the author of *A Sinhala Village in a Time of Trouble* (2nd edn 2000), and many articles on politics, religion and conflict in Sri Lanka.

Elizabeth Tonkin is Professor Emerita of Social Anthropology at Queen's University, Belfast. She first went to Africa as a teacher in Kenya and later did fieldwork in Liberia. She is author of *Narrating our Pasts* (1992) and co-editor of *History and Ethnicity* (1989) ASA27.

C.W. (Bill) Watson is a lecturer in anthropology at the University of Kent at Canterbury. He has been doing research in Indonesia and Malaysia for over two decades on subjects ranging from modern literature to Muslim politics. His major area of fieldwork is in Kerinci in central Sumatra. He is the author of *Of Self and Nation: Autobiography and the Representation of Modern Indonesia* (2000) and *Multiculturalism* (2000).

Chapter 1

Introduction

Towards an anthropology of elites

Cris Shore

Studying elites in an anthropological context

What makes an elite? How do elites in different societies maintain their position of dominance over subaltern groups? What legitimates the power and leadership of elites and how do they reproduce themselves over time? What can anthropology contribute to our understanding of elite formation and the politics of elite cultures and what can the study of elites offer anthropology? These are just some of the questions explored in this volume.[1] As the contributors suggest, the study of elites poses particular theoretical and methodological challenges for anthropology, a discipline that has long been concerned with issues of epistemology, reflexivity, representation and power.

The very idea of an 'anthropology of elites' might strike some as problematic and somewhat ironic. After all, what could be more elitist than anthropology itself, a profession steeped in the traditions and practices of Western middle-class academics, most of whom possess doctorates from the most exclusive universities, and whose scholarly output is aimed primarily for consumption by other Western, middle-class intellectuals? Indeed, the history of anthropology is the history of an intellectual elite, which, as historians of the discipline have shown, has developed its own particular discourses, rituals and exclusionary practices (Kuper 1996; Stocking 1992; Spencer 2000). Anthropology's elitism was manifest historically in its almost exclusive interest in exotic 'others' and its comparative neglect of social institutions and political processes in its 'own' societies.[2] Some critics argue that anthropology's unconscious elitism was also embedded in its traditional paradigm of 'scientific ethnography' – a paradigm that objectified its subjects while failing to acknowledge the discipline's own affinities with political hierarchy and European colonial rule (Grimshaw and Hart 1995: 46–7; cf. Asad 1973).

In one sense, therefore, exploring the behaviour and everyday practices of the rich and powerful rather than just those of the poor and powerless – or 'studying up' to use Laura Nader's (1972) expression – may offer an important counterweight to the elitism of anthropology itself, although it does not resolve the deeper epistemological problems that such 'Them/Us' or 'up/down' dualisms create in the first place (Herzfeld 2000). Nonetheless, an anthropology of elites is necessarily an exercise in political reflexivity since it obliges us to position ourselves more self-consciously in relation to the wider systems of power and hierarchy within which anthropological knowledge is constructed. It is encouraging in this context to observe the attention now being given to the anthropological study of the institutional contexts in which anthropology as a profession is embedded (Pels 1999; Spencer 2000; Strathern 2000). An anthropology of elites in this sense represents a further, albeit more politicised, extension of the idea of 'anthropology at home' (Jackson 1987).

If anthropologists constitute an intellectual elite, however, they represent only one kind of professional elite among many, and their status and influence is small beer compared to that of the more traditional 'strategic occupations' (or professional gatekeepers) such as lawyers, doctors, politicians, senior civil servants and company executives. Virtually every society has its privileged minorities: those who, for reasons of history, social status, economic position, political office or family connections, are the *de facto* power holders whose interests and normative values set the agenda and define the 'natural order of things'. 'The ideas of the ruling classes' wrote Marx and Engels over 150 years ago, 'are, in every epoch, the ruling ideas':[3] i.e., the class which is the dominant material force in society is at the same time its dominant *intellectual* force.

The ways in which elites attempt to maintain their hegemony in periods of rapid social and economic change are explored by several contributors to this volume (see Rowlands, Evans, Gledhill). However, whether the dominant elites in society constitute a plurality of competing interest groups, a single 'ruling class' or an example of what C. Wright Mills (1956) called '*the power elite*' continue to be questions of heated contention among social scientists.[4] A more interesting question perhaps, or at least a less abstract one, is how do elites maintain their authority and elite status? Here the question of 'legitimacy' and its cultural foundations is of paramount importance. In his pioneering book *The Politics of Elite Culture* Abner Cohen (1981) highlights a central problem faced by all dominant elites; namely, the need to reconcile the tension between 'universalism' and 'particularism'. To gain the support of subordinated groups, an elite must convince the masses that its sectional interests represent the wider public or national interest; i.e. it must seek to demonstrate its 'universalistic functions' of service to the public. As Cohen argues, rulers typically do this through the cultivation of mystique, dramatic performance, rhetorical strategies, or a combination of all three. The centrality of symbolism and power in the anthropological analysis of elites, what Kertzer (1988: 77) termed the 'ritual construction of political reality', is a theme vividly illustrated by Evers and Evans (Chapters 10 and 12 in this volume). However, in order to constitute itself as an elite in the first place an elite group must develop its own particularistic set of interests, norms and practices to differentiate itself from the masses. It must achieve 'distinction' in Bourdieu's (1986) sense. Exactly how they do this – the cultural resources they mobilise and the way they cultivate functions that are simultaneously both 'universalistic' and 'particularistic' – are central issues for anthropology.

To study elites anthropologically we must also consider the discursive frameworks in which elites are conceptualised and constituted in different cultural contexts. In virtually every society the power and legitimacy of elite domination are subjects of public interest and debate. For example, in the United States this often hinges around the question 'who rules America' and in critiques of its financial corporations (Domhoff 1967, 1979). Recent mass protests outside the World Trade Organisation talks in Seattle and Prague represent another kind of commentary on the influence of financial elites over the global economy. As Monbiot (2000) argues, the elites of financial corporations now exercise an unprecedented degree of direct control over many of those functions that were once considered strategic domains of states, from public transport systems, gas, water and electricity supplies, to universities, hospitals and prisons.

In much of the so-called 'developing world' the debate centres on problems of succession and the institutionalisation of those nationalist elites that led their countries to independence from colonialism. In Britain the issue often crystallises in debates about the monarchy, the private school system, the recruitment practices of universities like Oxford and Cambridge and the hidden influence of that entity which unites all of these areas, 'the British Establishment' (Sampson 1965; Nairn 1988; Paxman 1999). The very notion of 'the Establishment', the boundaries and membership of which are ambiguous and open to interpretation, highlights a key issue in the study of elites; how do we identify elites that do not recognise themselves as such? As Marcus reminds us (1983a: 9), in social science and casual lay usage 'elite is a term of reference, rather than self-reference'. Moreover, 'elitist' is also a term of abuse in many contexts. Is it enough, therefore, that we treat the concept of 'elite' as an observers' category rather than a self-description? And if so, what can such a conception tell us about the subjective aspects of elite cultures? From an anthropological perspective part of the measure of what makes an elite is not only possession of the trappings of power or reproduction over time, but the degree of self-recognition and consciousness of kind that exists among its members. In order to constitute themselves as a group rather than just a category, an elite must develop a common culture that is recognisable to its members. To become visible to itself, as Meisel put it, a new elite must 'develop three C's: consciousness, cohesion and conspiracy'.[5] Understanding how that consciousness is created and maintained lies at the heart of the project for an anthropology of elites.

To answer the question *what makes an elite?* we must first be clear about the definition and meanings commonly associated with this concept. For some anthropologists, the term 'elite' (like that of 'interest group', 'faction' and 'social network') is so protean and porous that it is almost devoid of meaning. The difficulty of defining who constitutes the elite and what powers they exercise in periods of social unrest is highlighted in this volume by Spencer's study of rural Sri Lanka and Watson's account of elite formation in Indonesia. Rather than using these concepts as fixed or tangible social science categories, Watson suggests we should treat them as heuristic devices, and with caution – using qualifying adjectives such as 'business', 'military', 'governing', 'modernising', 'religious', 'academic', or 'bureaucratic' to distinguish between the different varieties of elite. On the other hand, however, the word 'elite' is a cultural idiom and conceptual category that does render possible some sort of cross-cultural comparison and historical parallels that transcend culturally specific practices. To echo Marcus (1983a: 9), 'the concept suggests that the organization of these powerful groups can be mapped and described'. As a working definition, elites can be characterised as those who occupy the most influential positions or roles in the important spheres of social life. They are typically incumbents: the leaders, rulers and decision makers in any sector of society, or custodians of the machinery of policy making. Elites are thus 'makers and shakers': groups whose 'cultural capital' positions them above their fellow citizens and whose decisions crucially shape what happens in the wider society. Equally important, they are the groups that dominate what Elias (1978) called the 'means of orientation': people whose ideas and interests are hegemonic.

The very idea of 'elites' suggests qualities of 'agency', 'exclusivity', 'power' and an apparent separation from 'mass society'[6] – concepts that, in different ways, oblige us to consider related themes of stratification, hierarchy, brokers and causal agents behind events. Elites thus 'represent a way of conceiving power in society and attributing responsibility to persons rather than to impersonal processes' (Marcus 1983a: 10).

What then is the scope of an 'anthropology of elites' and how might the study of elites further anthropology's power of analysis – and, conversely its analysis of power? The case studies of elite cultures presented in this volume address these questions in a number of ways, drawing on examples from as far apart as Madagascar to Mexico via West Africa, Sri Lanka, Indonesia, Brazil, North America and Britain. Before turning to consider these, let me reflect briefly on insights gained from my own anthropological studies of elites.

Encountering elites ethnographically: from Euro-Communists to the European Commission

The idea for this volume began life a number of years ago with a deceptively simple set of questions concerning the operation of power within modern political systems. In the early 1980s I was carrying out ethnographic research on the Italian Communist Party (PCI), at that time the largest communist party in the Western world and arguably the most sophisticated in its development of Marxist theory. Studying such an organisation necessarily entailed delving into political theory, particularly that of Marx, Lenin and Gramsci, to whom the people I was studying claimed a special kind of intellectual kinship and historical affinity (Shore 1990, 1993). However, it also led me to read the work of many critics of communism, particularly those like Rosa Luxembourg (1961), Robert Michels (1959) and Milovan Djilas (1957) who highlighted the apparent oligarchical tendencies inherent in the Leninist party model. My own analysis, based on close observations of relations within the party apparatus, seemed to confirm their pessimism. They argued that 'democratic centralism', the organising principle that structures relations of authority within all communist parties, engenders not simply elitism, but authoritarianism and abuses of power. In short, Lenin's 'organisational weapon' designed to overthrow the tyranny of capitalism contained the blueprint for the tyranny of Stalinism. While this argument has been frequently extended by liberal critics to include all parties of the 'authoritarian left', few have commented on the fact that most private sector companies and government bodies are organised on similarly oligarchic and authoritarian bases. Authoritarianism in the business world, it seems, is a normative practice accepted without much criticism or comment. If corporations provide a model of good government, as some argue, then the study of corporate cultures offers an important context for examining changing ideas and practices of governance in general.

As with most anthropologists, my aim was to go beyond the abstract and deductive models of social science in order to understand the way social reality is constructed by the actors themselves; to grasp *their* conception of the world and the way they related to it as self-conscious agents. For Italian communists the problem was how to mobilise popular support against the ruling Christian Democrat elite that had dominated Italian politics and society since 1947. If understanding the process by which a corrupt and dynastic political class had established its hegemony over Italian society posed one set of questions for anthropology, so did explaining the extraordinary success of the PCI in creating a communist counter-culture in the 'Red Belt' regions of Central Italy. Was this self-styled 'mass Marxist party' an example of the 'revolt of the masses' as Ortega y Gasset had long predicted: evidence of the imminent decline of civilisation? Or was it yet another illustration of the very opposite: 'the revolt of the elites', as Christopher Lasch (1995) puts it? Italy is often characterised as a *partitocrazia*, a society colonised by its political elites through their party machines. The key question is what gives these parties their legitimacy? What is the relationship between the party elites and their membership, and to what extent did elites and masses share the same moral universe?

Tackling these questions necessarily entailed tracking the way events, persons and ideas interact with each other at various levels of analysis, local, regional, national and global. Popular communist culture included the party's extensive network of affiliated bodies and satellite organisations from women and pensioners' groups and youth organisations, to party-run bars, recreational centres and popular festivals, an organisational presence that extended into virtually all aspects of civil society and rivalled that of the Catholic Church. Being a 'mass party' (not simply a party *of* the masses) was, I learned, central to the identity and self-mage of Italian communists. This represented a major departure from the explicit elitism of the classical Leninist vanguard party model. However, I also became aware that a cultural gulf existed between the party elites – the permanent officials and 'Nomenklatura' – and the masses in whose name the leadership derived its legitimacy. Here was a party that espoused the language and symbolism of revolution while championing constitutionalism and the rule of law; whose mass membership were over-whelmingly working class and Marxist (often Stalinist), but whose leaders were increasingly liberal, revisionist and middle-class the higher up the party hierarchy one looked. The PCI was simultaneously a vindication and limiting instance of the pessimistic predictions of Michels and Djilas concerning the iron law of oligarchy and the emergence of the New Class. Was this revi-sionism by an enlightened bourgeois intelligentsia the reason for the party's success compared with other communist parties?

Reflecting on these paradoxes prompted me to rethink some of the assumptions of my own discipline, particularly the idea that fine-grained ethnographies of small peripheral communities necessarily provide a tool for probing larger-scale macro processes operating beyond the community. It goes without saying that the global and the local are closely connected and that often, therefore, the best way to analyse macro-level processes at the 'core' is to explore the way those processes manifest themselves at micro or local level. However, when studying elites we should be cautious about generalising from the micro to the macro. What happens at the local level is not a microcosm of, or synecdoche for, processes and formations occurring at the national or global levels. Even within a shared social system or political culture, elites and masses occupy a very different habitus. In short – and always bearing in mind the importance of context – the proper study of elite cultures is the habitus, networks and culture of elites themselves, including their informal and everyday practices and intimate spaces (Herzfeld 2000).

Ten years later the focus of my research shifted to Brussels and the ethnog-raphy of another political elite, the civil service of the European Commission, the European Union's executive body. Again, the research questions were deceptively simple. Given that so much power and decision making had passed from national capitals to the institutions of the European Community, it seemed appropriate to ask 'who *are* these officials and politicians at the "heart of the Union"' and, to paraphrase Geertz, 'what the devil do they think they are up to?' Besides the anthropological work of Handelman (1990) and Herzfeld (1992) on modern bureaucracy and its mystifications, my approach to studying this emerging technocratic elite was also influenced by Tony Benn, a veteran Labour politician and EU critic. Benn proposes 'five questions that one should habitually ask on meeting someone in power: What power have you got? Where did you get it from? In whose interests do you exercise it? To whom are you accountable? How do we get rid of you?'[7] These seemingly naïve questions provide an excellent starting point for probing the conditions of existence that give legitimacy to arguably any elite.

From this study two observations were particularly significant for an anthropology of elites. The first concerned identity formation and the processes by which a distinctive group consciousness and cohesion may develop, or fail to develop, among new elites. The research found clear evidence that a new kind of 'European consciousness' was developing, particularly among expatriate staff and politicians working within the EU's bureaucratic institutions. This raised another important issue about the extent to which bureaucracies may become repositories of meaning and identity for those who inhabit them, as Anderson (1983) illustrates in the case of the emerging post-colonial nations of Latin America. In this case, the EU's insti-

Figure 1.1   Heads of Government meeting as the European Council at Fontainebleau in June 1984, where the decision was taken to give an official boost to the concept of a 'People's Europe'. The Council agreed to set up a committee to examine ways to popularise the European Community and to promote the idea of European identity through targeted action in the cultural sector. Photo: European Council.

tutions had become crucibles for the construction of a new type of European subject: a transnational technocratic elite with its own norms, ethos and identity. From an anthropological perspective a process of identity formation or, *pace* Grillo (1980), 'ethnicisation' seemed to be occurring among these deterritorialised national officials and politicians who had gone to serve the European Union in Brussels. They were being transformed – or *transforming themselves*, depending on one's interpretation – into a unified 'supranational' elite with its own peculiar cultural practices, lifestyle and class interests. Consciousness, cohesion and conspiracy were all conspicuously present. This introduced a new dimension into the debate about the dynamics of European integration. The conflict between rival visions of Europe (notably 'supranationalism' and 'intergovernmentalism') that has preoccupied political scientists and EU scholars for the past four decades appears to be, at root, a struggle between old national elites and a new European transnational elite (Dewatripont *et al.* 1994: 41). Whether this EU elite will evolve into something resembling a 'New Class' or 'Nomenklatura', as the privileges gained by European civil servants and politicians are passed on to their children, remains to be seen.

My second observation concerned the relationship between theories of cognition and European integration. As predicted, there had been a marked shift of loyalties among staff in the European Commission; a transfer of allegiance from their countries of origin towards the EU and its institutions (the folk idiom for this process was *engrenage*). What was being witnessed here was a striking example of the way elite theory may itself function as an 'agent of consciousness' and vehicle for promoting elite ideology. In this case, 'integration theory', as developed by academics, was being used by EU officials to legitimise and inculcate the idea that the European Commission was the embryo of a future 'government of Europe'. In Stephen George's words (1985: 23):

> Encouraged by its success, the Commission appears to have come to believe the predictions of the neofunctionalist theory, that it was inevitable and that eventually unity would be achieved in its corner of Europe, and that it would emerge as the future government of this new supranational state.

Critics of classical elite theory have often observed that discourses about the 'inevitability' of, and 'necessity' for, elite rule are themselves part of the technologies used to naturalise and perpetuate elite domination. What was equally apparent from my study of the Commission, however, was the fundamental *lack* of legitimacy that has continued to undermine the EU's project for integration. EU institutions often proclaim themselves to be defenders of the 'European interest', but to follow Benn's analysis, they are accountable to no one and the peoples of Europe have no effective power to remove them from office. These two criticisms were highlighted in the Committee of Independent Experts' Report on fraud, mismanagement and corruption in the Commission – which precipitated the mass resignation of the Santer Commission in March 1999.

The EU's crisis of legitimacy (and 'democratic deficit'), I concluded, stems from a cultural deficit expressed most visibly in the absence of a self-identifying European people: a *demos* to lend credibility to the political system of the EU and its institutions. Elites by definition form parts of wider encompassing cultures. Like governments and bureaucracies, they require a general public to affirm their position of superiority; a mass citizenry that belongs to the same culture or imagined community – a community, moreover, that elites help to define. 'Elites command respect. When they lose it, they are no longer elites' (Herzfeld 2000: 233). Similarly, without what Gellner (1983) called the 'cultural branding of its flock', a political elite cannot acquire that respect in the first place, which makes its position extremely unstable. This explains the shift in thinking among EU strategists since the 1980s. No longer are they just focusing their attention on the creation of a supranational elite whose new 'European identity' will 'trickle down' to the general populace. Increasing emphasis is now placed on cultural actions to promote feelings of solidarity and belonging among the peoples of Europe. Europe's new technocratic elite appears to be following the all too familiar techniques of nation-building; its goal is to create a 'People's Europe' by inventing a 'European public' and engendering a sense of shared European citizenship and identity.

Why an anthropology of elites?

If the two case studies cited above indicate some of the issues and challenges for anthropology posed by the attempt to study elites 'from within', they also highlight the importance of studying elites in their wider social and historical contexts. When the proposal for a conference on 'elite cultures' was put to the 1997 annual meeting of the Association of Social Anthropologists it was enthusiastically supported, not only because the subject of elites is important *per se*, but also as a corrective to anthropology's seeming preoccupation with literary criticism, textual analysis, deconstruction and symbolism. One of the merits of a focus on elites is that it compels us to address wider issues of economics, politics and social change – themes eclipsed by agendas of post-modernism since the 1980s – thereby restoring a more sociological and historical perspective to anthropological analysis.[8]

The study of elites provides a useful focus for addressing a range of core anthropological and sociological concerns including language and power; leadership and authority; status and hierarchy; ideology and consciousness; social identities and boundary-maintenance; power relations, social structure and social change. This latter point is vividly illustrated by Raymond Williams. In his seminal book *Keywords* (1976: 112–15) Williams makes the important observation that shifts in the meaning and uses of the term 'elite' can be directly related to major social and historical changes and, specifically, to the transformation of the *ancien régime* social orders of Europe into the mass societies and nation-states of nineteenth-century bourgeois modernity. Prior to the eighteenth century, the term 'elite' was used in a more restricted sense to refer to the 'elect' (in the theological sense), meaning those formally selected or 'specially chosen' by God, or simply 'the most preferred and eminent persons' (Williams 1976: 112–13). After the eighteenth century, however, the word 'elite' began to be used more generally to express social distinction by rank, where it often became synonymous with 'best' and linked to feudal ideas of nobility and rank. Related to this were the ideas of 'quality', 'distinction' and 'choice', notions that were applied to things as well as persons. In the nineteenth century, the decline and disappearance of the feudal distinctions of rank and the emergence of new ways of appointing leaders based not on principles of heredity gave rise to the modern uses of the word, which were related to conscious arguments about class and power. The modern concept of 'elite' thus also carries the indelible stamp of nineteenth and twentieth-century social theorists, particularly their ideas about class and mass society. The point to stress here, as far as mapping the scope of an anthropology of elites is concerned, is simply that shifts in the social meanings and uses of the word 'elite' are themselves valuable sites for exploring important social and historical processes. This is a theme taken up by Keith Hart (Chapter 2 in this volume), who argues that the new world order today is closer to the *ancien régime* of pre-Revolutionary France than we might imagine.

A further merit of an anthropological focus on elites is that it opens up for debate an area which, with few notable exceptions, has been poorly researched within anthropology. While elites have been central concerns of sociologists, historians and political scientists for much of the past two centuries, anthropologists have paid relatively little attention to them and still less to the theoretical debates they have generated concerning power, the nature of class society, and modern forms of governance. This is not to say that anthropological research on topics such as 'political organisation', 'oratory and power', 'social stratification', 'ritual and leadership', 'networks' or 'kinship and ethnicity' has not provided valuable insights into the way some dominant minorities operate and their relationship to the cultures of which they form a part. However, despite the pioneering work of Cohen (1981) and Marcus (1983) and more recently Pina-Cabral and Pedrosa de Lima (2000) there have been few serious attempts to study elites ethnographically or to explore the politics of elite culture *per se*, particularly in 'Euro-American' societies.[9]

One reason for this is because anthropology's traditional research method of participant observation, personal involvement and long-term fieldwork does not lend itself easily to the task of analysing elites, most of which are, almost by definition, opaque or shielded from scrutiny by outsiders. One cannot simply pitch one's tent in the board room of the World Bank or the Pentagon, or unobtrusively observe the bargains being struck at a European Council of Ministers' meeting. The physics of presence – or as Gupta (1995:

376) puts it, the 'ontological imperative' of 'being there' – imposes a major obstacle to the project of studying up. Anthropology's commitment to the principle of consent adds further constraints. What if the elites we wish to study refuse to grant permission? Should the scope of anthropological enquiry be confined only to those groups that allow us access? And if so, under what terms and conditions? Despite some notable exceptions, most military, economic and political elites are unlikely to permit open and uncensored access to their internal organisation.[10] Indeed, the degree of control a group has over the way it is represented is part of the measure of elite power.

The study of elites thus presents us with some uncomfortable ethical issues. How far should the fact that they are likely to read what we write about them temper our analysis? Increasingly, it seems, anthropologists are being granted licence to study powerful national and transnational organisations (including the World Bank, the IMF, the BBC and the European Commission) but only on condition that the organisation retains a veto on what can be published. Under these conditions, the pressure to produce anthropological accounts that are not disagreeable to our interlocutors and funders becomes formidable. But if the price of access is *de facto* censorship (even of the self-imposed variety), what happens to the principle of academic autonomy and intellectual freedom?

The professional codes of ethics that govern anthropological research in Britain, the USA and elsewhere have traditionally stressed that anthropologists' 'paramount obligation is to their research participants' and that, where there is conflict, 'the interests and rights of those studied should come first' (ASA Code of Ethics 1999: 2).[11] This argument rests on two assumptions that have become increasingly problematic. First, that our research participants can be constituted as a unified body with a shared set of interests, and second, that anthropology, by definition, is the study of powerless 'Others'. What are the implications for anthropology, as Konrad asks (Chapter 14 in this volume), if the research participants are more powerful than the researchers? What happens when the research focus shifts from the traditional micro-level study of 'a people', to the study of the policies and practices of our own governments or corporate elites – those whose decisions shape the conditions of existence at local level?[12] What if our expanded definition of 'the field' includes the ethically ambiguous or corrupt practices of multinational companies or the activities of neo-fascists and racists (Holmes 2000)? Whose interests become 'paramount' in these instances? An anthropology of elites challenges both our assumptions about what constitutes the 'field' as well as some of our most deeply held notions about research ethics.

A further reason for the dearth of ethnographic studies of elites in Western societies is because in these societies such elites are often not recognised as part of the formal social structure. That is, they may constitute a *category* of persons, but not necessarily a group. Hence the importance of studying the informal dimensions of elite organisation, including patterns of friendship, kinship, ritual and symbolic behaviour. By examining elites ethnographically –

by 'probing their intimate spaces rather than relying on their formal self-presentations' as Herzfeld puts it (2000: 227) – we may offer up insights that challenge received wisdom about what constitutes an elite and how elites reproduce themselves.

For all its promise and potential, then, anthropology has made little impact when it comes to probing those intimate spaces of the modern state, bureaucracy or corporate power that play such an influential role in shaping contemporary Euro-American society. The anthropology of elites has been confined primarily to studies of other peoples' rulers and to familiar (and therefore relatively 'safe') themes such as leadership, castes, kingdoms, 'Big Men' and informal mechanisms of social control – yet even here the ethnographic picture is partial. The dynamics of elite culture remain something of a mystery. This represents a considerable shortcoming for a discipline that claims to study all of humankind. Despite this there is a growing recognition within the discipline that, to recapture its authority (Fox 1991), and relevance (Ahmed and Shore 1994), anthropology must focus its analysis more squarely on those institutions and agents of policy and decision making that operate beyond the locality as well as upon it. As Donnan and MacFarlane (1989: 6) put it, anthropology's remit also includes 'analysing the cultures of the policy professional [and] penetrating and uncovering the perceptions of those who seek to make their definitions of the world and its problems stick'. The work of Dell Hymes, Laura Nader and Kathlyn Gough in the 1970s – with its explicit focus on multinational corporations and 'hidden hierarchies' of power – began to do this. However, the theoretical and methodological issues raised by this call to 'study up' remain largely unexplored territory as far as anthropology is concerned. Once again anthropology would seem to be in danger of passing the buck, or so it might be argued, to sociology and cultural studies and other ostensibly more 'political' disciplines.

Studying elites: questions of method

If the argument *for* an anthropology of elites is relatively straightforward, *how* to study elites anthropologically is far more problematic. There is no simple solution to the methodological and ethical dilemmas discussed above. Moreover, the term 'anthropological fieldwork', as anyone who has been initiated into this peculiar anthropological rite of passage knows only too well, is a gloss that covers a promiscuous array of different research strategies, mostly qualitative, often anecdotal and invariably personal and subjective. That said, however, the contributors to this book provide at least four distinct answers to this question.

The first is that elites can only be meaningfully understood in their wider historical context; that is, as fluid and temporal entities whose powers and status rise and fall over time and in relation to broader economic and social changes. The extent to which local or regional elites are in fact 'epiphenomena' or by-products of processes determined elsewhere is also significant.

As Nugent remarks of the way local patterns of elite formation have been formed historically by national and supra-national financial interests seeking to exploit its resources, 'if one is looking for Amazonian elites, one could do worse than look *outside* Amazonia' (my emphasis). Nowhere is the union of history and anthropology – or anthropology and political economy – more necessary or more instructive. In short, elites must be viewed from a diachronic perspective and – like the concept of 'cultures' – as dynamic processes rather than static or bounded entities. The waxing and waning of national elites against the currents of historical change is a theme analysed in detail by Gledhill, Harvey, Watson, Nugent, Spencer and Tonkin, all of whom are concerned with developing Third World societies with long traditions of domination by colonial elites.

However, useful as such perspectives may be, historical and political economy approaches by themselves provide only half the picture and reveal little about what is at stake in local politics or what happens on the ground. Understanding the external conditions and interests that promote and sustain local or national elites must also be matched with an analysis of the norms, values and shared interests that characterise or unite such elites – hence the focus of this book on elite *cultures*.

A third answer to the question of how we might study elites anthropologically is by analysing their recruitment and the strategies they use to reproduce themselves over time. Here the concepts of *succession* and *reproduction* (both in the cultural and biological sense) are of paramount importance. Studying how elites ensure their survival requires close attention to their kinship structures and networks, as well as to the institutions for their selection and socialisation, which, as Tonkin and Eade demonstrate (Chapters 8 and 13, this volume), means a focus on schooling and the structures of elite education.

The fourth approach anthropologists might adopt is to analyse the language and practices through which elites represent themselves and the techniques they use to legitimise their position. One of the major ways in which elites maintain power and authority over the present is by 'monumentalising the past' (Herzfeld 2000: 234). 'Nationalism,' says Herzfeld (2000: 234), 'is in this sense a mass popularisation of elite tactics'. As Rowlands and Peers illustrate, heritage sites are fundamental (albeit contested) resources for both established and emerging national elites. Monuments (which include everything from statues and cenotaphs to museums, mausoleums and the Millennium Dome) not only venerate and commemorate the rulers and 'great men' of our age, they actively construct those histories by which people come to identify themselves. In this sense, they too become powerful technologies for shaping subjectivities and influencing how societies remember (Connerton 1989) – or the obverse; how they choose to forget (Forty and Kuchler 1999). From Gothic cathedrals and skyscrapers to ancestral tombs in Madagascar (Evers, Chapter 10 in this volume), and the infamous 'opera house in the jungle' (Nugent, Chapter 4 in this volume), monuments enshrine the status and authority of those who finance and commission them.[13] The invention of tradition and the appropriation of heritage are also themes germane to the study of elites and power.[14] As Evans's analysis of communism in Laos shows, the hegemony of ruling elites often rests on their ability to appropriate or mobilise those rituals and discourses that customarily symbolise legitimate authority. The tropes of kinship, inheritance and 'shared substance' have a special potency as a basis of community and solidarity among nationals. As Alonso (1994: 385) notes, 'so too does the substantialization of the state as a supersubject, and *paterfamilias*, an effect of power that Trouillot argues is key for moral regulation'. Citing Trouillot's work on Haiti, she observes that 'not only is this the dominant model of the state in Haiti, but it is "preferred by elites the world over because it gives them a choice role"'. Not surprisingly, perhaps, many of the ruling elites that feature in this volume represent themselves as 'fathers' and 'sons' of the nation, conceived as the political and moral community.

Scope of this volume

The aim of this book is not to rehearse familiar debates in sociology or political science regarding elites and society or elite theory; these issues have been extensively covered elsewhere by those disciplines. Rather, its objective is to explore, through ethnographic case studies, how anthropology might contribute to understanding the way elites operate: that is, the inner worlds of meaning and practice that define and sustain elite identities, the cultural mechanisms used to maintain their status, and the way elites relate to, and are embedded within, wider socio-economic and political processes.

In Chapter 2, Keith Hart uses his personal journey as a participant in the international development elite circles in the 1970s to reflect on the conditions of modern-day capitalism. Despite two centuries of globalisation he finds that an elite/mass dualism still provides a useful model for describing the political economy of contemporary world society. The legacy of the 'democratic revolutions' of the seventeenth and eighteenth centuries, he contends, is a world society divided into national fragments and as polarised and elitist as the pre-1789 *ancien régime* of France. The new world order – dominated by state capitalism – has restored the rule of elites at a global level. He concludes with a call for anthropologists to devote more energy to revealing and unpacking the structures of global inequality.

The remaining chapters are loosely divided into three thematic sections, the first, 'Elites, Politics and Peripheries', exploring elite politics in emerging, postcolonial societies. John Gledhill (Chapter 3) examines the striking historical endurance of Mexico's ruling Institutionalised Revolutionary Party or 'PRI', and the wealthy elite families allied to it. The apparent diversity of elite structures in Mexico, he argues, serves to disguise a chain of complicities and patron–client relations that have stifled movements for political and social reform. However, under the new regime of neoliberalism, the dignified masks of respectability that once lent authority to Mexico's rulers have slipped. The opportunities for amassing private fortunes have brought private sector entrepreneurs out of the shadows of the public imaginary and, following several high profile corruption scandals, into the foreground of public consciousness. Despite this – and the growing success of popular-based reformist coalitions – Mexico's financial and political elites remain firmly entrenched.

Chapter 4, by Stephen Nugent, examines the ephemeral and episodic nature of elite formation in Amazonia since the nineteenth century, a region that has witnessed a succession of different elites (colonial, church, military, industrial, commercial and scientific), each of which owes its rise to the exploitation of Amazonia's rich natural resources. Amazonian elites in the past were by-products of colonialism and national integration projects. Today instead they are closely linked to the global environmentalist agendas of the World Bank, USAID, scientists, NGOs and other experts. Ecologically informed reasoning and the imperatives of scientific, global management thus provide the conditions of existence for Amazonia's latest modernising elite. The chapter concludes by discussing the limitations of anthropology's traditional methods for understanding the way transnational connections impact upon local processes.

Chapter 5, by Penny Harvey, continues the debate about 'locating' elites in contexts where power is exercised through deterritorialised networks that are far less 'grounded' than our ethnographic fieldwork might imply. In this case, elites can be thought of 'as those who are *best able to avoid the constraints of location*' (my emphasis). The subjects of her study, the mestizo traders (or '*mistis*') of the Southern Peruvian Andes, derive their elite status both from their domination of local state institutions and their wider commercial links. They effectively straddle two worlds; politically and economically dominant in their rural heartland, yet socially marginal in the wider society beyond, where their racial classification as 'hybrids' (and therefore neither white nor indigenous) effectively excludes them from the national imaginary. However, *misti* families have learned to exploit their marginality as a way to consolidate local power and side-step control from the outside. The result is a Janus-like existence in which *misti* families must simultaneously demonstrate their attachment to 'traditional' practices (like speaking Quechua – but mainly in the intimacy of the home), while surrounding themselves externally with the symbols of 'modernisation', as if to mitigate the effects of their rural attachments.

Chapters 6 and 7, by Jonathan Spencer and C.W. Watson, also deal with rural elites in the peripheries of post-colonial societies, this time in the context of nationalism and social unrest. Spencer examines the rise of Sinhala Buddhist nationalism in Sri Lanka in the period after the landmark election of 1956, which heralded the demise of the old Western-educated Anglophone elite. However, contrary to received wisdom, Spencer highlights major continuities in personnel between 'old' and 'new' elites. While nationalism provided the new middle-class intelligentsia with a language for inviting the masses into history, as Nairn (1981) put it, some of the old elite also appealed to nationalist ideology in the cynical pursuit of their own limited political goals. However, nationalism once unleashed cannot be easily controlled and since the 1970s has fuelled successive waves of traumatic anti-state and anti-elite violence. Nationalism and violence are also central themes in Watson's study of elites and politics in Indonesia since the fall of Sukarno and the ascendancy to power of Suharto in 1966. Like Spencer, he uses ethnographic case studies to explore the linkages between centre and periphery, tracking the way individuals and families have moved from one sub-category of elite (military, administrative, party-based) to another (professional, university-educated, middle-class, business, religious). The ousting of President Suharto was achieved by an extraordinary alliance among elite sub-groups, but that unity was hard to sustain, and the structures that Suharto put in place are difficult to dismantle. Suharto's legacy is also witnessed in the distrust and scepticism that pervades political debates at all levels of Indonesian society. The unrest currently sweeping through Indonesia at a regional level thus represents a further realignment of alliances as the new political elites struggle to keep Indonesia together.

Part II, 'Elites, Hegemony and Tradition', explores *inter alia* the various strategies and tactics that political and cultural elites use to maintain their elite status and authority. Central to this is the way elites mobilise history, tradition and 'heritage' to shroud themselves with the veil of legitimacy and to define the social and political boundaries of inclusion and exclusion. Elizabeth Tonkin (Chapter 8) looks at the way incomers and immigrants in two different 'settler' societies in Kenya and Liberia adapted to their new environments. Her comparative analysis shows that the same ideologies, constraints and preoccupations with boundedness seem to operate in both white and non-white, non-colonial contexts – thus challenging many of the assumptions about the 'tensions of empire' implicit in recent post-colonial studies.

Chapter 9, by Michael Rowlands, also uses ethnographic comparisons from two societies to analyse the way political elites reproduce themselves. In this case, the focus is on the tactics used by governing elites in Mali and Cameroon to forge a sense of community and national identity among citizens. Central to these nation-building projects, as in much of Europe, have been the manipulation of history by intellectuals and the mobilisation of discourses on 'heritage' in the construction of an imagined community of nationals. While this approach has been used quite successfully in Mali, in Cameroon the state elite appears to have less of a 'nationalising ambition', preferring instead to engage in the more traditional politics of 'divide and rule'.

The political uses of discourses about origins are further explored in Chapter 10 by Sandra Evers who analyses the way the ruling Betsileo elite (the self-styled 'masters of the land'), in the Southern Highlands of Madagascar maintain their hegemony through the imprimatur of ancient custom and history. As Evers shows, the Betsileo are themselves recent immigrants to the territory they occupy. However, the key resource that confers legitimacy upon them is their ownership of ancestral tombs. By successfully portraying the status quo as a stable and timeless order – sanctioned by the authority of the ancestors – their elite status is confirmed and accepted, albeit grudgingly.

Chapter 11, by Laura Peers, concludes the section with a study of changing elites within the North American heritage industry, and more specifically, the issue of who controls the way 'Native American' museum sites are represented. As she demonstrates, the traditional bureaucratic and Eurocentric sense of the kind of narrative that public history sites should tell has been increasingly challenged since the 1970s by Native American and Canadian First Nation people. There is now a much greater degree of involvement and control by these groups in the heritage sites and a new 'heritage elite' is emerging. However, as Peers shows, displaying ethnographic museum artefacts to a multicultural audience is not without its tensions and difficulties.

Chapter 12, by Grant Evans, examines the curious case of the Communist regime in Laos. Having successfully presided over the fall of the old aristocracy in 1975, the ruling Communist Party has increasingly been obliged to selectively revive many of the traditional rituals of monarchy to shore up its nationalist legitimacy. Taking up Connerton's ideas about rituals, memory and the 'inertia in social structures' he points out why the Thai elite culture – and the Thai monarchy in particular – has come to occupy such an important role in Lao public culture. This leads him to reflect more widely on what Billig has termed 'banal nationalism', and the continuing charm and symbolic power of monarchy in general.

Part III, 'Elites, Professionals and Networks', shifts the focus towards elites in Britain with two case studies of highly educated professional groups. In Chapter 13 John Eade looks at the declining influence of the Catholic Church in England and the changing anatomy of Catholicism more generally. He asks, what relevance does this somewhat invisible ethnic group – what he describes as Britain's largest ethnic minority – have for wider debates about elites? One answer lies in what it reveals about the relationship between education and class. Using an ethnographic study of Catholic educational changes over the past century, he highlights the factors that have progressively eroded the old closed system of Catholic education in which the Catholic lay elite were traditionally socialised and where the 'Fortress Church' model was reproduced. Foremost among these today are the new avenues for social mobility now available to England's increasingly middle class Catholic population. The chapter goes on to discuss the way England's Catholic religious elite, having abandoned the fight over higher education, has sought to defend Catholic values and teaching at the level of secondary and primary schools.

In Chapter 14, Monica Konrad returns to the question of methods, arguing for a focus on 'actor-networks' as a way to study deterritorialised elites and tracking the ways information constitutes intersecting pathways of 'expert' power and knowledge. She explores two separate but interconnected elite cultures in the field of bioinformatics and 'pre-symptomatic' governance. The first case study examines how human genetics is linked to systems of accounting and to the British insurance industry (i.e. how underwriters make use of genetic information). The second analyses the use of expert knowledge and informational flows in promoting the status of molecular biologists who work on human genomic sequencing. As Konrad observes dryly: 'The new genetic technology "assists" ... not only the subfertile to procreative capacity, it helps biologists to continue to reproduce themselves into persons that matter'. Concluding, she returns to the debate about 'studying up', arguing that anthropology might successfully reinvent itself, as Nader proposed, if it ceases privileging the method of participant observation and focuses more on systems and relations of power that are not always visible to the naked eye. On this point, and on her call for greater political reflexivity, many of the contributors concur. The study of elite cultures challenges anthropology to rethink not only its methods and its ethics, but also its wider remit as a discipline concerned with all of humanity, including ourselves.

Notes

1   I would like to thank Stephen Roberts, John Eade and Susan Wright for their helpful comments and encouragement on an earlier draft of this chapter.
2   This is not to say that all anthropologists turned their backs on the structures and institutions of Western society. Tom Harrisson was an early critic of colonial society, although his contribution is often forgotten as Stanton (1997) points out. Similarly, Max Gluckman was an early pioneer of anthropological research into factory life and shop-floor relations in Manchester, but as Wright (1994) argues, this work represents the 'hidden history' of British anthropology.
3   K. Marx and F. Engels (1848) *The German Ideology* (Part 1: 'Feuerbach: Opposition of the Materialist and Idealist Outlook'). Source: Marxists Internet Archive, http://marxists.org/archive/marx/works/1845-gi/part_b.htm.
4   The conclusion reached by many scholars, including Marger (1987: 163), is that the United States today is closest to a power elite 'since (1) elite differences do not represent basic disagreements on essential issues of the political economy; (2) the corporate elite may not decide all issues, but it is able to set the agenda and boundaries of political debate; (3) the necessary overlapping of government and corporation gives rise to a natural elite cohesiveness, though not a conspiring group' (cited in Nagle 1992: 492).
5   Meisel (1962), cited in Cohen (1981: xvii).
6   'Apparent' because elites in fact actively create the 'masses' against which they distinguish themselves. This point is vividly illustrated in E.P. Thompson's classic work, *The Making of the English Working Class* (1968) and it features prominently in much of the theoretical literature on nationalism.
7   Benn, Tony (1993) Keynote Lecture on 'The Commonwealth of Europe Bill', Goldsmiths College, March. Also cited in Knowles (1998: 30).
8   Of course not everyone would agree with this analysis. For those cultural anthropologists who champion the 'symbols-and-meaning' approach, and for those who argue that anthropology should realign itself as a branch of cultural studies, this position is undoubtedly a retrograde one.
9   Thorstein Veblen's book *The Theory of a Leisure Class* (1899) arguably represents one of the first attempts to use anthropological concepts (particularly the idea of the

Potlatch and fighting with property) to study the competitive norms and behaviour of North American aristocrats, although Veblen himself was a sociologist.

10 Hugh Gusterson's study of US nuclear weapons scientists (1996) and George Marcus's study of American business dynasties (1983, 1986) are significant cases in point.

11 This sentence remains largely unchanged from the ASA's 1987 Code of Ethics – a document that was mirrored on the ethical guidelines of the American Anthropological Association.

12 For a useful anthropological discussion of the way localities are shaped by global flows of people, capital, ideas and information see, in particular, Appadurai (1991) and Friedman (1990). The implications of a focus on policy for anthropology is explored in Shore and Wright (1997).

13 In the case of Britain's controversial Millennium Dome in Greenwich, which cost close to a billion pounds and has been widely condemned as a failure, the ministers responsible for the project have been quick to distance themselves from it.

14 In addition to the well-known work of Hobsbawm and Ranger (1983), the archaeologist Michael Dietler (1994) provides some exemplary illustrations of this process in the case of France and former president Mitterrand's attempts to revive the Celtic heritage as the basis of French (and European) ethnic unity.

Bibliography

Ahmed, Akbar and Shore, Cris (eds) (1995) *The Future of Anthropology: Its Relevance to the Contemporary World*, London: Athlone Press

Alonso, Ana María (1994) 'The Politics of Space, Time and Substance: State Formation, Nationalism, and Ethnicity', *Annual Review of Anthropology* 23: 379–405.

Anderson, Benedict (1983) *Imagined Communities: Reflections on the Origins and Spread of Nationalism*, London: Verso.

Appadurai, Arjun (1991) 'Global Ethnoscapes: Notes and Queries for a Transnational Anthropology', in R. Fox (ed.) *Recapturing Anthropology*, Santa Fe, NM: School of American Research, 191–210.

Asad, Talal (ed.) (1973) *Anthropology and the Colonial Encounter*, London: Ithaca Press.

Bourdieu, Pierre (1986) *Distinction: A Social Critique of the Judgement of Taste*, Cambridge, MA: Harvard University Press.

Cohen, Abner (1981) *The Politics of Elite Culture: Explorations in the Dramaturgy of Power in a Modern African Society*, Berkeley, CA: University of California Press.

Connerton, Paul (1989) *How Societies Remember*, Cambridge: Cambridge University Press.

Dewatripont, M. *et al.* (1994) *Economic Policy Making and the European Union*, London: Federal Trust.

Dietler, Michael (1994) '"Our Ancestors the Gauls": Archeology, Ethnic Nationalism, and the Manipulation of Celtic Identity in Modern Europe', *American Anthropologist* 96 (3): 584–608.

Djilas, Milovan (1957) *The New Class: An Analysis of the Communist System*, New York: Praeger.

Domhoff, William (1967) *Who Rules America?*, Englewood Cliffs, NJ: Spectrum.

—— (1979) *The Powers That Be: Processes of Ruling Class Domination in America*, New York: Vintage.

Donnan, Hastings and MacFarlane, Graham (eds) (1989) *Social Anthropology and Public Policy in Northern Ireland*, Aldershot: Avebury.

Elias, Norbert (1978) *The Civilizing Process (vol. 1) The History of Manners*, Oxford: Blackwell.

Forty, Adrian and Kuchler, Suzanne (eds) (1999) *The Art of Forgetting*, Oxford: Berg.

Fox, Richard (1991) 'Introduction: working in the present', in R. Fox, (ed.) *Recapturing Anthropology. Working in the Present*, Santa Fe, NM: School of American Research Press.

Friedman, Jonathan (1990) 'Being in the World: Globalization and Localization', in M. Featherstone (ed.), *Global Culutre: Nationalism, Globalization and Modernity*, London: Sage, 311–28.

Gellner, Ernest (1983) *Nations and Nationalism*, Oxford: Blackwell.

George, Stephen (1985) *Politics and Policy in the European Community*, Oxford : Oxford University Press.

Grillo, Ralph (ed.) (1980) *'Nation' and 'State' in Europe: Anthropological Perspectives*, London: Academic Press.

Grimshaw, A. and Hart, K. (1995) 'The Rise and Fall of Scientific Anthropology', in A. Ahmed and C. Shore (eds), *The Future of Anthropology*, London: Athlone Press, 46–64.

Gupta, Akhil (1995) 'Blurred Boundaries: The Discourse of Corruption, the Culture of Politics, and the Imagined State', *American Ethnologist* 22 (2): 375–402.

Gusterson, Hugh (1996) *Nuclear Rites: A Weapons Laboratory at the End of the Cold War*, Berkeley, CA: University of California Press

Handelman, Don (1990) *Models and Mirrors: Towards an Anthropology of Public Events*, Cambridge: Cambridge University Press.

Herzfeld, Michael (1992) *The Social Production of Indifference: Exploring the Symbolic Roots of Western Bureaucracy*, Oxford: Berg

Herzfeld, Michael (2000) 'Uncanny Success. Some Closing Remarks', in J. Pina-Cabral and P. Lima (eds), *Elites: Choice Leadership and Succession*, Oxford: Berg.

Hobsbawm, Eric and Ranger, Terrence (1983) 'Introduction: Inventing Traditions', in E. Hobsbawm and T. Ranger (eds) *The Invention of Tradition*, Cambridge: Cambridge University Press, 1–14.

Holmes, Douglas (2000) *Integral Europe: Fast Capitalism, Multiculturalism, Neofascism*, Princeton, NJ: Princeton University Press.

Hymes, Dell (ed.) (1972) *Reinventing Anthropology*, New York: Vintage Books.

Jackson, Anthony (ed.) (1987) *Anthropology at Home*, London: Tavistock.

Kertzer, David (1988) *Ritual, Politics and Power*, New Haven and London: Yale University Press.

Knowles, Elizabeth (1998) *The Oxford Dictionary of Twentieth Century Quotations*, Oxford: Oxford University Press.

Kuper, Adam (1996) *Anthropology and Anthropologists. The Modern British School*, London: Routledge.

Lasch, Christopher (1995) *The Revolt of the Elites and the Betrayal of Democracy*, London and New York: W. W. Norton.

Luxembourg, Rosa (1961) *The Russian Revolution and Leninism or Marxism* (ed. B. Wolfe), Ann Arbor, MI: University of Michigan Press.

Marcus, George (ed.) (1983) *Elites: Ethnographic Issues*, Albuquerque, NM: University of New Mexico Press.

—— (1983a) '"Elite" as a Concept, Theory and Research Tradition', in G. Marcus (ed.), *Elites: Ethnographic Issues*, Albuquerque, NM: University of New Mexico Press, 7–27.

—— (1986) 'Appendix: Work in Progress', in G. Marcus and M. Fischer (eds), *Anthropology as Cultural Critique*, Chicago: University of Chicago Press, 169–77.

Marger, M. (1987) *Elites and Masses: An Introduction to Political Sociology*, Blemond, CA: Wadsworth.

Michels, Robert (1959) *Political Parties: A Sociological Study of the Oligarchical Tendencies of Modern Democracy*, New York: Dover.

Monbiot, George (2000) *Captive State. The Corporate Takeover of Britain*, London: Macmillan.

Nader, Laura (1972) 'Up the Anthropologist', in D. Hymes (ed.), *Reinventing Anthropology*, New York: Vintage Books, 284–311.

Nagle, John (1992) 'Recruitment of Elites', in M. Hawkesworth and M. Kogan (eds), *Encyclopedia of Government and Politics*, London: Routledge, 486–503.

Nairn, Tom (1981) *The Break-Up of Britain: Crisis and Neo-nationalism*, London: NLB.

—— (1988) *The Enchanted Glass: Britain and its Monarchy*, London: Hutchinson Radius.

Nelson, Brent and Stubb, Alex (1998) *The European Union. Readings on the Theory and Practice of European Integration*, London: Macmillan.

Paxman, Jeremy (1999) *Friends in High Places*, Harmondsworth: Penguin.

Pels, Peter (1999) 'Professions of Duplicity: A Prehistory of Ethical Codes in Anthropology', *Current Anthropology* 40 (2): April: 101–36.

Pina-Cabral, Joao de and Lima, António Pedrosa de (eds) (2000) *Elites: Choice Leadership and Succession*, Oxford: Berg.

Sampson, Anthony (1965) *Anatomy of Britain Today*, London: Hodder and Stoughton.

Shore, Cris (1990) *Italian Communism: The Escape from Leninism: An Anthropological Perspective*, London: Pluto.

—— (1993) 'Ethnicity as Revolutionary Strategy: Communist Identity Construction in Italy', in S. MacDonald (ed.), *Inside European Identities*, Oxford: Berg, 27–53

—— (2000) *Building Europe: The Cultural Politics of European Integration*, London: Routledge.

Shore, Cris and Wright, Susan (eds) (1997) *Anthropology of Policy: Critical Perspectives on Governance and Power*, London: Routledge.

Spencer, Jonathan (2000) 'British Social Anthropology: A Retrospective', *Annual Review of Anthropology* 29: 1–24.

Stanton, G. (1997) 'In Defence of *Savage Civilisation*: Tom Harrisson, Cultural Studies and Anthropology', in S. Nugent and C. Shore (eds), *Anthropology and Cultural Studies*, London: Pluto Press, 11–23.

Stocking, George W. (1992) *The Ethnographer's Magic and Other Essays in the History of Anthropology*, Madison, WI: University of Wisconsin Press.

Strathern, Marilyn (ed.) (2000) *Audit Cultures: Anthropological Studies in Accountability, Ethics and the Academy*, London: Routledge.

Thompson, Edward P. (1968) *The Making of the English Working Class*, Harmondsworth: Penguin.

Williams, Raymond (1976) *Keywords*, Glasgow: Fontana.

Wright, Susan (1994) 'Culture in Anthropology and Organisational Studies', in S. Wright (ed.), *Anthropology of Organisations*, London: Routledge, 1–31.

Wright Mills, C. (1956) *The Power Elite*, New York: Oxford University Press.

Chapter 2

World society as an old regime[1]

Keith Hart

I present my argument in two sections, corresponding to self and society, subject and object. In the first I will report on my personal journey as an ethnographer of the global elite concerned with development in the 1970s; while in the second, on the basis of further reflection, I suggest that contemporary world society might be thought of as being polarised between a rich elite and the mass of poor people. This leads me to conclude that humanity has failed to consolidate the advances in science and democracy that launched the modern age; and I ask why, after two centuries of the machine revolution, our world still resembles the old regime of agrarian civilisation. For whatever anthropologists may contribute to the study of elite cultures in the plural, I believe it is our duty to show the way towards grasping the human condition as a whole.

An ethnography of the development elite in the 1970s

When I finished writing my doctoral thesis in 1969, I felt that I understood Accra's street economy as well as the people who participated in it.[2] But, like them, I had no explanation for the great events which had shaken Ghana's political economy a decade after independence: the collapse of the cocoa price, the ensuing scarcity of goods, the army coup which overthrew Nkrumah. I had discovered an elective affinity in fieldwork with the lawless trade of Accra's slums. My method had been less to record the existing economic practices of Nima's inhabitants than to participate in them and challenge them, as an entrepreneur in my own right. I had been surprised by how easy it was for me to make money and how difficult to get rid of it. By the end of a stay lasting over two years, I had become a local big man, redistributing the profits of criminal enterprise through handouts, jobs and parties. I was ignorant of the history which might help me to account for this situation. Ghanaians wore cloth from my home town, Manchester, but I had little idea how it came about or what it meant.

Accordingly, I set out to learn more about the history of colonialism and of its successor, 'development'. More than anything, I wanted to enter the world of states and international agencies. So I joined an academic consultancy organisation at the University of East Anglia. Before long my conversations with development economists paid off and I was able to transform my Accra ethnography into a means of entering the debates of the day about urban unemployment in the Third World. I was helped in this by picking up 'economese' (how to sound like an economist without any formal training), through writing reports on West Africa for the Economist Intelligence Unit. These exchanges spawned the idea of an 'informal sector/economy' whose inter-disciplinary success as a concept is still a source of wonder to me (Hart 1973, 1992).

An initial foray into development consultancy as a 'manpower expert' in the Caribbean was followed by two heady excursions into the high politics of development: a mission in 1972–3 to write the development programme for Papua New Guinea's forthcoming independence (UNDP 1973) and an enquiry into Hong Kong's labour situation in 1976 (Turner et al. 1980). By the end of the 1970s, when I was able to convert a report for USAID on West African agriculture into a monograph on the region's political economy, I knew I had made good progress towards understanding the history of large-scale structures and processes. I did this by converting to Marxism and reading a lot; but also by carrying out a sort of ethnography into the elite circles who were responsible for development policy at that time.

One day Bert Turner, Professor of Industrial Economics at Cambridge, phoned me up at Yale. 'I need someone who can sound off about Third World cities at a moment's notice', he told me, 'and I thought of you.' The story that emerged is one I acquired by hearsay, but it went roughly as follows. James Callaghan's Labour government was under pressure from the parliamentary left and the unions to do something about Hong Kong. It was held to be scandalous that a Victorian capitalist colony could be allowed to exploit cheap Asian labour under a socialist government. Callaghan responded by promising a commission of enquiry into Hong Kong labour along the lines of the Donovan report on British labour relations a few years earlier. The Foreign Office then hit the roof. Britain maintained the fiction, for the benefit of the People's Republic of China (PRC), that Hong Kong was not a colonial state, but a municipal authority. A parliamentary enquiry would send entirely the wrong message. The idea was dropped and in its place a low-key academic enquiry was proposed, unpublicised and even secret, whose report might be delayed long enough for the heat to go out of the parliamentary issue. In any case, the report would not recommend substantial reform. Bert Turner and I were the academic enquiry. I did spend a few minutes considering the ethical and political dilemmas involved. But the chance of a month in Hong Kong overcame my doubts. Always the intrepid ethnographer!

Hong Kong was going through the long boom which allowed it to make the transition to prosperity in the 1980s. We discovered that one reason for this was the gap between local and global inflation rates. The latter was running at 15% in 1976, whereas Hong Kong's domestic rate was only 1%. Most of this was attributable to rent, since everything else (water, food, clothing, in short general wage goods) was supplied by the PRC at prices consistent with its own internal market. Almost all Hong Kong's production was for export and employers could distribute the inflation bonus between profits and wages at will. As it happened, the riots surrounding the Cultural Revolution in the late 1960s were still fresh in the memory and employers handed out wage increases freely in order to avert what they imagined could be union subversion under the direction of Beijing. So a communist state and a Labour government colluded in creating the conditions for one of the world's most successful capitalist economies.

This made it relatively easy to write a report saying that Hong Kong's workers needed no help from the British government. But I was given another task. Hong Kong's labour market was supposed to be as free as anywhere in the world. Indeed, Milton Friedman made a television documentary around that time highlighting Hong Kong as a leading example of the free market in practice. Employers told us that any attempt to rig wages would be thwarted by the extraordinary mobility of workers who could shop around between factories in the same high-rise buildings during their lunch hour, ready to exploit minor differences of pay at the drop of a hat. I didn't believe it; but the evidence was hard to find. We were supposed to be operating underground; but everyone knew who we were. My colleague preferred a confrontational approach which was easily rebuffed by the British businessmen and Chinese officials. I preferred stealth.

In exchange for lunch and flattery, I offered my services to businessmen seeking advice on whether to send their daughters to Oxbridge or the Ivy League. But my main hope for inside information was the personnel manager of the second biggest firm in Hong Kong. We met for drinks at his golf club. I was then invited for dinner and a game of bridge. This was obviously the cultural test. If I passed, I might be treated to some confidences. I am a good bridge player; but in the middle of the game, my host said, 'Didn't you say you were a classicist once, Keith? I like to read the Oxford Book of Greek Verse before bed. Let me show you my favourite poem.' I couldn't believe that he was going to test my competence in Greek, fourteen years after I gave it up. But he was. My heart sank when he picked out a passage from Pindar, the most obscure of Greek poets. When I looked at the passage he had singled out, I suddenly knew that he was a bluffer too, capable only of reading schoolboy Greek. The passage was very simple to translate and I congratulated him on the profundity of his choice.

After the game, my friend asked me to stay behind for a brandy and immediately said, 'I believe you would like to know how the labour market works here.' In short order he revealed that the top dozen firms met every Wednesday lunchtime and filled in a huge questionnaire, agreeing between them the wage level for every job in Hong Kong. This was then passed on to the government's labour office which published it as one of their own surveys of going wage rates. Everyone else negotiated in relation to these published government findings. He told me also that the Shanghainese cotton spinners met in a tea house every Tuesday afternoon for the same purpose. I later used this information in my report to the FCO to undermine Hong Kong's *laissez-faire* capitalist image. But, by then, as predicted, the heat had gone out of the Hong Kong question in British politics. I offer this example, warts and all, as a way of asking what anthropologists are prepared to give up in order to be temporarily assimilated in 'the flower of society'.

The other example is more conventional. I was recruited to a team, commissioned by the World Bank acting as executive agency for UNDP (United Nations Development Program), to draw up a development programme for Papua New Guinea (PNG) on the eve of independence. It was headed by Mike Faber, a general economist, and the other three members were an agricultural economist, an economist mainly responsible for mining and me with a wide remit in employment, education, health, social policy and local government. We spent three months in Australia and PNG during mid-1972, wrote a preliminary report and returned in 1973 for discussions with the newly elected Pangu party government of Michael Somare. The second time around we were reduced to two since the agriculture and mining experts had dropped out, possibly fearing that their consultancy careers would be wrecked by what one of them described as the lunacy advocated by Faber and Hart.

We arrived in Australia just when a quarter century of Liberal/Country party rule was expected to give way to Gough Whitlam's Labour party. The Ministry of External Territories (covering PNG) had been a Country party fiefdom. But, with the help of the Commonwealth Treasury, we found that PNG was a redistributive device for siphoning A$500 millions a year from taxpayers to three Australian interest groups: trading oligopolies (the usual story), civil servants (who enjoyed extraordinary conditions and pay), and farmers (who dumped subsidised rice and dairy products in PNG, hence the interest of the Country party). I early on formed the opinion that what was needed was a Nyerere-style rural socialist government aiming at self-sufficiency and thereby meeting the needs for both national autonomy and lower rates of Australian subsidy.

We soon ran into opposition. The chief World Bank representative was a career officer who had an annual season ticket with Pan-Am to carry his golf clubs into the first-class cabin, so that he experienced minimal delay on his way to the watering holes of the local elite. He believed in the World Bank's mission to maximise the profits of multi-national firms regardless of the returns to local populations. What we proposed in the way of grassroots development linked to an emphasis on the income of nationals he considered to be a 'racist' deviation from orthodoxy. Our proposal to renegotiate the terms of the Bougainville copper mine (then also the largest source of gold in the world) upset everyone: the colonial administrators who had arranged a notorious give-away, the operators (a subsidiary of Rio Tinto Zinc), the World Bank who believed a contract was a contract, the Department of External Territories and so on. In this climate of confrontation, the team found itself reduced to two.

Things improved on our return, however. The winning party in the country's first elections had used our preliminary report to campaign on 'eight points of development' drawn largely from our report. When Faber and I met the cabinet, the prime minister said, 'Gentlemen, before you came, we only knew of one model for development. Now we know there are at least two.' At which point, the World Bank official and the head of the colonial government's planning office leapt in to claim that they had been in substantial agreement with us all along and hoped that the new government would give them the business of implementing the development programme.

The main lesson I gained from this experience concerned the fragmentation and disunity of bureaucracies which often seem quite intimidating from the outside. In this case, although the principals in the mainstream institutions were ready to defend the status quo, others anticipated taking their place as a result of the Australian election and were prepared to support us. This was particularly true of officials from the Commonwealth Treasury who, it transpired, were the source of our appointment in the first place. Although it was hard going at times, it was possible to run with an idea through the bureaucracy and win. Generally, consultants legitimise decisions taken already; but sometimes an opportunity arises to make a difference, however small.

I was still in my twenties at the time, as I had been when I embarked on life as a criminal entrepreneur in Accra's slums. On both occasions, I was struck by the unequal social power that I wielded as a young Western ignoramus on the fringes of colonial independence. But both types of ethnographic fieldwork surely demonstrate how much the conditions of research are affected by the roles we assume in relation to the societies we study. I doubt if we tell our students enough about how the positions they occupy within the host society will affect the outcome of their research far more than a theoretical approach adopted in the insularity of the classroom. If we are serious about studying elites, this problem will become even more apparent. For going down the social spectrum, as well as allowing us to assume the mantle of populism, has masked political processes that are far more evident when anthropologists aspire to penetrate life at the top.

World society divided between a rich elite and the poor masses

For some time now, I have been aware that, to all appearances, I belong to the world's ruling class: white, middle-aged, middle-class men, the men in suits or just 'the suits'. The existence of this term means that we recognise the polarising tendencies of our world in terms of social categories. I would go further.

The world as a whole is now in much the same situation as were the advanced centres of agrarian civilisation before the modern revolutions which thought they had swept them away. It is hard for us to grasp that 300 years of political struggle and economic development have left world society in an analogous condition to that of the *ancien régime* in France during the 1750s, when Rousseau (1984) wrote his famous discourse on inequality. But how else can one describe a world in which a socially exclusive minority holds so much power over an impoverished mass whose powerlessness is now measured by how little money they have to spend? Who would have believed that the latest wave of mechanical invention would grant one man disposal of $60 billions and potential control of the global information industry, while billions of people lack material essentials, never mind the means of getting wired?

The project of imagining national communities, largely by means of statistical extrapolation, is little more than a century old. Even so, we now accept without question the idea that the Italians and the Spanish have the lowest birth rates in Europe or that Britain has sunk to being the eighteenth richest country in the world. Since the Second World War and the formation of the United Nations, it has become normal to collect statistics on the global population; but thinking about human society as a single entity has not yet taken hold. It is about time that it did. For ours is the moment of the formation of world society in a meaningful sense; and the fragmentation of perspective produced by national consciousness prevents us from imagining the human community as a whole. Numbers are one way of beginning that process.

There are two pressing features of our world: the development of markets, transport and communications since the Second World War has led to an unprecedented integration of global society as a single interactive network; and polarisation of rich and poor within national societies has been extended to huge and growing inequalities between continental regions. Becoming closer and more unequal at the same time is an explosive combination, since the normal method for dealing with inequality is to put distance between the classes, not to reduce it.

According to the United Nations *Human Development Report* (UNDP 1998), the world's 225 richest men (and they are men) own more than one trillion dollars, the equivalent of the annual income of the world's 47 per cent poorest people. Three of them have assets worth more than the gross domestic product of the forty-eight least developed countries. The West spends $37 billions a year on pet food, perfumes and cosmetics ('let them eat Pedigree Chum'), almost the estimated additional cost of providing basic education, health, nutrition, water and sanitation for those deprived of them. The rate of car ownership in industrial countries is 400 per thousand, but 16 in all developing countries. The rich pollute the world fifty times more than the poor; but the latter are more likely to die from the pollution. World consumption has increased six times in the last twenty years; but the richest fifth account for 86 per cent of it.

Even though relative deprivation is striking within nations (Bill Gates owns as much as the annual income of the 106 million least affluent Americans), solutions to the obscene inequality and ecological risks facing world society require us to focus on the global picture first. As a thought experiment, we could conceive of humanity as a unit stratified by wealth, race, age and gender. Women everywhere are struggling with the legacy of patriarchy. The world's poor, however, are concentrated in what came to be called the Third World and latterly the South, the outcome of Western expansion over the last 500 years and particularly of imperialism in the nineteenth century. The ideology sustaining this expansion was racism, the belief that the power of 'white' people derived from a biologically founded superiority to the 'darker races'. Although racism is nowhere officially sanctioned today, it still plays a major part in organising cultural responses to global inequality. Then also the world's young people are to be found predominantly in the South owing to a lag in the fall of birth rates there. For the age distributions of rich and poor countries are skewed heavily towards the old and young respectively.

There are, as I have said, tremendous inequalities within countries and regions; but it is not difficult to summarise the above description in terms of a two-class model. A rich, mainly white, ageing minority (about 15 per cent, if we take North America, Western Europe and Japan together) is surrounded by a majority (five-sixths of the total) which is on average a lot poorer, darker in colour and especially much younger. Seen in terms of the reproduction of humanity as a whole, we can say that a stagnant Western elite is about to be replaced by a hugely proliferating generation of non-Westerners from whom it is separated by a tradition of cultural arrogance and by ingrained practices of social exclusion.

The situation is not unlike that found in agrarian civilisations, where small urban elites sought to maintain control over rural masses condemned to drudgery and political impotence. The main difference between the two cases lies in the fact that modern world society is supposed to be organised by an ideology of human freedom and equality. This is the legacy of a democratic revolution, begun in the seventeenth and eighteenth centuries, which aimed to install rule by the people in general as the only legitimate form of government. The industrial revolution, which closely followed its political counterpart, implied that humanity might now be released from material as well as social constraints on its development. But the evidence of global inequality today shows that this emancipatory rhetoric is an illusion.

World society today is at base as rotten as the aristocratic regimes which preceded the modern age. Power has been concentrated into forms held against the people, first in the hands of owners of big money (capitalists) and then in a revived and strengthened state apparatus. In the second half of the nineteenth century, no major thinker envisaged the possibility of imposing state control on the restless energies of industrial/commercial society. Yet in the course of our own century, the rule of elites has been restored: state bureaucracy is absolute; and world society is divided into national fragments. There is no popular government anywhere; and most people have forgotten when they last took an active interest in such a possibility. The confusing part lies in the widespread use of a rhetoric derived from the democratic revolutions to cloak the purposes of those who reserve effective power to themselves. Western states are no more liberal than the Soviet Union was Marxist. At least the old regime of agrarian civilisation called itself what it was. The vast majority of intellectuals are complicit in the lies needed to sustain this latter-day revival of the state. Behind a smokescreen of democratic slogans, the bureaucracy relies on impersonal institutions to maintain grotesquely unfair levels of inequality.

One method for an anthropology of the contemporary human condition would thus be to conceive of world society as a single population divided into rich and poor or, if you like, polarised between a remote elite and the undifferentiated masses. This society is unsustainable, in that most of its members are exposed to conditions of poverty and violence that are humanly unacceptable, while a few enjoy the benefits of wealth in forms that were unimaginable before the Industrial Revolution. Moreover, a society so cruel and indifferent to the general human interest is heading for ecological disaster. Ours is a corrupt *ancien régime* that must soon find a new democratic revolution, if human intervention in the life of this planet is not to end in catastrophe.

The form of social organisation underpinning this universal crisis for humanity is state capitalism, the attempt to manage markets and money through nation-states. In whatever guise local elite cultures appear to us, we must first understand the general form before proceeding to analyse its variants. We know that agrarian civilisations ruled the earth for 5,000 years before the machine revolution altered the conditions of human life irreversibly. In 200 years the world's population has multiplied six times, the proportion living in cities has risen from 1 in 40 to 50 per cent, and energy production has grown at twice the rate of the people. This last statistic accounts for the fact that many people now eat more, work less and live longer; but the benefits of mechanisation are distributed most unevenly, with Americans consuming on average 400 times more energy than Ugandans, for example (World Bank 1998).[3] Up to three billion people, mostly Indians, Chinese and Africans, still work in agriculture with their hands; but the other half of humanity lives in the modern city or the urbanised countryside.

It would not be surprising if the latter, especially, held that we are now living in a world that has made a decisive break with the past. And this is indeed the case. Today's societies everywhere claim to rest on science and democracy, the twin foundations of modernity and the lasting legacy of the eighteenth-century revolutions. This modern religion is similar in many ways to older claims made on behalf of God, and with the same plausibility: if society is omniscient and good, how can there be so much suffering in the world? The obvious answer to this question is that society is not run by and for the people as a whole and, whatever its principles, they are not based on effective knowledge. Perhaps we are less emancipated from the past than we imagine and are further from a desirable future than we hope.

The breakout from agrarian civilisation was led by urban middle-class elements in a few places beginning with the Italian renaissance. This was not the first time: for a thousand years class coalitions based on property in land and money respectively slugged it out for control of Ancient Mediterranean society, before the Romans made the world safe for landed aristocracy. In the modern period, it did seem as if what its detractors call the bourgeois revolution was home and dry when mechanisation was married to capital accumulation. But this was precisely the moment when, fearful of the proletarian monster they had made, the middle classes shrank back and embraced an alliance with the military land-owning class. Society was reconceived as nations whose origins were shrouded in a rural past; and the counter-revolution took off with a vengeance. Marx was right to rely on a feudal metaphor for the new wage-labour system, since everywhere old forms of property and power were harnessed to the task of holding the workers down.

Even so, as the nineteenth century drew to a close, the issue was in the balance. The world was drawn together by a revolution in transport and communications (steamships, railways, the telegraph). The workers were concentrated in smokestack industries. Could they seize power from the owners and their allies? The issue was settled by the First World War, when governments discovered that they now possessed unprecedented powers of social mobilisation and control. Society was centralised at the top and twentieth-century state capitalism was inaugurated. Since then, until recently, when another revolution in transport and communications has begun to undermine territorial states, the question was not whether the people would win out or their rulers, but to which form of state people all over the world would be made subordinate. The middle classes abandoned their previous commitment to commerce in order to sup copiously at the trough of national bureaucracy, relying on their university diplomas for a lifetime of privilege as experts in social reproduction.

The result is that the middle-class revolution with which the modern age began has stalled, even regressed, first allying itself with landed power and then assuming the form of rule traditional for agrarian civilisation. As I have pointed out, no serious mid-nineteenth-century social thinker imagined that industrial/commercial society could be controlled from the top by a remote centralised mechanism. Yet a century later, most of us are conditioned to think that no other form of society is imaginable. The institutions of agrarian civilisation, developed over five millennia with a passive rural workforce in mind, are, in form if not in content, our institutions today: territorial states, landed property, warfare, racism, embattled cities, money as objects, long-distance trade, an emphasis on work, and of course world religions and the family. Consider what happened to all the wealth siphoned off by Western industrial states since the Second World War, the largest concentrations of money in the history of humanity. It went on subsidising food supplies and armaments, the priorities of the bully through the ages, certainly not those of the modern urban consumers who paid the taxes. No, we have never been modern, as Bruno Latour (1993) says. We are just primitives who stumbled recently into a machine revolution and cannot yet think of what do with it, beyond repeating the inhumanity of a society built unequally on agriculture.

Pierre-Philippe Rey (1973) sought to bring the West African colonial experience of capitalism and the original British case within the scope of a single explanation in *Les alliances de classes*. He argued that, wherever capitalism developed, the new class was forced into making compromises with the old property-owning classes in ways which made the resulting hybrid something specific to that society. Thus, the British industrialists had to make an alliance with the land-owning aristocracy in order for the factory system to flourish at the expense of feudal agriculture. Similarly, in West Africa the indigenous lineage elders made an alliance with the colonial authorities to supply the labour of young men to plantations and mines.

This kind of class alliance is depressingly familiar. It offers an example of the institutional complexity which more abstract economic theories tend to ignore; and which social anthropologists are trained to look for. In Britain, the industrial bourgeoisie was separated from the traditional landed aristocracy by region (North v. South); but their influence on national government was always limited by its location in London, the home of the mercantile and colonial elite. In the late nineteenth century, the industrial civilisation of regional cities (led by Manchester's cosmopolitan liberalism) was undermined by nationalism and financial imperialism based in London. The British economy never recovered from this process of political centralisation. It is not hard to tell a similar story about Rhineland capitalists and Prussian Junkers in Germany. Each national class compromise was historically distinctive, and this is why the capitalism of a country (Italy, Japan or wherever) is always different. There is no difficulty in tracing the local roots of elite cultures. It would be sad, however, if this ethnography of difference, like all the other ethnographies of difference which have become our professional stock-in-trade, ended up obscuring the social form which underlies the profound economic inequality of our world.

Humanity is caught between mechanisation and agrarian institutions; and the combination is potentially lethal. Its most striking pathology is the polarisation of rich and poor at every level of society. Nothing less than a world revolution is adequate to redressing such a situation; and it will not succeed without an appropriate explanation for the phenomenon in question.

My first observation is that we are living with the consequences of 5,000 years of agrarian civilisation (Childe's urban revolution, 1981) which cannot be discarded overnight. Agriculture as a mode of production relies on intensification of labour inputs, making people work harder for less; and the institutions we still live by were formed by small urban elites bent on controlling populations tied to the land. Half of the world's people are still living under conditions of traditional agriculture that do not afford them the means of participating fully in a capitalist economy driven by machines and money. They can join the rush to the cities or they can produce for the world market. The cities are themselves organised to sustain vast material inequalities between those who enjoy the benefits of machine civilisation and those who are largely excluded from it. And the latter are the majority in regions that have not yet mechanised production.

The second explanation for global inequality lies in capitalism itself. The system of money-making favours those who already have a large capital fund. Left unchecked, the rich will always get richer and the poor will stay poor. Modern capitalism has flourished when linked to machine production. These machines have hitherto been huge, centralised complexes (factories), so that power has gone to those capable of launching enterprises on a large scale, the owners of lots of money (capitalists, banks) and, more recently, states. Mechanisation too, in order to take root, requires cultural and social institutions (science, education, work discipline, finance, property law), which are unevenly spread between and within societies.

A major corollary of the above is the established tendency for labour markets to take on a dualistic character: two streams of workers, one highly paid in jobs using sophisticated machinery, the other performing tasks of little skill for low wages and in poor working conditions, often no better than those prevailing in traditional agriculture. Marx (1970) identified these trends in terms of the concepts of relative and absolute surplus value. Although squeezing profit out of sweat-shop workers is a naked form of exploitation, he considered that mechanisation allowed workers to be paid an even smaller share of the value of their production, despite their higher wages. This, after all, was why capitalists invested in machines. The migration streams of Europeans and Asians that ushered in the twentieth century world economy entrenched this dualism at the global level (Lewis 1978). Subsequently, both national and international institutions were developed to maintain the division in the interests of the rich and powerful. The chief function of these institutions, located in states and associations of states, is to justify inequality and to keep the poor in their place by controlling any movement which might undermine the separation of rich and poor. In a word, *apartheid*.

There is a cultural explanation too. If, as Max Weber (1981) insisted, it takes a cultural revolution to join the historical development known as capitalism, the means of altering the shape and dynamic of world society would seem to be even more daunting. A society formed by Western imperialism and served by an enduring legacy of racism is now governed by international institutions, dominated by the United States, whose chief purpose is to maintain the free flow of money (capital), to the benefit of those who already have lots of it. A world whose most inclusive body is the United Nations has enshrined national consciousness at the core of efforts to co-ordinate world economy. The territorial state and nationalism effectively reinforce indifference to others, leaving the world stage to be ruled by the most powerful, while undermining whatever sense of our common humanity might lead us to want to alleviate the horrors of poverty.

That the world economy is based on inhuman principles is a commonplace. Quite apart from whatever active role states and markets may play in promoting inequality, as impersonal institutions they place economic life on a footing where it is difficult for ordinary human beings to feel meaningfully involved with what is going on, even if they understand it, which is unlikely. Compassion and similar human qualities are unlikely to be influential in economic life when power seems to be concentrated in remote, faceless centres. The normal response to problems is to let 'them' (the powers that be, *les responsables*) get on with it. When confronted with the consequences of their own actions, people shrug their shoulders: it is nothing really to do with us. The case for a more human economy is this: that society will only be democratic and fair when people can assume meaningful responsibility for what they do.

Finally, we must turn to the specific developments in world economy of the last two decades, which I summarise as the rise of virtual capitalism. Virtual in two main senses: the shift from material production (agriculture and manufacturing) to information services and the corresponding detachment of the circulation of money from production and trade. This in turn is an aspect of the latest stage of mechanisation, the communications revolution culminating in the 1990s (Hart 2001a). The question is whether the same developments that have led to the recent integration of world society are the cause of its increasing polarisation. The answer, of course, is yes.

Long-distance trade in information services requires a substantial technical infrastructure. The internet has its origins in scientific collaboration between America and Europe during the Cold War. Its main language is English. The countries that led the industrial revolution in its first and second phases are thus well placed to take the lead in this third wave. Every stage of mechanisation has been initially concentrated in a narrow enclave of world society; and this one is no different. But diffusion of the new techniques has been quite rapid and decentralised. Mobile phones and videotape have brought telecommunications to many parts of the world where the old physical infrastructure was underdeveloped. Already some of the simpler processing tasks have been devolved to where educated labour is cheaper; equally the destruction of old manufacturing industries in the West has often been brutal. But the short conclusion is that many poorer regions appear to be stuck in phases of production that have been marginalised by this latest round of uneven development.

Spiralling markets for money in countless derivative forms have injected a new instability into global capitalism. The East Asian bubble of endlessly rising stock markets has burst, wiping out paper assets and devaluing currencies overnight. Mismanagement by the banks has reached colossal proportions. This apotheosis of capital, its effective detachment from what real people do, has made many huge fortunes, often for individuals controlling sums larger than the annual income of a dozen Third World countries. Here is certainly one of the motors of global inequality, money being made with money. Moreover, the money system has now reached a social scale and technical form that make it impossible for states to control it. This may be good news for democrats and anarchists in the long run; but in the meantime Hegel's recipe for state moderation of capitalism has been subverted, with inevitable results: rampant inequality at all levels and appalling human distress without any apparent remedy.

We are obviously at a turning point in human affairs. The present situation cannot continue indefinitely. It is no longer self-evident that being inside the virtual economy is a privilege. If the bubble bursts, people sitting on little plots of land in the countryside will count themselves lucky to have missed the bonanza. Development is no longer a linear process describing unequivocal winners and losers in the global economy, advanced and backward producers. The rules of the game are being rewritten so fast and with such uncertain consequences that it is no longer apparent who is best placed to benefit from them. The populations of America, Europe and Japan which have grown passively dependent on the impersonal institutions of state capitalism may be less well-placed than many others to learn patterns of economic activity adapted to a new age. But then the world's rural and urban poor are unlikely to be able to afford the price of participating in such an economy.

The word *elite* means the pick or flower of the crop, perhaps even the chosen few. It is a term redolent of an agrarian society run by those who believe themselves to be naturally, socially and spiritually superior to the masses. In other words, a form of society such as the one identified by de Tocqueville (1955) as the old regime, supposedly buried by the French Revolution. Contemporary world society has more in common with the old regime of agrarian civilisation than it does with the modernist rhetoric inaugurated by the democratic revolutions. This is not just because of the sheer gap in lifestyle and prospects between rich and poor; but because the ideology justifying global inequality is still identifiably racist, explaining difference as the expression of innate superiority and inferiority. The European empires have collapsed, but the people have not yet inherited the earth.

The intellectual tradition we know as anthropology should be capable of helping us to understand this anomaly and to remedy it. I have suggested that the methods of ethnography and global generalisation might be adapted to such a task. The term *elite* is a crude, even reactionary concept, not unlike *peasant*; but if it helps social anthropologists to focus on the causes of persisting human inequality, it will serve a useful purpose. I have concentrated here on sketching an approach to society conceived of in universal terms. This is in self-conscious contrast to the particulars of twentieth century anthropology's cultural relativism. But the point of having a sense of what humanity faces in common is to help us identify the particular trajectories of individuals and collectivities within it.[4] The global picture does not exist independently of our interactions with it. We alter society whenever we study it; and this is why, in the first part of this paper, I have described ethnography as a form of intervention, one perhaps of little overall consequence, but an active engagement with others nevertheless. In such a world, the universal and the particular need not be opposed and the contradiction between nineteenth and twentieth-century versions of anthropology might be overcome.

Notes

1   Closely based on the keynote address read at the conference, Part 1 is the first public airing of the experiences described there. Part 2 is drawn from my book *Money in an Unequal World* (Hart 2001a) and is amplified in another paper (Hart 2001b).
2   These opening paragraphs draw on an account produced for a volume on African enterprise edited by Stephen Ellis and Yves Fauré (Hart 1995).
3   In 1995 Americans each consumed 8,000 kgs of oil equivalent, compared with 22 kgs in Uganda.
4   I have begun to develop this approach with my collaborator, Vishnu Padayachee, in relation to the Indians of Durban, South Africa (Hart and Padayachee 2000).

Bibliography

Childe, V. Gordon (1981) *Man Makes Himself*, London: Moonraker Press.
de Tocqueville, Alexis (1955 [1856]) *The Old Regime and the French Revolution*, New York: Doubleday.
Hart, Keith (1973) 'Informal Income Opportunities and Urban Employment in Ghana', *Journal of Modern African Studies* 11: 61–89.
—— (1992) 'Market and State after the Cold War: The Informal Economy Reconsidered', in R. Dilley (ed.) *Contesting Markets*, Edinburgh: Edinburgh University Press.
—— (1995) 'L'entreprise africaine et l'économie informelle: réflexions autobiographiques', in S. Ellis and Yves Fauré (eds), *Entreprises et Entrepreneurs Africains*, Paris: Karthala et ORSTOM, 115–24.
—— (2001a) *Money in an Unequal World: Keith Hart and His Memory Bank*, New York: Texere; previously published as *The Memory Bank*, London: Profile Books, 2000.
—— (2001b) 'Money in an Unequal World', *Anthropological Theory* 1 (3: 307–330).
Hart, Keith and Vishnu Padayachee (2000) 'Indian Business in South Africa After Apartheid: New and Old Trajectories', *Comparative Studies in Society and History* 42 (4): 683–712.
Latour, B. (1993) *We Have Never Been Modern*, London: Harvester Wheatsheaf.

Lewis, W. Arthur (1978) *The Evolution of the International Economic Order*, Princeton: Princeton University Press.

Marx, Karl (1970 [1867]) 'The Fetishism of Commodities and the Secret Thereof', *Capital Vol. 1: A Critique of Political Economy*, London: Lawrence and Wishart, 71–83.

Rey, Pierre-Philippe (1973) *Les alliances de classes*, Paris: Maspero.

Robinson, Joan and John Eatwell (1974) *An Introduction to Economics*, Book 1, New York: McGraw Hill.

Rousseau, Jean-Jacques (1984 [1754]) *A Discourse on Inequality*, Harmondsworth: Penguin.

Turner, H.A. and Patricia Fosh (1980) *The Last Colony: But Whose?*, Cambridge: Cambridge University Press.

United Nations Development Program (1973) *Report on Development Strategies for Papua New Guinea*, Port Moresby: Government Printer.

—— (1998) *Human Development Report 1998*, New York: UNDP.

Weber, Max (1981 [1923]) *General Economic History*, Part IV, Brunswick, NJ: Transaction Books.

World Bank (1998) *Development Indicators 1998*, Washington, DC: IBRD.

Part I

Elites, politics and peripheries

Chapter 3

The powers behind the masks
Mexico's political class and social elites at the end of the millennium

John Gledhill

In this paper I survey the rise and apparent demise of the political machine that governed Mexico for the seventy-one years up to the presidential elections of 2000. Mexico's political and social elites should not be regarded as coterminous, though I will explore some of the connections between social power and status, on the one hand, and political power, on the other.[1] My analysis seeks to show how a national political elite was constructed in the course of the formation of the 'modern' national state, and how compromises were secured between contending elite factions in post-revolutionary Mexico. By highlighting the informal and less public aspects of this process, including their social etiquettes, I will also be able to illuminate less obvious causes of the ultimate disintegration of the old regime.

In a sense, that old regime was an object lesson in how political symbols and rituals derived from a revolutionary process could provide the basis for the enduring legitimacy of a system of rule. Yet it was always a contested system of rule, and the concept of 'legitimacy' relevant to this case needs further nuance. In Mexico, citizens constructed an imaginary of 'the state' (Gupta 1995) that recognised the corruption at the heart of politics while investing in the idea of using the law and bureaucracy as a means of solving their problems.[2] The imagined centre of power could be a source of valuable services, economic support and protection from the more powerful elements of a deeply unequal society. But it could also oppress those who pressed too strong a challenge to the various social 'pacts' on which the regime was based. In a sense, the regime of the Institutional Revolutionary Party (Partido Revolucionario Institucional, PRI) acted as a mask to the transcendent power of social elites, including elites that had survived the revolutionary upheavals of 1910 to 1920. It also fostered the emergence of new elite actors at different levels in society. Yet Mexicans were never naïve or complacent about the nature of social power, and for sixty years there was more to the regime than the revolutionary disguises embodied in its rhetoric. It fell when the system of power and compromises on which it was based ceased to work. Throwing off their old masks, members of the political class sought ways of conserving their authority while embracing neoliberal economics and aspects of neoliberal political ideology, but lost their solidarity in the process. The result has been a 'transition to democracy' in the electoral field, but it is not, as I will show, one that can be taken completely at face value.

In seeking to analyse processes at the national level, I will not eschew traditional anthropological analysis of local and regional processes. It is very important to recognise that elites exist at different social levels and in local and regional as well as national contexts. But I am also interested in redressing what I consider an imbalance in recent anthropological work on Mexico, and I begin by discussing this issue in more detail.

Re-making connections with the centre

Anthropological studies of Mexican politics have tended to concentrate on relationships between the national political centre and regional spaces. Studies of 'bossism' or *caciquismo* have broadened in recent years to address ways in which local processes shape national ones (Lomnitz-Adler 1992), with anthropological research being invoked against a 'state-centred' approach (Rubin 1996; Pansters 1997; Aitken 1999). A second focus has been on 'political culture', partly in an effort to reach a deeper understanding of how power relations actually work and partly to understand the limits of conflict and ebb and flow of popular social movements. Anthropologists have joined historians such as Mallon (1995) in illuminating the paradoxes of Mexican history through explorations of identity and historical memory (Nugent 1993).

As a result of these preoccupations, interest in elite culture and organisation has largely focused on elite–subaltern interactions and the emergence of new actors in regional landscapes. Thus, the rise of a new local elite in the indigenous municipalities of Chiapas in the 1970s was associated with the development of transport infrastructure and trucking. These new elements were able to articulate themselves to federal government agencies in a way that progressively diminished the need to dedicate resources to maintaining clientship networks with poorer people in their communities (Collier 1994, 1997; Escalante 1995). A massive increase in the state's direct role in the economy during the sexennials of Luis Echeverría and José López Portillo (1970–76, 1976–82) created new regional elites linked to the corrupt administration of state enterprises. These became a target for the hostility of increasingly disadvantaged private businessmen, drawing the latter towards a new activism in the political arena outside the framework of the PRI (Leyva Solano 1993; Bensabet Kleinberg 1999). There has, however, been less interest on the part of anthropologists in studying elite families and their networks in their own right.

A notable exception is a study of elite family history by Lomnitz and Pérez-Lizaur (1987), which offers useful insights into the reproduction of national elite culture and social organisation. For the most part, however, what anthropological literature does best is illuminate the way regional elite culture transforms as 'local' power is incorporated into wider networks. Frans Schryer (1990), for example, describes how the university-educated children of the rancher political bosses of the Huasteca abandoned old practices of family feuding orientated around hyper-masculine codes of status–honour for more 'civilised' forms of behaviour and the development of a commercial ranching economy. In the 1970s this transformation triggered violent agrarian insurrection on the part of an equally 'modernised' but increasingly alienated and impoverished peasantry. Such work has contributed to a more dialectical account of the dynamics of national history. A 'view from below' helps us appreciate that 'national' political labels may tell us little about what is at stake in local politics, offering a poor guide to the ideologies, social interests and conjunctural alliances underlying local conflicts (Zárate Hernández 1995). There are, however, drawbacks to failing to consider elite culture and networks at higher levels of analysis.

One problem is that of misconstruing what happens in regions as a consequence of their 'isolation from the national mainstream'. This is precisely what Mexican governments after 1994 (conveniently but, as we will see, falsely) identified as the root of the 'problem' in Chiapas, often seconded by left-wing critics of the regime who had a limited grasp of the real agrarian and political problems of the state. It is true that some important local developments, such as the rise of a left-wing municipal government pursuing Zapotec cultural politics in Juchitán in Oaxaca, were the results of conflict between the national state and an 'autonomous' local oligarchy – also opposed by the urban merchants (Campbell 1994; Rubin *op. cit.*). Yet this example demonstrates the extent to which Mexican history turned against such truly 'autonomous' local powers. History is even turning against the cultural processes through which regional power holders negotiated their relations with the executive branch of government in Mexico City: the deployment of an earthy provincialism in political rhetoric to assert the possession of a potentially troublesome local power base and popular support.

Lomnitz-Adler (1992) illustrates this with the case of Gonzalo Santos, the great *cacique* of San Luis Potosí, eventually forced into retirement by federal police action. In his quotidian use of expletives and masculinist brutalism, Santos projected his charisma over his *ranchero* followers and intimidated Mexico City technocrats and the educated children of regional elite families, whilst using a different, more respectful and appropriately ritualised code of etiquette in his linguistic transactions with indigenous communities. Such tactics are still evident in the behaviour of some regional bosses. The pronouncement on the 1999 election campaign to the party faithful of the disgraced ex-governor of Guerrero, Rubén Figueroa Alcocer, was the rather too colourful: 'Si Félix Salgado gana, ¡nos lleva a todos la chingada!'[3]

Yet although 'colour' in political performance is still appreciated, as evidenced by the successful campaign of the candidate of the right-wing National Action Party (PAN) for the 2000 presidential elections, Vicente Fox, plain-speaking is now generally embedded within a cosmopolitan image of 'the man of affairs'. Whilst other codes may still prove useful in rural areas, they increasingly appear an anachronism in a sophisticated urban society, in which many rural residents have actually participated at some point in their lives. Nor is Rubén Figueroa, despite his language, truly an anachronism. He was well connected in terms of business partnerships and position within national political networks. This brings me to another reason for being interested in elites in the present conjuncture. As I have argued elsewhere (Gledhill 1998; 1999), and illustrate again in the present discussion, an apparent revival of 'regionalism' in the 1990s was a symptom of the increasing incapacity of the national political apparatus to rule and a growth of factional conflict among the powers that stood behind it.

After President Calles established the PRI's first precursor, the PNR, (National Revolutionary Party), in 1929, Mexico 'enjoyed' stable civilian rule, without alternation of other parties in the presidency, until Fox's electoral victory in 2000. The PRI was not a 'political party' in the democratic sense. It was created to perpetuate the rule of the military strong-men (*caudillos*) who ultimately triumphed in the Mexican revolution. After the shift to neoliberalism in the 1980s, however, Mexico's reputation for political certainties began to unravel.

The country faced serious problems of 'governability'. Guerrilla movements emerged in the mountainous *sierras* (to walk the streets of poorer *barrios* in cities such as Acapulco). Personal security declined catastrophically. Politicians were accused of links with the drug cartels whose gunmen stalked devastated urban and rural landscapes.[4] Intra-elite conflict became overt in the wake of the assassination, in 1994, of President Carlos Salinas de Gortari's chosen successor, Luis Donaldo Colosio, in circumstances never clarified to the satisfaction of his family or the public. This was a disturbing development in a regime whose past coherence reflected the solidarity 'in the last instance' of its political class. Although 1999 ended with Salinas's successor in the presidency, Ernesto Zedillo, stage-managing a public reconciliation of the contending candidates for the PRI's presidential nomination for 2000, after bitter exchanges during the electoral process, ex-President Salinas remained outside this re-closing of ranks. Furthermore, gaps in the power structure created by dismantling state clientelism had been filled by an expanded national security apparatus, supported, in the case of Chiapas, by 'unofficial' paramilitary forces (Craske *et al.* 1998).

Mario Vargas Llosa described the PRI regime as 'the perfect dictatorship'. The Mexican people turned out to vote for PRI candidates without deployment of the coercive apparatus at the state's disposal. Yet under Zedillo, the Mexican congress ceased to be a rubber stamp for the executive. The PRI lost local and state elections, not simply to the PAN, which shared its commitment to free market economics, but to the centre-left Party of the Democratic Revolution (PRD) and the PT (Labour Party). At first sight, this

looks like a 'transition to democracy', as distinct from the transition to a negotiated 'alternation' between the PRI and the PAN that seemed the more likely
scenario after the PRD's crushing defeat in the 1994 presidential elections. Yet
the electoral process was diminished by high rates of abstention, still tarnished
by undemocratic practices on the part of all contenders, and accompanied by
symptoms of mounting 'disorder', including political scandals and drug-related
violence.

The first elections of the new millennium did, however, sweep the PRI
from power, not simply delivering Fox the presidency with an unexpectedly
handsome majority, but also inflicting possibly irreparable damage on the PRI
machine in the congress and the states. Fox's win was to a great extent built
on votes against the PRI rather than positive affirmation of his own policies,
in so far as these were clear. Although Fox was the candidate of the PAN, his
team included a number of prominent figures of the left as well as the right,
and his relationship with *panistas* advocating the implementation of conservative Catholic policies in fields such as abortion and education was
uncomfortable.[5] A politician who had himself apparently embraced some of
the principles of 'Third Way' social democracy Latin American-style, Fox's
continuing attachment to the PAN and big business background was nevertheless soon a cause of scarcely disguised political infighting within the new
administration. Within a year of Fox's accession to office, his foreign minister,
the leftist academic Jorge Castañeda, was revealing his own presidential ambitions. His political friends talked of creating a new centre-left party that could
offer positive benefits to the poorer citizens who had voted for Fox simply to
end the rule of the PRI. They certainly had much to be discontented about.

During the Zedillo administration, the numbers of urban Mexicans living
in extreme poverty doubled, to two out of every five inhabitants, while the
number living above the poverty line fell to less than a third of the urban
population (Boltvinik and Hernández 2000). The long-standing association of
rural areas with an even higher incidence of extreme poverty intensified, and
rural deterioration and escalating out-migration to the cities and United
States remained unchecked by the policies of the Fox government. The deterioration of both working and middle class living standards provoked by
Mexico's particular brand of neoliberal economics is not, as we will see, the
whole story of the fall of the PRI. But the continuation of a largely
unchanged economic model into a period of deepening recession provoked
by Mexico's increased dependence on the economy of its northern neighbour
places a serious question mark against the 'democratic' political future.

The question of who governs Mexico may thus be becoming secondary to
the question, not asked since the nineteenth century, of whether anyone can
govern Mexico. The first question is, however, important in a different sense,
since post-revolutionary Mexico was not, up to 2000, governed by a political
party, but by the PRI machine. In the next section, I offer a brief account of
this *ancien régime*.

The state, social elites and historical blocs in Mexico, 1910–88

The Mexican revolution was made possible by the dictator Porfirio Díaz's failure to transform a personalistic network of power relations into an institutionalised form of rule. Yet the state-building project of the successor regime which crystallised into Mexico's eternal ruling party was not radically distinct from its liberal precursor. Like the Liberals, the revolutionary *caudillos* found themselves locked in a struggle with the Catholic Church. This culminated in the Cristero rebellion of the 1920s, just as much a popular, grassroots movement as that of the peasant insurgents who fought for Zapata and Villa. The government's social base lay not in the countryside, but in an organised, anarcho-syndicalist, urban working class. It was only the military struggle against the Cristeros that drew Calles towards concessions to agrarian rebels.

The problem represented by the Cristiada was not resolved by President Lázaro Cárdenas's more radical agrarian programme in the 1930s, which extended land redistribution to resident workers on estates. Cárdenas did, however, embark on a comprehensive restructuring of the hegemonic apparatus. The army, in which the General exercised far more influence than his predecessors, became institutionally subordinate to civilian political authority. Although Cárdenas's own strategy was to include the military as a 'sector' (alongside peasants and labour) with its own voice within a revamped official party, his successor, Manuel Avila Camacho – also a military man – removed it. The result was an historic pact: the generals agreed to keep out of politics in return for a dignified public status and the right to enrich themselves. The Cardenista state embodied the project of top-down political control over popular movements that led many analysts to describe Mexico as a corporate state. Even the movement in Michoacán that served as Cárdenas's own regional power base in his ascent to national prominence lost its autonomy.

The Church, however, proved an intractable problem. The Cárdenas agrarian reform did not satisfy the entire rural population. A still weak hegemony was often instituted at local level through the violent forms of *caciquismo* illustrated by Friedrich's study of Naranja's 'princes' (Friedrich 1986). The successor movement to the Cristiada, *sinarquismo*, was the Mexican version of fascism, framed in opposition to Cardenismo's contradictions (Meyer 1977; Aguilar and Zermeño 1989).

Despite land reform and nationalisation of the oil industry, the outcome of the revolution was largely 'passive' in Gramsci's sense. Many Porfirian elite families emerged from the revolution with their fortunes intact. Those that did not were sometimes able to rebuild them by judicious intermarriage with the 'new rich' that the revolution itself produced, as illustrated in Carlos Fuentes's *The Death of Artemio Cruz*. Although the families of land-owning and commercial elites in provincial towns sometimes abandoned their places of origin as the revolution unfolded, many re-established themselves in Mexico City or other urban centres, sometimes with the personal assistance of the *caudillos*. Not only were the new rich born of the revolutionary process – which included the *caudillos* themselves – given the facilities to 'sanitise' their wealth, but an intense politics of compromise characterised even the 'radical' period under Cárdenas. Cárdenas's policies sought to encourage rapid industrial development (by transferring landed wealth to the industrial sector) and also allowed a smaller agrarian bourgeoisie to develop.

Cárdenas's social programmes were frequently undermined at the local level by the compromises made with existing elites. This politics of compromise reflected the interests of revolutionary *caudillos* in the private accumulation of wealth, to which Cárdenas was no exception, and the fact that the corporate state was more a project than a reality. The mass organisations created by the state existed everywhere on paper, and the president selected their national leaders. Yet in much of the country, including Cárdenas's own home turf in Michoacán, the 'masses' were far from being enthusiastic *cardenistas*.

The problem of hegemony did, however, ease over time, because Cárdenas laid the foundations for drawing 'the people' into a sense of national belonging in which state institutions were, at last, central. Many Mexicans still did not manifest a strong sense of national consciousness before the 1940s, and mass media also played an important role, alongside public education, in forging the *mestizo* nation. Popular forms of nationalism and liberalism were important elements in the political cultures of the strategic north and centre-west in the nineteenth century. Yet they were not linked to strong identification with national state institutions. The *raison d'être* of popular liberalism was opposition to the arbitrary forms of rule associated with elite actors controlling public administration. Securing a greater, if always sceptical, popular identification with the state was the achievement of the post-revolutionary regime, and it went along with a new social contract.

Although the bulk of public investment from the 1940s onwards was targeted at the private sector, the regime was able to extend its popular clientele by following up the land reform with an extension of social wage and welfare benefits to some sectors of the working class. It achieved less in this respect than the Soviet Union, although the capitalist character of the system allowed a more substantial improvement in private consumption standards for the more privileged, whilst public education offered children of peasants and workers ascent into a growing middle class. The post-revolutionary model of development still left vast multitudes without guarantees of employment, social benefits and inter-generational social mobility. The state did, however, respond to pressures from below, extending further concessions to the peasant sector, including more land reform, in the 1970s. The 'statisation' of the economy was a means of restabilising PRI hegemony through expansion of the networks and beneficiaries of state clientelism, funded by Mexico's oil revenues.

The partial truth of Vargas Llosa's description of the regime as 'the perfect dictatorship' lies in this achievement. Even the landless poor, the increasingly mobilised indigenous community, and the urban squatter movements, could find it meaningful to look to the state and the law for recognition and redress.[6] At the regional level, it led to the final breaking of truly autonomous local power, as in the case of Juchitán. Yet if we turn south from Juchitán to Chiapas, we also see how the integration of regional elites into national networks of power could perpetuate local injustices.

As I noted above, Chiapas is often misrepresented as a place where national state power failed to penetrate and where agrarian reform never happened. Yet the state's agrarian structure cannot be flattened into a simple opposition between big landowners (*finqueros*) and poor indigenous peasants (Van der Haar 1998). The major issue in the late nineteenth century was how the emerging planter class could unlock the labour of the highland Indian communities. The elites of San Cristóbal de Las Casas and Tuxtla Gutiérrez disputed the location of the state capital and the weight assigned to different modes of exploitation of the lower classes. As Jan Rus has shown, the 'War of the Castes' in Chiapas was not so much a rebellion as a massacre of people whose 'project' was simply to be allowed to practise their religion autonomously, peacefully cultivate their lands and control their own markets. *Ladino* aggression and the creation of a myth of Indian rebelliousness under-pinned imposition of the mechanisms needed to 'release' labour on the communities (Rus 1983).

In 1914, when the rebellions of Villa and Zapata forced the Constitu-tionalist President Carranza to abandon Mexico City, Chiapas also rose in arms under the 'Mapaches'.[7] The 'Mapaches' were smaller proprietors from areas beyond the Central Valley, whilst the upper strata of the Chiapaneco mercantile and land-owning elite collaborated enthusiastically with the Carranza regime (Benjamin 1995). The long-term effects of the Mapache uprising were 'reactionary'. Yet the reaction was not triggered by the central-ising efforts of the Carranza government. It was provoked by the abuses committed by the military units 'pacifying' the state and by the effects of Carrancista labour laws on middle strata whose economic position was precarious – the groups left behind by the willingness of regional elites to buy into national projects and embrace 'modernisation'.

The upper echelons of the Chiapaneco elite have not, therefore, been isolated from national networks in the twentieth century, and interventions by the centre have had important effects on the region's social history. Cárdenas used land reform to build a clientele. Communities such as Zinacantán only became communities of corn farmers thanks to agrarian reform, and their subsequent patterns of development reflect the way some groups within them gained membership of extra-community political networks (Cancian 1992; Rus 1994). The *priísta* bosses of highland villages in Chiapas today are the descendants of a generation of young village leaders and bilingual school-teachers whom Cárdenas backed as the instrument of 'state penetration'. In many ways, the post-Cardenista history of Chiapas was one of increasing indigenous assertiveness long before the Zapatista rebellion of 1994 (Van der Haar 1998; Villafuerte Solis *et al.* 1999), though the long-term result of this was a pulverisation of much of the peasant land base into infra-subsistence *minifundios*.

In San Cristóbal, the combined effects of the revolution and Cardenismo produced a massive emigration of the heirs of the *finqueros* and merchants of the Porfirian era by mid-century. This left smaller businessmen to exploit the new opportunities offered by the tourist trade. Ocosingo, the nearest major town to the Zapatista core area in the Selva Lacandona, resembles the Huasteca: a younger generation of university educated 'progressive' livestock producers, professionals and agroforestry entrepreneurs is displacing the 'traditional' rancher elite (Ascencio 1998: 5). Here, as in Comitán, where the sub-regional elite now consists of urban functionaries and businessmen (Escalante 1995: 30), new elite groups drew strength from their closer relationships with federal government agencies. This, in turn, increased their influence in state politics. Most of the agrarian problems of Chiapas are a reflection of the fact that national policies, such as promotion of extensive cattle raising, were pursued in the state under *priísta* governments whose members frequently entered the federal cabinet (Viqueira 1999).

Before looking at the contemporary power structures to which these regional elites are articulated, it will be useful to say a little more about the organisations that remained at arm's length from the PRI regime, the Catholic Church and the business class.

Catholic elite culture did penetrate the state through members of the elite who joined the 'revolutionary' camp without subscribing to militant secularist positions. Nevertheless, the Church possesses its own political extension in the shape of the PAN (and less reputably, in the past, the PDM). Salinas's removal of legal barriers to participation of the clergy in politics caused protest from those still wedded to the revolutionary tradition. Furthermore, one of the effects of the post-revolutionary state's struggles with the Church was its patronage of Protestant groups, such as the Luz del Mundo Church in Guadalajara. This was founded by a soldier and continued to enjoy close links with senior figures in the military as well as patronage from PRI governors, as a counterweight to the sometimes aggressive stance taken by Guadalajara's hierarchy against the national regime (González 1996). Opus Dei and Acción Católica have underpinned the reproduction of a Catholic elite culture which has continually sought to rebuild a mass base, especially amongst the urban petty bourgeoisie that votes for the PAN, often fortified in its militancy through training courses offered to the laity.

Although the long-run tendency after 1940 was towards compromise rather than confrontation, the Papal visit of 1999 created anxieties. Although the hierarchy (and the Vatican) originally cooperated with the Salinas government in its (pre-rebellion) attempt to remove the liberation theology-orientated Bishop Samuel Ruíz from Chiapas, political attacks on the bishop created a situation that threatened his personal security. Subsequent developments in the counter-insurgency campaign alienated less militant members of the clergy: the military not only closed churches but desecrated them in a manner reminiscent of the dark days of the 1920s. Since the Pontiff had an interest in human rights, and the failure of the regime to counteract growing poverty drew less radical bishops into a critique of neoliberalism, relations once again became delicate. In the event, however, the visit passed off in a manner that offered comfort to all sides.

Another central post-revolutionary issue was the role of business. Despite the state's implicit 'pact with capital', *capitalists* (generally referred to politely as *empresarios*, entrepreneurs) were not part of the official party structure. The state did sponsor the creation of quasi-official business groups, but in 1929 business established an autonomous organisation of its own, COPARMEX (the Employers' Federation of the Mexican Republic), as a result of a growing rift between the post-revolutionary state and the business elite of the northern city of Monterrey.

After the revolution the close-knit group of families that made up the Monterrey industrial and commercial bourgeoisie was forced to contend with a local labour movement determined to exploit the concessions that the federal authorities had extended to labour (Saragoza 1988). Led by the Garza-Sada family, Monterrey's businessmen sought to reach out to Obregón and Calles. Yet they soon discovered that 'revolutionary capitalists' had different interests to those whose wealth and power depended on business alone. As Saragoza puts it, where the state itself became a source of profit, and individuals' 'economic welfare was rooted in the state's domination if not control of Mexico's masses', 'political interests were primary' (1988: 205). When Cárdenas's reforming zeal forced a split with Calles, the Monterrey elite broke with both factions. They faced off federal labour laws, defended their company unions and company schools, and thereby secured unprecedented control over local social and cultural life.

Much of Mexico's business class was, however, content to leave the Monterrey elite to take the high ground of capitalist opposition to the regime alone. The 'bourgeoisies' of Mexico City and Guadalajara, and medium sized cities such as Querétaro and Aguascalientes, are not exact social equivalents of the Monterrey elite (Salmerón Castro 1996). This is not simply because the industrial and commercial structures of other cities differ from that of Monterrey. Entrepreneurial elites enjoyed different kinds of linkages to the state, with cliques controlling political power locally, and with the Church. Yet there was no need for the entire capitalist class to confront the regime. Informal channels of communication continued to secure specific concessions, whilst the economic muscle and combativeness of the Monterrey elite kept up pressure for concessions to be made.

Much of the private sector found state subsidies and protection attractive and was willing to tolerate the corruption and overmanning associated with the official union regime. In small provincial towns, however, entrepreneurs concentrated more on keeping the state off their backs (with its labour laws and inspectors in search of payoffs). Pursuing a strategy of spreading risks through diversification, such entrepreneurs often built networks and invested across the country, but adopted a cultural mask of intense localism to minimise their visibility (Forbes-Adam 1994). Where a local industrial class did develop, it tended to be antagonistic to the upper echelons of the social elite:

> Only thirty per cent of rich Mexicans invest in Mexican industry…They want to convert themselves into millionaires in the public sector but they aren't willing to invest in industry. They prefer their mansions, paintings, their big ranches.
>
> (Ex-president of CANCINTRA, Querétaro, cited in Keren 1997: 72; my translation)

Such sentiments also express growing disillusion with the disastrous process of public sector expansion during the oil boom of the 1970s. The nationalisation of the banks in 1982 ended the accommodation between business and the PRI state and provoked a shift towards radical right-wing leaderships in most of the business associations (Bensabat Kleinberg 1999: 74)

The long-term result was not, however, a radical rupture but a re-accommodation in which big business was invited to participate actively in the PRI (Bensabat Kleinberg 1999: 80). Since the PAN had already become more of a party of big business, with high profile businessmen becoming candidates for governorships, the political logic of the PRI's opting for the same strategy is transparent. Yet the interesting question is why business wished to work with the PRI rather than for a change of government. The obvious answer is that the PRI remained in power and had transformed its economic policies in a way that maximised the opportunities for big capital to prosper in the global marketplace.

The way connections within government can solve problems of market risk was dramatically demonstrated by the scandals surrounding the Zedillo administration's attempts to transform the private debts of some of Mexico's richest families into public debt in 1998 through the FOBAPROA (Fondo Bancario de Protección al Ahorro).[8] Despite a political furore, heightened by public suspicion that some of the fortunes at risk had illicit origins, the government persevered with measures that did little to satisfy the demands of Mexico's smaller businessmen and commercial farmers. The latter once again took their complaints to the streets through the *El Barzón* (The Yoke) anti-debt movement, initially established in the Salinas period. The rescue of Mexico's fourth largest bank at the end of 1999 alone cost one-and-a-half times Mexico's oil revenues for the previous year (*Mexico and NAFTA Report*, RM-99–11).

There are, however, two other possible perspectives on the rapprochement between big business and the PRI. One would point to the state apparatus's role in controlling the dissidence necessary to maintain the neoliberal economic model and the other to the transformations of the Mexican political class itself that lay behind the 'victory of the technocrats'.

Complicities and contradictions

This brings me to the powers behind the masks. Recruitment to high office has been structured by clique or *camarilla* networks (Camp 1996). Today's *camarillas* still connect with two original networks, one founded by Cárdenas, with roots in the military, and a second by Miguel Alemán, who became president in 1946. Alemán was the first university-educated civilian to assume presidential office. His *camarilla* might thus be described as the *camarilla* of the 'technocrats', though self-enrichment in office also made him a symbol of the venality of the civilian 'político'. These labels are not very meaningful in themselves, as individuals move from one *camarilla* to another. Yet 'technocracy' is structurally significant in recent presidencies: holders of US doctorates, both Salinas and Zedillo entered office young, and had less opportunity to develop *camarillas* centred on themselves. Zedillo was particularly weak, since, in contrast to Salinas, his social background was humble, and he was isolated from the PRI machine.

The *camarilla* structures regulated the division of public spoils and competition for high office. Over time their evolution created ramifying chains of social solidarity that broke down regional barriers and made the political class more unitary and less truly 'regional', even if particular families continued to dominate the politics of their home states. Because elite social networks also transcend party lines, *camarilla* mechanisms could continue to operate even with alternation of party government. This is especially important in the case of the centre-left PRD. Originally formed as a fusion of dissident *priístas* and left-wing parties, including the old Mexican Communist Party, it is now dominated by former *priístas* since more PRI politicians jumped ship after the PRD's electoral fortunes began to revive in 1997.

The coherence of the political class was a major strength of the *ancien régime*. At first sight, the cupola of power in Mexico seemed to be the presidency: for six years the incumbent enjoyed untrammelled power, but the rule of no re-election set limits to despotism. In a classic analysis, Frank Brandenburg (1964) argued, however, that the real summit was the head of the 'revolutionary family', a small network of leaders, including ex-presidents, who ran the country in general and the PRI in particular. One of Carlos Salinas's sins was to interfere with the established mechanisms for controlling political competition. Salinas wished his power to endure, and this obsession remained evident in his behaviour even after mounting scandal regarding his administration, and conflict with Zedillo, drove him abroad. When the trial of his brother Raúl, accused of intellectual authorship of the murder of his brother-in-law, came to judgement in January 1999, Salinas moved from exile in Ireland to Cuba, anticipating a triumphant return after the expected acquittal. Raúl was in fact sentenced to fifty years, an outcome that signalled deep divisions within the revolutionary family.

Lázaro Cárdenas's son Cuauhtémoc's defection from the PRI to challenge Salinas in the 1988 elections made it more likely that the power groups that stood behind the state would become openly competitive, but Salinas had defused the immediate threat posed by Cárdenas and the PRD by 1992. The Chiapas rebellion and political murders of 1994 helped the PRI win the presidential elections, as a 'politics of fear' gripped the populace (McDonald 1997). It was the crash of December 1994 that changed the scenario radically. The effects of open intra-elite competition were made more dramatic because many members of that elite lost their dignified masks in the process.

The most obvious dropping of masks was that of the '*narco-políticos*'. One example in 1999 was the governor of Quintana Roo, Mario Villanueva, accused of links with the Ciudad Juárez and Cali cartels. Yet although arrest warrants were issued, Villanueva walked past his guards and fled to Cuba. More importantly, scandal ran deep in the Salinas cabinet. Mario Ruíz Massieu, once deputy attorney general and brother of the politician for whose murder Raúl Salinas was convicted, committed suicide in a Texas prison while awaiting trial for money laundering. Shortly afterwards, former FBI agent Stanley Pimental alleged that money from drug trafficking had ended up directly in the President's office. Pimental argued that the PRI had provided protection to the drug cartels throughout its history (*Mexico and NAFTA Report*, RM-99–10).

A favourite target of press speculation based on supposed 'leaks' from official sources was Carlos Hank Gónzalez. Once a schoolteacher, he was Mayor of Mexico City under López Portillo (1976–82) and Minister of Agriculture under Salinas (1988–94). Mexicans frequently use the expression 'rich as Hank González' in casual conversation and *Forbes* estimates his fortune at one hundred million dollars. His principal role in politics was that of a kingmaker, with a strong personal *camarilla*, centred on the state of Mexico but of much wider extension. A number of his protégés held high office earlier in the Zedillo administration. Both his sons have been active in a variety of business enterprises, including transport companies (supposedly used for shipping narcotics) and casinos and racetracks (supposedly used for laundering money) (*Proceso*, 7 November 1999). The family brought the wrath of the Federal Reserve Board down on its head following an attempt to take control of a US bank (*La Jornada*, 6 June 1999).

Within Mexico, the Hank clan was popularly seen as an archetypal example of a Mafia-style family, using its wealth to influence politics from backstage, and affording its patronage and protection to organised crime. The Hanks themselves vigorously contest these charges. The family hired former

FBI and DEA agents to demonstrate that hard evidence was lacking for any of the accusations laid against them, and managed to secure the endorsement of two former US ambassadors to Mexico (*Proceso*, 28 November 1999). The position of the Zedillo government was that such accusations were slanders, while the Clinton administration adopted a 'refuse to confirm or deny' posture.

When power relations are built in a 'shadow state' on the basis of operations in 'informal' or 'illegal' markets, 'facts' tend to become systematically murky, and misinformation as abundant as information. Nor is this a problem restricted to the Mexican side of the border. I have argued elsewhere that the United States had a vested interest in leaving the issue of drugs and politics in Mexico live but unresolved. It supplied leverage in dealings with the PRI government on matters such as the NAFTA and immigration policy (Gledhill 1999). I also argue that, in Latin America in general, the drugs economy and shadow state are products of what Poole and Rénique (1991: 191) term the 'unutterable connections' established by US domination over the region. From the standpoint of both counter-insurgency geopolitics and political economy they are systemic global phenomena rather than 'pathologies' rooted in the peculiarities of Southern political cultures. Some 'facts' are, however, relatively uncontested, even if their implications are subject to official denial.

One of the persons to enjoy close relationships with both the Salinas brothers and Carlos Hank was Carlos Cabal Peniche, an overnight millionaire whose rise also involved patronage from figures in the Catholic Church and participation in the BCCI scandal (Gledhill 1999). Cabal went on to invest in a range of industrial enterprises which shared the common characteristic of making extensive use of the chemical precursors used in the production of cocaine, along with banks and currency exchanges, investments that in this context suggest money laundering. When Cabal's banks foundered, he faced criminal charges, and was gaoled in Australia subject to extradition procedures. His career manifested the entire web of connections established between the formal political sphere, privatisation of public enterprises and 'legal' and 'illegal' economic activities during the Salinas era. He embarrassed the Zedillo government greatly from his prison cell by speaking to the press about his financial contributions to PRI electoral campaigns. These, he asserted, did not simply include the gubernatorial campaign of Roberto Madrazo Pintado, unsuccessful contender for the PRI's presidential candidature in 2000, who returned, with Zedillo's blessing, to re-assume the governorship of Tabasco state after the contest, despite the opposition of some members of his own party.[9] The PRD opposition claimed that Madrazo won his governorship with a higher level of electoral expenses than those that put Clinton into the White House, and Cabal subsequently claimed that other electoral beneficiaries of his enforced generosity were Luis Donaldo Colosio and Zedillo himself. Whilst this and other assertions continued to be denied officially, what cannot be denied, since it is a matter of public record, is that Cabal Peniche moved freely within the inner circles of Mexico's political and social elite. These relationships underpinned his brief moment of glory as the model entrepreneur of a 'new' Mexico.

The elite power blocs that constitute a 'shadow state' were always there in post-revolutionary Mexico. Yet it is still important that so many dignified masks began to slip in the 1990s, since the political rituals of the old order were also made less meaningful to most Mexicans by the traumatically socially polarising consequences of neoliberal economics. As things stand, recent Mexican history seems to express contradictory tendencies. On the one hand, we have a flowering of pro-democracy, civic and human rights movements. On the other hand, despite the existence of this type of public culture, powerful political actors managed to defend their impunity, even in the face of major popular mobilisation. Minor figures such as governor Villanueva and a few army officers were officially charged with links with drug-traffickers. Yet Villanueva courted disaster by exciting Zedillo's political hostility, and his case needs to be set against the extended political survival of governor Madrazo. Madrazo's rehabilitation after his intemperate challenge to Francisco Labastida for the PRI nomination demonstrated that the warring factions of the political class were prepared to close ranks to ensure the continuity of their power.

Although this was to prove too little too late, the compromises that actors in the formal, electoral, sphere of politics may be obliged to make with the structures of shadow state power remain a live issue throughout Latin America and beyond. As William Reno has remarked in the context of Africa, shadow state structures may become an *alternative* institutionalisation of power that can achieve long-term stability (Reno 1995: 183). A country's place in the global economy can establish long-term relationships between control of informal markets and the exercise of political power, relationships in which foreign companies become elements in the power networks of these actors. The boundaries between roles in the public and private sector become blurred, as more former state functions are privatised. Informal entrepreneurial activity becomes a means not only of exercising power but also of occupying formal positions in the political field. Southern shadow state actors are vulnerable to abandonment by their foreign corporate allies and to regulatory interventions by more powerful states interested in avoiding scandals at home (of the kind provoked by the BCCI affair). Yet their local social power is such as to throw doubt on the capacity of an untainted 'civil society' to enforce political accountability.

Chaos or recomposition?

Mexico in the final years of unbroken PRI rule illustrates a more general process in which effective power gravitates towards 'shadow state' networks. What makes it an interesting case is that a different kind of state existed not very long before. 'Corruption' and clientelism were structurally integral to the old regime. It was not, however, a regime which needed to 'armour its hegemony with coercion' in the way that it did in the second half of the 1990s, and it was remarkable for its ability to accommodate, if not comprehensively satisfy, a broad range of conflictive forces.

The contemporary alliance between Mexican big business and US capital is a strong one, perhaps made even stronger by the election of Fox (an old personal friend of George W. Bush). The only demand that alliance makes of government is that it creates conditions that enable it to prosper. In most respects, the groups that constitute the shadow state share these economic interests and partner transnational capital in their 'legitimate' (and perhaps some less legitimate) activities. The greater intervention of the United States in Mexico's internal affairs problematised the position of those involved in 'illegal' activities, since some had to be sacrificed for the sake of appearances. Reduced levels of elite solidarity removed traditional guarantees – as the Salinas family discovered. Yet enormous efforts were made to create a web of confusion that made it difficult to incriminate anyone of anything in a court of law. In this sense, complicity between those at the top of the pyramid was a continuing feature of the system.

At the close of 1999, the 'revolutionary family' still seemed set to survive into the next millennium. Facing an opposition lacking alternative economic projects that had a clear a priori appeal to a sceptical electorate, the PRI seemed likely to retain the presidency. Electoral processes had already given opposition groups an opportunity to try their luck at governing. Yet it was difficult to administrate localities with diminishing fiscal resources and multiple sources of public disorder, including flourishing criminal organisations which still enjoyed protection from other instances of power (civil, military and police). There were positive possibilities in a more open political environment for local alliances and compromises to ameliorate the social effects of constant economic shocks. Ordinary Mexicans displayed resilience in devising coping strategies, including strategies that depended on cross-border movement, some of which provided opportunities for moderating the repressive capacities of security forces (Besserer 1997). Yet permanent crisis is not necessarily conducive to collective action.

Salinas's achievement was to convince ordinary people that the left-wing opposition could no longer return the country to the old order. Individuals and families set about solving their own problems, drawing on their social networks and any patrons who might offer a helping hand. Thoughts turned away (in disillusion) from politics, and solidarities narrowed: individualism, familism and the exclusion of others from claims offered fertile soil for neoliberal values to take root. When Mexico's capitalists fail to manage their affairs successfully, on the other hand, it is the taxpayer who foots the bill, and transnational corporations that take control of the assets.

This continues to be the case even after the fall of the PRI. Fox sought to solve the problems of increasing public expenditure with a regressive fiscal reform proposal that increases indirect taxes on items that poor people consume. He gave the green light to Citybank's takeover of Mexico's largest domestic banking group, an issue made yet more controversial by scandals surrounding both banks in relation to earlier connections between power and illicit wealth. He is in favour of an aggressive capitalist transformation of the poor southern regions of Mexico through the development of an extractive economy linked (in a somewhat contradictory way) to biodiversity, energy and tourism. Yet what finally defeated PRI rule was intra-elite conflict coupled with the system's increasing failure to deliver anything other than mass impoverishment and growing personal insecurity (despite a growing militarisation of the national security apparatus, directed against organised social movements, that proved counter-productive).

With their masks removed, and reciprocity at a low ebb,[10] the figures that stood behind the PRI ceased to be able to draw convincingly on the reformist rhetoric of the old order. They became vulnerable to political challenge because they ceased to embody what people had valued about that order (despite recognising its inner corruption). They could not reorganise themselves effectively to present a face that could establish alternative grounds for claiming to represent the public interest. Their public internal feuding and violence undermined the myth of a coherent, centralised and stable state controlled by backstage actors of unlimited power. In presiding over the dismantling of a sectoral society, leaving so many individuals socially incapacitated under conditions of growing income polarisation, and failing to stop 'disorder', the PRI abandoned the terrain on which it could play successfully on the politics of fear.

In voting against the PRI, many electors no doubt hoped that the new government would mete out some punishment to the former political class, without reflecting too deeply on whether the economic alternatives on offer would prove an improvement. Fox won because he was the candidate who had garnered enough support from dissident elite figures to seem strong enough to win, while also embodying in full measure the hyper-masculinity and personal eccentricities of a 'modernised' *caudillo*. Yet the symptoms of 'disorder' that Mexico's neoliberal transition provoked may prove nothing more than unavoidable glitches in the renegotiation of power relations as far as elites are concerned. Even if they prove more enduring, it is now impossible to go back to the Mexico of the past.

What will happen in the future depends in part on whether Mexico's northern neighbour is willing to support political forces that are less convenient from the point of view of US interests but more likely to disrupt the chain of complicities that protected the powers behind the masks. This is also a choice that confronts the more civilised members of Mexico's social elite, for whom the defence of privilege has so frequently counselled caution in political engagement and tacit acquiescence in the absence of a rule of law from the lives of less fortunate citizens. Part of that choice must involve making some connection between the fact that Mexico is a country that suffers from problems of extreme wealth as well as from problems of extreme poverty.

Notes

1   One of the issues explored in the original version of this paper that will have to be left on one side here for reasons of space is the role of university intellectuals, including anthropologists, in Mexican politics. Suffice it to say that academics as public intellectuals played a very important role in both the construction of post-revolutionary nationalism and in giving some credence to aspects of 'neoliberal reform'. On the other hand, the toleration of intellectual dissidence has been crucial to Mexico's image over the years, although it had strict limits under the PRI regime, especially when intellectual dissidence outside the upper levels of the social elite translated into activism. The intimate social networks of the national elite are central to an understanding of the limits of political action by intellectuals.

2   We could contrast Mexico with some other Latin American countries, such as Colombia, by arguing that in the case of Mexico the workings, rituals and practices of power encouraged a majority of social actors to invest in the idea of political rule. In Colombia, the sanguinary confrontations between 'Liberal' and 'Conservative' factions during *La Violencia* of 1946–58 produced a system of elite alternation in power that left political rule itself with minimal legitimacy, reinforcing a deep social ambiguity towards all forms of authority, at all levels in society (Jimeno 2001). There is a very low level of subscription to the idea that the existing state can be made to work for anyone. Very large numbers of people are allied, by subscription or conscription, with projects to reconstruct a 'corrupt' state by destroying it, in the case of the guerrillas, or fulfilling the 'ordering' functions the official state is incapable of filling, in the case of the paramilitaries.

3   'If Félix Salgado [candidate of the PRD-PT centre-left alliance] wins, we're all well and truly shafted!'

4   Mexico has four major cartels. Estimates of their economic power vary from 4.39% of gross domestic product on 1998 figures by the Mexican Public Prosecutor's Office, to 20.7% according to the calculations of the US Drug Enforcement Agency (*Proceso*, 24 June 2001).

5   Although Fox himself is a committed Catholic, his moral standing was problematised by his personal relationship with his political adviser and spokeswoman, Martha Sahagún. Both were divorced, and annulment of Martha's earlier marriage, to a son of one of the PAN's founders, a native of the intensely conservative town of Zamora, Michoacán, was out of the question. The couple finally celebrated a civil marriage in 2001, with the Church maintaining a stance of disapproval.

6   Whilst, as in other Latin American countries, the law functions most of the time to disempower the poor and privilege the 'connected' (DaMatta 1991), the possibility of achieving a 'connection' that would enable a group of claimants to secure land rights or other concessions was not a total illusion. It served as the experiential underpinning of an imaginary of the state that Monique Nuijten aptly describes as 'the hope generating machine' (Nuijten 1998). The fact that ordinary people constructed a model of the power elite behind the state as corrupt was actually quite helpful in maintaining a commitment to engage with the bureaucratic agencies through which 'the state' was actually 'known' in real life and misconstrued as centralised and coherent.

7   The name 'racoons' refers to people who move at night and eat raw maize from the fields (*milpas*).

8 This was replaced at the end of the year by the IPAB (Instituto para la Protección al Ahorro Bancario). For further discussion, see Gledhill (1999).
9 Fox initially seemed willing to reach an accommodation with Madrazo at the beginning of his presidency, when the latter was again bidding for the national PRI leadership in the wake of the electoral catastrophe. Madrazo's selection as new PRI leader might have eased the new government's position in the Congress. His business interests in the south-east of Mexico, linked to those of the Hank–Salinas group, were also useful in the context of establishing Mexican economic dominance in Central America under the former regime's 'Plan Puebla-Panama', which Fox enthusiastically endorsed. Yet Madrazo's efforts to rig the 2000 state elections in Tabasco were so strikingly incompetent that the Federal Electoral Commission had little choice but to take the unprecedented step of ordering a new poll, while Madrazo himself made a discreet exit to the USA.
10 As Chabal and Daloz remark, in the African context, corruption is entangled in the instrumentality of a political order based on vertical ties (and very blurred boundaries between the 'public' and 'private', 'state' and 'society') yet also closely associated with positive ethical values of 'reciprocity'. Thus:

> Provided the beneficiaries of graft do not hoard too much of what they accumulate by means of the exploitation of the resources made available to them through their position, and provided they redistribute along lines that are judged to be socially desirable, their behaviour is deemed acceptable.
>
> (Chabal and Daloz 1999: 99)

In Mexico, similar principles traditionally applied and may continue to be important in the future. But their scope narrowed substantially in recent decades. Local elites tied to national bureaucratic and political networks became less dependent on mobilising local clienteles (Collier 1994). The scope of 'official' vertical patronage ties became increasingly selective, targeted on key organised groups threatening to derail the neoliberal model that could not so easily be repressed, while the net value of clientelistic handouts was reduced by deteriorating general economic conditions. Both local political factions (including those of the opposition) and shadow state actors continued to demonstrate the political instrumentality of these kinds of relations, but within relatively narrow social as well as political fields. This explains why the new regional *cacicazgos*, such as those of Figueroa and Madrazo, provoked strong local opposition and violence, while the impact on a national political order still very different from that of most African countries was not sufficient to sustain PRI rule.

Bibliography

Aguilar Valenzuela, Rubén and Zermeño Padilla, Guillermo (1989) 'De movimiento social a partido político: de la UNS al PDM', in Jorge Alonso (ed.), *El PDM: movimiento regional*, Guadalajara: Universidad de Guadalajara.
Aitken, Robert (1999) 'Localizing Politics: Cardenismo, the Mexican State and Local Politics in Contemporary Michoacán', Leiden: Leiden University Ph.D. thesis, Research School CNWS.
Ascencio Franco, Gabriel (1998) 'Clase política y criminalización en Chiapas', *Ciudades* 40: 3–6.
Benjamin, Thomas (1995) '¡Primero viva Chiapas! La revolución mexicana y las rebeliones locales', in Juan Pedro Viqueira and Mario Humberto Ruz (eds), *Chiapas:*

Los Rumbos de Otra Historia, Mexico City: Universidad Nacional Autónoma de México, 175–94.

Bensabet Kleinberg, Remonda (1999) 'Strategic Alliances: State-Business Relations in Mexico Under Neoliberalism and Crisis', *Bulletin of Latin American Research* 18(1): 71–87.

Besserer, Federico (1997) 'La transnacionalización de los oaxacalifonianos: la comunidad transnacional y multicéntrica de San Juan Mixtepec', paper presented to the XIX Colloquium on Regional Anthropology and History *Fronteras Fragmentadas: Género, famila e identidades en la migración mexicana al norte*, held at the Colegio de Michoacán, Zamora, Mexico, 22–24 October 1997.

Boltvinik, Julio and Hernández Laos, Enrique (2000) *Pobreza y distribución del ingreso en México*, Mexico City: Siglo XXI Editores.

Brandenburg, Frank (1964) *The Making of Modern Mexico*, Englewood Cliffs, NJ: Prentice Hall.

Camp, Roderic A. (1996) *Politics in Mexico*, New York and Oxford: Oxford University Press.

Campbell, Howard (1994) *Zapotec Renaissance: Ethnic Politics and Cultural Revivalism in Southern Mexico*, Albuquerque, NM: University of New Mexico Press.

Cancian, Frank (1992) *The Decline of Community in Zinacantán: Economy, Public Life, and Social Stratification, 1960–1987*, Stanford, CA: Stanford University Press.

Chabal, Patrick and Daloz, Jean-Pascal (1999) *Africa Works: Disorder as a Political Instrument*, Oxford, Bloomington and Indianapolis: The International African Institute in association with James Currey and Indiana University Press.

Collier, George A. (1994) 'The New Politics of Exclusion: Antecedents to the Rebellion in Mexico', *Dialectical Anthropology* 19(1): 1–43.

—— (1997) 'Reaction and Retrenchment in the Highlands of Chiapas in the Wake of the Zapatista Rebellion', *Journal of Latin American Anthropology* 3(1): 14–31.

Craske, Nikki *et al.* (1998) *Chiapas, Before It's Too Late… A Report by an Independent Delegation to Chiapas, Mexico, March 1998*, Bristol: Bristol Chiapas Support Group.

DaMatta, Roberto (1991) *Carnivals, Rogues and Heroes: An Interpretation of the Brazilian Dilemma*, Notre Dame and London: University of Notre Dame Press.

Escalante Gonzalbo, Ma. de la Paloma (1995) 'Cambio y política modernizadora en Chiapas', in Diana Guillén (ed.), *Chiapas: una modernidad inconclusa*, Mexico City: Instituto de Investigaciones Dr. José Luis Mora, 11–41.

Forbes-Adam, Victoria (1994) 'Profit and Tradition in Rural Manufacture: Sandal Production in Sahuayo, Michoacán', Ph.D. thesis, University of London.

Friedrich, Paul (1986) *The Princes of Naranja: An Essay on Anthrohistorical Method*, Austin, TX: University of Texas Press.

Gledhill, John (1998) 'Neoliberalism and Ungovernability: Caciquismo, Militarization and Popular Mobilization in Zedillo's Mexico,' in Valentina Napolitano and Xóchitl Leyva Solano (eds), *Encuentros Antropológicos: Power, Identity and Mobility in Mexican Society*, London: Institute of Latin American Studies, 9–28.

—— (1999) 'Official Masks and Shadow Powers: Towards an Anthropology of the Dark Side of the State', *Urban Anthropology and Studies of Cultural Systems and World Economic Development* 28(3&4): 199–251.

González, Fernando M. (1996) 'Guadalajara en los tiempos de la amenaza comunista', in Humberto González Chávez and Jesús Arroyo Alejandre (eds), *Globalización y regionalización: el occidente de México*, Guadalajara: Universidad de Guadalajara, 173–94.

Gupta, Akhil (1995) 'Blurred Boundaries: the Discourse of Corruption, the Culture of Politics, and the Imagined State', *American Ethnologist* 22(2): 375–402.

Jimeno, Myriam (2001) 'Violence and Social Life in Colombia', *Critique of Anthropology* 21(3): 221–46.

Keren, Donna J. (1997) *Trabajo y transformación económica de Querétaro*, Querétaro: INAH, COBAQ, Instituto Municipal de Cultura.

Leyva Solano, Xochitl (1993) *Poder y desarrollo regional: Puruándiro en el contexto norte de Michoacán*, Zamora: El Colegio de Michoacán and CIESAS.

Lomnitz-Adler, Claudio (1992) *Exits from the Labyrinth: Culture and Ideology in the Mexican National Space*, Berkeley, CA: University of California Press.

Lomnitz, Larissa Adler de and Pérez-Lizaur, Marisol (1987) *A Mexican Elite Family, 1820–1980: Kinship, Class, and Culture*, Princeton, NJ: Princeton University Press.

Mallon, Florencia E. (1995) *Peasant and Nation: The Making of Postcolonial Mexico and Peru*, Berkeley, CA: University of California Press.

McDonald, James H. (1997) 'A Fading Aztec Sun: The Mexican Opposition and the Politics of Everyday Fear in 1994', *Critique of Anthropology* 17(3): 263–92.

Meyer, Jean A. (1977) *Le sinarquisme: un fascisme mexicain? 1937–1947*, Paris: Hachette.

Nugent, Daniel (1993) *Spent Cartidges of Revolution: An Anthropological History of Namiquipa, Chihuahua*, Chicago: University of Chicago Press.

Nuijten, Monique (1998) 'In the Name of the Land: Organization, Transnationalism and the Culture of the State', Ph.D. thesis, Wageningen: Landbouwuniversiteit Wageningen.

Pansters, Wil G. (1997) 'Theorising Political Culture in Mexico', in Wil G. Pansters (ed.), *Citizens of the Pyramid: Essays on Mexican Political Culture*, Amsterdam: Thela Publishers, 1–37.

Poole, Deborah and Rénique, Gerardo (1991) 'The New Chroniclers of Peru: US Scholars and their "Shining Path" of Peasant Rebellion', *Bulletin of Latin American Research* 10(2): 133–91.

Reno, William (1995) *Corruption and State Politics in Sierra Leone*, Cambridge: Cambridge University Press.

Rubin, Jeffrey W. (1996) 'Decentering the Regime: Culture and Regional Politics in Mexico', *Latin American Research Review* 31(3): 85–126.

Rus, Jan (1983) 'Whose Caste War? Indians, Ladinos and the Chiapas "Caste War" of 1869', in Murdo J. MacLeod and Robert Wasserstrom (eds), *Spaniards and Indians in Southeastern Mesoamerica: Essays on the History of Ethnic Relations*, Lincoln, NB: University of Nebraska Press, 127–69.

—— (1994) 'The "Comunidad Revolucionaria Institucional": The Subversion of Native Government in Highland Chiapas, 1936–1968', in Gilbert M. Joseph and Daniel Nugent (eds), *Everyday Forms of State Formation: Revolution and the Negotiation of Rule in Modern Mexico*, Durham, NC: Duke University Press, 265–300.

Salmerón Castro, Fernando I. (1996) *Intermediarios del progreso: política y crecimiento económico en Aguascalientes*, Mexico City: CIESAS.

Saragoza, Alex M. (1988) *The Monterrey Elite and the Mexican State, 1880–1940*, Austin, TX: University of Texas Press.

Schryer, Frans J. (1990) *Ethnicity and Class Conflict in Rural Mexico*, Princeton, NJ: Princeton University Press.

Van der Haar, Gemma (1998) 'La campesinización en la zona alta tojolabal: el remate zapatista', in María Eugenia Reyes Ramos, Reyna Mogel Viveros and Gemma van der Haar (eds), *Espacios Disputados: Transformaciónes Rurales en Chiapas*, Mexico City: Universidad Autónoma Metropolitana and El Colegio de la Frontera Sur, 99–113.

Villafuerte Solis, Daniel *et al.* (1999) *La Tierra en Chiapas: Viejos Problemas Nuevos*, Mexico City: Plaza y Valdés, S.A. de C.V.

Viqueira, Juan Pedro (1999) 'Los peligros del Chiapas imaginario', *Letras Libres* 1: 20–8, 96–7.

Zárate Hernández, José Eduardo (1995) 'Agricultural Modernization and Political Recomposition in El Llano Grande', in Sergio Zendejas and Pieter de Vries (eds), *Rural Transformations Seen From Below: Regional and Local Perspectives From Western Mexico*, La Jolla, CA: Center for U.S.–Mexico Studies, University of California at San Diego, 9–21.

Chapter 4

Gente boa

Elites in and of Amazonia

Stephen Nugent

Discussion of Amazonian elites is a diffuse matter: a hodgepodge of historical examples and a few ethnographic illustrations. One reason for this is that Amazonian class structure – difficult to ignore in a discussion of elites – is hard to grasp because of the vagueness of the idea of a generic Amazonian society. It's difficult to approach structured anything in a domain consistently defined as socially amorphous and naturally rigid, and as we are frequently reminded (by anthropologists, historians, ecologists, planners – just about everyone), there is not a single Amazonia anyway, but at best a mosaic of bits of Amazonia.

If that be the case, it might be asked 'why even bother to introduce Amazonia into a symposium on elites?' There are two answers. One, in light of the anthropological ambition to 'study-up' – substantially unfulfilled despite a number of case studies – any discussion of elites in Amazonia could join the masked ranks awaiting the long-deferred analysis. I am not sure I have much to offer on that front. The second answer, however, may provide a more useful entrée. Maybe elites *per se* do not provide as useful a starting point as does a consideration of the conditions of existence necessary for the emergence of elites. In part, this strategy is informed by a desire not to enter into either a definitional debate about the relationship between political and economic power (see Marcus 1983: 14) or a debate about the role of elites, but it reflects an admiration for the kind of empirical study represented in the work of Domhoff (1967, 1974), Shoup and Minter (1977) and Chomsky and Herman (1988), the latter of whom define the target of analysis with particular clarity: *cui bono*.

There is an additional reason for citing these works as starting points, and that is in all the concern is less to categorise elites than it is to examine the institutional conditions under which elites are socially reproduced. The elites who are the focus of the studies above comprise a singularly useful starting point given not only the hegemonic role of the US in the post–Second World War period, but the high level of interaction between military/state and corporate interests, and increasing concentration and centralisation of elite power with significant responsibilities for the administration of development abroad under the linked idioms of modernization and neo-liberalism. There is, in short, a monumental elite apparatus with dynamic properties of interest not just in the analysis of elites themselves, but also in their capacity to reproduce abroad – in Brazil and Amazonia.

In terms of Amazonia and elites, let me give an example of what I have in mind. In the post-Second World War period, Brazil – a great number of authors have argued – adopted a particularly aggressive posture with regard to a technocracy-led model of national development. According to Foresta (1991: 7):

> In few countries were the ideals and practices of national development woven more tightly into public life than in Brazil. A planning mentality permeated the federal government after 1945, and development plans were a regular feature of the national economy by the end of the decade.
>
> In addition to establishing a national development bank and a federal planning structure, Brazil actively collaborated with many multi-lateral and bi-lateral development agencies such that former President Kubitschek, upon coming to power in 1956, could declare Brazil ready to achieve 'fifty years progress in five.'
>
> (Foresta 1991:7)

The commanding position of a state apparatus committed to 'development' resulted in what Evans (1979) refers to as a tri-pod structure (*tri-pé*): a bureaucratic state one of whose primary functions is to broker deals between fractions of national capital and foreign capital such that the state apparatus itself frequently appears to be empty; it is continually defined and redefined by the kinds of accommodations sought between national and international capital (one consequence of which, of course, was an incapacity to mitigate the effects of enormous debt burdens in the 1980s and 1990s; see Branford and Kucinski (1988)).

This is the kind of externality alluded to above: the conditions of existence of elites in Brazil are not narrowly defined in terms of Brazil *per se*. Brazil's long-standing, high-level economic and political links with the US (see J. Kippers Black 1977) provide a matrix in which elites are bearers of values which bespeak an international system as much as a national one. This is not to say that there are not specifically Brazilian factors that inform the shaping of an elite or elites. The power of rural oligarchies dating from the eighteenth century is still potent and provides the basis for enduring battles by regional powers for central state dominance. Disgraced former President Collor may have been chief of state, but from the perspective of many in the centre-south he was merely a flag-bearer for rustic gunmen from up north. Similarly – and despite the complete inversion of political values – the election of Erundinha as the first Workers' Party mayor of Sao Paulo was resented, or so it was reported, not so much because she was PT, a former social worker, or a lesbian, but because she was a north-easterner ruling a major southern city. Similarly – in relation to the effective power which regions hold over the centre – a recent economic crisis, which led to a major devaluation of the *real* (of the order of 30 per cent), was instigated by the refusal of a state governor – Itamar Franco, formerly known as 'Elvis isn't dead' because of his modest quiff – to repay to central government revenues it was owed. Franco was a dispossessed presidential candidate and ex-president carrying on a feud with his successor via the power still granted him as a state governor far removed from the centre of power.

This diffusion or decentralisation of national elite power is obscured to a significant degree, especially when viewed from outside Brazil, by the symbolic presence of the state, especially in the form of the extensive lexicon of acronyms representing the numerous federal agencies. Clearly, this is hardly unique to Brazil, but the branding of the state (and, by association, its elite) is belied on the ground. This is not, I hasten to add, simply a matter of there being a discrepancy between regional and national elites. It is an original condition of the notion of a national, Brazilian elite post-republic, the restatement of a debate over national identity conducted by men of letters and men of science representing the schools of law and medicine, museums and institutes engaged in defining modern Brazil from the diverse vantage points of Rio, Sao Paulo, Salvador, Belem and Recife (see Schwarcz 1999 for extensive discussion).

In summary, the category 'elite' in Amazonia – if one is seeking a benchmark according to which to compare regional elites with national elites – can lead down two paths: ethnographic/historical documentation of what passes as the local category/categories, or examination of the conditions which make possible (or preclude) the emergence of that category as socially potent. The argument sketched here is that Amazonian elites have to be approached indirectly, that is not as a fixed feature of the social landscape, but as episodically shaped by the role of the state in the world system.

Historical background

It is important, if obvious, to note that there are no examples of pre-modern Amazonian elites which feed into contemporary configurations of Amazonian elites. This is not to say that within the collective domain of indigenous societies questions of the role of elites are not pertinent – see, for example, the battles with UNI, the Union of Indigenous Nations – but except in symbolic fashion, indigenous peoples have not been able to assert themselves nationally (or regionally, in Amazonian terms) in a way which draws them into discussions of elites (notwithstanding the tendency to attribute 'chieftainship' to indigenous spokesmen). Amazonian elites are by-products of the colonial experience and thereby represent quite specific inscriptions of attempts to draw the region into empire, the state and the world economy. Certainly, there is an Amerindian dimension to elites, but given the marginalisation of 'the Indian problem', there is no opportunity to address this except obliquely (but see Ramos 1998).

Early attempts to establish a quasi-feudal system in Brazil through land grants resulted in notably non-feudal outcomes: export plantation agriculture and commercial exploitation of extractive products. In Amazonia, the former was not a significant development, while the latter was, albeit on a scale which hardly transformed the region's class structure except through the decimation of peoples haphazardly drawn into the commerce of *drogas do sertão*. Elites were imports, in the form of church, military and colonial personnel. Of these, only church operatives can claim a continuity of position, but the degree to which they constitute an elite – as opposed to representation of a remote, alien elite society – is modest. Indeed, attempts to re-romanise the Church at the end of the nineteenth century – in the face of rising popular Catholicism – failed to re-establish the official Church's hegemonic position.

The mid-nineteenth century presents, I think, an early and key example of the diffuse qualities of Amazonian elites. The focal event was the *cabanagem*, a civil war based in the estuary of the Amazon – in the cities of Belém and Cameta – but extending upriver to Manaus as well. There is relatively little published about the *cabanagem*, but in that there are clear differences about both the definition and role of elites.

Following Brazil's independence from Portugal in 1822, Amazonia, although far removed from centres of power, was engaged in a dispute about the consequences of national independence. While some commentators view the *cabanagem* primarily as a rebellion reflecting the interests of various disenfranchised groups – Indians, *caboclos*, runaway slaves – most also address the central role of elite fractions espousing quite different post-independence strategies: monarchism, republicanism or autonomy for the as-was Estado de Grão-Pará (basically the contemporary federal states of Pará and Amazonas). The outcome (in the 1840s) was unambiguous: Amazonia did not achieve independence, and the civil war (which also involved several foreign powers) resulted in the loss of about a quarter of the population of greater Belém.

Whatever the composition of a vestigial regional elite at that time, the dramatic growth of the extraction and trade of rubber ensured over the following half century consolidation of a new kind of elite, that mediating between a disperse population of tappers and their commercial agents and the large trading houses in Belém and Manaus in negotiation with extra-Amazonian commercial entities (in New York and Liverpool, primarily).

Although the rubber trade in Amazonia is conventionally depicted as a 'boom', there is good reason to question and reject that characterisation. For one thing, the rubber industry in Brazil prevailed – in terms of near-monopolistic production of *hevea brasiliensis* – for almost one hundred years, less a boom than a well established, although easily forgotten, durable industry of extraction. Second, the industry was highly stable: from the time exports were first recorded (in the early 1820s) until the introduction of South-east Asian estate rubber, exports grew annually, as did prices; and throughout this period (1820–1911) the mode of extraction hardly altered (dispersed semi-autonomous tappers linked through local merchants to regional export houses) while improved transport and increasing demand in diverse industrial sectors (abroad) led to replication of existing production regimes rather than their transformation. With the commercial valorisation of Amazonia as an economic domain, two quite different versions of elites emerged. One of these – still in place, albeit vestigially – is represented in the Amazonian trading families which served as the link between dispersed local producers and remote industrial consumers. They persist today (if, at times, in memory only) as the 'traditional' powers of the region, *comerciantes* whose post-rubber activities included the maintenance of the exchange of forest products for national and international imports. The second version of elites is better known. It is represented in the Opera House in Manaus (and monumental colonial buildings of Belém), in the tales of profligacy and conspicuous consumption, in the romantic superimposition of European decadence onto green hell.

The absence of that second elite following the collapse of the rubber industry is part of a larger characterisation of Amazonia between c.1915 and 1970: a stagnant and backward place that could hardly sustain a basic livelihood, much less an elite.

The tension between local elite and elite valorised by external factors is addressed by Victorian naturalists recounting their engagement with local 'society' during the course of their investigations of Amazonia in the mid- to late nineteenth century. On one hand, there is in the background the opening up of Amazonia commercially and scientifically, and on the other hand there is the painful adherence to social conventions assumed by local elites, for example, the dressing for dinner in climatologically painfully inappropriate outfits suitable for gentry (see Bates 1864; Wallace 1889).

Local manifestations of elites

Following the construction of the Transamazon Highway (c.1970), a new kind of elite was constructed, one largely predicated on the promise of future development of an Amazonia which would no longer have to be apologetic about its marginalisation from the apparatus of modernity. In this section I discuss a number of appropriations of eliteness effected by people in Santarem who were either affiliates of 'traditional' elites, and looking to up-grade as agents of national modernisation, or who were actual agents of programmes of 'national integration' (the official cover term for modernisation initiatives grouped under or associated with the Transamazon).

One of the immediate effects of the Transamazon on local societies long insulated from any substantive participation in national society was the introduction of the possibility of institutionalising local social differences according to non-local forms of status marking. Two are noteworthy. The first concerns new opportunities for social differentiation and definition of an elite through a monument: the Hotel Tropical. The second concerns local redefinition through exploiting already existing resources: traditional social clubs.

Hotel Tropical was part of a network of five-star hotels constructed in collaboration with the national airline – Varig – in the years immediately following the Plan for National Integration. While the Hotel served international visitors – a few – its signal contribution locally was to provide a setting for social activities accessible only to the Santareno bourgeoisie: air-conditioned cinema, swimming pool, extensive dining and conference facilities, salons for photoshoots of socialites. Hotel Tropical became, in the mid-1970s, a cardinal reference point for the *gente boa* ('fine' people, gentlefolk) of this paper's title.

The Yacht Club (*Iate Clube*) was a complementary development, a social club not far from Tropical in a squatter neighbourhood adjacent to the Santarém–Cuiaba road connecting Santarem to the Transamazon. Here, at weekends, Santarem's traditionally powerful families entertained themselves and new members of the Santareno elite, especially those entrepreneurs from the South associated with the gold industry (at that time focused in Itaituba). The Yacht Club was an extension of a traditional form of social club based on occupation, or residential or class affiliation, but whereas its predecessors were rather ossified – in some cases objects of ridicule for their archaic pretensions, even by members – the Yacht Club was defiantly neo-Amazonian: elaborate barbecues, water-skiing, volleyball. It also represented a significant departure in terms of public display of elite affiliation. Members might previously have spent weekends at their interior ranches, but the Yacht Club provided a new urban focus for class-solid activities.

The point here is hardly profound, but worth stating: the new manifestations of elite behaviour represented in Hotel Tropical and the Yacht Club were direct reflections not of an internal Santareno dynamic – not that such did not exist – but of the impact of an external dynamic in the form of state-led modernisation, the prime beneficiaries of which were those whose local standing as privileged Santarenos – educated, materially well-off, politically connected – allowed them to exploit the possibilities which accompanied state provision of a new infrastructure: road network, hydro-power, technical assistance for agricultural and animal husbandry, credit facilities.

The impact of changes wrought by national integration is not confined only to novel domains such as Hotel Tropical and the Yacht Club, but also includes the strengthening of pre-existing institutions whose importance is exaggerated or enhanced with the expansion of state-led activities. For example, the role of elite educational institutions is significantly altered. Pupils at such schools in the pre-Transamazon period might have been expected to proceed from local secondary schools to federal university and then on to careers outside the region. Post-Transamazon, they might be expected to return to the *municipio* and be absorbed within family enterprises (as lawyers, agronomists, veterinarians).

A pause

Thus far I have sketched some background material pertaining to elites in one Amazonian sub-region with no purpose greater than that of establishing the historical contingency of elites. One of the implications of Operation Amazon and its successor, the Plan for National Integration, however, is not merely that the territory of Amazonia be incorporated in a substantial sense within the nation, but also that it be administered according to the protocols of national, not regional, society. This is obviously a grey area, especially given the durability of the image of Amazonia-permanent-natural-frontier as well as the dynamism of a vast, largely unregulated regional economy, but it is worth looking at those elite institutions which now command power on behalf of the region whether or not they are of the region.

A working definition of elites offered by Chomsky (1992: 139) includes the following elements:

- those in a position to make decisions which affect crucially what happens in society at large;
- those in a managerial position with regard to political and economic institutions;
- those ideological elites who control the media.

These represent groups that are interconnected and share a common set of values and associations, determining a basic framework of what happens in society ultimately rooted in economic power.

None of these, I would argue, is significantly represented in Amazonia. Rather, such elite interests which prevail in Amazonia are mediated through national and international elites. This is not to deny the existence of Amazonian elites in many guises, but it is to argue that the crucial elite agenda is set elsewhere. In terms of element (1), for example, and not with-standing the considerable power of local regional elites, about half the territory of Amazonia falls within the control of Calhe Norte and the Greater Carajás Project (Hall 1989). In the case of the former, this is under the direct supervision of the federal armed forces. In the case of the latter, this is a private, corporate state. Control from afar is not a novelty. Following the imposition of National Security Status on the land bordering the national highways project in the region (of which the Transamazon is the centrepiece, although preceded by the Belém–Brasilia highway), the administration of federal lands fell to the National Institute of Colonisation and Agrarian Reform (INCRA). In areas of particularly heightened land conflict, federal intervention in the form of dedicated agencies was instituted (such as GETAT, responsible for administering the Tocantins/Araguaia region).

With regard to element (2), two examples: the Free Trade Zone of Manaus was established in 1967, to create within central Amazonia a commercial entrepôt to attract foreign capital in search of ecologically sound investment conditions (low wages, state subsidy). The result is an enclave economy with few coordinated backward linkages and with national/international, not regional priorities. Second, with regard to element (2): SUDAM, one of the most powerful agencies of the PIN period – the Superintendency of Amazonian Development – was mainly responsible for granting subsidies to large-scale cattle ranches, a major – if not the most important – stimulus to deforestation. More than 12 per cent of Amazonian forest is now cleared, virtually all of this post-1970, and virtually all of this under the careful super-vision of SUDAM.

In terms of element (3), Brazil has a highly centralised television broadcast system dominated by a few key (non-Amazonian) corporations. Amazonia is distinctly national in terms of its media.

In summary, if one is looking for Amazonian elites, one could do worse than look outside Amazonia.

Passing elites

Aside from diverse local Amazonian elites, those elite interests represented episodically in Amazonia have converged around one dominant theme: natural Amazonia – source of raw materials and tropical preciosities – requires high level management (elites), not local talent (junior/middle management, peasants, fishermen). In this section, I suggest that one of the reasons for the ephemerality of a durable notion of Amazonian elites is the ephemerality of Amazonia's being conceived of as a social landscape rather than, default posi-tion, essentially a natural landscape.

Elites in colonial society were representative of an empire charged with civilising the heathen hordes. Given the relatively small contribution of Amazonia to imperial coffers – unlike other regions – the role of elites was in crucial respects depressed: ruling a backwater. By the mid-eighteenth century, and under the rubric of the Pombaline reforms, Amazonia was the target of a policy of miscegenation simply to maintain an adequate colonial population in the region. By the mid-nineteenth century – following the *cabanagem* – Amazonian society was described by travellers in a way which hardly disguised the privileges of colonial overseers, but which hardly revealed an 'Amazonian society' in which the command of elites was a prominent feature. Both Bates and Wallace present portraits (of Santarém, for example) in which co-existing social groups and classes were horizontally rather than vertically arranged. There is no question of any other than white dominance, but the features of an elite society which they recorded seem to have more salience for an enclave elite adhering to European styles and customs than it did for society overall. Both, in fact, note the apparent absurdity of elite conventions:

> Some adhere to the black cloth coat and cravat, and look most uncomfortably clad with the thermometer from 85 to 90 in the shade.
>
> (Wallace 1889: 6)

> Much ceremony is observed in the intercourse of the principal people with each other, and with strangers. The best room in each house is set apart for receptions, and visitors are expected to present themselves in black dress coats, regardless of the furious heat which rages in the sandy streets.
>
> (Bates 1864: 210)

The slow growth of the rubber industry saw the emergence of a new Amazonian elite, one with a commanding position *vis-à-vis* local/regional society, but also incomplete in terms of shaping the overall class structure of Amazonia given its client status in relation to industrial consumers of rubber. The industry in Amazonia did not include significant processing of raw rubber, hence there was no consolidation of elite positions through the elaboration of technical and socio-economic complexity. Once Amazonia's monopoly position as global supplier of *hevea brasiliensis* declined, the region's elite apparatus also retired. There were residues in the form of monuments (Opera House, Teatro de Paz), commercial infrastructure (warehouses, wharves, *aviamento* system), but elites were represented as commanders of decline rather than foci of a new Amazonia.

The next local elite – still in formation – is also tied to the cycle of waxing and waning fortunes of an Amazonia whose social landscape is redefined according to the global appeal of its natural landscape. If one returns to the elite elements provided in Chomsky's definition, there is a sub-group which has the form: researchers, policy makers and commentators whose credibility derives from their claims to be able to relate the local to the global, Amazonia as focal site of global environmentalist attention. The case to be made here is that if there is an Amazonian elite, it is one which makes most sense in light of the specific features of the Brazilian state (corporatism, neo-liberalism, advanced dependent-development and old-fashioned *pistoleiros*), Brazil's major-player status as semi-autonomous US client, and the apparatus of an aggressive, centralised, constantly detestable federal administration, not in narrowly regionalist terms.

Eco-elites

There is a tendency to associate the growth of the environmental movement/eco-politics with grassroots, populist initiatives, and while there is little doubt about the bottom-up development of the movement as a whole, it is also the case that a co-opted environmentalism features strongly in top-down, managerial and globalising agencies such as the World Bank, USAID, ODA/DIFID, the Rockefeller Brothers Fund, FAO, UNDP and so on. Regardless of the motives of the latter – and the record is replete with examples of what appear to be profoundly anti-environmentalist activities promulgated under the guise of eco-philanthropy/aid – there is a shared, albeit contested, agenda of environmental concern which has been closely linked with development policies in Brazil and elsewhere since the 1960s. Beyond the shared agenda, there is also a record of collaborative activity among researchers, activists and development entities which obscures in crucial respects the diversity of goals. Two examples come from Amazonia. The first concerns a set of theories glossed as Pleistocene Refuge Theory, according to which certain bio-domains are rated as more valuable than others on the grounds that they represent primordial bio-diversity, hence the proposal to designate certain areas of Amazonia as more appropriate for insulation from the effects of modernisation (on the assumption that generalised despoliation is inevitable). Such theories have been engaged by planners and researchers in marking priority conservation areas and represent a significant collaboration between policy makers and scientists of impeccably elite credentials. The second example is a biological reserve – Mamiruá – in Western Amazonas, near Tefe. Established as a research station supporting work in the biological and natural sciences, Mamiruá is now a federal biological reserve supporting, at one end, extension work for public health and education and, at the other, work in the biological sciences conducted by international heavyweights (such as the late William Hamilton who provided key work in the maths of sociobiology).

In both cases, the relationship between scientific research and policy is overt, but implausible. The scientific research is long-term; the policy implementation on the basis of speculative claims is immediate. The likely resolution of the disjunction between the status of the speculative scientific claims (extremely high) and the realisation of informed action/policy (extremely low) is a no-brainer. Amazonian elites are not even in the frame.

These are merely examples, but indicative ones. They represent a general trend in Amazonia (and Brazil) well-documented in an obscure book published in Brazil in 1992, *An Organic Artifice: Transition in Amazonia and Environmentalism* (*Um Artificio Organico: Transicao na Amazonia e Ambientialismo*) (Arnt and Schwartzman 1992), which reveals the extent to which the environmentalist, grass-roots movement is institutionally constrained by an agenda seized by global funding agencies. NGOs (and the expertise they represent) are not aspirant players, they are already accommodated. This is not to say that they are all of a type – the Rubber Tappers' Union is not incorporable within Electrobras's Department of the Environment – but it is to say that they operate within a shifting system largely administered from far afield (from countries, say, in which crucial issues involve specious guarantees that hardwood garden furniture comes from sustainable sources). *An Organic Artifice* itself was made possible through the largesse of the Ford Foundation (and was specifically sponsored by FF operatives celebrated – in previous incarnations – for their basic science, not policy, work), despite the fact that the book implicitly attacks precisely the role of non-Amazonians/Brazilians in the environmentalist agenda-setting process.

The agenda-setting power of eco-politics has resulted in a wide range of progressive interventions in Amazonia, many backed by authoritative reports by respected experts. At one extreme we have the *Nossa Natureza* (Our Nature) programme launched by ex-president Sarney, a bilious and vacuous campaign meant to flag the state's interest in matters Amazonian/ecological. At the other end we have indigenous and peasants' rights groups for which the emergence of eco-politics provided a crucial tool for political mobilisation. As important as efforts tied to ecologism have been in shaping late-modern Amazonia, the fact that they have been so whole-heartedly adopted by those interests which have themselves fomented the crisis should give pause.

What kind of elite is this?

From many vantage points ecological research in Amazonia has a deserved scientific reputation. Wallace's close affiliation with Darwin is well known, and he and Bates and Spruce are renowned for their path-breaking work. Richards' analysis of the short-nutrient cycle, Falesi on soils, Goulding on fish, Condamine, von Humboldt, Sternberg, Schultes, Prance, Miller... There is a long list of scientific work which, however incohesive – not surprisingly, given normal science protocols – still bears the cachet of 'science'. Referring to this work in shopping-list format draws attention to the fact that despite the absence of a plausible elite/authoritative take on Amazonian ecologism, command of the ecology agenda is sufficient to award authority. It is also noteworthy that while such a list is strongly non-Amazonian/Brazilian, that predominance is cast against a denuded background. There is an Amazonia that is canopy forest, *candirú*, *caxaça*. There is no Amazonia with analogues of Geronimo, Sitting Bull, or Rachel Carson or Swampy. Chico Mendes is a potent candidate, but it was precisely his efforts to equate social justice with ecological justice that led to his assassination. Crudely, but I think accurately put, the administration of Amazonian affairs by an external elite is valorised by recourse to an acritical ecological idiom which has historical depth and scholarly legitimacy, but which has been overwhelmingly motivated by concerns for the administration of empire.

I have put it crudely, but I think this is appropriate to the circumstances. The caricature of Amazonians provided by elite commentators and administrators in this century has shifted from slap-dash peasant, slashing and burning, idly paddling remote oxbows, stopping off only long enough to kill endangered mega-fauna, to wise forest manager who carefully ensures a mode of existence (however poorly remunerated) balancing social and natural demands. That portrayal itself may be caricature, but it draws attention to a major sleight of hand: what the pre-environmentally-aware Amazonian and the post-environmentally-aware Amazonian are doing for a living is hardly different. What is different is the definition of its significance, and that definition has not been reshaped so much by the internal dynamic of Amazonia as by the constructions put on it in the name of environmental conservation, on an agenda formulated far outside Amazonia, by elites effectively, those in a position to make decisions which affect crucially what happens in society at large, those in managerial positions with regard to political and economic institutions, those who select media agendas.

Closing comments

Anthropological approaches to the study of elites have, by and large, taken as the units of analysis local systems in which the embedding of political, economic and cultural power results in some kind of claim (contested or not) to privilege. What I have sketched above is somewhat different, local configurations of power which, however relevant they are to daily conduct, seem less important (or explanatory) than do superordinate and non-local structures, in the case of Amazonia ones informed by the convergence of a path of state-led development and a path of scientific research, a convergence which achieves high ecological and ideological fit. Implicit in this is a case made for Brazilian and Amazonian exceptionalism. Amazonians are implicated in an unresolved national debate about elites which has, since the late nineteenth century, been embedded in the discourse of raciology conducted, at the national level, through the formation of research institutes attempting to define the distinctiveness of Brazilian miscegenation by recourse to elite prescriptions borrowed from abroad (Schwarcz 1999) just as, I would argue, current questions about elites in Amazonia are significantly shaped by dependent affiliations with elites abroad (the 'development community').

Anthropological studies of elites are typically constrained by the fact that research depends on some version of consent (implicit or explicit). While we are generally able to practise research on others on the basis of a complex, but still quite overt, socio-political asymmetry, the study of elites is awkward and requires a different strategy since they are by definition under less obligation to consent to being studied. Given the lack of access to elites, there are two (not mutually incompatible) strategies available. One is to focus on accessible elites and limit the anthropological remit to the ordained asymmetrical programme (that is, accept the relative implausibility of 'studying-up'). The other is to disregard the conventional anthropological definition of elites and look instead at effective elites, those who shape the terms of debate including those terms regarding the definition of elites. For some anthropologists the latter option defeats the anthropological project. For others though it is a test of the adequacy of anthropological method and perspective that despite years of admonition to direct the anthropological gaze upward, there is still so little to show.

Bibliography

Arnt, A. and Schwartzman, J. (1992) *Um Artifício Organico*, Rio de Janeiro: Editora Rocco.

Bates, H.E. (1864) *The Naturalist on the River Amazons*, London: John Murray.

Black, J.K. (1977) *United States Penetration of Brazil*, Philadelphia: University of Philadelphia Press.

Branford, S. and Kucinski, B. (1988) *The Debt Squads*, London: Zed.

Chomsky, N. (1992) *Chronicles of Dissent*, Monroe, Maine: Common Courage Press.

Chomsky, N. and Herman, E.S. (1988) *Manufacturing Consent*, New York: Pantheon.

Domhoff, R. (1967) *Who Rules America?*, Englewood Cliffs, NJ: Prentice-Hall.

—— (1974) *The Bohemian Grove and Other Retreats*, New York: Harper & Row.

Evans, P. (1979) *Dependent Development*, Princeton, NJ: Princeton University Press.

Foresta, R. (1991) *Amazon Conservation in the Age of Development*, Gainesville, FL: University of Florida Press.

Hall, A. (1989) *Developing the Amazon*, Manchester: Manchester University Press.

Marcus, G. (ed.) (1983) 'Elite as a Concept, Theory, and Research Tradition', in *Elites: Ethnographic Issues*, Albuquerque, NM: University of New Mexico Press.

Ramos, A. (1998) *Indigenism*, Madison, WI: University of Wisconsin Press.

Schwarcz, L. (1999) *The Spectacle of Races*, New York: Hill and Wang.

Shoup, L. and Minter, W. (1977) *Imperial Brain Trust*, New York: Monthly Review Press.

Wallace, A.R. (1889) *A Narrative of Travels on the Amazon and Rio Negro*, London: Ward and Lock.

Chapter 5

Elites on the margins

Mestizo traders in the southern Peruvian Andes

Penelope Harvey

When the Pope visited Cusco in 1985 I found myself standing on the side of the road next to a wealthy lawyer and his wife. It was 6 am. People were anxious to get a good view of the Pope as he drove by, and were even hoping that he might stop and exchange a word or give a blessing. It is cold at that time of day, but I was surprised to see this couple 'dressed up' in indigenous garb. He wore a coloured ceremonial poncho and a *chullu*, the knitted hat that peasants and herders wear to keep out the cold. She was in wide homespun skirts with a jacket and shawl. They explained that the Pope had made it clear that he was visiting the poor people of Peru. And they were not going to let their wealth stand in the way! But they had not dressed up to trick the Pope. They experience the poverty of their nation in relation to more developed parts of the world. And they also felt an affinity with that understanding of the poor as the more deserving, more authentic, more community-oriented people whom the Pope had singled out for favour. As educated middle-class Cusqueños and Quechua speakers they would have been actively engaged in what is seen as a collective social responsibility to carry forward the values of their authentic indigenous Inka heritage for the future of the nation. Thus, the lawyer and his wife were ready to present themselves to the Pope as representatives of the deserving poor of Peru and had taken the precaution of dressing appropriately lest the Pope failed to see beyond the wealthy middle-class professional exterior.

The identification of 'elites' is of course a contextual issue. Cris Shore and Steve Nugent invited us to think with the idea of elites as those who, collectively, occupy the most influential positions or roles in the governing institutions of a 'community', the leaders, rulers and decision-makers. In similar vein George Marcus defines 'elites' as 'those with political power and who control distribution of resources in their locale' (Marcus 1998). The 'elite' to which I refer in this chapter is a group of *mestizo* traders, locally known as *mistis*, whose power is based in the control of state institutions in rural areas of the Southern Andes. I am referring to control of the political and juridical offices of mayor, governor and judge in small rural towns, which they have used historically both to acquire land and labour in an economy where both commodities are scarce, and to secure favourable conditions for the conduct of long-distance trade between the Amazonian regions and the urban centres of the Andes and even the coast. Much of this trade is semi-clandestine, involving the movement of gold, coca and precious hardwoods – all products which are highly regulated by the state. *Misti* men control this trade, spending most of their time away from home, either driving their huge Volvo trucks long distance, or moving around more locally in pick-ups, distributing goods and collecting debts. The issue of place and location is important in this work for while these *mestizo* families demonstrate the translocality of power and the subsequent importance of personal mobility, their case also reveals how important it is to establish a grounded local context for the legitimate exercise of power.[1] The ethnography of this group is drawn from my fieldwork in one small Andean town, a district capital with a population of some 1,500 people, a day's journey by lorry from the capital of the Department of Cusco.

It could be argued that anthropology, and particularly the anthropological method of participant observation, has a tendency to over-locate the study of elites. It is certainly the case that the methods employed in my Peruvian research made it both possible and inevitable that I would identify *local* 'elites', situated groups of people, rather than the less grounded, 'deterritorialised' networks through which power is exercised at a global level. And such 'elites' are perhaps by definition marginal in times when we might be more inclined to think of 'elites' as those who are best able to avoid the constraints of location and who no longer need the grounded legitimacy that my Ocongate traders sought.[2] But the ethnographic study of the accessible is not condemned to localism. For it is important to understand both how marginality is constituted in processes of social, cultural and political location that extend far beyond the place in question, and how power is exercised in particular places through relationships that extend beyond that place.[3]

Making difference matter in the Southern Peruvian Andes

When I first arrived in the small rural town where I was to spend nearly three years during the 1980s, I was told that it was not really a suitable place for anthropologists. There were other foreigners in town, a Dutch doctor, and a Catholic NGO staffed by two Spanish priests, two nuns and several workers from the urban centres of Lima and Cusco. These people, who were working in the area to try and improve the lot of the rural poor, told me that Ocongate was to the local hinterland, what Lima was to the nation. Expecting me to work on the margins, they wanted to warn me that I should not stop in Ocongate. They claimed that traditions had degenerated and there was a fully monetised economy. The local people were basically interested in trade and in migrant labour in contrast to those living in the rural hinterland who were still engaged in a traditional agricultural and herding economy. These foreigners on the whole had very little time for the residents of the town. They understood the local *mistis* to be largely responsible, if not for the economic difficulties of their favoured target population, then at least for their inability to do very much about it. The priests were liberation theologists fully prepared for political engagement with poverty, but perhaps less prepared for the complexity of local politics in which they had become embroiled. One key area in which they had decided to intervene was in the marketing of agricultural produce and wool. This trade had been controlled by the town's more wealthy traders who were used to buying up what was produced in the surrounding area, storing it in their spacious and secure houses and, when they had sufficient quantity to make the journey worthwhile, transporting it (in the lorries that they owned) to urban centres where they could sell it on for a healthy profit. It was very difficult for small producers to compete with those who owned transport, who were able to trade in bulk, and who knew the ways of the city. The priests had decided to operate as rival middlemen. They also owned transport and large secure premises. The idea was that they would buy up local produce at a better price than the local *mistis*, and in this way they would be able to undermine the latter's stranglehold on local trade. At the same time they would train the small producers to work together and build an autonomous base for trading direct with the city.

The problem, which the priests had not forseen, was that they themselves had unwittingly stepped into a scenario in which both the local *mistis* and the very people that they were intending to help simply saw them as a rival elite faction. In terms of local politics this meant that the priests soon found themselves on the verge of being evicted from the town altogether. Using the kinds of tactics that elite families would quite routinely use against each other, the priests were accused of political subversion. In the endemic local factionalism, ruling families had always used alliances with urban political elites to get their rivals imprisoned. Thus, as power bases shifted in the regional and national centres, so local family fortunes waxed and waned. At a time when the Maoist guerrilla group, Shining Path, was beginning to establish itself in the Andean region, the local *mistis* had managed, through accusations of communism, to bring in the army to turn the mission over in a search for arms. They did not find any, but by the time I arrived towards the end of 1983 the battle lines were clearly drawn and while the *mistis* threatened the priests and did what they could to subvert their activities in the area, the priests in turn directed all their resources and energy (including their religious ministrations) to people living outside the town. However their lives were further complicated by the fact that local people generally understood the battle as a fight between elites. There were many rumours that the priests were building up stocks of potatoes and wool to sell to Europe for far greater profits than the local *mistis* would exact in Cusco. There was also considerable reluctance to relinquish the benefits of the kinds of unequal, yet symbiotic relationships which the *misti* elites built up with people in the more rural areas. For many people the *mistis* were seen as far more trustworthy or at least more fathomable.[4] The *mistis* were seen as themselves more local than the priests. For a start they spoke the same language (as bilingual Quechua and Spanish speakers), and more ironically the *mistis* clearly shared the same religion. This lack of trust on religious grounds arose because the priests were making a deliberate effort to demystify Andean Catholicism. They played down the performance of their priestly role. They would arrive in the church for mass in jeans, carrying their vestments in a plastic bag, and dress at the altar. They refused to use the elaborate paraphernalia of high Catholic ritual (except when forced into it on certain occasions of successful political finessing by the *mistis*), and they were at pains to point out to people that the images of the saints were only plaster figures who should not be attended to in such a way as to prevent people from taking matters into their own hands. This kind of approach lost them a lot of local support. I remember an old man of peasant origins who kept a small chapel, dedicated to the local miraculous Christ, and furnished with an oil painting of this Christ figure which was highly revered in the area. The priests had told him that he might as well throw the paintings in the river. He had concluded that they were not Catholics at all, but evangelical Protestants, outsiders who did not understand and were antagonistic to local people. In short, by applying a rather crude Marxism to local relations of power, labelling the *mistis* as the bad oppressors from whom they tried to liberate a subordinated population, the priests had failed to grasp two key points: namely, that by getting so openly involved in politics they were seen locally as a rival elite faction (offering the same kinds of protection and favour to clients that other elites offered), and they were not necessarily the best bet, for despite their clear connections to the outside – after all they were Europeans and priests – their local credentials were very shaky and their motives somewhat suspect.

I was also warned in the city of Cusco, by some local intellectuals, that Ocongate was not a particularly useful place for anthropologists to study as the local elites were very idiosyncratic. These *misti* families were not the traditional landed elites of Southern Peru (to whom I return below), but were people who had made their money in trade, taking advantage of the road that was built to connect the city of Cusco to the lowland city of Puerto Maldonado. From the outside then these local elites were characterised to me as (1) the *mestizo* oppressors of local indigenous populations and (2) an upstart nouveau riche class of traders, neither authentically indigenous, nor members of the aristocratic land-owning classes.

This reaction to the Ocongate *mistis* is interesting as it provides a clear indication of how such local elites can be seen as marginal in wider contexts. The rural *mestizo* has long been a problematic figure in Peru, vilified in a process of nation building that worked around the opposing poles of indigenous and white identities with no positive space for the hybrid national. I need to unpack this history to explain the intrinsic marginality of this particular social group. De la Cadena (1998, 2000) tracks the ways in which Peruvian intellectuals have struggled with how to locate the *mestizo* in the national project. She argues that the gradual replacement (from the 1930s onwards) of 'race' by 'class' in both political rhetoric and intellectual production had the effect of institutionalising what she calls the 'silent racism' of academic and political practice. By the 1930s the Peruvian nation had been powerfully imagined as a place of racial and geographical division – the highland area inhabited by dark-skinned *serranos* (highland people), the coast, particularly Lima, by whites. The distinction was a moral one that could, however, be transcended by education. This transcendence was achieved most effectively by a group of *serranos* (the *indigenista* intellectuals who came to power in the 1920s) who challenged the Lima political elites and came to occupy the highest positions in the national public and political administration – including the presidency itself. Peruvian indigenist politics was built on an appeal to the spiritual purity of indigenous peoples – the pre-Hispanic, Quechua speaking Indian agriculturalists:

> Asserting their lofty intellectual status, *serrano* academics, disregarding their physical appearance, displaced the definition of 'mestizos' from themselves to ignorant and immoral 'others'. This curbed Limeño references to *serrano* intellectuals' phenotype, and ultimately moulded a definition of race that emphasised innate intelligence and morality and acquired education as its defining traits.
>
> (de la Cadena 1998: 147)

Her point, and one most pertinent to the case that I am describing, is that Peruvian intellectuals were able to 'unmark' their phenotype and geographical placement, but the residue of this process was an implicit division within the remaining highland population, that is the division between the indigenous agriculturalist (the spiritual source of *indigenista* politics) and the *mestizo*, 'a despicable regional character, a deformed Indian that had left the heaven of the *ayllu* and abandoned agriculture, their inherent activity' (de la Cadena 1998: 148). De la Cadena graphically illustrates the ways in which the *mestizo* was depicted with a quotation from the work of Luis Valcarcel, one of Cusco's most prominent *indigenistas*, writing in the 1920s:

> The horrible silence of mestizo towns. The midday sun wanders with leaden feet across the plaza. Then it leaves, setting behind the walls, sheds, the tumble-down church, the shabby houses ... worms lost in the subcutaneous galleries of this decomposing body that is the wretched mestizo town, men surface now and then, the sun chases them away, they return to their burrows ... What do these troglodytes do? They do nothing.

They are the parasites, the scum of the sewer ... the master of the wretched mestizo town is the quack lawyer ... the quack lawyer is secretly feared and abhorred ... He exploits the whites and the aborigines equally. Lying is his job. Just as the gentleman is the highest product of the white culture, so the quack lawyer is the best that our mestizo towns have created.

(de la Cadena 1998: 148–9, from Valcarcel 1925: 44)

As the language of ethnicity came to replace that of race in Peru, the concept of mixture remained problematic. The *mestizo* continued to be either the degenerate peasant, and local abuser of power, or the tormented misfit, torn between the authentic purity of the Indian and the intellectual fulfilment of white elites. And despite a change in language, racial categories stayed firmly attached to particular activities in a way that got carried forward into later discourses of class. By the 1960s and 1970s the *mestizo* or *cholo* political leader was by definition a member of the urban proletariat. The idea implicit in this process is what de la Cadena characterises as 'the redemptive power of education'. Education transforms race such that the educated peasant is by definition a *cholo* or *mestizo*, but his place for the future of the nation becomes the city and not the rural areas.

The Ocongate priests therefore, despite the fact that they themselves were foreigners steeped in the philosophy of liberation theology, were involved in reproducing hegemonic ideas about the racial character of local *mestizo* elites as they fought to liberate the indigenous agriculturalists from their sway. The identification of these *mestizo* traders as elites by the outside NGO reflects the somewhat awkward relationships that anthropologists tend to construct with the elite groups they study. The priests' intentions in criticising the practices of these traders, and in attributing them with the power to perpetuate social inequality in the region, is undoubtedly motivated by a wish to attribute responsibility to particular persons rather than to the impersonal processes of the market, or the neo-liberal state. As Lukes has argued, we want to know whom to hold responsible for the effects of power (Lukes 1986: 13). The priests want the local notables to take responsibility for the position they occupy in the locality, to recognise the problems they cause and to do something about it. They also clearly want to distinguish their own elite status from that of these powerful traders. They are anxious to disrupt the comfortable establishment alliance between church, state and market. Indeed their position as radical theologians is premised on the disruption of the ways in which this alliance is consolidated in the practices of the more conservative sectors of the Catholic church. But in the process the priests attribute too much personal power to these families and overlook the ways in which they are caught up in a much wider global history – in which priests and anthropologists are also entangled.

The emergence of the Ocongate 'elites'

Ocongate today is the district capital of a region which was once dominated by one of the largest *haciendas* in Southern Peru. Lauramarca was a huge, primarily herding estate of some 64,000 hectares, with lands ranging from the *coca* growing lowlands to the high *puna* pastures. In the nineteenth century the *hacienda* was owned by the Saldivar family. This family controlled the whole region by denying any autonomous access to land, systematically encroaching on the legally established community lands of its periphery. At this time the Saldivar family also controlled the local market. They bought all local produce and resold it to *mestizo* merchants from Ocongate once a week at a Sunday market. These landowners quite unashamedly exercised what Nugent has termed 'aristocratic sovereignty' which he defines in the following way:

> Aristocratic sovereignty was based on the assertion of fundamental, inherent, and qualitative differences among people who occupied the various categories of society. Distinctions based predominantly on race (Indian, *mestizo*, white), gender (female and male), ancestry (Spanish or not), and land ownership segregated the population into what were (in theory) fixed and inherited social categories that did much to prescribe the life possibilities of the people who occupied them. Roles of leadership and control in virtually all domains – economic, social, political, military, legal, and religious – were reserved for the white, male elite of Spanish descent (who likewise reaped most of the benefits of dominating the social order ... The ongoing public expression of one's relative status in the regional social order was encoded in forms of dress, in patterns of socializing and 'cultural' affectations ('European' versus 'Indian'), in deferential patterns of behavior and speech, in forms of livelihood, and in the ability to occupy important positions in public life. The sum total of these constantly reiterated distinctions helped lend an air of naturalness and inevitability to aristocratic sovereignty.
>
> (Nugent 1997:15)

The Lauramarca *hacendados* were thus distinguished from local populations not simply by their wealth, but also by their education, their clothing, their speech. Their power over those who lived on their land was absolute. They are remembered as having had the power of life and death which they exercised in an arbitrary fashion, motivated by greed.

By the turn of the century some *mestizo* traders, with an eye to finding a way into the local market, controlled so violently by the landlords, clashed with the Saldivar family in a confrontation that is remembered for various reasons relevant to my current argument. In the first place one of the local authorities was taken prisoner by the Saldivars and humiliated, treated like an animal, whipped and forced to eat hay. Hundreds of people marched on the *hacienda* to release him, and in the struggle the landowner was shot. There were two important consequences of this. The army was called in to restore order, and the townspeople were treated very harshly. It would be several more decades before the *mestizo* traders would be in a position to establish firm alliances themselves in the cities. It was clear that at this time their actions were seen as an outrage against the social order. However, they did manage to move the market out of the *hacienda* and into the town, a move which they used to consolidate their own trading activities. There was thus an interesting entanglement between the *mestizo* traders and the peasants – both enemies of the *hacienda*, both persecuted by the army but for very different reasons. The *mestizos* were basically trying to ensure the freedom to establish and benefit from local markets and to wrest control of these from the land-lords. The peasants were struggling against a hugely abusive regime in which their livestock was regularly stolen or expropriated on the grounds that it might pollute the landowners' stock, they were sold into slavery, women were raped, and anyone was liable to be shot down.

Nevertheless the Peruvian state had been founded in 1821 on Enlightenment values, set up in the name of new liberal principles of democracy, citizenship, private property, individual rights and protections (Nugent 1997: 13). However the state was weakened by the wars of independence and required the support of the traditional landed elites, and it was the best part of a century before these Enlightenment values began to motivate action rather than simply appear as political rhetoric. In the Southern Peruvian Andes the latter half of the nineteenth century was particularly violent. There was a demand for alpaca wool on the international market and indigenous herders (who owned most of the alpacas) began to attain economic positions that they could never previously have imagined. The response of the local land-lords throughout Southern Peru was to find new, usually violent, ways to keep these Indians in place (Poole 1988; Flores Galindo 1977; Jacobsen 1993). However throughout this period, as Nugent has shown so well for the Chachapoyas region of Northern Peru, there was a rhetorical lip service paid to the values of 'popular sovereignty', a rhetoric that in some ways confirmed the power of these elites because they so blatantly did not live by the precepts they would proclaim on ritual occasions. However, by the 1920s and 1930s the traditional landed elites throughout Peru began to lose their grip on power. Aided by the 'massive dislocations in culture and economy experienced throughout Peru as a by-product of the late nineteenth-century crisis in global capitalism … marginalized middle sectors of the local population coalesced into a "movement of democratization", and declared themselves the defenders of popular rule and the enemies of aristocratic privilege' (Nugent 1997: 313). In the Chachapoyas region of Northern Peru that Nugent has studied, the 'revolution of 1930' ousted the local landed elites. In Cusco the move was not as definitive but there were also rebellions throughout this period. The Saldivar family sold the *hacienda*, but sold it on to new owners who continued their violent treatment of local people (Gow 1976). Relationships with urban politicians, judges and military personnel ensured the continuity of the landed elites.

However, this was also a time when the Ocongate *mistis* began to support more openly the projects for political and national integration, actively seeking a state presence to challenge the dominance of the landowners. In Ocongate it is clear that from this period both state education and commerce and accumulation came to be seen as positive forces locally, and these were all domains controlled by the *mistis* – traders, muleteers, teachers, public employees. For the central Peruvian administration, the archaic landed elites were increasingly felt to be blocking the project of national integration, a project which was manifest most visibly in Peru by an obsession with transport and road building. Nugent talks of the obsession of the middle sectors with roads, and it was an obsession in which Ocongate elites were fully engaged. The road from Cusco reached the town in 1938.

The relationship between the peasantry and the *misti* traders was ambiguous during the first half of this century. On the one hand the *mistis* were seen as outsiders, people who were not in any way the natural allies of the peasants. When the Saldivar family offered to sell the *hacienda* in the 1930s, it was mooted that the peasants themselves should buy the land. However they feared that such a gesture would be futile as there was a sense that they would never be able to lay effective claim to the land.

At this time the *colonos* attempted to buy Lauramarca. The Saldivars were quite willing to sell and a deed of sale was drawn up in which the *colonos* were to make a downpayment in cash and pay the balance in annual quotas generated by the sale of their livestock and the produce from the demesne lands. But those *colonos* employed by the *hacienda* as supervisors (accountants and overseers) were against the sale – no doubt seeing it as a threat to their own interests. They successfully convinced their fellow *colonos* that they were incapable of running Lauramarca by themselves; and even if they did succeed in buying it the *mestizos* of Ocongate would soon move in and take over:

> How are we peasants going to buy it? We're used to being ordered about by the *mistis*. You think we're going to be free? The *misti* is always a *misti* and will cheat us…The *misti* of Ocongate will definitely take over this property. When you let the patron go, we'll be kicked out.
>
> (Gow 1976: 153–4)

Nevertheless it also appears to have been the case that the presence of *misti* traders in some of the communities on the edges of the estate did protect the peasantry from some of the worst excesses of the landlords in the 1950s and 1960s. They made no direct intervention, but the landlords found it harder to wipe out villages in which there was a resident *misti* population. They could be treated like animals but not with the same impunity as landless peasants.

The *mistis* of Ocongate were also openly courting a state presence in the town, looking for an alternative source of power and influence than the families of the landed elites who treated them as racial inferiors and blocked their commercial interests.

The changes which marked the end of the landed elites in central Peru were thus felt in Ocongate but in different ways. For a start the landlords of the huge Lauramarca estate had more power. They were not locked in endemic battles with rival landowners. The outcome of the eventual transfer of power also left the Ocongate *mistis* in a position from which to inherit some of the landed elites discourses and practices of power. The *hacienda* was expropriated in 1969, and passed into the hands of the bureaucrats and technicians of the agrarian reform.

What interests me in particular about the Ocongate *mistis* is how, in the absence of the large landowners, they began to reproduce the disjuncture that the Chachapoyan landed elites had demonstrated. Continuing to use the language of popular sovereignty as political rhetoric, they recouped many of the strategies of power from the landed elites for the perpetuation of their own elite position in the locality. The exercise of power in Ocongate continues to be overtly coercive. The coercion is directed in many ways to the production of absolute categories of difference which the *mistis* then selectively transcend in various ways.

The exercise of power on the margins

As were the old landed elites, the *mistis* are groups of men allied through marriage in a local context of factionalism and paternalistic control. They exercise their power through control of state institutions and their subsequent ability to manifest both their autonomy and their ability to coerce others with relative impunity. In some senses they maintain distinction through land and have always taken land where and when they could, and have come to control the best-irrigated fields in the area, on which they can raise quality cattle and crops. However agriculture in itself could not support the kinds of categorical difference which they erect around themselves.

It is commerce, not land, that underwrites their power. However, success in commercial activity is predicated on quite different relations of production, both locally with clients/customers and in the cities where they are always aware of the possibility that they might be forced to inhabit the uncomfortable racial placement of the rural *mestizo*. Trade offers a more fragile relation to resources than the old landed elites enjoyed and the Ocongate *mistis* thus also have to find ways to engage with people both locally and at a distance. In this context, what they do is take up a Janus-type existence in which they seek both to 'modernise' their immediate environment, surrounding themselves with powerful symbols of distinction to mitigate the effects of their rural attachments, while at the same time bolstering these attachments primarily through recourse to a gendered division of symbolic labour – in order to maximise local trust and acceptability.

The elite families to whom I refer are all confident bilinguals. Spanish is their language of preference, particularly in public and always in political debate, but Quechua is the language of affect often associated with a Quechua-speaking mother or nursemaid. Quechua thus becomes the language of the most intimate spaces of the home, the kitchen and the hearth, but also of the day-to-day business interactions with local people. In most of the families the women run shops through which they dispense goods and more general patronage while simultaneously gathering information about anything and everything that is going on locally. They would always know exactly where I had been and what I had been up to, who I had been drinking with, if I had been dancing. They also know about and support local religious practices both in relation to public Catholic ritual and in the more intimate offerings made to the powers of the landscape. They take the trouble to stock the sweetest coca and to have the right ritual elements for small sacrificial offerings which are made (and which they themselves make) at various times of the year. *Misti* family houses are distinguished by their fortress-like quality and by the elaboration of spaces with specific functions, most notably their formal dining rooms used to entertain and impress. Yet their kitchens are often constructed in more local style. They prefer to cook on wood burning adobe stoves. They are larger and more elaborately constructed than many perhaps, and are certainly used to prepare a more elaborate cuisine, but the kitchens will have guinea pigs living on the mud floors as in all other houses of the area.

Debt collection makes trade a difficult task in the immediate locality and traders are adept at exploiting local idioms of collaboration in order to forge close relationships with their client base. Perhaps most significantly, they make strong fictive kinship links with the rest of the local population through the institution of *compadrazgo* and through the adoption of poor children into their households. These children are brought up as members of the family and confer local parental status on families who send their own children away to school and might otherwise have far less intense relationships to the school and medical post locally than they might want.

In terms of public spaces, these families are at the forefront of campaigns for modernisation, for drinking water, for electricity, for a telephone, and most importantly for improved schools and an improved road. In some ways it is clear that such facilities enhance their own comfort, and also enable their trading relations. As importantly they consciously work against the image of the 'wretched *mestizo* town' I referred to earlier. Nevertheless, they also know that there is a limit to their possibilities in this respect, for living as they do, and more particularly where they do, they will always be racial 'others' in the eyes of their urban patrons. It is here that the mobility of the elites is so important. Not only are the men constantly on the move, but once their children reach the age for secondary education, they are sent to the cities. On the whole they expect their children to go on to university and acquire a professional training and to make the contacts and links that they need for effective connection to outside power. Some members of the family will however return. In the one elite family that I was very close to, the only son had even dropped out of school altogether to accompany his uncle and learn the skills of the local *misti* trader but he carried on his education by correspondence.

This strong connection between these elite *misti* families and the outside world is very important. In many cases the families have come from outside in the past two to three generations, but they are not outsiders because of the various ways in which they have embedded themselves in the place, building the town around themselves and their activities. They brought the state institutions, they built the market place, brought the road (with on-going and committed campaigning to prevent urban planners taking other routes), they are the most active in public Catholic ritual, they built the schools. In some ways, as the priests first suggested to me, it might appear that in fact the town is itself 'the outside'. However, this appearance of modern institutions and infrastructure in the locality has to be understood in the wider framework of a more general desire among the wider population of the locality for an active state presence in the region, as protection against and counter-balance to the arbitrary brutality of previous regimes. These new elites are not the old landowners. They are very coercive in the exercise of power but they do not engage in the kinds of theatrical violence through which former elites could demonstrate their ability to act with total impunity. Now the exercise of power requires a more liberal idiom, but a liberal idiom that nevertheless perpetuates a clear sense of racial difference, achieved through the constant assertion of the importance of their links to the outside, of their education and of their successful engagement with the market economy. As local authorities they delight in imposing their own particular version of the state and actively promote the public celebration of school and the other local civic institutions, where possible fining people who try to avoid doing things their way. In some senses then, they play the rhetoric of liberal democracy to the hilt but use it to coerce others locally.

However, precisely because of their knowledge of the city, the elites in Ocongate also understand perfectly well that the metanarratives of modernity will not deliver. Expectations of modernity have to be measured, they know that they have to cover their backs. The city is not the answer for them; if it were they would have moved there already. Most of them own houses in the city in which the school-age and university-level offspring live. However it is precisely in the city where they feel their marginality most strongly. For here it is that they are subject to the discourses of exclusion, discrimination and disrespect.

When I returned to Ocongate in 1997 after a long absence, one of my closest women friends from one of the local *misti* families revealed her own fears about the future of the area in terms that I had never previously heard

Figure 5.1 Drinking together at a local festival

her use. This is a woman who sits at the heart of one of the key elite families of the region. While her brothers conduct long-distance trade, she sits in the well-stocked shop and exercises what I had always understood as a benign control over the many people who came her way, asking for work, for loans, for shelter, for food. This family had enabled my entry into the field. Through a long-distance network of connections that linked a local Cusco anthropologist with her brother, a writer and a poet who teaches at the local university, I had first come to Ocongate in the company of another brother, the eldest. This brother runs the family business and has been mayor several times. He never married but has a close relationship with his divorced sister who keeps the house and the shop while he drives around the country. In some respects I was very lucky with this family, as in the current adult generation they are the least factionally embroiled of the five or so families to whom I have been referring in this paper. However the situation had been very different in their parents' times. Their father had been imprisoned and imprisoned others in his turn in local family battles between elite families. As part of this local contest for power, their parents had built up a very close clientele of over a hundred godchildren, who they could still call on a generation removed for various kinds of service and preferential access to goods, to labour and to information. It was to one of these families that I was sent when they found out that I wanted to do an anthropological study. And it was clear that these godchildren had no very direct option to refuse my cuckoo-like arrival in their house. Nevertheless they also appeared to have a genuine bond of affection for this elite family, there was a mutuality and a respect in the relationship that in some senses worked for both sides.

I was then not prepared for the strong sense of racial abuse which attached to the fact that for the first time the mayor had been elected from a local peasant household. This man is an unusual figure in the community. He had left home at a relatively young age and moved to Lima where he had managed to get a university place to train as a nurse. This university was closed down for student activism in the 1970s and he never did qualify as a professional, and he returned to Ocongate politicised, disgruntled and looking for ways to change his own luck. He had been working as a migrant labourer when I had left the village. What interested me was the fact that local knowledge of his parents' origins precluded his acceptance by the elite families despite the fact that he had lived in cities and received a relatively high level of university education. Had he been prepared to make alliances with the *misti* families or to have changed his life-style to mark difference in a *misti* way, I suspect that his origins could have been erased. However, his political support was not based in the town itself, but in a new generation of educated voters living in the Ocongate hinterland. The fear of the local *misti* families is that, for the first time in Peruvian history, they can no longer claim an exclusive right to local political office. Their own campaigns to modernise the area, to build up the school and extend the reach of state institutions have produced a literate electorate eager to invest in their own communities rather than in the town of Ocongate itself. My friend declared that they would probably all have to move out of Ocongate now that the indigenous peasants from the surrounding areas had the electoral majority. She was already engaged in an on-going struggle with the present mayor, whom she dismissed as ignorant and incompetent. But to her this was nothing compared to the humiliation that the town would suffer once the inevitable happens and they elect a peasant or herder from the outlying areas. When that happens, she declared, 'we will tie him onto a donkey and send him back. How is someone from the *puna* going to represent the town in Cusco? People in Cusco are going to think that we are all like donkeys and sheep.' Her problem is different, but her response follows similar notions of racial difference that motivated Saldivar to tie the then mayor of Ocongate to a mule and feed him straw.

Despite protestations to the contrary I suspect that the *misti* elites are not yet ready to leave Ocongate. Their position is strong despite the change in who comes to hold political office locally. I suspect that the office will become more functional and less powerful. Education works at all levels simultaneously and the mechanisms of differentiation are still very strong. As the children of peasant farmers and herders come to hold local office, the children of *misti* elites are achieving better positions in other towns and cities, even abroad. In this way the *mistis* can increasingly by-pass the local town authorities, while increasing their abilities to embellish their own households with foreign goods as living proof of difference within the locality.

Forced to inhabit 'race' on the margins, these *mestizo* traders use their own children and their wives to mitigate their anomalous position. They send their children away to consolidate their connections to the urban educational centres which offer racial redemption and they leave the women at home to maintain the close local relationships through which they legitimate their elite status in the town. And in the process they straddle two alternative bases for a claim to elite status. One is elaborated through the manifestation of difference and distance and is built on the marks of distinction associated with class difference and expressed through notions of a racial divide. The other is elaborated through an insistence on exceptional status and moral worth via connection to an enduring indigenous identity. The educated children of the Ocongate traders feel particularly able to exemplify this status in their elaboration of generic indigenous culture in the locality, just as the lawyer and his wife did on the occasion of the Pope's visit to Cusco.

Local understandings of power and of dependence resonate with the ways in which the 'indigenous' has been imagined by and for the nation.[5] The legacy of such imagination is twofold. A deep sense of racial division and of discrimination towards those who are thought to hold the nation back from modernising and from prosperity and a deep sense of the rights afforded to those who can demonstrate connection to legitimate and authentic indigenous heritage. The Ocongate elites reproduce this script and benefit from their capacity to move between its key frames of reference. But they also find themselves trapped in the structures of coercive marginality which they help to sustain. Their deepest fear is that the contemporary neo-liberal state might offer more opportunities and greater 'rights' to the educated children of peasant farmers and herders. These young people might be able to lay claim to the margins more effectively than they can. Their situation is echoed by that of national political elites, who have had to concede what were once assured offices of state to new political actors, to Fujimori elected in the 1990s to chants of '*chinitos y cholitos en contras de los blancos*' (the Chinese and the urban Indians against the whites) and to Toledo in 2001 who exploited his provincial origins and campaigned as a *cholo* (an urban Indian/peasant), albeit a cosmopolitan *cholo* with degrees from Stanford and Harvard.[6] Ironically, it is precisely at the moment when localism becomes the new global currency for political actors, that the *mestizo* elites are most under pressure to construct an indigenous modernity that can compete with the new ethnic politics of indigenous elites. Perhaps far from being the manipulators of the system in the terms explained to me by the priests, these families might in fact become the victims of the racial divisions that they have fostered but which now they might be prevented from straddling by the new brand of indigenous activism that seeks to challenge the equation of 'indigenous' with 'marginality'.

Notes

1   See Gupta (1995) for a discussion of the need to problematise the relationship between translocality and localisation in relation to the ethnography of the state.
2   Nugent (Chapter 4 in this volume) draws attention to the difference between accessible and effective elites, making the point that anthropologists usually study the former rather than the latter.
3   See Gupta and Ferguson (1997) for discussion of processes of social, cultural and political location. I have also found the work of Tsing (1993, 1994), Ferguson (1994) and Stewart (1996) extremely useful for the focus on how marginality is constituted and to what effect.
4   See Poole (1988) for a detailed discussion of how the powerful local landlords in the isolated regions of the department of Cusco used to exercise their power both through control of local state institutions and through their own cultural embeddedness in the region.
5   See Gupta (1998: 165–83) for a useful discussion of competing understandings of indigenousness.
6   I am grateful to Wendy Coxshall for keeping me informed of these matters, and for pointing out the irony of the fact that while Fujimori's non-white status was emphasised by the self-evident differences between him and his white opponent Vargas Llosa, Vargas Llosa was a full and open supporter of Toledo in the 2000–2001 campaign!

Bibliography

de la Cadena, M. (1998) 'Silent Racism and Intellectual Superiority in Peru', *Bulletin of Latin American Research* 17 (2): 143–64.
—— (2000) *Indigenous Mestizos: The Politics of Race and Culture in Cuzco, Peru, 1919–1991*, Durham, NC: Duke University Press.
Ferguson, James (1994) *The Anti-Politics Machine: 'Development', Depoliticization and Bureaucratic Power in Lesotho*, Minneapolis: University of Minnesota Press.
Flores Galindo, A. (1977) *Arequipa y el sur andino: ensayo de historia regional (siglos XVIII – XX)*, Lima: Editorial Horizonte.
Gow, D. (1976) 'The Gods and Social Change in the High Andes', Ph.D. dissertation, University of Wisconsin, Madison.
Gupta, A. (1995) 'Blurred Boundaries: The Discourse of Corruption, the Culture of Politics, and the Imagined State', *American Ethnologist* 22 (2): 375–402.
—— (1998) *Postcolonial Developments: Agriculture in the Making of Modern India*, Durham, NC: Duke University Press.
Gupta, A. and Ferguson, J. (1997) *Anthropological Locations: Boundaries and Grounds of a Field Science*, Berkeley, CA: University of California Press.
Harvey, P. (1999) 'Culture and Context: The Effects of Visibility', in R. Dilley (ed.), *The Problem of Context, Perspectives from Social Anthropology and Elsewhere*, Oxford: Berghahn, 213–35.
Jacobsen, N. (1993) *Miracles of Transition: The Peruvian Altiplano, 1780–1930*, Berkeley, CA: University of California Press.
Lukes, Steven (ed.) (1986) *Power*, Oxford: Basil Blackwell.
Marcus, George (1998) *Ethnography through Thick and Thin*, Princeton, NJ: Princeton University Press.

Nugent, David (1997) *Modernity at the Edge of Empire: State, Individual and Nation in the Northern Peruvian Andes (1895–1935)*, Stanford, CA: Stanford University Press.

Poole, D. (1988) 'Landscapes of Power in a Cattle Ranching Culture of Southern Andean Peru', *Dialectical Anthropology* 12: 367–98.

Stewart, K. (1996) *A Space on the Side of the Road: Cultural Poetics in an 'Other' America*, Princeton, NJ: Princeton University Press.

Tsing, A. (1993) *In the Realm of the Diamond Queen*, Princeton, NJ: Princeton University Press.

—— (1994) 'From the Margins', *Cultural Anthropology* 9 (3): 279–97.

Chapter 6

The vanishing elite

The political and cultural work of nationalist revolution in Sri Lanka

Jonathan Spencer

These activist elements, with their grass-roots support and knocking at the doors of privilege, were composed of vocal Buddhist monks, ... pious Buddhist members of temperance societies, village elites of vernacular teachers, ... ayurvedic physicians, ... and the newly rich merchants and *mudalalis*, who were the objects of the snobbery and disdain of the traditional rural headmen and chiefly families and the English-educated professionals and estate owners. The so-called social revolution of 1956 reflected the interests of these segments of the population, who were the touchstone for the masses at large.

S.J. Tambiah (1986: 133–4)

On the mother's side [she] is the descendant of one of the most enlightened and picturesque Sinhalese personalities of colonial times ... [His home was] but a remote hamlet in the highlands of Ceylon. But with this village we associate Sinhalese cultural influences on account of this remarkable figure who was the embodiment of what was best in the old Kandyan aristocracy – dignity, patriotism and gallantry. His heart was with the simple village folk. While he occupied a prominent position among the feudal chiefs of the time he stood out from among them as an erudite scholar and a cultivated man.

Extract from popular biography of nationalist politician (1960)

We were used to these people [local landlords] coming and asking for their share of the harvest; when they came and asked for our votes we gave those too.

Sharecropper reflecting on the Sinhala
nationalist election victory of 1956 (1983)

Kolambata kiri, apata kekiri! (Colombo gets the cream, we get cucumbers!)
Youth slogan of the 1980s

The study of nationalism poses a real challenge to many of the less sophisticated assumptions which have informed the anthropological study of politics. Surveying the political wreckage of the late twentieth century, it is particularly hard to reduce nationalism, and the suffering and sacrifice made in its name, to the kind of narrow instrumental explanations which have characterized certain strands of 'classic' political anthropology (Spencer 1997). A discussion of nationalism cannot avoid a discussion of power, but the power involved is not necessarily (or usually) the property of a particular individual or segment of society. To unravel the workings of nationalism, we need to look to arguments which enable us to discuss power in non-instrumental terms. The two outstanding theoretical contributions to such a discussion are those of Arendt (1970), who locates power in collective action and collective agency (and differentiates power from coercion and violence), and Foucault, for whom power is diffuse, pervasive and productive. Whatever one makes of the coherence or otherwise of Foucault's writings on power, his work has at least had the salutary effect of disengaging the issue of power from models of instrumental action. Arendt's ideas are part of a wider concern with democracy and public argument, and this is a connection I want to explore at the end of this chapter.

What I propose to do in the rest of this chapter is examine critically the use of the notion of an 'elite' as a key agent in a particular moment in the history of nationalism in Sri Lanka. I suggest that the invocation of 'elites' as actors in discussions of nationalism has the effect of smuggling in an instrumental reading of nationalism, which can then be presented as an ideology serving the 'interests' of a particular group, the 'elite'. Instead I want to follow my colleague Thomas Blom Hansen (1999) in linking nationalism to issues of democracy, and drawing out some implications for the study of power and the usefulness or otherwise of the term 'elite'.

The rural elite and the received wisdom

In 1956 something happened to the pattern of Sri Lankan politics from which the country has yet to recover. For the first time since independence eight years earlier, the ruling party was comprehensively defeated in a general election. Its opponents, led by the charismatic S.W.R.D. Bandaranaike, swept to power on a tidal wave of mostly rural populism. The key issue was language, and the election is remembered as the victory of 'Sinhala Only' as the national language, and therefore as a defeat for the non-Sinhala-speaking minorities on the island.

There is, though, a widely accepted sociological reading of this moment which complements the ethnic interpretation. The 1956 election, it is said, was a victory for a new kind of Buddhist activism, and the key agents in this new activism, as well as Buddhist monks themselves, were said to be members of a group variously described as the 'rural' or 'vernacular intelligentsia' or 'elite'. The election represented a victory for this group against the old English-educated elite who had dominated the island's politics and government up to that point. By the early 1960s it was possible for an outside observer to speak confidently, in the past tense, of the 'eclipse of the Western-educated urban elite' (Geertz 1973: 272) and for modernisation enthusiasts to write books with titles like *The Emerging Elite* (Singer 1964) to describe the country's changing political scene.

By the 1970s, though, this Western-educated elite showed signs of a surprising academic comeback. What was now felt to be remarkable about the political landscape was precisely the endurance of the 'old' elite families (Jiggins 1979). One influential, and still compelling, argument from the late 1970s claimed that the gap between the elite and the masses, not that between Sinhala and Tamil, was 'the principal cleavage' in Sri Lankan politics (Manor 1979: 22). A major work of the mid-1980s, Mick Moore's *State and Peasant Politics in Sri Lanka*, devotes several pages to the paradoxical survival of 'elite dominance' after 1956, through a period of often apparently radical national politics (Moore 1985: 205–13). In an update from the early 1990s, although Moore cites recent research which suggests that political leadership had grad-ually spread beyond the 'elite' and into people of 'more middle-class status', he also notes that, through most of the 1980s, the real power holders, the President's inner circle, remained dominated by members of the old elite (Moore 1992: 71–2).[1] Not surprisingly Moore highlights the accession to the Presidency of a low-caste urban politician, R. Premadasa, in 1988 as a possible watershed in the slow expansion in the social distribution of political power. Premadasa, though, was assassinated in 1993 and his most recent successor, Chandrika Kumaratunga (elected in 1994), is S.W.R.D. Bandaranaike's daughter and a member of the same powerful family that has supplied two former prime ministers, as well, further back, as a succession of leading 'native officials' under the British. Moore's 1985 work is almost the last serious, empirically based, survey of the political sociology of Sri Lanka. Since the mid-1980s, almost all attention has focused on the ethnic crisis and the esca-lating civil war, and somehow issues of the distribution of power and resources within the polity have lost their academic urgency, even if, as I shall argue in due course, perceived distributive injustices continue to fuel the conflict itself.

These issues, to some extent, raise straightforward empirical questions – to what extent has power remained concentrated in the hands of the same fami-lies since independence? – which require empirical answers. It goes without saying that a lone ethnographer is not the most appropriate source for these answers. Instead, I want to focus on another issue raised in my opening quotes about the events of 1956: the supposed tension between the old, urban or Westernized elite and the village or rural elite, said to have been key agents in the political changes of that year. Using the view from one particular corner of the island, I want to see what this tension can tell us about the political sociology of nationalism. What emerges from my story, I believe, is a potential division between the political and the cultural work of nationalism, and between a notion of the elite as a real group of people, concerned above all to retain their power and privilege, and a different sense of elite to denote a certain kind of cultural position and a certain kind of cultural work. The first notion is of an elite as above all an exclusive group, the second is of people described as 'elites' who in fact operate as agents in a process of democratic inclusion.

Let me use my opening quotations to set out the argument that follows. The first quotation, from Tambiah's valuable overview of political decline in Sri Lanka, sets out the conventional view of the events of 1956. The activists in the 1956 election were Buddhist monks and lay-people, as well as 'village elites': Sinhala-medium teachers, practitioners of Ayurvedic medicine, and *nouveau riche* merchants. Ranged against them were 'traditional rural headmen and chiefly families and the English-educated professionals and estate owners' (Tambiah 1986: 134). Yet, as my second and third quotation demonstrate, the national and local political leadership in this campaign clearly belonged to that second category. S.W.R.D. Bandaranaike himself was the Oxford-educated son of the most prominent 'native' official of his day. Brought up a Christian, he converted to Buddhism upon the arrival of universal suffrage in the 1930s. On his return from Oxford in 1925, he had to apologize for his inability to respond to the assembled crowds of welcome on his father's estate in anything but English. By the 1950s, despite a considerable reputation as an orator in Sinhala, he publicly confessed to continued difficulty in reading it (Manor 1989: 56, 230). The politician whose biography I quoted at the start came from a family of powerful landowners in the area where I conducted my own fieldwork in the 1980s. Her brother was elected as MP for the area in 1956, in an election my informant remembered best not for its democratic fervour, but more as an extension of existing share-cropping relations: 'when they came and asked for our votes we gave those too'.

In the next section of the paper I will sketch in the historical and political story behind that informant's quote, stressing the role of the colonial state and the colonial imagination in the making of a 'feudal' elite in this area. I then briefly look at comparative examples of elite formation elsewhere in Sri Lanka in the late colonial and post-colonial context. In the section after this, I will turn my attention to the chimerical village elite of Sinhala-medium school-teachers, Buddhist activists and the like. Here I suggest that the use of the term 'elite' is problematic, but that, while the invocation of a clear group or stratum is probably deeply misleading, the kinds of cultural processes attributed to this group are real enough. In the final section I will broaden and extend the argument, partly to criticize the sociological naivety of much anthropological writing on nationalism, and partly to examine the implications of my analysis for more recent political developments on the island. Here, I shall return to the last of my opening quotes – 'Colombo gets the cream, we get cucumbers' – in order to look at the unresolved tensions, inherited from the politics of the 1950s, which lie behind the political violence of the 1980s and 1990s.

The old county families

My concern in this section is with 'the old Kandyan aristocracy', members of the highest stratum of the dominant *goyigama* caste known as the *radala*. My evidence comes from one corner of Sabaragamuva Province, many miles from the centre of pre-colonial power in Kandy itself. I have elsewhere (Spencer 1986: 48–85) described the fortunes of this group in some detail, and here I want instead to paint a broader portrait of local power relations in the colonial period. There are four overlapping points to be established here. Firstly, colonial rule from the first was heavily dependent on the mediation of a handful of inter-related local families, who supplied the personnel for a stratum of powerful local officials. Secondly, these families greatly increased their command of material resources in the course of the colonial period, not least through legal and sometimes illegal exploitation of privileged access to the machinery of the colonial state. Thirdly, although early British officials viewed local society through the prism of their own colonial sociology – in which the 'leading families' had a central part – this colonial sociology hardened and developed into increasingly baroque formations in the course of the nineteenth century. Finally, with the beginning of electoral politics in the 1930s, complex representations of rural change – which systematically obfuscated the real processes of elite dominance – became the currency of mass political symbolism.

Sri Lanka was one of the most deeply colonized places in Asia. The coastal areas, known as the Low Country, were controlled by first the Portuguese, then the Dutch, from the late sixteenth century onwards. The mountainous interior remained nominally independent until the early nineteenth century, when divisions within the ruling stratum at Kandy allowed the British to march in and assume control of the whole island. Within two years, though, a major rebellion broke out, led at first by a pretender figure claiming to be the legitimate heir to the last King, but quickly taken over by leaders from the pre-colonial aristocracy. The rebellion was eventually suppressed at great human cost and the aristocratic leaders executed.[2]

My story starts during the rebellion. In Sabaragamuva, a few key figures from the old aristocracy supported the British against the rebels. One of them, described by one British official as 'this faithful adherent to Govt.' and 'one of our most loyal chiefs', used his new influence with the British to increase his own power and land-holding. ('His avarice is insatiable' was a less complimentary comment from another official.) His influence in the area itself was less impressive – even tenants on his own lands (including the village where I conducted my own fieldwork 150 years later) ignored his appeals and went over to the rebels. Nevertheless, he was promoted to the position of *disava* (provincial governor) by the British, and received the grant of rights in a village previously held by the King in reward for his support. For the rest of the century, this man's children and grandchildren dominated the area in which I was to conduct my fieldwork, filling the various higher positions

which the colonial authorities reserved for the local *radala*. By the end of the
century, the familiar colonial adage – 'find a chief' – had been worked up into
a strong, internally consistent, vision of the proper order of rural society in the
area. Whereas in the early years of British rule, the 'Kandyan chiefs' were seen
as potentially duplicitous, a necessary evil to be tolerated rather than celebrated, by the end of the century a different note was creeping into official
representations of them:

> The landed class, on which Government so largely depends for its influ-
> ence and assistance in the administration of native interests, partly no
> doubt owing to causes beyond control, but mainly, in my opinion, to the
> direct action of Government, is steadily losing its position and character
> in Sabaragamuva, being unable to maintain itself through the loss of
> revenue and services formerly enjoyed.[3]

That was a Government Agent writing in 1886. His successor, writing a
decade later, took a more optimistic view, although his language bears a
moment's reflection:

> A hearty welcome from & a good understanding with, the leading fami-
> lies is a grand standby. The old families of Sabaragamuva have fairly held
> their own – Doloswela, Wanigama and others have died out owing to the
> Kandyan chiefs having such small (legitimate) families. But those which
> remain have become aggrandized territorially and most of them are effi-
> ciently represented.
>
> This is v. different from the history of the old county families of tun
> korles [another Kandyan province] which have almost all of them died
> out or fallen into hopeless decay.[4]

The surreal implication that actually we are talking about rural Hampshire
rather than rural Ceylon is strengthened by these comments, again from a
Government Agent, this time in 1919 concerning the heir to one of these
families:

> The training of this boy is a matter of very great importance and it would
> not be a bad thing if the Education Department could keep him and
> other chiefs' sons under their special care. They should be taught to ride,
> to shoot, to love country pursuits and how best to manage the large
> uncultivated tracts of country which they will inherit.[5]

Several features of this emergent colonial sociology require comment. First
of all, by the end of the nineteentth century, it was firmly taken for granted by
colonial officials that these families were the 'natural' intermediaries between
government and the mass of the rural population, and thus that their sons

would naturally inherit their fathers' positions. Their situation was not, though, utterly secure and as doubts about their possibly declining fortunes arose, so it became necessary for government to offer more active support of its favoured class. Finally, these families, as Kandyans and as members of the 'first-class Goyigama' (the official euphemism for the *radala* sub-caste), were implicitly opposed to less reliable intermediaries: low country Sinhala, members of other castes, *nouveaux riches* who had risen to prominence along the coastline south of Colombo.

These ideas coalesced to most striking effect during the period when Arthur Gordon was Governor from 1883 to 1890. Gordon, who had already made his mark as Governor of Trinidad, Mauritius, Fiji and New Zealand, seems to have carried his own social evolutionary certainties from one colonial setting to another. Fiji, he decided for example, was like the Scotland of the recent past – 'feudal rather than primordial' in Nick Thomas's (1994: 157) gloss. Similarly Ceylon, in his view, was hierarchical:

> Governor Gordon wrongly concluded that the caste hierarchy of Ceylon contained a *goyigama* aristocracy and that no other caste deserved honors and privileges equivalent to those to which the *goyigamas* were entitled. Furthermore … he considered the Kandyan chieftains as the archetypes of this aristocracy.
>
> (Peebles 1973: 338)

Throughout the century, the leading family of my story had been petitioning government for recognition of a large land claim, based on the village ceded to them after the rebellion in the early years of British rule. Gordon, to the consternation of subsequent officials, conceded the family's claim to these lands, and from then on, they lived as absentee landlords for huge tea estates, leased and operated by British agency houses.[6] They also found other ways to explore the new opportunities offered by British rule, most notably by acting as go-betweens for the same agency houses who systematically bought up villagers' rights in highlands for estate development. Their role as privileged intermediaries for the colonial state provided other benefits. The villagers I spoke to remember paying shares of their swidden harvest to the local *valavva* ('manor house' in the colonial idiom), presumably as protection against the state's attempt to regulate and stop this kind of agriculture altogether.

Although the archives are full of evidence that the 'old county families' frequently exploited their masters' indifference to local circumstances in order to turn a fast, and sometimes questionably legal, buck, this does not seem to have substantially undermined colonial faith in their role as natural rulers of their appointed countryside (Meyer 1992; Spencer 1986: 70). That view was based on a vision of them as above all traditional owners of paddy-growing villages, whose inhabitants looked up to them as their natural superiors. In fact, by the turn of the century, in this area at least, a large share of their income seems to have derived from their ownership of estate land, most of which was managed by European companies. In this respect they were rather more like the colonial elite elsewhere in the island than conventional wisdom suggests. In the Low Country, the areas longest colonized by Europeans, new capitalist groups emerged in the course of the nineteenth century. As the government sold off Crown land for estate development, these new capitalist groups were able to shift their fortunes out of socially dubious activities like the arrack trade, and into more apparently prestigious and 'traditional' areas like large-scale land-holding. Many of these new capitalists came from castes which were unprivileged in the old order, but they were joined by Low Country representatives of the 'first-class *goyigama*' who, like their counterparts in the Kandyan areas, used their easy access to the colonial state to accumulate land on a huge scale (Peebles 1973, 1995; Roberts 1982).

Until recently, though, a very different picture of landholding and power in colonial Ceylon has prevailed. The major change in the colonial period, it was argued, was the emergence of a rural dual economy divided between a plantation sector, owned and run by Europeans and worked by immigrant Indian Tamil labour, and a traditional small-holding sector, based in paddy agriculture and impoverished and squeezed by the alienation of land around the villages to the plantations. This vision of rural history in the colonial period was taken up by nationalist leaders around the turn of the century and vigorously propagated by elite politicians in the era of mass politics from the 1930s on. (It is also uncritically reproduced, in Marxist, feminist, Marxist-feminist, and I dare say deconstructionist form, in some academic work up to the present.) What this version of the history of rural crisis systematically effaced was the role of the indigenous elite in land acquisition and the expansion of plantation agriculture: instead blame for rural poverty was displaced onto two different outsider groups, the European planters and the Indian labourers on the tea estates (Samaraweera 1981; cf. Moore 1989; Spencer 1992). Thus it was that one of the new government's first moves after independence was the disenfranchisement of Tamils 'of Indian origin' living and working in the estates, allowing major Sinhala land-owners to pose as guardians of peasant tradition against the depredations of 'alien' commercial agriculture.

The 'village elite' and the work of nationalism

Space does not allow a full exploration of the fate of the 'old county families' after independence in 1948. Suffice it to say that, from 1956 until 1977, they provided all the MPs for the constituency in which I worked. In 1977 the United National Party (UNP) won a landslide victory over the Sri Lanka Freedom Party with which these families were closely associated. Locally, this was presented in terms of a victory over feudalism: one of the UNP's slogans was *radala balaya epa* (we don't want *radala* power), and the local UNP organizer in the village in which I worked, like others in the constituency, celebrated by renaming his dog Bandara (an 'aristocratic' name associated with the *radala* families). But the new MP, though ostensibly very different (a Muslim rather than a Sinhala Buddhist), was also the son of a large local landowner and close associate of the same 'old county families'. Nationally, members of these families are again well represented in the PA government which came to power in 1994.

It seems to me that there can be little problem in applying the term 'elite' to this small circle of families, tightly bound by repeated inter-marriage at the same level, often bitterly divided in their competition for the spoils of the colonial state, but nevertheless quite clear about the appropriate necessary distance between themselves and the lower orders of colonial society. And, despite the complexities of subsequent political change, it is quite clear that at least some of them have proven remarkably adaptable to the era of mass politics, to the extent that we might talk of them as the unexpected inheritors of the populist revolution of 1956. They are not, for all that, the progenitors of that revolution, and here we encounter a rather different group of people to whom the term 'elite' has been applied: the supposed village elite.

This group appears with suspicious clarity, suspiciously early in writing on the events of the 1950s. To some extent, the language used to describe the group varies. One contemporary journalist refers to them as the 'Sinhalese middle class of small businessmen, school teachers, ayurvedic physicians and other sections of the intelligentsia with an oriental outlook' and goes on to describe them as 'the national bourgeoisie and petit-bourgeoisie' (Pieris 1958: 4–5). Wriggins, in the best analysis of the time, also talks of a 'village middle-class', but he too identifies the same list of key figures: 'the Buddhist monk, the village school master, the indigenous doctor, the Village Headman, and the elected chairman of the Village Committee' (Wriggins 1960: 39). Geertz, characteristically, manages his own ornate rephrasing, describing this group as 'consequential rural personages' (1973: 272), but again listing the school teacher and the ayurvedic physician, *et al*. More recent writers, though, have used the term 'village elites'. The fullest description of this group can be found in Singer's 1964 *The Emerging Elite*, where he devotes six pages to his description of the 'rural elite' which includes 'Buddhist priests, traditionally influential families, vernacular schoolteachers and ayurvedic physicians' (Singer 1964: 137). All this is prefaced with a cautionary warning that this group does not possess 'an awareness of common interests and bonds with other members of the group', and that it might be better to talk here not of '*an* elite' but of '*many* elites' (Singer 1964: 136). (This pluralizing note occurs in a chapter which has already reported on 'the civil service elite', 'the military elite', 'the trade-union elite' and 'the urban business elite', not to mention 'the political elite' which gets a separate chapter of its own.) Although Singer's is the fullest description of the rural elite, he refers to very little empirical data about rural social structure or the elite of any particular village, apart from a single reference to a survey of landlessness, and a brief quotation from Ryan's *Caste in*

Modern Ceylon (1953). The group reappears in Tambiah's (1986) survey of the background to the current crisis. And, more recently still, James Manor, in his biography of the nationalist leader, refers to S.W.R.D. Bandaranaike's links with 'key elites in the villages where most of the votes were – teachers, priests, ayurvedic physicians and small businessmen' (Manor 1989: 183; see also 197 and *passim*).

I want to suggest that, as a group, the rural elite is a chimera, an empty category generated by the need to identify an interest group on which to pin responsibility for the nationalist mood of the mid-1950s. This is not to say that village school teachers and monks do not exist, nor to suggest that they are unconcerned with maintaining the dignity of their position in local life. It is, though, to suggest that the political work carried out by school teachers, monks and the like in the early 1950s was not the work of an elite in the sense of a closed group of powerholders. Had it been so, it would not have worked. There *are* excellent accounts of local elite politics in Sri Lanka, which do show the existence of a relatively closed and self-conscious stratum in rural areas, eager to monopolize access to the state and state resources (for example, Alexander 1981; see also Obeyesekere 1974), but these studies do not talk of school teachers and Buddhist monks and ayurvedic physicians, but of land-holders, political brokers and the like. The villagers I asked about the events of the 1950s remembered not the role of monks or school teachers, but the effortless transition from landlord to political representative: 'We were used to these people coming and asking for their share of the harvest; when they came and asked for our votes we gave those too.'

One of the most striking features of the Sri Lankan political field is what could be called the 'structural opacity' between town and country, which ensures that powerful urban figures know little or nothing at first-hand about the problems and aspirations of those living in poor, rural areas. In a situation like this, one of the key valuables traded in local politics is information, with MPs heavily dependent on district and village party bosses for access to reliable knowledge of local problems (Gunasekera 1994). This opacity is itself one strong cause for suspicion of the 'rural elite' formulation that emerged so quickly to explain Bandaranaike's 1956 election victory. It also means that we have very little reliable information on local politics in the 1950s.[7] Instead, I shall shift from history to ethnography, and describe some of the work of nationalism in the village where I carried out fieldwork in the early 1980s, in the hope that this will also illuminate the politics of the 1950s.

Less than a fortnight after I had moved into a village in Sabaragamuva Province in early 1981, I received a visit from a local school teacher. He had come, he said, to tell me some of the history of the village. In particular he gave me a detailed account of various local place names: that hill over there is named the 'hill of the milk-boat' because, in the days of the Sinhala kings, a herdsman used to keep his cows on the hill, below which there was a great tank or reservoir, recently restored. Because the milk was transported across the tank by boat, the hill was known as the hill of the milk-boat. The hill itself, he continued, was used for beacon fires, lit to warn the forces of the Kandyan king of the approach of European soldiers to the south. The name of the old village on its side (on which the modern village name is based) came from the word meaning a trail blazed along a path, or more generally a sign or marker; it was so called because of the signal fires that used to be kindled on its summit. A couple of days later, exactly the same story was told me by the *gramasevaka*, the minor local official who now filled the role of the colonial village headman.

Neither the school teacher nor the *gramasevaka* were natives of the village, having settled there twenty and ten years earlier, respectively. What they were doing – in telling me this unsolicited tale of the village past – was actually providing a new, and potentially less embarrassing, version of the local past, a version in which local memory was over-written by national political concerns. When I gave my address to Sinhala friends outside the village, they often queried the village name which didn't sound 'right' for a Sinhala village. Later in my fieldwork, I discovered that older villagers would say this was probably because it was a Tamil name of some sort, and point out phonetic similarities to certain common Tamil words. On one occasion, when a young man started to do this in my presence, he was quickly corrected by a companion, who invoked the authority of the school teacher to explain why this 'Tamil' story was incorrect. The context for all this, of course, was the politicization of the country's past, in which archaeological evidence, Sinhala place-names, sacred bo-trees, were all taken as evidence of Sinhala occupation of the whole island, and thus refutation of Tamil claims for their own distinctive homelands in the north and east. The existence of a 'Tamil' mark on the landscape, so far from the disputed north and east, in its own modest way threatened to confound this whole project.

This moment was, I would suggest, paradigmatic of a whole area of cultural work, of which the school teacher was one of the village's most industrious agents. The teacher was not, as I mentioned, a native of the village. Rather, he had been born about fifteen miles away beyond the nearest small market town. His family were middling prosperous farmers, holding the few acres of paddy land that raised them above their share-cropping and labouring neighbours. He had been schooled locally, before going away to study at the provincial capital forty miles away and subsequently finding employment as a government schoolteacher. When he arrived in the village in the early 1960s he was its only government employee. Very soon he married a woman from one of the better-off village families and thus acquired a world of kin in his new home. ('Better-off' in this case was a relative condition – the village as a whole was extremely poor at that time.) At work and on all public occasions he wore national dress (*jatika āndum*) of white shirt and sarong with black Western shoes. By the time I started my fieldwork he had been transferred to a school about ten miles away, but he remained the dominant figure in those areas of village life that centred on the Buddhist temple, such as the lay society that administered temple affairs and organized the celebration of major collective rituals, or a newly formed co-operative society which provided for funerals and other emergencies. He was chairman of both these bodies and a prominent speaker at all their public meetings. He also spoke at many of the funerals and weddings I attended.

Let me take a second, contrasting, example. If my first figure was a model of public piety, my second is somewhat less so. This is the dog-owning village UNP boss I have already mentioned. Like the school teacher (who was his most bitter political opponent) he was an outsider who had first settled, then married, into the village. His father was a man of distant Low Country origin, the owner of a small store in the nearest market town. In the early 1970s, this man had taken on the lease of one of the village's two small general stores, and swiftly married the daughter of one of his new neighbours. His elder brother was the chief UNP organizer in the constituency. When their candidate and party proved victorious in the 1977 election, the younger brother gave up his stores and took up the position of government cultivation officer and local representative of the UNP party machine. He rarely bothered with the pious appurtenances of national dress, but preferred to wear trousers for all his official and semi-official business. A local representative of a Muslim MP, and a man with his own considerable reputation for drinking and fighting, most of the time he all but abandoned the terrain of competitive Buddhist piety to his opponents.

So, for example, when both men made speeches at a village wedding in late 1983, not long after the anti-Tamil riots which swept the country in one week in July, the UNP boss chose to stress relatively neutral images of community: we are all kin in this village, all united, all relatives. The school teacher, though, used a much more charged rhetoric of nationalist difference: our host is a good Sinhala Buddhist man, he has only Sinhala Buddhist blood in his body, this is how it should be in this country, which is a good Sinhala Buddhist country. These speeches were as much about village politics as they were about the immediate circumstances of the wedding. The party boss drew on the facts of kinship to stress his own claim that all his efforts were focused on a single goal: the unity of the village. But, his own local alliances closed down some obvious rhetorical options. He owed his position to an outsider, the Muslim MP, and so he worked to link the day's events with an ideal of unity based on locality and kinship, rather than blood and religion – an ideal often drawn upon by national political figures in 'statesmanlike' mode. The school teacher suffered no such qualms. For him, the wedding was as much an occasion for the celebration of difference – the difference of being Sinhala and being Buddhist – as well as an opportunity to restate his grievances against his political opponent. Every mention of Sinhala and Buddhist could be implicitly opposed to Muslim and Christian and Tamil. Muslims and Christians were the party boss's allies, and were outside the charmed circle of Sinhala Buddhist nationhood, while the Tamils were the old enemies who had so recently – and brutally – been reminded of their 'proper' place in the country.

The party boss, whatever his public position, was certainly no less chauvinistically anti-Tamil or anti-Muslim in private than the school teacher. But his own political circumstances, and the fact that in areas of competitive piety he could not hope to compete with the teacher, constrained him on this occasion. His greatest skill was his capacity to improvise, not least in public speaking where he could, briefly, convince his audience to believe the most counter-intuitive claims. The previous year, for example, he and his immediate friends had thrown their weight behind a small Buddhist festival organized by a group of very poor and very marginal recent immigrants to the village, migrants from far afield who had settled as encroachers on state-owned land on the fringe of the village. The festival offered, among other things, a rare chance to upstage their political rivals in a public display of Buddhist identity. At the festival itself, which was attended by several hundred people, including his main political enemies as well as his allies, the UNP boss produced a speech of great power and audacity. He started with the immediate circumstances – the 'little' people who had organized the event, their aspirations to raise the funds so that one day they could endow a temple of their own – before linking them, first, with his own political position:

> It is only 'our' people, the UNP, who do anything for the little people in this village; all the big people are with the [opposition] SLFP and don't care for the poor people out here on the edge of the village. To show that we care I have written to the Prime Minister and told him about these people and their needs and [his voice, by now, rising triumphantly] *he has written to me* and promised that the government will build a model village on this very spot so that these people will have proper houses to live in. *I have the letter here*!

Of course he didn't, and to this day there is no sign of a model village anywhere in the area. As one of his opponents remarked sardonically afterwards, if he had really received a letter from the Prime Minister everyone for miles would have heard about it as soon as it arrived. The model village was swiftly forgotten, but it had served its immediate rhetorical purposes. The model village movement, which the then Prime Minister was leading, embodied an especially tangible kind of nation-making. All over the country, people were being moved into the new uniform dwellings being constructed under the Prime Minister's programme, and the press was full of references to the movement which self-consciously combined allusions to an idealized rural past while promising an improved and 'developed' future.[8] The village boss's improvised connection linked the immediate local event to national political culture, by borrowing or stealing a central symbol from that culture. Like his enemy's speech at the wedding, the movement was again from local circumstances to national imaginings.

What these figures share, of course, was a position as half-insiders, half-outsiders, and the capacity to tell a particular kind of story, one that linked the local to the national, and the past to the present. 'All great storytellers,' Benjamin reminds us, 'have in common the freedom with which they move up and down the ladder of their experience' (Benjamin 1973: 102). Storytelling, he claims, belongs above all to the artisan class, in which 'was combined the lore of faraway places, such as a much-travelled man brings home, with the lore of the past as it best reveals itself to the natives of a place' (Benjamin 1973: 85). Neither of my examples were artisans as such, but they were travelled men of a sort: they had differing experiences of life in the town, and could cope better than most with the differing worlds of town and country, separated in terms of class, consumption habits, and sometimes language. Both were noticeable for their ability to deal with the social demands of life outside the village: the school teacher could speak in English with visiting officials, while the party boss was always available when the inevitable bottle of arrack was passed around in the back of the jeep on such occasions, and was able to trade jokes and stories with the best of them. Other people had some of this experience of rural and urban styles of life and expression, most notably the village priest who had a Sinhala-medium degree from the University of Colombo, but he was a very reluctant public performer, preferring instead to spend his time with the handful of regular visitors who would gather at the temple to discuss the news and share his knowledge of the wider world.

There are a number of other people whose lives and activities seem to fit the pattern I have been describing, especially the young people whose education had taken them out of the village and who, on their return, were so active in the work of remaking the village in terms of a certain Buddhist or nationalist respectability.[9] Many of these young rural modernists were the most active figures in the anti-state violence of the 1980s which swept the south of the island. The party in whose name that violence was carried out – the JVP or People's Liberation Front – combined appeals to Sinhala nationalism, denouncing the government as traitors to the Sinhala people, with sharp anti-elite invective. The slogan I quoted at the start of the paper – 'Colombo gets the cream, we get cucumbers' – dates from the time of the JVP terror and state counter-terror. Similar processes have been at work in Tamil areas and have provided some of the fuel for the continuing insurrection against the Sinhala-dominated government: 'In Colombo the schools have marble toilets', as one young LTTE cadre put it in a BBC film some years ago. Both the JVP leader, Rohan Wijeweera, and the LTTE leader, Prabakharan, came from poor but respectable, rural or suburban, educated but not elite, backgrounds. Both are (or were: Wijeweera was arrested and murdered by government forces in 1990) spell-binding orators, able to weave together appeals to the inclusionary vision of the nation with resentment at continued exclusion from the tables of the powerful.

It seems to me perfectly reasonable to see figures like Wijeweera and Prabakharan as rooted in the same life-circumstances, and the same personal and political dilemmas, as my school teacher and the party boss and the young men and women who organized rituals of Buddhist respectability at the village temple. It also seems to me reasonable to read backwards from these examples, and others like them, to those who were described as the 'rural elite' in the 1950s. If we do that, then we get a rather different, but I think more plausible, understanding of what happened in the politics of the time. Instead of under-standing the work of the 'village elite' as the work of a discrete interest group, lobbying for its share of state resources – better salaries for Sinhala teachers, state support for ayurvedic medicine, etc. – we might do better to think of this as a moment of radical democratic energy. The people who made up the chimerical village elite were, above all, the conduits for a far more inclusive political rhetoric, dominated for the first time by the first person plural. The slogan still associated with the celebrations after Bandaranaike's election victory was simple but telling: *ape anduva*, our government.

Those people I met in the 1980s, whose social situation and political activity seemed most like the 'rural elite' of the 1950s, are most easily identifi-able, not in structural terms – as members of a closed, or would-be closed stratum – but from their position in processes of cultural production and reproduction. Their quintessential representative is probably the school teacher, the person whose role it is to reproduce the official view of the past and the present in the schoolroom, but whose informal activities complement this by articulating and re-articulating accounts of local community and belonging which bring together the idiosyncrasies and needs of the particular place with the big, transcendent verities of nationalist ideology.

Two caveats are in order here. Firstly, I have highlighted the explicit articu-lation of nationalist ideology, whereas much of the local work of nationalism is implicit – the construction of national subjectivities – and located in the quotidian operations of nationalizing institutions like schools. Secondly, I have granted a kind of sociological self-evidence to my village cultural brokers. In fact their presence in the village is itself a product of real social and political processes, and there is another history that can be told here. In this village, the school and the temple arrived together in the early 1940s. The temple was built as part of a policy of self-conscious 'colonization' of the rural periphery by activist monks operating out of one central temple at the nearest small town. The school was established by the first monk to move into the village, then, under an official scheme of the time, adopted by the state in the late 1940s. This spread of crucial institutions of cultural production and reproduc-tion was an island-wide phenomenon at the time, coeval with the emergence of mass politics. But, although the changing state was an important factor in this process, either it was not directly involved in the process (as in the building of new temples), or only became involved after local activists had started the process (as in the spread of rural schools in the 1940s). It would take another, much longer, study to deal properly with the emergence in the 1950s of a 'rural elite' of monks and school teachers and cultural activists, but one thing is clear: their appearance as a coherent political entity at the time is as much a symptom as a cause of the nationalizing processes attributed to them.

The genie in the bottle

The story I have sketched in here is obviously schematic and over-general-ized. It would seem, though, to correspond to the account of nationalism provided by Tom Nairn (in his pre-Gellnerian, world-systems phase) in which nationalism is crucially important to elites on the periphery as the most effec-tive means of mobilizing popular support: 'The new middle-class intelligentsia had to invite the masses into history; and the invitation card had to be in a language they understood' (Nairn 1981: 340). So, in my account of this process, the 'national elite', as represented by immensely wealthy and powerful figures like Bandaranaike, needed others, the 'middle-class intelligentsia', to do their ideological work for them, to provide 'a language', a set of powerful symbols, which could be understood by 'the masses'. And, over time, the elite endures and the masses find themselves still excluded from the tables of the rich.

That, I think, is too partial an account of what has happened in Sri Lanka. Certainly, there is plenty of evidence that from the 1930s on, elite figures self-consciously, and often cynically, employed the popular appeal of nationalist ideology to fight their own more limited political battles. But there is even more evidence that nationalist ideology, once unbottled, refuses to go away, and those animated by its appeals do not always listen to the commands of its supposed elite masters. That, certainly, has been the experience of Sri Lanka since the 1950s. Since the early 1970s the country has experienced at least three waves of traumatic anti-state violence. Two, in 1971 and 1987–90, were the work of the Sinhala JVP. The third, and most lasting (since the mid-1970s), is the work of the Tamil LTTE. All have been based in a combination of deep nationalism and anti-elite resentment. As such, they are, in obvious and non-obvious ways, part of the continuing consequences of the revolution of 1956. The obvious link is, of course, the fact that the radical Sinhala nation-alism of the 1950s was a language of exclusion for Tamil-speaking minorities, and the LTTE are merely the last stage in a long process of alienation and opposition in the North and East. Less obvious, but just as important, is the fact that violent youth movements, in both North and South, have been based in very similar social and cultural predicaments and, in their own disturbing way, often speak a language of democratic inclusion.

I think my case has a number of implications for an anthropology of nationalism. First of all, a great deal of recent anthropological writing on nationalism has concentrated on disembodied 'readings' of nationalist symbols and ideology, with little or no attention to the contexts and agents involved in their use. This trend is so widespread it would be unfair to single out particular authors. In so far as nationalism *is* situated in a socio-political context, this is usually done by invoking 'national (or nationalist or nationalizing) elites'. I hope that my example has shown that the promiscuous use of the term 'elite' obscures as much as it reveals.[10] What is left especially murky are the agents and processes whose cultural work is so important to the dissemination of nationalist ideology. Vague allusions to 'national elites' (who almost always live elsewhere, beyond the margins of the ethnographer's attention) inevitably create a top-down picture of nationalism, an ideology simply imposed from above on local people. For a country like Sri Lanka, where nationalism, democracy, egalitarianism, and sometimes anti-elitism, have been so powerfully conjoined, and where the fruits of that conjunction have at times been so pathological, this simply will not do.

Instead, I think we need to look more closely at these links between nationalism, democracy and egalitarianism. Hansen's (1999) account of the rise of the BJP in India situates the movement within a more encompassing democratic revolution, whose consequences are as much social and cultural as 'political' in any narrow sense (see Kaviraj 1998). In different ways, my two local political leaders may be seen as agents of such a revolution, whose efforts are focused on inclusion rather than exclusion, on a large rather than a small 'we'. This appeal to inclusion also forms the basis of such power as they may be thought to possess. What power they have is much more fragile and evanescent than the power of the 'old county families'. It is in many ways performatively based – so long as they command an audience, and their audience colludes in the terms of their performance, they remain men of importance. If their words fail to chime they are just ordinary men with loud voices. This opens up new questions – too complex to be explored here – about the variable repertoires of power available to agents in differing political and historical contexts. But these questions, and others about the cultural consequences of democracy, are, it seems to me, the most exciting ones facing any new anthropology of politics.

Acknowledgement

Most of the field and archival material on which this paper is based was collected while I held a research studentship from the Social Science Research Council in 1980–84, supplemented by material collected on a succession of trips in the 1990s, supported by the University of Edinburgh and the British Council in particular. Some of the argument on power and democracy reflects more recent work conducted while I was the holder of a Nuffield Social Science Research Fellowship. I would like to thank Thomas Hansen for his last-minute efforts to breathe intellectual life into this paper.

Notes

1 Moore is citing Tara Coomaraswamy's Sussex DPhil thesis, which I have been unable to consult while writing this paper.
2 For a full account of these events, see Peiris (1950).
3 Administration Report for Sabaragamuva (1886: 157).
4 Government Agents' Diaries, SLNA 45/29, 20/7/1896.
5 Government Agents' Diaries, SLNA 45/337, 7/9/1919.
6 Full references can be found in Spencer (1986: 67–70).
7 Anthropologists of the time, you may recall, were rather more fascinated by cross-cousin marriage and the internal politics of Cambridge theory (Leach 1961; Yalman 1967); Obeyesekere's early 1960s fieldwork produced the first ethnographically convincing work that really addressed rural power relations (Obeyesekere 1967; but see also Tambiah 1963).
8 See Brow (1996) for an excellent ethnography of the unforeseen consequences of the building of one such model village.
9 I have described one such young man, and linked his preoccupations to themes from the political violence of the late 1980s in another paper (Spencer 2000).
10 See, for example, Peebles' trenchant comments on the use of the term 'elite' in the work of Michael Roberts (Peebles 1995: 12–14). Roberts himself defends his usage as an alternative to a structural definition of 'class' (Roberts 1982: 10; see Cohen 1981: 232–3).

Bibliography

Alexander, P. (1981) 'Shared Fantasies and Elite Politics: the Sri Lankan "insurrection" of 1971', *Mankind* XIII 2: 113–32.

Arendt, H. (1970) *On Violence*, New York: Harcourt, Brace & World.

Benjamin, W. (1973) 'The Storyteller', in H. Arendt (ed.), *Illuminations*, London: Fontana, 83–109.

Brow, J. (1996) *Demons and Development: The Struggle for Community in a Sri Lankan Village*, Tucson, AZ: University of Arizona Press.

Cohen, A. (1981) *The Politics of Elite Culture: Explorations in the Dramaturgy of Power in a Modern African Society*, Berkeley, CA: University of California Press.

Geertz, C. (1973 [1963]) 'The Integrative Revolution: Primordial Sentiments and Civil Politics in the New States', in C. Geertz, *The Interpretation of Cultures*, New York: Basic Books, 255–310.

Gunasekera, T. (1994) *Hierarchy and Egalitarianism: Caste, Class and Power in Sinhalese Peasant Society*, London: Athlone.

Hansen, T.B. (1999) *The Saffron Wave: Democracy and Hindu Nationalism in Modern India*, Princeton, NJ: Princeton University Press.

Jiggins, J. (1979) *Caste and Family in the Politics of the Sinhalese 1947–76*, Cambridge: Cambridge University Press.

Kaviraj, S. (1998) 'The Culture of Representative Democracy', in P. Chatterjee (ed.), *Wages of Freedom: Fifty Years of the Indina Nation-State*, Delhi: Oxford University Press, 147–75.

Leach, E. (1961) *Pul Eliya: A Village in Ceylon*, Cambridge: Cambridge University Press.

Manor, J. (1979) 'The Failure of Political Integration in Sri Lanka (Ceylon)', *Journal of Commonwealth and Comparative Politics* 17 (1): 21–46.

—— (1989) *The Expedient Utopian: Bandaranaike and Ceylon*, Cambridge: Cambridge University Press.

Meyer, E. (1992) 'From Land-Grabbing to Land Hunger: Highland Appropriation in the Plantation Areas of Sri Lanka during the British Period', *Modern Asian Studies* 26 (2): 321–61.

Moore, M. (1985) *The State and Peasant Politics in Sri Lanka*, Cambridge: Cambridge University Press.

—— (1989) 'The Ideological History of the Sri Lankan "Peasantry"', *Modern Asian Studies* 23 (1): 179–207.

—— (1992) 'Retreat from Democracy in Sri Lanka?', *Journal of Commonwealth and Comparative Politics* 30 (1): 64–84.

Nairn, T. (1981) 'The Modern Janus', in *The Break-up of Britain*, 2nd edn, London: Verso.

Obeyesekere, G. (1967) *Land Tenure in Village Ceylon*, Cambridge: Cambridge University Press.

—— (1974) 'Some Comments on the Social Backgrounds of the April 1971 Insurgency in Sri Lanka (Ceylon)', *Journal of Asian Studies* 33 (3): 367–84.

Peebles, P. (1973) 'The Transformation of a Colonial Elite: The Mudaliyars of Nineteenth-Century Ceylon', Ph.D. thesis, University of Chicago.

—— (1995) *Social Change in Nineteenth Century Ceylon*, New Delhi: Navrang.

Pieris, D. (1958) *1956 and After: Background to Parties and Politics in Ceylon Today*, Colombo: Associated Newspapers.

Pieris, P. (1950) *Sinhale and the Patriots 1815–18*, Colombo: Apothecaries' Co.

Roberts, M. (1982) *Caste Conflict and Elite Formation: The Rise of a Karava Elite in Sri Lanka, 1500–1931*, Cambridge: Cambridge University Press.

Ryan, B. (1953) *Caste in Modern Ceylon*, New Brunswick, NJ: Rutgers University Press.

Samaraweera, V. (1981) 'Land, Labor, Capital and Sectional Interests in the National Politics of Sri Lanka', *Modern Asian Studies* 15 (1): 127–62.

Singer, M. (1964) *The Emerging Elite: A Study of Political Leadership in Ceylon*, Cambridge, MA: MIT Press.

Spencer, J. (1986) 'Tenna: Peasant, State, and Nation in the Making of a Sinhalese Rural Community', DPhil. thesis, Oxford University.

—— (1992) 'Representations of the Rural: a View from Sabaragamuva', in J. Brow and J. Weeramunda (eds), *Agrarian Change in Sri Lanka*, New Delhi: Sage, 357–87.

—— (1997) 'Post-colonialism and the Political Imagination', *Journal of the Royal Anthropological Institute*, 3 (1): 1–19.

—— (2000) 'On Not Becoming a "Terrorist": Problems of Memory, Agency and Community in the Sri Lankan Conflict', in V. Das *et al.* (eds), *Violence and Subjectivity*, Berkeley, CA: University of California Press, 120–40.

Tambiah, S. (1963) 'Ceylon', in R. Lambert and B. Hoselitz (eds), *The Role of Savings and Wealth in Southern Asia and the West*, Paris: UNESCO, 44–125.

—— (1986) *Sri Lanka: Ethnic Fratricide and the Dismantling of Democracy*, London: I.B. Tauris.

Thomas, N. (1994) *Colonialism's Culture: Anthropology, Travel and Government*, Cambridge: Polity Press.

Wriggins, W. (1960) *Ceylon: Dilemmas of a New Nation*, Princeton, NJ: Princeton University Press.

Yalman, N. (1967) *Under the Bo Tree*, Berkeley, CA: University of California Press.

Chapter 7

The changing nature of elites in Indonesia today

C. W. Watson

The study of Indonesian elites in the twentieth century has been well served by historians. They have written some highly illuminating studies of the operation of elite groups at a local, regional and national level, studies which have been informed as much by anthropological and sociological methods and insights as by historical ones *tout court*. Anthropologists have only lately come into this field but the recent anthropological work has been of an outstanding quality. Thanks to the researches and the example of historians, anthropologists have been able to set their study of local politics firmly within a diachronic account of the evolution of powerful interest groups and kinship networks over a historical period stretching at least as far back as the beginning of the twentieth century. Where the anthropological studies have been especially good, in particular the works of Antlöv (1995), Bowen (1991), Kipp (1993) and Schulte Nordholt (1987), is in demonstrating the articulation of the local with the regional and the national, an accomplishment which reflects their intimacy with the local situation and the ease with which both conceptually and geographically they are able to move from the periphery to the centre to observe the dynamics of the exercise of power, patronage and prestige.

In all the discussions about elites, however, there has been a certain taken for granted quality of what the word entails and only a very rough-and-ready attempt to introduce analytical qualifications. Van Niel, for example, in his book entitled *The Emergence of the Modern Indonesian Elite* (1960) refers to functional (administrative) elites and political elites, both groups within the broader category of a Western educated modernising elite. In his case the distinction works well in drawing our attention to the formation of different groups within the colonial polity. However, as the twentieth century progresses and one tries both to make sense of the proliferation of factions and rivalry in arenas of political and economic power, and to create further categories of, for example, military elites or business elites, the boundaries around which are often highly porous, then problems of definition can often prove intractable. And this is simply to limit the discussion to the new urban centres. In rural areas where there is often reference to village elites, of which there are categories of political, religious, and landowning, the problems multiply. Spencer's point in this volume (see Chapter 6), drawn from his experience of rural Sri Lanka, about the emptiness of the category of elite at this level is well taken, and we should take care if we want to preserve the analytical usefulness of the term.

My limited purpose here is to demonstrate that in fact there is, if used cautiously, a continuing usefulness in the notion of elites, especially if taken in conjunction with other concepts to explore the political realities of Indonesia. The particular contribution which anthropologists can make to this exploration lies in contextualising the operation of elites both spatially, by showing, as they have done in the past, the linkages between centre and periphery, and temporally, in following the movement of individuals and families from one sub-category of elite into another. My own acquaintance with Indonesia now stretches back over thirty years, and during that time I have been mixing with and observing elites in both Jakarta and in rural areas. With respect to the latter most, but not all, of my work has been done in Kerinci in central Sumatra, and consequently I draw my examples from there. Both my own more general experience and the reading of the ethnographies of others suggest to me that the Kerinci case, *mutatis mutandis*, is applicable to the wider Indonesian scene. In the first part of what follows I provide a brief synopsis of political development in Indonesia up to 1969 relying on standard accounts; in the second part I extend the description up to the present, this time relying on my own observations and presenting two short case studies to illustrate the points I make about the rapidly changing dimensions of elite formation in the second half of the twentieth century; and finally I return to the question of the continuing utility of the term elite and what the anthropological contribution to discussion of it in Indonesia might be.

Historical context: 1900–69

The histories of what might conveniently be termed the modernising national elites of Indonesia in the twentieth century have been well documented. In the pioneering work referred to above Van Niel (1960) described how from the beginning of the century the Dutch carried into effect a policy of modernisation, throughout the archipelago but especially in Java, by means of incorporating a Western educated native cohort of civil servants and officials into the colonial administration. Many of these Western educated school graduates, rather than take up employment in government service for which they had been trained, preferred to avail themselves of the new opportunities being created in the fast-growing towns in Java. Some went into journalism and publishing, catering for the newly created and rapidly expanding literate population. From the ranks of this group there soon emerged nationalist opposition to Dutch colonial rule (Blumberger 1987, Shiraishi 1990). And at a slightly later date, around 1927, this nationalist movement became consolidated under the leadership of a more highly educated stratum of the native 'traditional' elite who had entered the professions as doctors, lawyers and engineers and who saw themselves as part of a global anti-colonial movement with which many of them had come into direct contact during further education in the Netherlands (Ingelson 1979).

Very much sharing Van Niel's approach, Sutherland (1979) has described in detail how one group within this elite, the Javanese aristocracy, the so-called *priyayi* class, responded to Dutch encouragement and developed a culture of service which seemed to demonstrate a continuity with their own traditional patterns of obligation and duty, although in the new dispensation this was predicated on a different set of assumptions of the rewards of service – fixed salaries and accountability rather than tribute and patronage. The distinguishing characteristic of this administrative elite was that it developed a sense of overriding loyalty to the notion of the State and a commitment to the bureaucratic procedures that were necessary to the tasks of administration required of them. In this way they brought about what has subsequently been labelled the *Beamtenstaat* (the Bureaucratic State) which, according to commentators such as Anderson (1990) and McVey (1982), has determined the character of all subsequent polities which have emerged in Indonesia immediately after independence and even after the apparent dramatic shifts which occurred when the so-called Old Order of Sukarno was replaced by the New Order of Suharto.

Less frequently cited than these accounts but equally thoroughly researched (Siegel (1969) Castles (1972), Liddle (1970), Kraan (1980), Williams (1990), Reid (1979)), there have been studies of the character of local elites and the tensions which sometimes arose between those representatives of ruling classes who had benefited from the patronage of the Dutch and a new more democratically inspired stratum, also Dutch-educated, who were challenging the older establishment in a competition for power and influence at a local level.

A further dimension to these local conflicts and in some cases inextricably woven into them was a conflict among religious elites that has also engaged the attention of historians. At the same time as modernising initiatives were being encouraged by the Dutch, a modernist Muslim movement had been introduced into the archipelago in 1912 deriving its inspiration from the Egyptian moderniser Mohammad Abduh. In Indonesia, as elsewhere in South-East Asia (Benda 1970), the modernisers met strong opposition from an entrenched establishment of local religious scholars who saw their authority being eroded and who distrusted the new scholarship. This frequently led to a polarisation at a local level between the *kaum muda* (young group) and *kaum tua* (old group) that brought about divisions within local communities, which in some areas even seventy years on have not healed. The position of the Dutch *vis-à-vis* this conflict was ambivalent. On the one hand they applauded the modernist thinking of the *kaum muda* as represented in the modernist organisation, the Muhammadiyah, which had established schools, polyclinics, orphanages and even a scout movement along Western lines (Alfian 1982); but on the other hand they deplored the challenge to the traditional structures of authority, the secular hierarchies and their religious supporters, whose positions they had endorsed and on whose support they had come to rely. The emergence of local conflict both seemed to threaten internal stability and herald the creation of a political opposition to Dutch colonial rule.

When the Pacific War broke out in 1942, although the composition and definition of these different elites were still fairly fluid and individuals could retain friendships across the dividing lines of their different political and religious opinions, sharper demarcations developed between the groups as each began to take on a recognisable distinctive shape. At the apex of political power were the upper echelons of the native bureaucracy, men who worked closely with senior Dutch officials and were rewarded with prestigious positions and the titles and trappings of high office; men like Achmad Djajadiningrat who had reached the pinnacle of authority with his appointment to the highest governing body in the Dutch East Indies, the Raad van Indie (see Watson 2000: 38–69). Personally devout though many of them may have been, they shared the Dutch distrust of religious politics and the ambitions of those whom they saw as potentially dangerous fanatics.

The radicals for their part felt that the tide of colonial history was on the ebb, and, although in 1942, from their places of exile and detention, their immediate future did not seem promising, they were not overly downhearted (Watson 2000: 70–105). Within the population at large, their ideas at that time were not (*pace* Shirashi 1990) widespread or influential (O'Malley 1980) but nonetheless they were heroes to a younger generation and there was a strong bond of solidarity among them. (See the autobiographical novel by Soewarsih Djojopuspito (1941) for a wonderful evocation of this group at that period.) As might have been expected, since they shared a common educational background with the bureaucratic elite, they too felt a certain hesitancy about the direction which Islamic modernism was taking, although some did in fact become the leaders of a modernist Muslim political streaming. At a local level, in the rural areas and outside Java, the disputes between *kaum muda* and *kaum tua* had by 1942 lost some of their earlier intensity, and the young Turks of a decade or so previously were now taking on the role of modernisers rather than political activists.

With the coming of the Japanese the influence of the different political groupings was reversed. Although the bureaucrats continued to play an important administrative role, since the Japanese could not afford to dispense with them, they were regarded with suspicion, and at a local level they were not treated with any of the respect that the Dutch had shown for them. The radical non-cooperators were on the other hand courted by the Japanese. Members of the Muhammadiyah, for example, were sought out and given positions of responsibility. Although with hindsight after the war many realised that they had been duped by the Japanese – for a spectacular instance of this in relation to the prominent religious leader Hamka, see Watson 2000: 106–29 – at the time, as committed nationalists, they felt that they were contributing to the imminent independence of Indonesia. Moreover, despite their ultimate disillusionment with the Japanese they did derive some advantage from the period in terms of having gained the direct political experience of inserting a modernist Muslim voice into the debates of the time, establishing networks across the archipelago (and into Malaya) and thus preparing themselves for the major role which they would play in the post-independence Indonesia of the 1950s.

In the mythology surrounding the critical period of the revolution between 1945–50, when the Indonesians were fighting the Dutch, the impression is created that the population was united in its efforts to resist the return of colonialism. The reality is somewhat different. Several of the local aristocratic families appeared to be willing to accept the Dutch once more, an attitude for which they paid a heavy price in the so-called social revolution, which led to their massacre. Even among those groups that were hostile to the Dutch there was considerable rivalry that led to outbreaks of violence and fighting among themselves. The Communist Party, for example, found itself outmanoeuvred by the established government forces and was all but destroyed in a confrontation in Madiun in Central Java in 1948. In other cases people used the cover of the general turmoil and uncertainty to settle personal scores. In terms of the emergence of elites, however, the most important feature of this period is the coming into being of a military elite which developed a corporate sense of identity as well as a local ethos built upon regional divisions.

After the withdrawal of the Dutch in 1950 and the consolidation of a new democratic machinery of government, there was less fluidity in membership of elite groups. In effect one sees the development of the classical elite dilemma in the years which follow: while satisfying their supporters that their demands are being met, elites are struggling to maintain their power and influence at the centre by compromising among themselves, employing a combination of cajolery and threat. Events between 1950–65 can be interpreted as the playing out of these elite rivalries through the mechanism of party politics.

It is, then, through party political machinery that elites throughout Indonesia exercise their influence, and the history of the period 1950–60 can be viewed as an engagement in an intense struggle throughout the archipelago among party members to promote their representatives into influential positions in the local administration, in government departments, in schools and universities and in the police and armed forces. Of the political parties through which the elites operated, the most significant were the PNI, the secular Nationalist party, the Masjumi, the modernist Muslim party, the NU, the 'conservative' Muslim party – largely confined to Central and Eastern

Java – and the PKI, the Communist party. The other smaller parties clustered around these larger ones and formed ad hoc alliances with them.

The other major contender among the elites was the armed forces which, despite attempts to clip its wings, gradually over the decade of the 1950s had emerged as perhaps the most powerful single institution within the state, and one which despite President Sukarno's best efforts could not be brought entirely under the control of the government (Sundhaussen 1982 and Crouch 1975).

In the two years preceding the coup attempt of 1965 and the massacres that followed there had been an extraordinary build-up of tension in Indonesia as a consequence of the very sharp exacerbation of political confrontation and elite competition. When Suharto took over from Sukarno in 1966, he and his advisers embarked on a thoroughgoing reorganisation of those political structures that were regarded as responsible for bringing about the polarisation of the earlier period. He was in an enviably strong position from which to carry out this restructuring since he was the head of the armed forces, now regarded as the saviours of the nation, he had eliminated the only parties which could have offered any resistance to his proposals, the PKI and the left of the PNI, and he had the support of all the decision-making pragmatists in the civil service and also of the modernist and conservative Muslim groups.

The recent past: 1969–99

The rest of my paper is an attempt to describe what has happened to elite formations in the last thirty years, and whereas my analysis of the preceding period has been drawn from summary and selection of the works of historians and political scientists, the following description tries to adopt a more anthropological perspective in so far as it is based on personal observation and a close engagement with changes in Indonesia over this recent period, observing not only the shifting politics of a Jakartan elite but also seeing at close hand the workings of a local elite and the connections between centre and periphery.

Three features characterise the changes in the composition of elites in Indonesia in the period after 1970: the undermining of the influence of the religious elites, both those of a modernist and those of a conservative persuasion, the growing power of an administrative elite associated with the new State party GOLKAR, and the creation of a new middle class comprising both professionals and a business elite in Indonesia which begins to exert increasing influence on Jakartan politics from the early 1980s. A corollary of this last phenomenon is that as the middle class increases its influence so the military elite, which dominated Indonesian politics up to that time, declines in direct proportion to the rise of the middle class. All these developments at the centre have immediate consequences for political and economic activity in the *daerah* (the periphery, i.e. the regions outside Jakarta), as we shall see.

Religious elites in Java were able to wield influence in the Sukarno period both because of their close associations at the village level with the rural population for whom they acted as cultural brokers (Geertz 1960) and because their membership of NU allowed them to extend a certain amount of patronage to those who appealed directly for help. NU leaders could approach their counterparts within the PNI, for example, whose members dominated the civil service, to request political favours. In 1966 the PNI's influence had declined while the NU was still influential; thus it might have been anticipated that a religious elite would have increased its standing in rural areas, as might the modernist Muslim leadership which had been partially rehabilitated by the New Order government. In the event Suharto and the military, fearing the competition which a revived Muslim politicisa-tion would bring to the political arena, by a series of organisational manoeuvres simply dismantled the old party political structure.

It took some time for the specific nature of the tactics employed and their effectiveness to be fully appreciated, and throughout the 1970s Muslim groups were still trying to mount opposition campaigns particularly in the run-up to the elections. Election results, however, demonstrated how futile this opposi-tion was. GOLKAR representatives campaigning for their party at the local level used a combined carrot and stick approach. The carrot was to offer inducements to influential religious leaders to persuade them to join GOLKAR, a move which met with rejection in the first half of the 1970s but which by the end of the decade was beginning to have some effect. The stick, administered most frequently in the immediate run-up to elections, was a devious campaign of terror and intimidation. To the population at large it soon became abundantly clear that the best channels through which to seek patronage were through GOLKAR and the civil service. If religious leaders had access to these channels then all well and good; if not, then one aban-doned them and looked for more powerful patrons. The Muslim elites, then, although they still enjoyed respect and deference on account of their religious scholarship and their past services to the local community, ceased to function as politically significant voices.

Case 1: The Kiyai of Lubuk Dalam

(NB. All names in the case studies are pseudonyms.)

H. Wahab had been very active among the *kaum muda* group in Kerinci in central Sumatra in the early 1930s. As the son of a wealthy property owner he had been sent away to acquire an advanced religious education in one of the modernist schools in West Sumatra. On his return he had come into conflict with his father's generation for challenging some of the traditional village customary practices which in his opinion were not consistent with Muslim beliefs. Although the local Dutch officials were not very happy about his Muhammadiyah sympathies, they reached a *modus vivendi* with him and his like-minded friends, and by the early 1940s they were all happily playing tennis together. In the Japanese period and during the Revolution his stock rose as he became the most important regional official with good links to the modernist Muslim leaders of the Masjumi political party throughout the archipelago. His downfall came when, along with much of the leadership of the Masjumi, he was on the wrong side in the Sumatran PRRI rebellion against Sukarno in the mid-1950s. When the rebellion was crushed, he was imprisoned for a number of years.

When the New Order came to power he once more became a person of influence and respect in Kerinci and was often consulted by the new local administration. In the 1970s, however, when it became clear that he did not intend to get drawn into GOLKAR and would be supporting the new Modernist Muslim party, PARMUSI, the local administrators turned against him. Outwardly they still showed him respect and sent him occasional gifts, but in the lead-up to the 1975 election, groups of rowdies had been hired to stone his house at night and carry out systematic intimidation to the point that for the duration of the final election campaigning he had decided to leave Kerinci. In the years which followed he had continued to be quite outspoken in his opposition to GOLKAR, and he had maintained close links with his erstwhile Masjumi friends, visiting them whenever he was in Jakarta. His political influence, however, was insignificant. Nonetheless he was recognised as a member of the Kerinci elite, was widely respected as a religious scholar and through personal friendships and kinship links was still able to help and support others through acts of minor patronage. He had very quickly perceived how important a good modern education was to be for the life-chances of his children and encouraged them to pursue higher education, paying for four of his sons to go through expensive training in medical school. None of them followed his footsteps to become religious teachers.

H. Wahab's case illustrates the consequences at a local level of the strategies planned and implemented in Jakarta. As far as the modernist Muslim elite was concerned this pattern was repeated throughout the archipelago. This group were still held in respect but to all intents and purposes they had had their day. Their place was taken by those government officials who were automatically recruited into GOLKAR and used GOLKAR networks. At the same time, to offset the possibility that these would become petty autocrats, their power was counterbalanced by an elaborate system of local security in which the heads of local army garrisons and local police chiefs were also able to exercise a considerable amount of independent authority. There was thus always a potential for rivalry at this level leading to the replacement of the head of either the civil or military authority. Who would go would depend on the strength of their personal links of patronage leading back to the centre in Jakarta. For the most part, however, differences and disputes rarely led to head-on confrontations, and a compromise was usually reached, particularly from the mid-1970s onwards when there was sufficient money dropped into the local regional economies to allow all the various factions to prosper.

One further move served to consolidate the power and the influence of the civil service down to local village levels throughout Indonesia. In 1979 a restructuring of village government (Watson 1987) led to the position of village head being incorporated into the structure of government administration. Prior to that, the lowest level of government official had been the *camat*, a sub-district head. There had always been a potential for tension in the relations between *camat* and village heads since the latter, however much they might have been pre-selected by the local administration, always risked posing a challenge to their authority if they decided to voice villagers' grievances. Now, however, with this restructuring and a monthly salary drawn from the government the village head became less a people's representative than the lowest level of authority mediating the government's writ (Antlöv 1995: 198–201).

At the same time as this strengthening of the civil service was occurring, the growth of the economy was also making possible the rapid rise of an urban middle class, particularly in Java (Tanter and Young 1990). It is difficult, however, to regard this new class as an elite. They were comfortably off and were now in a position to benefit from the educational opportunities which they had enjoyed some 15–20 years earlier. They were still, however, dependent on linkages with influential businessmen and military figures mostly resident in Jakarta. The latter constituted the real urban elite which began to dominate the economy. What could be observed was the close cooperation between corporate business, largely in the hands of the Indonesian Chinese, and retired senior military figures who – again provided that they toed the New Order line (see Jenkins 1984 for details of what this meant) – were able to engage in exactly those kinds of negotiations in relation to major government contracts at the centre which officials on a considerably more minor scale were conducting in the regions. This cosy relationship persisted for about fifteen years between 1975–1990, with the government allowing it to develop unchecked and facilitating it through both ensuring political stability and keeping in place protective measures to support this new business elite. Inevitably, however, this protective system, riddled as it was with inefficiencies and hedged in by cumbersome regulations, could not be maintained forever.

Changing global circumstances, of which the most important were the fall in oil prices leading to an economic strategy of diversification and an ever-increasing competition to attract foreign investment, led from the mid-1980s onwards to shifts in the orientation of the Indonesian economy, which in turn fed into the political debates of the time about the need for greater openness and accountability. These global changes also coincided with the rise of a new professional elite and the transformation of the attitude of the older elites, which now began to act more independently and flex their muscles.

Case 2: The Ph.D. in international relations

Ati's father was a lecturer in a university in Bandung who had never been particularly politically active, although his broad sympathies lay with the Masjumi and the modernist Muslim groups. He was a Minangkabau from a relatively humble non-elite background from the highlands of West Sumatra and had originally come to Java to complete his education in the early 1950s. His experience working for further degrees in the USA and Britain in the 1950s had given him a strong attachment to Western liberal values, and he was widely read. When the opportunity came for him in the late 1970s, as it did for many other senior civil servants, foreign office officials and members of the military elite, to go abroad, he went to England with his family and stayed in London where his daughters had the opportunity to go to secondary school and then on to university where they did very well. When he returned to Indonesia in the mid-1980s he was initially intimidated by the hierarchical organisation of the bureaucracy in the university, and by the way in which civil society was still cowed by the authoritarian senior military figures who appeared to be so influential at local and national levels. Whenever I met him in those latter years of the 1980s he would tell me ruefully of some new encounter with petty bureaucracy or the assertiveness of the military. He would also recount with amusement the actions of some of his more confrontational friends whom he admired but whom he felt misunderstood the realities of power within the society. Gradually, however, as the years went by he seemed to lose his apprehension of the military presence and found that much to his surprise there was more scope for open discussion than he had realised. Consequently, he and his friends, all of whom like him were senior academics with considerable experience of studying abroad, would frequently meet and discuss politics quite openly.

Meanwhile Ati had also returned from abroad, and with a Ph.D. in international relations she soon found a position as a senior researcher in LIPI, the national research institute. She was by this time also married to a man who had graduated from the prestigious technical university, ITB, in Bandung and who was employed by a big multinational firm working in Indonesia. Although she understood very well the nature of Indonesian politics, she had no direct experience of Indonesian political culture. This in fact worked to her advantage since, far from being intimidated by the administrative hierarchies as her father had been, Ati was quite ready to speak out and express her opinions, and in the circles in which she moved in Jakarta this straightforwardness was respected. Her English was perfect and she had excellent links with foreign embassies by whom she was constantly invited to receptions or conferences abroad, as well as on one occasion having been offered the opportunity by the US State Department of work experience in Washington. Consequently, she very quickly became a member of the bureaucratic elite, at the same time sharing a more general perspective common to a growing number of young professional intellectuals, many of whom like her had been educated abroad. By the mid-1990s this group were all living comfortable middle-class lives in Jakarta and the other big cities in Java with spacious houses, all modern conveniences, the opportunity of regular trips abroad and the usual concerns for their children's education and how to provide the latter with the kind of academic head-start from which they themselves had bene-fited. At the same time, whenever they thought about it, when for example they were pressed for their opinions by foreign friends, or when they or their friends suffered personal frustrations as a consequence of the political system, they expressed an increasing irritation at *Cendana* politics, the actions taken by the President's family, resident in Jalan Cendana, which seemed designed only to perpetuate a personal dynasty. Since, however, Ati's own interests were not much affected she was prepared to tolerate these abuses of democracy and on the whole was not sympathetic to radicals whom she felt did not understand political realities. As for the military, although Ati and others recognised the power which they wielded, they were not affected by them, and their personal relations with top military figures were good. If asked to explain her personal political orientation Ati would say that her views were analogous to the old PSI of the 1950s, Sjahrir's party, made up of Western educated prag-matic decision makers, well represented in senior positions in the civil service, influential in policy making, but politically insignificant in terms of the weight they carried in the legislative assembly. She would not, however, have been receptive to the criticism, frequently made of the PSI, as possibly applying to her, namely that intellectual bureaucrats like her were simply remote from the situation on the ground and were unable to understand the discontent and anger of the majority of the population who felt powerless in the face of the structures by which they were constrained. When, through the creation of ICMI, the association of intellectual Muslims, in the late 1980s, Suharto, as part of his strategy to seek support and construct a counterweight to the military, restored Muslim political opinion-makers to the political stage, Ati was one of those whose status was enhanced. She was asked to become a member of the ICMI think-tank, CIDES, which was set up by Suharto's close ally, B.J. Habibie, to whom she became even more closely linked after his elevation to the Presidency in 1998 and for whose new Habibie Center – modelled on the Carter Center – she continues to work.

Ati's championing of Habibie placed her firmly in the camp of those professionals and intellectuals who felt that he provided the best chance for the immediate political and economic stability of the country. In the climate of the time, however, it also set her very strongly against those of the anti-Habibie camp with whom she was previously united in a common dislike for *Cendana* politics. To understand how this polarisation within the elite occurred, we must return to the circumstances leading up to the downfall of Suharto.

When the Indonesian economy began to go under in the late summer of 1997, Suharto felt that he was secure, thanks to the way in which he had insured his position by playing his potential rivals off against each other. Oppositional voices within the army had been deftly sidestepped and current military leaders were all personally loyal to him. Muslim intellectuals had been co-opted into supporting him – the only Muslim voices expressing any opposition were Abdurrahman Wahid and Amien Rais. The professionals were still doing well. The senior professional bureaucrats were, it is true, pressing for urgent reform, but they had no muscle and could safely be ignored. A growing number of NGOs had also sprung up in the 1990s and were often very vocal at a local and national level about environmental and rights issues without, however, making much significant impact. Students too made strident demands for a more open democratic system and many gave their support to Megawati, the daughter of Sukarno, the former president, but, initially at least, they were ineffectual and Suharto could always rely on the army to deal with them if things got out of hand.

Ultimately, however, student demonstrations which had built up a momentum in the run-up to the Presidential election instead of subsiding increased in intensity, this time supported by their parents' generation (Watson 1998). The economic situation was deteriorating rapidly as Suharto and his business allies appeared unwilling to accept the measures which the senior Indonesian technocrats overseeing the economy were urging upon him. The upshot of the increasing tension over the months between March and May was that the intellectual elite, former ministers, senior figures in the circle of government advisers, and younger intellectuals including Ati and her friends, recognised that Suharto would have to go.

The eventual ousting of Suharto came about through an extraordinary alliance among different elite sub-groups. In effect all factions, or at least all the influential voices within the factions at the time, were united in opposition to Suharto, his family, their cronies and hangers-on. However, that unity was hard to sustain. For one thing there was still a lot of opposition to Habibie, the new president, who was seen to have been one of those closest to Suharto who had benefited from his years in office. The secular nationalists, those who clustered around Megawati, were in particular hostile to him, and they included a number of younger intellectuals. Like Ati they had been educated abroad but did not share her political opinions. And finally there was a general suspicion of the residual influence of GOLKAR. Although it too appeared to have been completely discredited at all levels, national and regional, because of its close association with the New Order and the arrogance with which it abused its powerful status, there were signs that under its new chairman, Akbar Tanjung, a man widely admired for his integrity, it might still command a lot of support. In fact in the elections held in June 1999, especially in the regions, including Kerinci where its members remain influential, GOLKAR was very successful.

The unrest which is now sweeping through Indonesia at a regional level can be attributed to a number of causes, but if one confines analysis to a perspective on elites, one can in broad terms argue that what is happening is a further realignment of alliances. The administrative elites and their GOLKAR supporters who had appeared so invulnerable to attack now find themselves under siege. The armed forces, who over the years had seen their authority decline in relation to the civilian administration, are now much less likely to intervene on behalf of that administration with whom they worked so closely in the early years of the New Order, and anyway they are too busy guarding their own backs.

Kerinci has been no exception to the general pattern. There were demonstrations in the summer of 1998 against the local administration which was accused of corruption. The district head, the Bupati, was forced to keep a low profile and stayed out of Kerinci for most of the time. In order to try to restore some stability to the area those Kerinci people who reside outside the region and live in the large towns on Java and Sumatra, where they keep in touch with each other through regular meetings and get-togethers, decided to return to Kerinci and pool their ideas on what needed to be done. Among the most active of this group were H. Wahab's children. Now firmly established in professional careers their opinions carry considerable weight in Kerinci. They are in regular contact with their relatives there and return at least once or twice a year for ritual celebrations and religious holidays. Among the group of returnees there was a general consensus that senior figures in the GOLKAR/Government Administration who had been responsible for the mismanagement of the region should not be allowed to regain power. To this end they were campaigning that one of their own number should be appointed as the new Bupati. Here, however, consensus began to break down since who the most suitable candidate might be was disputed among representatives of various sub-regions within Kerinci. Eventually a compromise was reached, and the new Bupati, a retired army officer, seems to have the confidence of the professional elite who are now in a stronger position than they have been for fifty years, in fact since the time that H. Wahab was district head. The GOLKAR civil servants, however, continue to be responsible for local administration, and to judge by electoral results at least still have considerable local support.

Conclusion

The detailed description of recent events in Indonesia contextualised within a potted history of elite formations in the twentieth century was designed to illustrate that although a focus on elites, especially when hedged by qualifiers, can sometimes be conceptually difficult to offer a satisfactory account of who constitutes the elites and what power and influence they exercise and how permanent they are. Historical events and global shifts in international politics have such immediate and dramatic consequences that it seems impossible to observe continuities of the kind to which we are accustomed in, say, the analysis of class and capitalism in Western societies or of a landowning aristocracy in feudal or post-feudal societies.

In specifying the distinctiveness of an anthropological perspective for an understanding of the rise and fall of categories of elites in situations such as that found in Indonesia, anthropologists, whether they are working with urban elites in positions of power and influence or whether they study leadership in small rural communities, tend to work by drawing upon their experience of the immediate and particular. Other social scientists customarily proceed from the general to the particular, thus from categories to local description. The various Western social science approaches to Indonesia have over the years veered between the two extremes, at times over-emphasising culturalist approaches, at other times adopting a more general political-economy perspective (Robison 1981). Anthropologists by the nature of their discipline steer a middle path between the two, but always begin from experience in the field. It is this experience of the individual and the particular which always provides a useful corrective to any attempt to force analysis of the data to conform to some pre-existing framework.

Elites, factions and interest groups are very slippery protean entities in the context of the realities of Indonesian politics, and rather than attempt to use the concepts as hard and fast social science categories we should treat them heuristically to be exploited if and when they suit us. The Indonesian example demonstrates that the growing complexity of the organisation of the state in the last thirty years has brought about a comprehensive realignment of political and social relations. Although it is sometimes possible to trace elements of former elite structures in contemporary configurations, most notably in the apparent resurrection of the old political parties, the NU and PNI, reflected in the positions of the president and vice-president, superficial similarities can be deceptive, and it is clear that earlier elite taxonomies derived from and applied to an understanding of the first six decades of the twentieth century are today no longer satisfactory. Furthermore, the emphasis of historians and political scientists on using the description of elite politics at the centre as a measure for an assessment of the politics of the nation is demonstrably inadequate in helping us to understand the post-1998 turmoil in the country. Much of this turmoil has taken place in the *daerah* and its scale has taken observers by surprise: both local observers and social scientists failed to pick up any indications of later eruptions of violence in the Moluccas, Sulawesi, Kalimantan, or even, though on a much smaller scale, Kerinci. With hindsight one might suggest that the reason for the failure lies in the undue confidence which both placed on their perception of local elites and leaders whom they knew and understood and whom they felt could be relied on to contain confrontations which might arise along lines of ethnic or religious cleavage.

A sharper attention should have been paid to the way in which new forces had emerged, as a consequence both of the economic restructuring which had taken place over the past three decades and as a result of significant changes in the demography of local regions arising from the substantial development of opportunities for geographical mobility and subsequent spontaneous transmigration. (In fairness I should say that studies of Java and Bali by Antlöv (1995), N. Schulte Nordholt (1987) and H. Schulte Nordholt (1991) had noted the tensions there.) Herein lies the final point which needs to be made regarding the study of elites in Indonesia and I suspect in many other countries: the tendency to identify elites and employ the concept to search for continuities in styles of postcolonial political action needs to be constantly reexamined. However radical and innovative the concept may have been in an earlier period (Vincent 1990: 362–3), its limitations are now obvious. Rapidly changing socio-economic conditions inevitably mean not only equally rapid transformations in the character of elites but also the emergence of new types of associations and political groupings – ethnically based, voluntary, student-based, religious, regional – within civil society. Consequently, while not abandoning altogether a focus on elites, both policy makers and anthropologists would do well to locate their analysis within the context of new structures and social formations. The changes wrought by the latter have dramatically and qualitatively altered social values and political behaviour. In these circumstances, then, if we still wish to persevere with a concept of elites to assist our understanding, the least we should do is to acknowledge an anthropological truism: only contextualise.

Bibliography

Alfian (1982) 'Islamic Modernism in Indonesian Politics: The Muhammadijah Movement During the Dutch Colonial Period (1912–1942)', unpublished Ph.D. thesis, University Microfilms.

Anderson, B.R. O'G. (1990[1983]) 'Old State, New Society: Indonesia's New Order in Comparative Historical Perspective', in B. Anderson, *Language and Power: Exploring Political Cultures in Indonesia*, Ithaca, NY: Cornell University Press, 94–120.

Antlöv, Hans (1995) *Exemplary Centre, Administrative Periphery: Rural Leadership and the New Order in Java*, Richmond: Curzon Press.

Benda, Harry J. (1970) 'South-East Asian Islam in the Twentieth Century', in P.M. Holt, Ann K. Lambton and Bernard Lewis (eds), *The Cambridge History of Islam*, Cambridge: Cambridge University Press, vol. 2A, 182–207.

Blumberger, J. Th. Petrus (1987[1931]) *De nationalistische beweging in Nederlandsch-Indie*, *KITLV*, Dordrecht: Foris Publications.

Bowen, John R. (1991) *Sumatran Politics and Poetics; Gayo History, 1900-1989*, New Haven, CT: Yale University Press.

Castles, Lance (1972) 'The Political Life of a Sumatran Residency: Tapanuli 1915–1940', unpublished Ph.D. thesis, Yale University.

Crouch, Harold (1975) *The Army and Politics in Indonesia*, Ithaca, NY: Cornell University Press.

Feith, Herbert (1962) *The Decline of Constitutional Democracy in Indonesia*, Ithaca, NY: Cornell University Press.

Geertz, Clifford (1960) 'The Javanese Kiyayi: The Changing Role of a Cultural Broker', *Comparative Studies in Society and History* 2: 228–49.

Ingleson, John (1979) *Road to Exile: The Indonesian Nationalist Movement, 1927–1934*, Singapore: Heinemann Educational Books.

Jenkins, David (1984) *Suharto and His Generals. Indonesian Military Politics 1975–1983*, Ithaca, NY: Cornell Modern Indonesia Project, Southeast Asia, Monograph Series No. 64.

Khaidir Anwar (1980) *Indonesian: The Development and Use of a National Language*, Yogyakarta: Gadjah Mada University Press.

Kipp, Rita (1993) *Dissociated Identities. Ethnicity, Religion, and Class in an Indonesian Society*, Ann Arbor, MI: University of Michigan Press.

Kraan, A. van der (1980) *Lombok: Conquest, Colonization and Underdevelopment 1870–1940*, Singapore: Heinemann Educational Books.

Liddle, R. William (1970) *Ethnicity, Party and National Integration: An Indonesian Case Study*, New Haven, CT: Yale University Press.

McVey, Ruth T. (1982[1977]) 'The Beamtenstaat in Indonesia', in Benedict Anderson and Audrey Kahin (eds), *Interpreting Indonesian Politics: Thirteen Contributions to the Debate*, Ithaca, NY: Cornell Modern Indonesia Project Southeast Asia Program, Cornell University, Interim Report Series Publication No. 62.

Nordholt, Henk Schulte (1991) *State, Village and Ritual in Bali*, Amsterdam: VU University Press for Centre for Asian Studies Amsterdam, Comparative Asian Studies 7.

Nordholt, Nico Schulte (1987) *Ojo Dumeh. Kepemimpinan Lokal dalam Pembangunan*, Jakarta: Sinar Harapan.

O'Malley, William (1980) 'Second Thoughts on Indonesian Nationalism', in J.J. Fox, R.G. Garrault, P.T. McCawley and J.A. Mackie (eds), *Indonesia: Australian Perspectives*, Canberrra: Australian National University, 601–13.

Reid, A. (1979) *The Blood of the People: Revolution and the End of Traditional Rule in Northern Sumatra*, Kuala Lumpur: Oxford University Press.

Robison, Richard (1982[1981]) 'Culture, Politics, and Economy in the Political History of the New Order', in Benedict Anderson and Audrey Kahin (eds), *Interpreting Indonesian Politics: Thirteen Contributions to the Debate*, Ithaca, NY: Cornell Modern Indonesia Project Southeast Asia Program, Cornell University, Interim Report Series Publication No. 62, 131–48.

Shiraishi, Takashi (1990) *Age in Motion: Popular Radicalism in Java, 1912–1926*, Ithaca, NY: Cornell University Press.

Siegel, James (1969) *The Rope of God*, Berkeley, CA and Los Angeles: University of California Press.

Soewarsih Djojopoespito (1941) *Buiten Het Gareel*, Utrecht: W. de Haan.

Sundhaussen, Ulf (1982) *The Road to Power: Indonesian Military Politics 1945–1967*, Kuala Lumpur: Oxford University Press.

Sutherland, Heather (1979) *The Making of a Bureaucratic Elite: The Colonial Transformation of the Javanese Prijaji*, Singapore: Heinemann Educational Books.

Tanter, Richard and Young, Kenneth (eds) (1990) *The Politics of Middle Class Indonesia*, Clayton: Centre of Southeast Asian Studies, Monash papers on Southeast Asia No. 19.

Van Niel, Robert (1960) *The Emergence of the Modern Indonesian Elite*, The Hague and Bandung: Van Hoeve; republished for the KITLV, Leiden by Foris Publications, 1984.

Vincent, Joan (1990) *Anthropology and Politics: Visions, Traditions and Trends*, Tucson, AZ: University of Arizona Press.

Watson, C.W. (1987) 'State and Society in Indonesia', Canterbury: Centre of South-East Asian Studies, Occasional paper No. 8.

—— (1998) 'Military's Might in Indonesia', *Times Higher Education Supplement* 15 May.

—— (2000) *Of Self and Nation: Autobiographical Representations of Indonesia*, Honolulu: University of Hawaii Press.

Williams, Michael C. (1990) *Communism, Religion, and Revolt in Banten*, Athens, OH: Ohio University Center for International Studies, Monographs in International Studies, Southeast Asia Series No. 86.

Part II

Elites, hegemony and tradition

Chapter 8

Settlers and their elites in Kenya and Liberia

Elizabeth Tonkin

Introduction

Anthropologists and historians are giving more attention to colonisation, and to 'settler societies', which tend to be seen as dominant and European (but see Stasiulis and Yuval-Davis 1995). I argue that incomer groups are subject to certain constraining choices wherever and whenever they attempt to move in among other peoples. I consider two African cases: Kenya, which is generally taken to be exemplary of white British settler colonisation, and Liberia, where the dominant settlers were black Americans with limited support from the United States.

In both countries there were numerous competing incomer groups. The dominants did not form 'the elite'. Rather, elite formation was *internally* contested alongside wider group conflicts for overall control. These two sometimes opposed processes work together.

The actual uncertainties, compromises and 'tensions of empire' (Cooper and Stoler 1997) are increasingly recognised, though with a tendency to assume the operations of white racism and imperialist ideology. Anthropologists can challenge this essentialism if aware of actors' temporalities – the temporal contexts in which the political, economic, security and social relations of settlers and their *sending communities* may radically change.

Of course, scholars work with different definitions of colonisation and imperialism, whether stressing the commonalities of empire building throughout history, or arguing that the formation of European empires in the nineteenth century is tied to the rise of industrial capitalism. I use the wider perspective to focus on the general structuring and dynamics of incomer communities, but stress actors' temporalities in 'the colonial period'.

General conditions and relations of settlement

Looking at examples reveals generalisable imperatives for incomers, and constraints upon them. Thus, the Latin *colonia* named settlements of pensioned legionaries (OED). The Greek trading-post type (*ἀποικία*) was sited on offshore islands or defensible peninsulas (see for example Ascherson 1996). The *incomers* had either to impose themselves on *locals*, or negotiate with them, or try both strategies. Unless incomers assimilate, these imperatives remain. Keeping social organisation, language and economy different may facilitate mutual accommodation and promote trade (Barth 1969). Relationships with other incomers, as with locals, or between settler and metropole, are all bargains, even if enforced ones, which need ideological support for cultural and social reproduction.

As the settling communities' relationship with locals may and usually does change, so does that with their communities of origin. Will they continue to help defend or finance them? The senders' interests in their offshoot may weaken; the incomers may become alienated from the metropole and try to escape its control. Imperial powers may protect incomers or conquer locals as the Romans did, but incomers may also negotiate security locally.

Incomers will want sexual relationships, with outside partners if need be. The community's future ranges between assimilation – in a sense to disappear – and pluralism, in which different groups are kept culturally or religiously distinctive, or segregated: without exogamous sex or marriage, the group must reproduce itself internally. Whatever the solutions, *all* the relationships I have noted indicate group negotiations of power.

The case studies

Choices and researchers' formations

Kenya and Liberia are two Sub-Saharan African states in which I lived during years preceding key political changes. I use my memories as evidence, to be critically judged like any other, realising too that my intellectual outlook has been cumulatively affected by each successive milieu in which I have worked. These include the contrasts of Nigeria, colonised, but not considered settled (and see Phillips 1989) and Northern Ireland (see for example Clayton 1996). Many citizens of Birmingham, where I was a university lecturer, have been 'colonisin' Englan' in reverse'[1] and show that 'immigrants' may also be 'settlers'.

History: Kenya and Liberia

I summarise the historical background of Kenya and Liberia extremely briefly, with the risk of traducing complexities that have been very significant,[2] for the period when both began to be named states. I do not consider Kenya after independence in 1963, or Liberia after 1980, when there was a military coup against the settler regime.

Kenya

European incursions into what became Kenya were recognised formally by the Foreign Office's agreement with Sir William Mackinnon to operate the

Imperial British East Africa Company in 1888. This failed financially and the Foreign Office took the territory over as a Protectorate in 1895, transferring the administration of Kenya to the Colonial Office in 1905. In 1963, the British government granted the colony independence.

Imperial foreign policy was to secure the headwaters of the Nile, and thus access to Egypt, so a railway was built from the coast to Uganda, completed in 1901. 'The Scramble for Africa' had by then spurred German, French, Belgian and Italian as well as British competition, in waves of dominationist sentiment which often connected Christian dreams of conversion to those of economic wealth ('commerce') and fantasies of improved imperial status in Europe (see for example Galbraith 1972).

Explorers, followed by missionaries and later IBEAC agents, walked into East Africa from around the mid-nineteenth century. The British used their long-standing consular base in Zanzibar, administered from India before the Scramble (Mangat 1976: 467–8). Missionary agitation against 'Arab' slavers, who were settled there and active on the mainland, was much supported by British public opinion, and led to military action in Buganda. Muslims became moral opponents as well as economic ones. The railway required financing and, as soon as it was built, European settlement was presented as a means of revenue for it, since the Highlands of Kenya were found to be temperate (rising above 5,000 feet) and apparently lightly populated. At first, however, the region was envisaged as appropriate for Indian settlement, as a colony for India's excess population.

Liberia

In America, colonisation societies sent black settlers to the west African region they named Liberia from 1821. Their aims were complex and contradictory (see Tonkin 1981): ostensibly aimed at 'civilising and christianising Africa' by converted African ex-slaves, the white senders also wished to remove freed blacks from the United States, whether for anti- or pro-abolitionist reasons. In 1847, the Commonwealth of Liberia was constituted as an independent republic, and has frequently been cast as one of the two sub-Saharan African countries that were never colonised (the other was Ethiopia). This has led to treating the state as 'neo-colonial' (see for example Hlophe 1979).

Such a model makes the United States the coloniser, but its early role was limited. A class-based model also underplays conflicts between incomer groups and the contestation for elite status within the group of 'Americo-Liberians', who became dominant. I shall argue that their actions were characteristic of what is assumed to be (white) metropolitan-origin colonisation. Americo-Liberians also imitated the legal, military and administrative structures of neighbouring African colonies, whose rulers made economic demands on Liberia and had economic desires for it, that only from the 1920s were entertained by the United States, whose 1930s Loan Agreement forced considerable Firestone Rubber plantations into Liberia. Neo-colonialism became more apparent after the Second World War, with major investments in 'Cold War' communications infrastructures and considerable US interests in iron ore.

Who were the settlers?

These accounts of Kenya and Liberia, drastically truncated as they are, point to complex and changing involvements between incomer groups and their senders. The British in Kenya and black Americans in Liberia also found themselves involved with many other incomer groups. I discuss these competitors equally briefly, contrasting the contexts in which communities and would-be ruling elites struggled to establish and maintain themselves. The terms 'settler' and 'colonist ' have been frequently used for self and other refer- ence in both countries. As will be seen, they also point to complex settings and can mask realities.

Africans

The African communities inhabiting present-day Kenya and Liberia were themselves uncentralised and mobile incomers (compare Kopytoff's 1987 model of an expanding frontier of differentiating groups). White Kenyans and Americo-Liberians allied with locals (see for example Low and Smith (1976) and Berman and Lonsdale (1992) for Kenya), as they struggled first for local autonomy and later for territorial rule. The superficial accessibility of land brought Europeans and Africans into increasingly unequal conflict. More sophisticated whites could assert their quest for *lebensraum*, which was achieved by the fittest incomers – themselves. Most incomer groups in Kenya attempted to exclude 'natives' from authority and power, but Americo- Liberians also used strategies of selective incorporation. Both means helped to consolidate social identities, as I shall note.

Arabs and Swahili in East Africa

Arabs had long negotiated settlements with locals on the East African shore- line, operating a historic trading diaspora from Oman. Their descendants included *Swahili* (which like the cognate *Sahel* refers to margins), who with indigenous Africans had settled in complexly differentiated and stratified communities for which Arabs formed 'the fundamental reference category, reinforced by wealth and military power' (Constantin 1989: 148), an elite which became mainly cultural. The Americo–Liberian colonists settled in this way too, though intended to be agricultural 'pioneers' (Tonkin 1981).

To British incomers, Arabs were initially significant competitors and enemies, conceptualised as far-reaching, even through today's Sudan. But they had no one unified, powerful metropole to support them, and they declined. The 1964 Zanzibar revolution showed Africans could still regard them as alien incomers, though many had assimilated, as Swahili, such that no scholars can comfortably delineate two separate categories.[3] Marriage, concubinage, incorporation of clients as well as of slaves all meant that it is now referentiality by selves and others that is their focal characteristic.

Indians and Lebanese

Contacts between Africa and the subcontinent were very old and diverse with Indian long-distance traders preceding British incursions; later, too, Indians financed Zanzibari Arabs (Churchill 1908: 49). They soon moved into Kenya as civil servants and personal servants to the British, and into many forms of commerce (Mangat 1969, summarised in Mangat 1976). Since this community ('Asian' after Partition) was always at least three or four times as large as the European one, and 'it is difficult to think of any significant sector ... where Asian capital, entrepreneurial ability and skills have not made an appreciable contribution' (Ghai 1965: 103), it is surprising how little it is discussed in recent scholarship. By 1963, Kenya Asians numbered c.180,000 with 85 per cent living in the five largest towns (Ghai 1965: 92). They included members of most professions, civil servants of many grades, policemen, a wide range of skilled craftsmen and mechanics, wealthy industrialists and merchants of all levels including small rural shopkeepers.

Colonial studies discourse focuses on conflicts between white settlers and native Africans in Kenya, using a political economy model of the colonial state. In fact, Europeans long felt threatened by Indians, not Africans, and fought successfully to exclude them from land and political power. That success is one reason for the scholarly inattention. However, a 'settler' elite was largely secured by this struggle, in a racist campaign, 'the Indian Question,' from 1902, peaking in 1923.

Asians were a focus of European insecurity expressed as pollution, whether from plague, unsanitary behaviour that required their segregation, or hints of bestial (especially homosexual) practices.[4] Politicians – conflating the social and moral – claimed that boundary-breaking would harm child-like Africans, not themselves. African interests would be furthered by limiting Indian advancement (partly true). Missionaries concurred: Hindus, Muslims and Sikhs were unsavoury role models. By the end of the colonial period, despite their continued struggles politically, Asians remained the middle tier of a white-controlled hierarchy in which they were segregated from Europeans and Africans. Whites monopolised many social occasions, forms of transport, land and housing locations and there were tripartite health and education services.

In the many self-differentiated Indian groups[5] caste hierarchy survived and Muslim Ismailis became influential but no single elite developed; and one cannot reduce Asians to 'the merchant class'. Although Europeans always represented Asians as money-makers and clerks, they really had a much more complex relationship with them. From an early dependence on their capital and mercenary soldiers, whites came to rely on Asian bureaucrats and police officers. Asians in turn could rationalise their social and political limitations *vis-à-vis* Europeans as superiority over Africans, until it became clear Africans were going to get power. European presentations of Asians also occluded the common wish of the administrative and settler elites to exclude lower class white immigrants (who in Rhodesia did 'Asian' work).

Liberia never developed such a substantial median community.[6] Lebanese replaced the white traders who opened up coastal commodity and retail business before the First World War. Both groups often had relationships and children with African women, but were dispersed and not numerous. As with other middlemen, however, including Kenyan Asians, they could become the focus of resentment at point of sale or debt, deflecting recognition of exploitation away from higher scale political and economic actors. The real medians in Liberia were 'Civilised natives', who had access to some posts and superior opportunities within the state, distinguished from 'Tribal' natives culturally, sometimes legally too, in a changing category (Tonkin 1981; Brown 1982) which created exclusionary but permeable frontiers (see below).

Military co-optation

To sketch the fluctuating mosaics of incomers in Kenya and Liberia shows they were interdependent in both, but variably and unequally so over time. In both countries security needs led to alliances and co-optation. In Kenya, 'military service and civil administration were synonymous during the early years' (Moyes-Bartlett 1956: xvi). British officers were always supported by native troops,[7] initially Indians from 'martial' communities, but also by local 'friendlies' fighting against rival neighbours, and rewarded with loot. The Foreign Office deprecated this practice, preferring corps 'turned' from fighting the British, like Sudanese and Somalis (some settled in Kenya; see Moyse-Bartlett (1956: 84); Parsons (1997)), and in 1905 the King's African Rifles were set up. So, throughout a thoroughly brutal 'pacification' (detailed in Berman and Lonsdale 1992), locals in Kenya as well as many other incomers fought for the British.

Americo-Liberians soon fought too. From the 1870s, throughout the First World War and the 1930s depression (see for example Martin 1968; Sullivan 1985; Tonkin 1978–9) they were opposed by locals, who also fought against exploitative administrators (see for example Hlophe 1979). A Liberian Frontier Force was set up as part of the 1912 Loan Agreements, in which USA, France, Britain and Germany financed the bankrupt state. In 1915, Liberia received US military help, including black American officers. But indigenous people soon became incorporated into the army. In the 1930s

Sasstown war against the government, Kru fought neighbouring LFF Kru and were beaten by a Vai commander. Historically, Americo-Liberians sought to dominate the security forces, but by the 1970s, few were in the army and police (Hlophe 1979: 271). Non-commissioned indigenes fronted the 1980 coup that toppled Americo-Liberian dominance.

The Europeans

In an often cited passage, Winston Churchill wrote amazedly after a seven weeks' visit to Kenya in 1907 (1908: 20–21) about the conflicting views and interests of the volatile, tiny group of Europeans. Insightfully noting the complexity of relationships between them, and of 'the white man *versus* the black, the Indian *versus* both', he also realised that the 'settlers' – 'up-country' farmers – were only one component of the 'Unofficials', but did not mention the missionaries, or the tradesmen and professionals ('commercials') whom perhaps he did not meet.

Officials and missionaries: contradictions of 'trusteeship'

If European domination was achieved militarily, after the initial years of infor-mality noted by Moyse-Bartlett it was administered within the British Colonial Service by 'Officials'. Members of specialist and technical services like doctors and nurses, teachers, agriculturalists and vets, and members of the Public Works Department (PWD) formed over 80 per cent of the provincial administration by the 1930s (Berman 1990: 85); local government included Nairobi City Council employees. Up to independence, whites usually headed all these sectors. Below them was a largely Asian world of clerks, with Africans in the lowest jobs; in education, European men and women headed and largely staffed the government Asian and African secondary schools.

Though the class social solidarity of Europeans is much stressed by commentators noting that the (top) administrators' public school background matched that of many farmers, yet, as the range of government services expanded so did its members' social and educational background and their social norms. For Britons, *class*, would be, even if unspoken, a pervasive, complex divisor: hands-on, technological work, as in the PWD, had no social cachet. Social deference was thus mixed (compare for example Cooper and Stoler 1997; Stoler 1989).

Senior colonial officials formed an administrative elite since they were backed and financed by the British government and its military forces. 'Trusteeship' of the natives was Officials' policy, but unofficial representatives on the Legislative Council (with a European franchise from 1920) could press for liberals to be sacked. In 1923, when the Colonial Office was promulgating some rights for Asians, opposed farmer settlers planned a loyalist mutiny, and to kidnap the governor. But hopes that army officers would support them against the government, as in the 'Curragh mutiny' before Irish independence, were it seems fanciful, and the conspirators were limited to noisy demonstrations.

Senior Officials and missionaries felt responsible for raising African status, unlike influential 'Unofficials'.[8] Missions normally became established under government protection and control though some had preceded both trade and the flag. Some missionaries shared the public school, ancient university background of senior officials, others were lower class by upbringing and nonconformists or fundamentalists by conviction. Many evangelicals were American. Whereas leaders of the Church Missionary Society and Church of Scotland Mission are frequent voices in colonial records, Catholics seem absent. In earlier years, few were from Anglophone countries.

Like officials, missionaries ultimately identified with other Europeans, though they sometimes opposed them. Service to Africans was their *raison d'être*, but they also found 'mission boys' stroppy ('cheeky') and preferred unspoiled natives, though missions were providing Western education needed by all incomer sectors. After independence, they were criticised as paternalists (see for example Oliver 1952; Welbourn 1976; Kipkorir 1980). It was equally a contradiction – for them – that they educated Africans into nationalism, through schooling and the Gospel message. They built up African churches, but there is silence in the literature about Protestant clerics' acceptance of racial segregation: I recall services at the Anglican Cathedral and Presbyterian Kirk as all-white.

Such ideological contradictions, and charges that missionaries were mealy-mouthed against injustice, are as notable in Liberia (see for example Wold 1968; Tonkin 1981). More attention in the nineteenth century was paid to Americo-Liberians than to natives. Some of the first southern American missionaries brought their slaves (Martin, cited in Tonkin 1981: 314). But church leadership became a route to political success for all, the president's denomination ranking highest. This politicisation of Christianity co-occurred with the commercialisation of administration (see below).

The Unofficials

Although the stereotype whites in Kenya were farmers, these were always a minority overall within white settlement. Nevertheless, such Europeans styled themselves, very early, as, collectively, agricultural pioneers committed to settling, to contrast them (inaccurately) with Indians 'unsuited' therefore to buy land. By 1931, the Kenya Census enumerated 28 per cent Europeans in agriculture, 24 per cent in commerce and 20 per cent in government (Kennedy 1987: 198, Table 6). 'Commerce' then excluded 'professions' and 'industry': in 1962, there were over 90 classes of industry (including agriculture and government service), with more 'directors and managers' than 'farmers'.

Europeans often aimed to get rich quick and get out, and landowners were not actually committed settlers in distinction to home-based civil servants.

These often bought farms (or later, retirement homes); land ownership by Officials was permitted after 1919 precisely to encourage blending. Office workers and shopkeepers likewise might stay for life, while few farmers kept their land beyond one generation. Land sales were frequent; many went bankrupt. Asians became predominantly urban but by the 1950s most Europeans were too. The majority lived within greater Nairobi, 82 per cent of them in its most prosperous quarter (Morgan and Shaffer 1966: 15; Morgan 1967: 106). For us (since I was one) this meant a comfortable suburban life with cheap domestic labour and disposable income for safari and coast tourism. Most Europeans had never been on a farm.

Creating an elite

Power, capital and representation in Kenya

> No one had shrewder capitalist instincts than that atavistic circle which included Cranworth, Delamere, the Cole brothers, Finch-Hatton, and Grogan. The sheer scope of their property holdings and financial dealings made them a dominant economic force in the colony. The gentlemanly contingent as a whole were refugees not from capitalism but from indus-trialism and its corollaries. Property and profit were among the central preoccupations of the society they made in Kenya.
>
> (Kennedy 1987: 47)

Lord Delamere led the Europeans till his death in 1931. These largest land-holders operated along with syndicates of fellow aristocrats and South African financiers (Kennedy 1987: 23, 30). *Land* (see below) and Europeans as aristo-cratic farmer pioneers still image Kenya and are popularised through film and television. It was a misleading picture even of the small group who became an 'Unofficial' elite and claimed to represent all whites. Most farmers struggled because they lacked capital. The earliest white incomers included very poor Boers (Kennedy 1987). Capital gains came from land speculation (see for example Sorrenson (1968) and the sardonic McGregor Ross (1927), Director of Public Works until pushed to retire).

'Elites are those who get the most of what there is to get in any institu-tionalised sector of society ... usefully studied by asking what communities they represent or dominate' (Marvick 1996: 27–8, following Lasswell). This perspective illuminates both Kenyan and Liberian politics. Delamere invested heavily in the Kenyan agricultural industry, was a 'foxy' and relentless political operator, wooed classy visitors from Churchill to the Prince of Wales and British ministers, and regularly led deputations to England where he culti-vated influentials, though on his last visit he found them unsympathetic (Huxley 1935).

Delamere and his circle built a non-Official elite through political effectiveness (see for example Dilley 1966[1937]). They also used social access to win over, bully or subvert top Officials, but failed ultimately to oust them. Their policies were supported by earlier governors anxious that agriculture support colony finance and sharing the dream of a 'white man's country' (Mungeam 1966), which was a powerful part of Delamere's political populism. Delamere also spoke for 'Commercials' who opposed Indian advancement. Wider ideologies of group reproduction and land issues supported this elite and so outlived Delamere, but the *senders'* support declined, the representatives of large scale overseas capital became too important to ignore (see Berman 1990); white farmer-settlers became commercially and politically marginalised. The 'Mau Mau' revolt brought African independence, not a settler-run state.

Land: practice, ideology

Cultural representations are ideological weapons (Cooper 1997: 409) and the elite image of *land* proved inclusionary for upper-class senders and Kenyan whites. Land contestation remained the theme of all political action. No one should diminish the resultant injustices to Africans (see for example Sorrensen 1968). But European advocates and opponents of settlement shared assumptions about land[9] which often ignored African constructions and used imagery that separated land from labour, for which European demand was chronic. Europeans saw land as a finite, territorial good. Lonsdale (1992) has argued that for Kikuyu, 'the land is the people' (see above).

The land was also imaged as wild *landscape*, lyrically described and photographed (as in Huxley's life of Delamere). Widespread emotional attachment to it justified settler dominance and linked urbanites to farmers, though these were often tenants of financiers and bankers. Hauntingly lovely to me too, it included Africans only as exotic props. Now, Kenya is tourist-packaged as landscape peopled with 'wild' life.

Group reproduction

The elite's racist ideology was also supported through processes of group reproduction, such as *education* and the control of *sexuality*. Education was segregated racially (as African, Arab, Asian, and European) till the 1960s. There were some private preparatory schools, the wealthiest (including Asians) could send their children Home, and a convent supported female gentility. With these significant exceptions, whites received a common education.[10] This came via boarding schools which developed grammar rather than public school values when many teachers were beneficiaries of the British 1944 Education Act; pupils were from all walks of life.

Controls on sexuality and marriage likewise intensified racial, not specifically elite solidarity, though there were aristocratic family linkages. A considerable comparative literature on sexuality for coloniser and colonised shows how public relationships between them became limited or suppressed, with Freudian – and Douglasian – stress on boundary-keeping. Stoler (1989, 1997) and others have shown how colonial *mestizo* communities formed a social *limen* between white dominants and natives, often challenging European boundary-making. In Kenya, the (endogamous) Asian threat obviated any 'Eurasian threat'. But initially, sexual relations with female locals were common in all incomer groups, unregulated and generally known about. Thereafter – for officials from 1909[11] – they became generally deprecated but not at all eradicated (White 1990). In public, racial segregation was socially patrolled.

Elite status in Liberia: incorporation and exclusion

Finally, I compare and contrast the construction of eliteness in Liberia, where, as in Kenya, the proportion of dominant incomers was tiny – 0.6 per cent in the 1960s (Clapham 1976: 130–1). Many were slaves only emancipated on condition they went to Liberia. For the first fifty years, 'mulattos' dominated, some having capital from their white fathers and more education. The True Whig Party, which then ruled till 1980, succeeded against them by incorporating some 'recaptives' – enslaved Africans captured by the US Navy before arrival in the Americas. Unlike Kenya, selective incorporation became a strategy of group reproduction. Americo-Liberian settlers created a new form of family (see for example Hlophe 1979). Officially structured by Christian monogamy, this included the children of indigenous women ('outside wives') and wards who became dependants and supporters.

The near identification of public office with economic opportunity in a patron–client mode of government has been identified as a means of continued Americo-Liberian dominance (see for example Liebenow 1969; Clapham 1976). Political, administrative and commercial functions were fused as scarce resources in a poor and undeveloped country. Gradual inclusion of 'natives' in a legislature formally copied from the USA gave them little power since it was (and is) dominated by the President. An exclusionary elite was competitively reproduced in this personalised climate. Settlement origin helped, since settlements had unequal access to the capital, as did financial resources and social connections with power brokers which enabled networking and clientage. In the end, however, birth connections remained the best guarantee of loyalty for those at the top – who were killed in the 1980 coup partly because of this exclusiveness.

Cultural representations self-identified colonists, who claimed Christianity, English and 'civilised' customs including Western clothes and houses modelled on those of southern American plantations (see Figure 8.1); their social cohesion was also promoted through church membership and Freemasonry. However, these attributes could all be taken on by natives, who thereby became 'Civilised'. Thus the strategy of selective incorporation contained the seeds of its own dissolution, but its social and economic exclusiveness bred hostility just as the discriminatory segregation of Kenya had done.

Conclusions

Once the options for, and practices of, incomers are recognised as widespread and commonplace, real specificities in so-called settler societies can be more easily identified, as I have sketched for Kenyan whites and Americo-Liberians. Ongoing support by senders is most important, and self-identification with senders strengthened 'the consciousness of kind' (see Chapter 1) and thus the cohesiveness of the wider European community in Kenya, and also of the Americo-Liberians, who took pride in American values and imagined institutions even though these had often in reality excluded blacks. Similarly, pride in Britishness included colonial governance, even while this was being opposed by the elite who were claiming to represent all Unofficials. They not only relied on the senders' finance and military power to control the indigenes but also attempted to manipulate successive British establishments in their own favour. This was impossible for Americo-Liberians.

The 'three Cs' quoted by Shore in Chapter 1 operated in the elite contests of both countries. Wider European cohesion in Kenya was promoted by Delamere's elite with their conspiracy theories about Indians and, later, Africans, while the often small, bickering and isolated Americo-Liberian settlements were brought together by their fear of indigenous uprisings. Their cultural consciousness included much disparagement of 'country' or Tribal

Figure 8.1 Settler house in 1970s Liberia

ways, even though they might in fact share these (Tonkin 2000). Elite contests were also marked by internal conspiracies.

Recent work on European colonisation has been powerful and based both on anthropological and historical understanding (see Pels 1997), but has not explored the use of cultural politics in achieving elite status within competing incomer groups. These processes are common to Kenya, where I have focused on one 'aristocratic' settler elite, and Liberia where I generalise processes of elite formation and maintenance. My minimal sketch of Arab/Swahili history suggests that as one incomer group becomes politically successful over all, and the rest simply struggle against further discrimination, elite competition becomes more limited for the rest, who then aim for niche success or becoming a cultural reference point. But that does not mean their struggles should be ignored: analysing the maintenance of elite cultures and power in Kenya and Liberia shows the importance of seeing how *all* the component communities of a state are held together and apart.

Acknowledgments

I thank anthropology seminar participants at Queen's University and LSB College Dublin for comments, and Dr. W.T.W. Morgan for documentary help.

Notes

1   Booth (1984: 61), citing the Jamaican poet Louise Bennett.
2   The literature on Kenya is extensive, slimmer on Liberia. I therefore usually cite a single in-depth source with wide references.
3   For the 1962 census, 'the decision … hinged principally on whether they or their family head were paying African Poll Tax or Arab Personal and Hospital tax' (Census 1962: 57).
4   Thus the East African Women's League petitioned Field Marshal Smuts's wife: 'We, the women of Kenya, humbly implore your assistance to protect us and our children from the terrible Asiatic menace that threatens to overwhelm us' (Ross 1968[1927]: 348).
5   According to Bharati, 'there is virtually nothing of sociological significance about the minority which would hold for all its constituent groups' (1965: 15). I am ignorant about Asian elite contestations.
6   Of African Liberian incomers, those more comparable with Arabs and Swahili include 'Fanti', Ghanaian-origin fishermen, and 'Mandingoes', a term conflating very different groups including Muslims, long-distance *transporteurs* from Mali, and local Mande-origin communities: this inclusive categorisation can be and is used to exclude any component sub-group as alien.
7   Apart from some NCOs, white other ranks hardly fought in Kenya before the Mau Mau insurgency. Many British troops were stationed there for Far Eastern postings in the Second World War (see White 1990) and post-Suez (Berman 1990: 350–2). The 1962 census reports them as 25.3 per cent of adult European males.
8   The aggressiveness of Major Grogan, 'a good sound system of compulsory labour would do more to raise the nigger in five years than all the millions that have been sunk in missionary labour for the last fifty' (in Ross 1968[1927]: 88), is a

consistent hallmark of European public discourse, let alone what was said informally; these tones tend to get flattened in scholarly summary.

9 'The Irish question' was seen by many as a question of land and a Colonial
   Secretary, Lord Lansdowne, led Southern Unionists as a Kerry landowner
   (Mansergh 1991: 48–9). Quite a few settlers came from Ireland, including
   members of great landlord families like Delamere's first wife and her Cole
   brothers; later incomers saw Kenya as an escape from the Civil War and the Free
   State which would give them land again (Duder 1993).

10 The Boers did not achieve secondary schools of their own till the very end of the
   colonial period. They were among the farmers with illiterate children before the
   government education service became established (Mungeam 1978; Kennedy
   1987: 169).

11 The Crewe Circulars, which 'prohibited liaisons with indigenous women in
   various parts of the empire,' were provoked by complaints against a District
   Officer in Kenya (Strobel 1991: 4).

Bibliography

Ascherson, N. (1996) *Black Sea: The Birthplace of Civilization and Barbarism*, London:
   Vintage.
Barth, F. (ed.) (1969) *Ethnic Groups and Boundaries*, Bergen-Oslo: Universitets Forlaget.
Berman, B. (1990) *Control and Crisis in Colonial Kenya: The Dialectics of Domination*,
   London: James Currey.
Berman, B. and Lonsdale, J. (1992) *Unhappy Valley: Conflict in Kenya and Africa*, London:
   James Currey.
Bharati, A. (1965) 'A Social Survey', in D.P. Ghai (ed.), *Portrait of a Minority*, Nairobi:
   Oxford University Press, 13–63.
Booth, T. (1984) 'We True Christians', Ph.D. thesis, University of Birmingham.
Brown, D. (1982) 'On the Category called "Civilized" in Liberia and Elsewhere',
   Journal of Modern African Studies 20 (2): 287–303.
Census 1962 (1966) *Kenya Population Census 1962, Vol IV: Non-African population*,
   Nairobi: Ministry of Economic Planning and Development.
Churchill, W. (1908) *My African Journey*, London: Hodder and Stoughton.
Clapham, C. (1976) *Liberia and Sierra Leone: An Essay in Comparative Politics*,
   Cambridge: Cambridge University Press.
Clayton, P. (1996) *Enemies and Passing Friends: Settler Ideologies in Twentieth Century
   Ulster*, London and East Haven: Pluto Press.
Constantin, F. (1989) 'Social Stratification on the Swahili Coast: From Race to Class?',
   Africa 59 (2): 145–60, special issue, 'Social Stratification in Swahili Society'.
Cooper, F. (1997) 'The Dialectics of Decolonization', in F. Cooper and L.A. Stoler
   (eds), *Tensions of Empire: Colonial Cultures in a Bourgeois World*, Berkeley, CA:
   University of California Press, 406–35.
Cooper, F. and Stoler, L.A. (eds) (1997) *Tensions of Empire: Colonial Cultures in a Bour-
   geois World*, Berkeley, CA: University of California Press.
Dilley, M. (1966[1937]) *British Policy in Kenya Colony*, London: Frank Cass.
Duder, C. (1993) '"Men of the Officer Class": The Participants in the 1919 Soldier
   Settlement Scheme in Kenya', *African Affairs* 92: 69–87.
Galbraith, J. (1972) *Mackinnon and East Africa 1870–1895: A Study in the New 'Imperi-
   alism'*, Cambridge: Cambridge University Press.

Ghai, D.P. (1965) 'An Economic Survey', in D.P. Ghai (ed.), *Portrait of a Minority*, Nairobi: Oxford University Press, 91–111.

Hlophe, S. (1979) *Class, Ethnicity and Politics in Liberia 1944–1975*, Washington, DC: Washington University Press.

Huxley, E. (1935) *White Man's Country: Lord Delamere and the Making of Kenya* (2 vols), London: Chatto and Windus.

Kennedy, D. (1987) *Islands of White: Settler Society and Culture in Kenya and Southern Rhodesia 1890–1939*, Durham, NC: Duke University Press,

Kipkorir, B. (ed.) (1980) *Biographical Essays on Imperialism and Collaborators in Colonial Kenya*, Nairobi: Kenya Literature Bureau.

Kopytoff, I. (1987) 'Introduction', in I. Kopytoff (ed.), *The African Frontier*, Bloomington and Indianapolis: Indiana University Press, 1–84.

Liebenow, G. (1969) *Liberia: The Evolution of Privilege*, Ithaca, NY and London: Cornell University Press.

Lonsdale, J. (1992) 'The Moral Economy of Mau Mau: Wealth, Poverty and Civic Virtue in Kikuyu Political Thought', in B. Berman and J. Lonsdale (eds), *Unhappy Valley: Conflict in Kenya and Africa*, London: James Currey, 315–504.

Low, A. and Smith, A. (eds) (1976) *History of East Africa*, vol. III, Oxford: Clarendon Press.

Mangat, J. (1969) *A History of the Asians in East Africa 1886–1945*, Oxford: Clarendon Press.

—— (1976) 'The Immigrant Communities (3) The Asians', in A. Low and A. Smith (eds), *History of East Africa*, vol. III, Oxford: Clarendon Press.

Mansergh, N. (1991) *The Unresolved Question: The Anglo-Irish Settlement and its Undoing 1912–72*, New Haven and London: Yale University Press.

Martin, J. (1968) 'The Dual Legacy: Government Authority and Mission Influence among the Glebo of Eastern Liberia, 1834–1910', Ph.D. thesis, Boston University.

Marvick, D. (1996) 'Elites', in A. Kuper and J. Kuper (eds), *The Social Science Encyclopaedia*, 2nd edn, London: Routledge.

Morgan, W. (ed.) (1967) *Nairobi: City and Region*, Nairobi: Oxford University Press.

Morgan, W. and Shaffer, M. (1966) *Population of Kenya: Density and Distribution*, Nairobi: Oxford University Press.

Moyes-Bartlett, H. (1956) *The King's African Rifles: A Study in the Military History of East and Central Africa*, Aldershot: Gale and Pollock.

Mungeam, G. (1966) *British Rule in Kenya 1895–1912*, Oxford: Clarendon Press.

—— (ed.) (1978) *Kenya: Selected Historical Documents*, Nairobi: East African Publishing House.

Oliver, R. (1952) *The Missionary Factor in East Africa*, London: Longmans Green.

Parsons, T. (1997) '"Kibra is our blood": the Sudanese Military Legacy in Nairobi's Kibera Location 1902–1968', *International Journal of African Historical Studies* 30 (1): 87–122.

Pels, P. (1997) 'The Anthropology of Colonialism: Culture, History, and the Emergence of Western Governmentality', *Annual Review of Anthropology* 26: 163–83.

Phillips, A. (1989) *The Enigma of Colonialism: British Policy in West Africa*, London and Bloomington: James Currey and Indiana University Press.

Ross, J. McGregor (1968[1927]) *Kenya from Within: A Short Political History*, London: Frank Cass.

Sorrenson, M. (1968) *Origins of European Settlement in Kenya*, London: Oxford University Press.

Stasiulis, D. and Yuval-Davis, N. (eds) (1995) *Unsettling Settler Societies*, London: Sage.

Stoler, A. (1989) 'Rethinking Colonial Categories: European Communities and the Boundaries of Rule', *Comparative Studies in Society and History* 31(1): 134–61.

—— (1997) 'Sexual Affronts and Racial Frontiers', in F. Cooper and L.A. Stoler (eds), *Tensions of Empire*, Berkeley, CA: University of California Press, 198–237.

Strobel, M. (1991) *European Women and the Second British Empire*, Bloomington, IN: Indiana University Press.

Sullivan, J. (1985) 'Fishers, Traders, and Rebels: The Role of the Kabor/Gbeta in the 1915 Kru Coast (Liberia) Revolt', in J.C. Stone (ed.), *Africa and the Sea*, Aberdeen: African Studies Group, 48–63.

Tonkin, E. (1978–9) 'Sasstown's Transformation: The Jlao Kru *c.*1888–1918', *Liberian Studies Journal* 8 (1): 1–34.

—— (1981) 'Model and Ideology: Dimensions of Being Civilized in Liberia', in L. Holy and M. Stuchlik (eds), *The Structure of Folk Models*, ASA Monograph 20, London: Academic Press, 307–30.

—— (2000) 'Autonomous Judges: African Ordeals as Dramas of Power', *Ethnos* 65 (3): 366–86.

Welbourn, F. (1976) 'The Impact of Christianity on East Africa', in A. Low and A. Smith (eds), *History of East Africa*, vol. III, Oxford: Clarendon Press, 383–422.

White, L. (1990) *The Comforts of Home: Prostitution in Colonial Nairobi*, Chicago and London: Chicago University Press.

Wold, J. (1968) *God's Impatience in Liberia*, Grand Rapids, MI: W.B. Eerdmans.

Chapter 9

Cultural heritage and the role of traditional intellectuals in Mali and Cameroon

Michael Rowlands

Introduction

My aim is to compare two attempts in West Africa to create a common discourse allowing diverse 'citizens' to imagine themselves, in Anderson's words, as a national community (Anderson 1983). Redolent of European nineteenth-century cultural histories, the re-establishment of the tyranny of tradition in the late twentieth century continues to stress continuity and sameness as the ideals for nation building and long term security (see Stolcke 1995:4). Underpinning ethnic cleansing and other barbarities, a 'politics of belonging' requires simple and expedient means of defining inclusion and exclusion in terms of rights to reside, to own property or simply the right to live which as often as not is defined by claims to have a unique history. Equally reminiscent of nineteenth-century European cultural histories, the task of creating a unique history in the late twentieth century has been the work of academics, intellectuals and others whose job it is to excavate the subterranean layers of the collective consciousness.

This Gramscian theme resurrects the distinction between organic and traditional intellectuals as a useful starting point for discussion (Gramsci 1971: 5). If the organic intellectual was self consciously aware of the vanguard position he/she should play in mobilising political action, Gramsci saw the traditional intellectual as the producer of forms of knowledge that pre-existed such self-conscious states. Defined by an earlier historical moment, they continue to exist through periods of fundamental change in the organisation of society. He argued that new groups moving towards dominance usually try to make use of traditional intellectuals to further mass acceptance of their hegemony. In Europe these intellectuals were the teachers, priests and folklorists who garnered local knowledges threatened with extinction, formed local history and antiquities societies and defended the redoubt of local knowledge against the rationalism of practical consciousness. This 'heap of passive sedimentations' in Gramsci's vision accounted for the persistence of groups and continuities in traditionalising discourses. The linkage he made between intellectual discourse, production and power without mechanically reducing one to the other has been widely influential. Developed most notably in anthropology by Feierman in his book *Peasant Intellectuals*, he describes how in Tanzania the discourses of traditional chiefs, healers and diviners over cleansing and harming the land were drawn into the service of colonial authorities and modern politicians through the intermediary of an educated elite (Feierman 1990).

It is these ideas that I wish to bring into the discussion of how elites manage and manipulate traditional discourses in the service of their interests. I compare two cases in West Africa (Cameroon and Mali) that share a Francophone colonial past, and yet demonstrate markedly diverging postcolonial state trajectories. My argument is that in one case, Mali, the state elite does manage to produce a sufficiently compelling image of the nation state by harnessing the past and present as unity. Ideas of the heritage of Mali conjure up in the national imagination that sense of simultaneity close to what Benjamin called messianic time; that something which has always been and will be again in the future but *meanwhile* can be grasped in an instantaneous present (Benjamin 1973: 265). In the other case, Cameroon, the state is a source of neither meaning nor security. Powerful ties and loyalties bind urban based elites to their villages and regions of origin as a primary source of cultural meaning. In Cameroon, the state fails to provide a discourse in which all 'citizens' can imagine themselves as a national community. Quite the reverse to the situation in Mali, the state is the actual source of devolutionary tensions between ethnic regional blocks, which since the 1990s has reached new heights with political liberalisation. The question I raise in this paper therefore is descriptive: how have the educated elite in these two settings harnessed their ' traditional intellectuals' to serve such divergent trends?

Conceptualising the local

In many parts of Africa in the 1990s, authoritarian regimes have proved adept at managing demands for political reform by seeking new ways of establishing control over local populations. In an era of 'political liberalisation', regimes that were long used to exercising authoritarian power suddenly needed to find ways of mobilising mass support. The rhetoric of 'nation building' has taken on new forms of expression as the option of ethnic clientship politics backed by coercion has been modified in order to give more room for the development of a local politics that reaffirms allegiance to the 'village' or 'community'. When 'elections' can have real meanings, then the need to control votes has the paradoxical effect of encouraging a politics of autochthony or 'belonging' (see Geschiere and Gugler 1998).

Political liberalisation has also resulted in a striking intensification of debate over who has the right to belong. Who really belongs where, and how this is to be judged, has led to violent exclusions of people from areas and towns where they have lived for long periods – in some cases for generations. In many parts of West Africa, distinguishing people as native to an area and others as strangers is nothing new. The idea that places have stranger quarters or that there should be a special treatment of strangers (usually extremely generous and hospitable I might add) is part of the culture of West Africa and other parts of Africa. An ideology of who has the right to settlement or land has also been matched by ideologies of prestigious stranger origins confirming political claims to the right to rule. In Cameroon for example for many years there has been a debate over the so-called 'Tikar problem' (Chilver and Kaberry 1971). Various chiefdoms of the western Grassfields region trace their origins from a vaguely defined but extremely important ritual centre called Tikar from where they are said to have originated. Chiefs and notables recognise relations with each other in terms of shared origins and by rights to ritual objects and knowledge that were originally brought from Tikar. There are good reasons to believe that colonial concepts of land codified in 'customary' law led to this freezing of history and the creation of a mythical space in which claims to legitimacy could be made (Fisiy 1995). The result was to reduce a fluid and dynamic precolonial pattern of movement and exchange of people and things to a more fixed pattern of permanent ownership and induced stability of settlement. Post-independence political elites continued these fictions of private ownership in order to allocate resources for themselves and their clients. More recent neoliberal ideas have promoted individual ownership based on the standard argument that private property would encourage investment and commitment to development and the intensification of production. What this also appears to include, in the light of World Bank pursuit of administrative decentralisation policies, are moves to re-establish historical rights on land and other resources by privileging the idea of primary ownership. This idea has of course to be based on something and increasingly this seems to be the espousal of proving primary origins; the particular association of a people with a sense of place or a site that they claim to own.

As general theorists of globalisation have emphasised recently, an increased sense of belonging and locality is a general phenomenon accompanying flows of people, finance and media. Appadurai, writing on the production of locality, emphasises the affirmation of cultural difference and locality as a paradoxical consequence of a world in flow (Appadurai 1996). Closure is the local response by which means people regain a purchase on disquieting events. Hence a stress on autochthony and roots is now found everywhere and has become a major issue in the redefinition of national origins, ethnic regionalism or debates about the disjunction between the nation and the state (the point about the hyphen made by Appadurai). We have to assume that reconciling flow and closure also assumes local variants. Xenophobia in Eastern Europe is not necessarily the equivalent of ethnic politics in West Africa. In particular it assumes in a very generalised sense that closure should be formed around something, usually of an essentialising character, in order for exclusion of 'strangers' to be justified. My argument is that this sense of closure is

mediated through elites who adopt or can invent the role of organic intellectuals linking tradition to the state.

In contemporary Cameroon, it is not unusual to be asked where you come
from. For the expatriate it means that the non-Cameroon world is ranked in
terms of the importance of the resources and contacts he/she might provide.
Britain, although an anchoring point for Anglophone identity in Cameroon,
is an impoverished ally and low on the scale of priorities. The Netherlands has
a particular reputation for toughly negotiated 'help', whilst America is the
nirvana accessed through a lottery for green cards. Within Cameroon the
question is directed to establishing one's ethnic origin so one can judge where
the respondent's primary loyalty will lie. Ideas of relative closeness in kinship
terms are heavily mediated by ethnic/regional loyalties in the search for status
and security.

In Yaounde or Douala – the two principal cities of Cameroon – the local
indigents are defined as either Ewondo/Beti or Douala and in both cases
identity is increasingly defined as the fear of becoming a minority 'in one's
own city'. In the case of Douala, this fear of minority status goes back to the
1930s when Bamileke migrants from the Grassfields region (widely respected
and feared for their dynamic, entrepreneurial spirit) bought land from the
Douala to grow coffee and as migrants gained a solid economic foothold on
the coast. The Douala response was to invest heavily in urban land, to
modernise and build to meet the needs of a colonial and post-colonial administration. But in the 1990s the fear of being outvoted in new democratic
elections by the descendants of Bamileke migrants has led to violent clashes.
The need to gain control of 'ethnic homelands' has resulted in the formation
of a wide range of local and regional elite associations often with the support
of government. The 1972 constitution of Cameroon declares that the rights of
individuals are enshrined in the principle that every man has the right to
protect his regional and ethnic identity. In the new 1996 constitution this was
changed to protect the rights of autocthonous minorities by extending the
category of indigenous peoples, which in Cameroon had meant forest
pygmies or nomadic pastoralists, to include all citizens wishing to defend their
minority, ethnic status. To participate in municipal or parliamentary elections
meant that you now had to belong to a ward based on ethnic origin before
you were entitled to vote. Considerable advantages exist in building alliances
with other smaller groups to form 'indigenous' ethnic regional blocks that can
dominate local elections. In the case of Douala this has led to the formation
of SAWA, a regional movement of coastal peoples formed as an
autochthonous minority to combat the possible dominance in local elections
of Bamileke and other Grassfields migrants. The principal opposition party –
the SDF (Social Democratic Front), a largely Grassfield and in particular
Anglophone party – had won five of the mayor elections in Douala in 1996
which set off large-scale demonstrations in the city. The Grassfielders were
characterised as ungrateful migrants who had been given land and opportunities

to work by the 'native' Douala but were now intent on taking over and driving them out. The government intervened to show that they could protect minorities against 'stranger' migrant majorities. President Biya signed a decree appointing 'indigens' as government delegates in the metropolitan councils where the SDF opposition had won the municipal elections.

Indigenous politics in Cameroon in the 1990s became a pattern of shifting regional ethnic alliances within which people moved for influence and success. No matter what influence elites may have exercised in their home regions through access to the state, this was weakened unless they could convert patronage into local power and influence in their home areas. Those repositories of traditional knowledge in the village or chiefdom that elites had previously paid respect but considered to be of little political importance suddenly became the source of local influence for urban-based political elites. The chiefdoms of the Grassfields region are recreated in the urban settings of Yaounde or Douala as literally the village in the town (by comparison to Clyde-Mitchell's description of 1950s migration on the Copper belt (see Ferguson 1999)). Traditional institutions and associations have branches in town; the chief will have a town palace; people of the same village will live together in town, go to restaurants and bars run by people of their chiefdom and take jobs in ethnically run businesses. Members of successful elite groups in town will be given prestige titles in the village to mark the important contributions they have made to the community (Fisiy and Goheen 1998). And the widespread belief and resilience of beliefs in occult forces is generally interpreted as a resource of personal and collective power used to guard against various forms of marginalisation by elites (Geschiere 1997)

What accompanies these practices is a traditionalising discourse that emphasises how nobody can escape from their origins. A strong conception of 'returning to the village' evokes a physical, relational and metaphysical space. Everyone outside of it is a stranger immediately barred from certain kinds of knowledge and special skills. Who actually belongs is an emotionally loaded issue and is bound up with where you should be expected to be buried and where you should build a house. There are constant references to the fact that however far you feel you may have travelled and distanced yourself from your origins, in the end you will be buried on ancestral land. This defines you as indigenous and your living anywhere else for however long a period, and even over several generations, will define you as a stranger. This does not mean that this ideal of belonging could not, particularly in the past, have been manipulated to create new localities, for example by electing to be buried in town. But in the 1990s the right to be buried as a stranger has become more contested. Is it Bamileke land in town where your father is buried and would this be recognised as such back in the village? Cases of burials being dug up and the bodies transported back to the village for reburial are now becoming more frequently cited as the prerequisite for claiming local political support by a member of an elite association.

Architecture and a sense of place have taken on new roles as markers of ethnic affiliation. Indigenes are expected to build a house on village land to which eventually they will retire and under which they will be buried. Taking a pride in the heritage of chiefdom, a pride in one's origins, in communal beliefs and in material culture has become a feature of an ethnic identity. Heritage is understood as an 'old fashioned' museological view of culture, which you can have more or less of and from which you can be deprived, quite literally by your opponents destroying it or stealing it. Among the Bamileke in the last ten years, new palaces have been built with towering roofs and adorned facades, symbols of their defiance to the general hostility they feel is expressed against them. The powers that enable village elites to gain success in the outside world are constantly related to powers derived from membership of special associations in the chiefdom or from the powers inherited from dead ancestors. In the Grassfields, elites are considered to be the servants of the Fon; they are his 'new' sorcerers who now go out and gain 'modern' forms of wealth and power equal to the triumphs of hunting, warfare and trading that were characteristic of the past. Now they go out and conduct forays in foreign lands to capture wealth and resources for a Fon and his people (Fisiy and Goheen 1998). Men and women are given special honorific neo-traditional titles to illustrate their importance to the chiefdom. And these conferments were the subject of endless disputes by holders of 'authentic' titles who accused chiefs and elders of selling titles to elites to gain their patronage.

But in the 1990s, this traditionalising of elites was further refined to define a particular 'ethnic way of life'. The Grassfields region in Cameroon is characterised by powerful chiefdoms dating back many hundreds of years. Their relationship with colonial authority was marked by considerable ambivalence but the ritual/sacred powers of chiefs allowed considerable manoeuvring in the relationship between people and the administration. The replacement of colonial authority by a one-party state brought little change in this situation. But the advent of multiparty politics forced the chiefs to make more open political commitments to political parties. They became more caught up in the turbulence of elite politics and they were more prone to manipulation by their politicised elites. Fisiy and Goheen describe the super-inflation of traditional titles in Nso' at this time, creating new titles for families living in the urban village than those at home and consequently a rural/urban divide in traditional statuses and protocols (Fisiy and Goheen 1998: 390).

Following Wolf and others, it is relatively easy therefore to describe the position of urban elites in Cameroon as brokers or gateway keepers in the relation of tradition and the state. The pre-eminence of loyalty to home region creates numerous vertical and horizontal ties and in particular cultural associations that aim to ensure the maintenance of rural ties among members in town or abroad. Among the Grassfields chiefdoms this results in active appropriation of a hierarchical system of values and symbols, whereas elsewhere in Cameroon more straightforward displays of wealth and power in consumption define 'big men' as those who have a special, if predatory, relationship with the state. In either hierarchical or egalitarian modes, elites maintain predatory contact with the state to nurture and allocate the accumulation of wealth and titles at the local level.

During the political upheavals of the early 1990s with the pressures of political liberalisation, elite associations became more important as brokers between state power and local allegiance (Nyamnjoh and Rowlands 1998). Politicians, depending on the control of mass support for votes, returned to their regions of origin to ensure their popularity as representative elites. Multipartyism encouraged regionalism and commitment to place by establishing the need to define who 'belongs' in voting terms. Situations where 'stranger' populations dominated the voting patterns and brought in ethnic 'outsiders' to represent local populations created ethnic tensions and polarised expectations that elites should favour locals over strangers. Since it is the position of the president of the republic that holds the system together, it was formerly impossible for those in power to be disloyal to him. Cameroon is totalitarian in the sense that the 'state serves the people only to the extent necessary to ensure that people will serve it'. And this depends on the extent to which elites deserve and are served by a president. In this respect recent devolutionary trends have made the centralised state power, perhaps only temporarily, uncharacteristically dependent on local elites and their capacity to deliver voting support for incumbent power holders. Regional ethnic politics and the delivery of the 'block vote' reinforces the predatory relation to the state to which the latter can only respond with increased threats of violence to maintain control when the customary acts of patronage are no longer sufficient. The state as a reified space is described as a bazaar where, given access, elites can foray and capture wealth, a place to be captured and pillaged rather than imagined and adhered to. In these circumstances, external agencies take on increasingly neo-colonial forms as they defend themselves against the crudest forms of pillaging of their budgets by locating aid and development finance in 'offshore accounts' or by reifying the infrastructure of local development and keeping it firmly in the hands of expatriate control.

Traditionalising discourses in Cameroon also encourage the idea that the 'local' is not just one place but is dispersed in terms of urban and village networks. The 'village' can be as much in the capital, or a provincial town, as in the chiefdom proper. And it is this institutional pluralism, supported by neo-traditional discourses, that has been reinforced, in particular by a decade of political liberalisation. Dispersed elites, by exercising a stranglehold on access to resources (land, forests, mineral rights, water and so on), encourage strong centrifugal tendencies in Cameroon. Besides the figure of the president and personal commitment to the ruling party, there is little available to provide a unified vision of Cameroon to surpass an all-pervasive sense of the merits of ethnic diversity. In certain contexts this unleashes another paradox, the more the local identity becomes necessary for mobilising local support for political power, the more there has been a tendency to argue for the removal of local identities from national politics. In 1993 for example a group of Bamileke intellectuals published a report recommending the de-politicisation of traditional chiefship: 'the traditional chieftainship must turn its back on all enterprises of an electoral nature and respect the customs … chiefs are deeply involved in partisan politics. This attitude runs counter to what the chief's role should be: to defend all of the inhabitants or citizens of his polity, regardless of their political affiliation' (Malaquais 1997: 514). The writers of the report recommend that the palace of a traditional chief should be a place where people come to revive their cultural identity, which had been lost during the colonial era. Chiefs are urged to build cultural centres or local museums where they could meet their constituents, each centre would have a hall or auditorium where up to 600 people could meet; a library and video centre where the archival resources, oral traditions and material culture of the chiefdom could be kept and stored. Some of the major chiefdoms in the Grassfields such as Bandjoun or Bamoum have already established museums as monuments to the ruling dynasties. In fact, the politicisation of local origins has resulted in some cases in emptying out any explicit political content precisely in order to constitute the chiefdom as a site of pure cultural origins redeemed of any political associations. Building a house is meant to create a site for future burial, a place to return to in cases of misfortune when you need to consult elders and diviners. But paradoxically the form it takes is increasingly less than culturally pure. Dominic Malaquais, in describing contemporary Bamileke architecture, shows how the plan of one Bamileke architect responsible for building one of these cultural centres is distinctly hybrid. On the one hand he declares, 'We are in a society which suffers from a veritable cultural chaos – a true crisis of identity – the principal role of the chiefdom must be to resolve this problem.' On the other his recommendations on the architectural style chosen to help achieve this aim are distinctly un-Bamileke, being a combination of a Bamoum prototype palace (modelled on King Njoya's 1905 palace) with an entrance style borrowed from the entrance of the Sultan's palace at Rey Bouba from the far north of Cameroon and a roof copied from houses in the Bamenda region. A trans-ethnic architectural style is advocated which is an odd choice for a cultural centre that is meant to remind Bamileke youth of their cultural and ethnic origins. Warnier has also noted that the upper echelons of the Cameroon elite are increasingly becoming trans-cultural/ethnic, so that among the rich and powerful, pure ethnicity is fast making way for a 'metissage' of cultures and identities (Warnier 1993).

Elite associations are heavily involved in encouraging a politics of localised but hybrid autochthony in Cameroon, and the state finds many advantages in promoting this to intervene in local politics. Cameroon is described in official discourse as a country of great linguistic and cultural diversity, which has managed to avoid the ethnic violence of some of its neighbours in Central Africa. The notion of *convivialité culturelle* is used to describe Cameroon as a land united by diversity, constantly needing to balance the tensions of a triple colonial heritage and other multiple identities that have made it 'Africa in miniature'. It alludes to the idea that by transcending local differences, a spirit of mixture and conviviality identifies Cameroonian and national success as a commonality. It also has the paradoxical effect of re-traditionalising the chiefship by demanding that fons/chiefs and important notables should shrive themselves of a secularised pursuit of political and business ambitions and instead return to a true vocation of being an authentic arbiter of tradition. But such localisation by elites and politicians underestimates the power this gives chiefs and elders to re-assert their authority and shrive themselves of the ambivalence inherited since colonial times. If the chiefs/fons want museums and cultural centres to define their re-traditionalised status, then elites appear to have more nationalising ambitions, to create a more technocratic and eventually less ethnicised basis for their politics. Whilst both tendencies lead to the devolution of 'tradition', the first asserts it as a pure and homogenous cultural state into which their elites have to be induced whilst the second, by attempting to usurp tradition as a hyperreal and mobilising identity, hybridises its cultural form, thus making it at the same time everywhere and nowhere.

Le 'top-down'

The situation of Cameroon is not unique either in Africa or other parts of the world, in particular where there is a long-term pattern of regimes ruling by stressing ethnic diversity and the need for a strong centre capable of overcoming divisive boundaries. The emphasis on belonging and autochthony does appear to be less divisive in countries where politicians succeed in describing the nation as a unity and could either emphasise or suppress these differences almost at will. It is therefore quite surprising that relatively few African states have been able to effectively use the past – in particular a glorious past – as a means of maintaining unity.

Since the writings of Renan on nationalism, it has been almost unthinkable for the idea of the nation to exist without being embedded in a glorious past. When the French President François Mitterrand declared at the opening of the archaeological excavations of Mont Beauvray, 'Bibracte [its Roman name] is a sacred site where the first act of our French history was played out', his intention was not just to claim that the nation owed its origins to a common ancestor who resisted Roman occupation but also that the resulting Gaulish-Celtic confederacy symbolised France as the first of many unities in difference in the face of external opposition. This Francophone ideal of the nation, not surprisingly, was disseminated within its colonial empire with varying degrees of success.

The extent of this did rather depend on what historical resources were available to be captured in this manner. Mali held a particular attraction for French rule because of its imperial histories. Heir to the empires of Ghana, Mali and Songhai and the later kingdoms of the nineteenth century that French colonial rule effectively dismantled and in part emulated, Mali has a past that allows the contemporary state a basis in shared unity. There are many signs that the merits of this are well recognised. There are over 300 monuments and memorials in the capital Bamako, a number relating to colonial battles and triumphs by French armies that are preserved and maintained alongside more ancient accomplishments of the nation of Mali. One of the stories attached to President Konare (who was professionally trained as an archaeologist) is that soon after inauguration he was being driven through the capital when he noticed that a French colonial building was being demolished for a new hotel to be built. Leaping out of the presidential car, he ordered the demolition to be halted and had a heritage order slapped on the building.

Mali is the home of three World Heritage Sites, each of which has a state-financed cultural mission to preserve and restore it and encourage tourism. The promotion of 'patrimoine culturel' as the embodiment of national treasures is a hotly debated issue in Mali. For the cultural missions, it means containing the past and preventing any loss of cultural property through illegal activities and smuggling of antiquities. The missions organise sensibilisation programmes intended to educate local people in the value of heritage and the loss to national identity if they facilitate the pillaging of archaeological sites and the selling of antiquities to dealers. The idea is strongly voiced that culture and identity precedes development and the merits of retaining national heritage for tourism. For the National Museum, 'patrimoine culturel' is a selective idea based on a qualitative assessment of national treasures. The fact that most of these now reside in foreign museums and private collections is a source of anguish. Every attempt is made to purchase back such treasures when they appear on the international art market or compel other museums to repatriate 'stolen property'. Finally there is a view that 'patrimoine culturel' represents the hidden and suppressed creativity and talents of the Malian people. Repressed by colonialism and poverty, traditional skills and creativity need to be rediscovered and revalorised in new modernising settings. This is part of the mission statement of the Ministry of Culture and Tourism, whose job it is to 'intervene' and bring these hidden elements of the Malian way of life into the light of day and capitalise on their artistic production for the purposes of cultural and institutional development and tourism.

These differences of view emerge in the concrete settings of heritage projects and disputes over what is considered 'of value' and worth preserving. A 'Western' philosophy of 'restoration' is deployed primarily as an expatriate exegesis on the value of particular sites, buildings and objects as repositories of cultural capital. The World Bank, for instance, has recently made a long-term loan for the restoration of the mosques of Timboctou based on the advice of the Getty centre. The Minister of Culture hotly disputed the need for this loan, arguing that it would add to crippling debt without visible benefit and the mosques did not need this amount of money spent on them anyway. Financing the development of national music, theatre and dance was the more pressing concern according to her. At present there are over a dozen major 'heritage projects' either in hand or planned for Mali, principally based on external funding. How Malians come to see themselves through 'the tourist gaze' is a fascinating aspect of this process that I have no space to develop here, but it does suggest that managing heritage is a hotly contested issue within the national elite.

In Mali, a national elite can be defined as those who participate in a debate on the development of national cultural heritage. Ideas of citizenship and the capacity or will to identify oneself or others as Malian is crucially bound up with sensitising various abstract categories like the 'peasantry', 'women' and 'ethnic groups' to a sense of common heritage. The national theatre in Bamako has produced a play on the plundering and illicit export of cultural heritage which a group of actors take round the villages near the major heritage sites. The performance is accompanied by a travelling exhibition on the archaeology of Mali and someone from the Musée National du Mali will give a talk on the effects of the plundering of archaeological sites and how the village will benefit if they set up a 'youth committee' to prevent it. As a means of the state intervening at the local level, these 'sensibilisation' programmes are seen by everyone in the same light as development projects; suspect unless they have clear resources attached (Bedaux and Rowlands 2001).

By comparison with Cameroon, the role of both the organic and traditional intellectual is integrated in state heritage institutions in Mali. The cultural centres concerned with maintaining World Heritage Sites are funded by the Ministry of Culture to employ 'local experts' in traditional or indigenous knowledge to relate their aims to local communities. The Musée National du Bamako has a separate agenda to collect and document the material culture of different ethnic groups and fund research on the cultural heritage of Mali. Finally archaeological surveys and ethnographic research are recognised by the Institut des Sciences Humaines. The 'top-down' agenda of all these structures is basically similar; to reinforce the cultural identity of Mali, promote tourism and development and sensitise the population to their proper civic responsibilities.

Discussion

Elites in both Cameroon and Mali play brokerage and gate-keeping functions in the classic manner described by Weber. But in the dialectics of 'belonging' and 'longing' described by van der Veer and others, there is an identification with origins that shapes the role of elites. 'Belonging' in the case of Mali is co-ordinated around developing a sense of being 'Malian' that is quite explicitly

authoritarian.Yet in Gramscian mode, it relies on the harnessing of local sentiments by engaging the writings of *marabouts* or encouraging peasant
intellectuals to value ancestral pasts for harnessing a sense of longing for the
creation of a national culture. Elite associations operate in similar mode in
Cameroon by harnessing local sentiments and 'traditionalising' discourses from
the village to their position. But for effect, each must stress a singularity that
defines itself against another. Moreover the power of the president lies in his
role as master juggler, playing one off against the other. It is symptomatic of
the situation that there have been plans and the budget available for over eight
years to build a national museum for Cameroon and yet nothing has been
agreed nor a foundation stone laid.

In both cases but with almost opposite effects, the study of elite cultures
illustrates the inadequacy of making a split between civil society and tradition
– between subject and citizen – as a characteristic of the postcolonial state in
Africa (cf. Mamdani). The two are not so clearly separated and the continuing
importance of the 'traditional' in the links between rural and urban, between
civil society and custom means that everyone participates in both as a crucial
part of their identification.

Acknowledgments

Research on which this article is based was supported by the Suatsoma Fund.
I am also grateful for the support of Institut des Sciences Humaines and the
Musée National in Mali, and of R. Bedaux of the Museum of Ethnology
Leiden.

Bibliography

Anderson, B. (1983) *Imagined Communities: Reflections on the Origins and Spread of Nationalism*, London:Verso.
Appadurai,A. (1996) *Modernity at Large*, Chicago: University of Chicago Press.
Bedaux, R. and Rowlands, M. (2001) 'The Future of Mali's Past', *Antiquity* 75: 872–6.
Benjamin,W. (1973) *Illuminations*, London: Fontana.
Chilver, E. and Kaberry, P. (1971) 'The Tikar Problem: A Non-Problem', *Journal of African Languages* 10 (2): 13–14.
Feierman, S. (1990) *Peasant Intellectuals*, Madison,WI: University of Wisconsin Press.
Ferguson, J. (1999) *The Expectations of Modernity*, Berkeley: University of California Press.
Fisiy, C. (1995) 'Chieftaincy in the Modern State: An Institution at the Crossroads of Democratic Change', *Paideuma* 41: 49–62.
Fisiy, C. and Goheen, M. (1998) 'Power and the Quest for Recognition: Neotradi-tional Titles Among the New Elite in Nso', Cameroon', *Africa*, 68 (3): 383–402.
Geschiere, P. (1997) *The Modernity of Witchcraft: Politics and the Occult in Postcolonial Africa*, Charlottesville,VA: University of Virginia Press.
Geschiere, P. and Gugler J. (1998) 'Introduction: the Urban-Rural Connection – Changing Issues of Belonging and Identification', *Africa* 68 (3): 309–19.

Gramsci, A. (1971) *Selections from the Prison Notebooks*, New York: International Publishers.

Malaquais, D. (1997) 'Architecture, Landscape and the Design of Space in a Chieftaincy in the Bamileke Highlands', Ph.D. thesis, Columbia University.

Mamdani, M. (1996) *Citizen and Subject: Contemporary Africa and the Legacy of Late Colonialism*, London: James Currey.

Nyamnjoh, F. and Rowlands, M. (1998) 'Elite Associations and the Politics of belonging in Cameroon', *Africa* 68 (3): 320–37.

Stolcke, V. (1995) 'Talking Culture: New Boundaries, New Rhetorics of Exclusion in Europe', *Current Anthropology* 36: 1–24.

van der Veer, P. (1994) *Religious Nationalism: Hindus and Muslims in India*, Berkeley, CA: University of California Press.

Warnier, J.-P. (1993) *L'Esprit d'entreprise au Cameroun*, Paris: Karthala.

Chapter 10

The construction of elite status in the extreme Southern Highlands of Madagascar

Sandra J.T.M. Evers

The rural region between Ambalavao and Ankaramena (about fifty kilometres to the southwest of Ambalavao) in the extreme Southern Highlands, hereafter referred to as the 'Region', was the focus of research I carried out over a ten-year period (1989–99).[1] As my research progressed, I increasingly concentrated on the village of Marovato,[2] which proved to be fertile ground for examining the emergence and consolidation of an elite grouping.[3] Since Marovato's inception during the 1930s, the first settlers of the village had entrenched their status by using the ideology and terminology of tombs and ancestors. They mobilised their interpretation of history and culture to maintain boundaries of exclusion and lend legitimacy to their authority.

Topographically, the Region is a hilly transition between the Highlands and the arid semi-desert flatlands of the South. Settlement of the zone between Ambalavao and Ankaramena is relatively recent. Towards the end of the nineteenth century, the no-man's-land (*efitra*) located between the territories occupied by the rice-growing Betsileo in the Southern Highlands and the cattle-raising Bara and Antandroy further South was settled. The first arrivals in the area were runaway slaves who were followed at a later stage, after the abolition of slavery by the French in 1896, by ex-slaves. Whether or not these migrants originated from the Betsileo region – the area between Ambositra and Ambalavao – they assumed the Betsileo name.

The first settlers are estimated to have arrived in Marovato between 1930 and 1967.[4] They describe themselves as *tompon-tany* ('masters of the land'). Current socio-economic relations and *fomba gasy* (Malagasy customs) are viewed by them as a stable and timeless system. The *tompon-tany* use the imprimatur of ancient custom and history to confer legitimacy upon present-day regional and local socio-economic configurations. Reality, however, is much more grounded in the recent past. For example, the *andevo* ('slave' or 'slave descent') status of certain migrants was imposed by the *tompon-tany*. The *andevo* are socially ostracised and economically marginalised by the *tompon-tany*, who justify this by invoking the name of the ancestors, as the *andevo* are deemed to have no tombs, whereas the *tompon-tany* do.

This raises the question of how these *tompon-tany* were able to create an ancestral community in which the position of all the inhabitants of Marovato is determined by the presence or absence of a family tomb. And even more striking, as will be discussed later in this chapter, is that those labelled *andevo* by the *tompon-tany* not only accept the underpinnings of the system but also assume their role as the principal actors in its perpetuation.

Exclusion of non-Betsileo

Up until the nineteenth century, the names of local groups throughout Madagascar were geographical indications or referred to certain characteristics of the group (Sick 1984: 185–200). For example, Antandroy, the people who live in the semi-desert of the extreme South, means 'people of the land of thorns' (referring to the plants there). During the nineteenth century, the Merina attributed the name 'Betsileo' ('the many invincible') to the occupants of the Southern Highlands due to their fierce resistance to Merina expansion. Merina hegemony hardened their consciousness of themselves as a separate entity. Subsequently, the French colonial government (1896–1960) created eighteen distinct 'ethnic' groups. Thus, the people of the Southern Highlands over time 'became' Betsileo (Kottak 1980: 5, 48, 49, 101). When present-day Betsileo migrate to other parts of the country they continue to refer to themselves as Betsileo. Before looking in more detail at the Betsileo group, I will briefly describe the settlement history of the Region.

Until the latter half of the 1960s settlement in the Region and acquisition of land were relatively easy. Occupying this land gave these people the opportunity to attain the status of *tompon-tany* ('masters of the land') by establishing a family tomb,[5] thereby conferring upon it the status of ancestral land.[6] These pre-1967 migrants currently form the established group of the Region.[7] They call themselves Betsileo and stress that they have commoner (*olompotsy*) or even noble (*hova* or *andriana*) origins. Based on reports of slave settlement in the *Archives d'Outre Mer*, it appears more likely that this migrant group is of slave descent.[8]

I tried to verify whether the migrants who became *tompon-tany* were of actual free origin. Most were willing to tell me where they originally came from, and I was able to check some of their claims. I visited seven villages that were said to be the *tanin-drazana* of seven *tompon-tany* families in the Region. I found their relatives, but it was difficult to tell whether the villages really were their *tanin-drazana*. Often these relatives also turned out to be migrants, who had themselves only recently become *tompon-tany* by establishing a family tomb on their newly acquired land. Moreover, I was restricted by the fact that questions about descent might be considered offensive. People of free descent are generally not reluctant to discuss their family tomb. Indeed, they are proud of it and showcase their social status by speaking of it. People of slave descent, however, feel that by talking about ancestral land and tombs, they might reveal either the absence of a tomb or its recent pedigree. Because of this, determining people's origin turned out to be a hazardous adventure. After several long trips (ranging from 15 to 50 kilometres on foot) to places that people had identified as their *tanin-drazana*, I decided that it would be more fruitful to examine perceptions and claims in this regard, which I felt was almost if not as important as reality. Thus, it is not necessarily the authentication of the free origin of the *tompon-tany* which confirms their status, but its legitimisation through the tomb.

A migrant could only aspire to *tompon-tany* status in the Region if he possessed land. It is precisely this *sine qua non* that presented an obstacle for post-1967 migrants. This later wave of migrants moved to the Region for three main reasons. The first group of Antandroy, Bara and Betsileo were fleeing the terror of the cattle thieves in Southern Madagascar. The second group included people of slave origin who hoped to start afresh by moving to another region. The third group of migrants came for economic reasons, as the Region is renowned for its manioc harvests.

Settlement was to prove more arduous for these latter migrants. By the end of the 1960s, all available land in the former no-man's-land had been claimed by the *tompon-tany*. In 1967, the *tompon-tany* of the Region apparently held a meeting where all unclaimed land was divided between them, and that land would henceforth only be leased and not sold. This amounted to nothing less than a *de facto* exclusion of the later migrants from the ranks of the *tompon-tany*.

These *tompon-tany* are now very selective in accepting migrants into their villages. In principle, they only allow family members to live with them. Non-Betsileo Malagasy are rejected outright. To justify this, the *tompon-tany* stereotype them as 'different people' (*olona hafa*). Migrants of non-Betsileo origin are often the victims of prejudice, but none more so than the Antandroy, who are referred to as *olona ratsy* ('bad people'). The Antandroy are not allowed to reside in Betsileo villages. Nor do the *tompon-tany* allow them to lease land. In this way they hoped to rid themselves of the Antandroy. Yet the Antandroy have stayed to this day, living in small hamlets where their basic means of livelihood is rearing cattle.[9] The Antandroy have no tombs in the region. When someone of their community dies, he is transported back to his ancestral land or buried near the mountains.[10] Antandroy hamlets are located close to the road (RN7), at a distance of between one to five kilometres to the East or West of the little town of Ankaramena. Their settlements are scattered, composed essentially of a few families dwelling in little huts.

Betsileo *tompon-tany* identify the 'otherness' of the Antandroy by pointing to differences in speech, physical appearance and behaviour. This task becomes more delicate when the *tompon-tany* attempt to demarcate other Betsileo on the basis of their supposed slave origin. The following section will discuss how the labels of *andevo* and 'outsider' are attributed to Betsileo migrants despite the fact that they cannot be distinguished by physical appearance.

Figure 10.1 Village in the extreme Southern Highlands of Madagascar

Identifying the 'others' within the Betsileo group

Every Betsileo migrant (*mpiavy*)[11] who wishes to live in Marovato must first report to the members of the *tompon-tany* village council. This council unites the heads of the five largest *tompon-tany* families of Marovato. They always demand to know where the applicants' ancestral land and family tomb are located. Their aim is to gain an understanding of the origins of the newcomer. Any migrant who is vague about his descent is presumed by the *tompon-tany* to be of slave origin, since all free-born persons in the Highlands have ancestral land and a family tomb in their native region. *Tompon-tany* refer to Betsileo who cannot name their *tanin-drazana* as people who do *tsy misy tantara* ('not have a history') or have *very tantara* ('lost their history'). This is an automatic cause of marginalisation, as their past has given them no status or claim to recognition.[12]

Over the last few decades, the *tompon-tany* have only allowed migrants deemed to be of slave origin to settle in Marovato if they are prepared to live in the Western periphery. Migrants of free origin, meanwhile, may locate in the Eastern part of the village. Anyone now living in West Marovato is considered by other villagers to be a member of an inferior group. Betsileo ideology associates the West with all that is bad and evil. Its very land and location are viewed as impure. No Betsileo of free descent would consider living in the

Western periphery.[13] The people who dwell in West Marovato are referred to as *andevo*.[14] Villagers of free descent designate them as *olona maloto* ('impure' or 'dirty people'), whereas they call themselves *olona madio* ('pure' or 'clean people').

These abstracts,[15] taken from my fieldwork diary (1992), show the impact that these labels have upon migrants who dwell in West Marovato.

> To the Northwest of the village centre are a few yards of open field, mostly occupied by pigs searching for whatever food they can find. At night, the villagers use the field as a latrine. Just prior to reaching the field, one passes the hut of Velo (32) and Zafindravola (30).
>
> It is early in the morning on May 22 when Ramosa, my assistant, and I visit Velo and Zafindravola. Their hut is built of low-quality laterite and is divided into two parts by a piece of cloth. The right space is used for cooking over a wood fire. On the left side, Zafindravola and Velo sleep with four children: three girls who look to be between the ages of four and seven and a little boy who is just under a year old. Velo is not the father of the two eldest girls. Zafindravola says that they were born before she knew Velo. The fathers are 'unknown'. The family moved to Marovato in 1988.
>
> Velo: 'When we came to the village, I went to see the village leader. His name is Rafidy Andriana. I told him that we really would like to live in Marovato. First, he asked me with how many we were. I told him with four, my wife was pregnant with another baby. His second question concerned our *tanin-drazana* ('ancestral land'). Well, I answered him that we came from a village near Fianarantsoa but he wanted to know the name. I just could not remember. He replied that he could not accept us and that we had to leave. But we could not leave, Zafindravola was very pregnant. He said that he had to consult his ancestors on this matter. We waited three days. We slept at the riverside. His son came to see us and told us that his father had received a dream in which the ancestors had spoken. We were allowed to live here. We had nothing. We had to build the house ourselves. Nobody helped. We also could lease some land from a family who has a lot of land in Marovato. I try to cultivate it now but it is far away, near the mountains, and there are too many stones in the ground. I have nobody to help me.'
>
> Zafindravola: 'The house was not even finished when I got my baby. I was alone. Nobody came to see her. I could not understand it. It was not clear. I was very sad.'
>
> Velo quickly interjects: 'Later someone told me that we live in the wrong part of Marovato, the *maloto* part which is reserved for people who do not have a *tanin-drazana* and a *fasana* ('tomb'). That is why people speak ill of us. I went to see the village leader again and told him that we do not belong here but he thinks we do.'

Bia (60) lives in Southwest Marovato. She denies being *andevo*: 'I am from an *andriana* family.' But whereas all *andriana* ('noble descent') are *tompon-tany* and live in relatively well-kept dwellings in North and South Marovato, Bia's hut is in very poor condition. It is only about six square metres. She shares it with her daughter (18) and her son (17).

11 May 1992: Bia claims she was born in Ambositra in the Northern Betsileo area. At a very young age, she married Rakotozafy, Bia: 'He is *andriana*, just like me.' After thirty-five years of marriage and four children, her husband ended the marriage because she was beyond her fertile years and he desired more children. Bia: 'After he left me, I fled Ambositra with my two youngest children, as the other two were already married. I was embarrassed and hurt. I did not know where to go.' She led a nomadic life for some years and when she heard that in Marovato she could cultivate manioc, Bia decided to give it a try.

In 1989, her case was discussed by the members of the *tompon-tany* village council. They decided that she could settle in West Marovato. The village elder, Rafidy Andriana, leased her some land. Marovato did not bring Bia what she hoped: 'I had so many dreams when I came here, but I have been sick ever since my arrival. Maybe because of the change of climate or maybe because I do not feel welcome here. People never accepted me.'

After asking Rafidy Andriana[17] four times about Bia, he declares that he thinks that she is of slave descent and therefore should live in West Marovato.

It is noteworthy that the *andevo* label is imposed upon the newcomers by the *tompon-tany*. The fact that migrants are unable to prove their free descent by means of a family tomb and ancestral land does not necessarily mean that they are of actual slave descent. Sometimes their place of origin and family tomb are too far away for the *tompon-tany* to verify. In such cases, the *tompon-tany* leave the newcomers with two options – either to depart or to establish themselves in the Western sector. Bia (see case above), for example, by agreeing to live in West Marovato, 'became' an *andevo* in the eyes of the other villagers, despite her vigorous claims to be of noble descent. Thus, *tompon-tany* shape the destinies of newcomers by ascribing their social identities. These identities heavily condition the day-to-day life of the *andevo*, and even form part of their own conceptual scheme.

Internalisation of the *andevo* label is one of the most significant elements of social relations in Marovato. This is poignantly demonstrated by the *andevo* bowing to passing *tompon-tany* nobility, and in their self-imposed adherence to *olona madio* rules of avoidance. The internalisation of inferiority also is clearly visible in West Marovato. The *andevo* display a number of different behaviour traits from other villagers. Firstly, none of them ever shakes hands to greet me, which is the usual village practice. They also seem to suffer from 'amnesia' when I inquire about their place of origin. The other villagers are always proud to identify the land of their ancestors as this legitimises their current social status as people of free descent. Another distinguishing facet of life in West Marovato is that every household acts as a different socio-economic unit, hardly interacting with other villagers. The household works its own plot of leased land and the women cook individually whereas in the rest of the village both women and men usually undertake their daily activities on a communal basis.

Having learned my lesson during futile attempts to verify the roots of those who currently call themselves *tompon-tany*, I knew that checking the actual origin of the migrants in West Marovato would serve no useful purpose. Once again, social constructions take on lives of their own through the prejudice against migrants in West Marovato. This is further reinforced in the cultural idioms employed by the elite, as is displayed in *tompon-tany* calling the migrants in the Western periphery *olona maloto* ('impure' or 'dirty people') while they call themselves *olona madio* ('pure' or 'clean people').

Social marginalisation of the *olona maloto* is articulated through the anxiety villagers of free descent have of being polluted by the *andevo*. Not only do they feel superior to 'impure' people, they also keep a great physical distance from the inhabitants of the Western periphery. Villagers who come into contact with *olona maloto* immediately become 'impure', and this pollution can only be eradicated by being ritually cleansed by the oldest member of the former royal family near Anjoma, a village located approximately twenty kilometres northeast of Marovato.

To conclude, the Marovato population is principally organised into two binary classifications which are fundamental points of reference for social relations in the village: firstly the *tompon-tany* ('masters of the land')–*mpiavy* ('migrants') dichotomy and secondly the distinction between *olona madio* and *olona maloto*. The second binary opposition overlaps, but is not identical with the first. Although all *tompon-tany* are *olona madio*, not all *mpiavy* are considered to be *olona maloto*. Only those who cannot demonstrate free descent through possession of ancestral land and a family tomb are labelled *andevo* and *olona maloto* by members of the *tompon-tany* village council. They are ordered to settle in the Western periphery of Marovato. This geographic marginalisation of the *andevo* is a visible expression of the conceptual boundary between the *olona madio* and the *olona maloto*. However, despite the *tompon-tany* classification system and their insistence on the *fady* ('taboo', 'forbidden') of social contacts between *olona madio* and *olona maloto*, there can be no doubt that the principle of keeping at a 'safe' distance from *olona maloto* is sometimes best honoured in the breach, as demonstrated by the seven mixed marriages in Marovato, which will be discussed in the next section.

Perpetuation of elite status: marriage and land

Marriages are a significant tool used by the *tompon-tany* elite to maintain their superior social position. This has far-reaching consequences for the *andevo*, some of which can perhaps best be illustrated by the following cases.

Voahangy (24), whom villagers consider to be an *andevo*, married into the *tompon-tany* family of Ragaby. His family compound is located in North Marovato. It consists of various small huts surrounding his brick house. Voahangy and her husband Rakoto (41) dwell in a tiny hut just opposite the house of Ragaby.

Ramosa, my assistant, and I visit them on the 2nd of June (1992). The hut accommodates eight inhabitants: Rakoto, who is the nephew of Ragaby, his wife Voahangy and their daughter. They each already had one child prior to marriage. These children are part of their household just as are two children of Rakoto's deceased sister. Maro, the father of Rakoto, also lives with them. He is the brother of Ragaby. Rakoto came to Marovato in 1988. Despite his short settlement history, he is perceived as *tompon-tany* due to his family affiliation with Ragaby.

Rakoto was forced to flee his birthplace Ihosy, when he fell victim to the cattle thieves. They burned his house to the ground. Rakoto was able to escape the inferno in time, but his wife was burned alive. Traumatised by the memory of this incident, he left Ihosy with his father, whose wife also had recently died. They took Rakoto's only child (who he managed to save while running out of the burning house) and the two children of his deceased sister. They all hoped that the settlement in Marovato would provide them with a secure future.

In 1991, Ragaby ordered his brother to find a wife for Rakoto. Maro contacted several fathers with available daughters in the village, all of whom came from free descent families. Unfortunately, the fathers of the eligible brides quickly refused after having inspected Rakoto's financial position. Materially, he had nothing to offer, since he had lost everything in the Ihosy fire. Maro: 'It was difficult. I thought I would never find a wife for my son. There was only one solution … West Marovato!' It was late at night when Maro knocked on the door of Ratsimbazafy, who had five daughters of marriageable age. Maro: 'I only went after the villagers had withdrawn on the grass mat for the night so they should not notice me.' For Ratsimbazafy, Maro's arrival was a dream come true since he had great difficulty in finding husbands for his daughters. He selected Voahangy because she was the eldest and already had one baby. Ratsimbazafy: 'Rakoto is a good husband for her. She remains in Marovato and I can call on her when her help is needed.'[18]

That same night the marriage arrangements were made. Ratsimbazafy settled for a *tandra* ('bridewealth') of four chickens, and within the week Rakoto and Voahangy were husband and wife. The marriage, however, was received as an affront by other villagers of free descent. To this day, the mention of this mixed marriage provokes harsh criticism. Ragaby was particularly blamed just after the marriage, which was considered to be a serious violation of *fomba gasy*.[19] But Ragaby remains stoic: '*Fomba gasy*? It is also *fomba gasy* that you can get cleansed by the oldest member of the former royal family in Anjoma. I go to see him every week, so everybody should be happy.' This seemed sufficient to silence some villagers, but did not prevent the *tompon-tany* nobility from speaking ill of Ragaby. Not unexpectedly, Rafidy Andriana is harshest in his criticism: 'I am sure that my ancestors will one day rectify this violation of *fomba gasy*.'[20]

Soon after, a member of Rafidy Andriana's own family was revealed to be *andevo*.

It is the third of June when I hear about this from my informant Ravonjy, who lives in a village near Marovato. Ravonjy: 'He obviously did not check her out sufficiently. I know for a fact that the wife of his nephew is the sister of Lalao.' Lalao is married to Ratsimbazafy and is the mother of Voahangy (cf. former case).

Ramosa, my assistant, is very upset upon hearing the news. He obviously fears that Ravonjy is right and is even more concerned about the reaction of his father.[21] I try to console him and say that I do not believe that Lalao and Tsija (27), the wife of Rafidy Andriana's nephew Rakazy (39), actually are sisters since I have never seen them together.

12th of July: Today there was a reunion of the elders from all the villages near Marovato. They discussed what should happen with Rakazy and his wife Tsija; she is now openly acknowledged to be the sister of Lalao and therefore seen as an *andevo*. So, Ravonjy seems to have been right after all.

The elders decided that Rakazy and Tsija do not need to get a divorce, the usual solution imposed when mixed couples are discovered. They arrived at this decision because the couple already has two children together. Tsija and the children, however, will not be allowed to enter Rafidy Andriana's family tomb.[22]

16th of July: I saw Rakazy today at the river and I asked him what he thought about the decision of the elders.

Rakazy: 'You probably think that I should be happy, because they said that I do not have to leave my wife. But my father is buried in Rafidy Andriana's tomb and I want to be reunited with him when I die. I cannot take my wife and children with me, they cannot enter. So I will be alone. This I fear. It is not good to be alone. I better try to find another wife and get children with her so I will not be alone, later.'

The heads of *tompon-tany* families regard keeping their families 'pure' as one of their most important tasks. 'Pure' primarily signifies that no *olona maloto* should be admitted into their families.[23] 'Pure' also means adhering to the dictates of their ancestors as understood by them. The *tompon-tany* are able to satisfy the first requirement by arranging marriages for their children with marriage partners whose genealogical roots can be identified as 'free'. The second they claim is achieved by marginalising the *andevo* as the 'Others'.

The *tompon-tany* feeling of superiority is also reinforced by their control of new migrants to the village. Whereas the *tompon-tany* were once the newcomers to the region, by supervising the admission and eligibility of other people into the village they began to perceive themselves increasingly as the establishment of Marovato. In fact, they now refer to themselves openly as the old guard of the village. The *tompon-tany* are well aware of the importance of projecting a good image of themselves, while depicting the *andevo* as 'outsiders'. *Tompon-tany* describe themselves as the 'backbone' of the Marovato community. The responsibility to ensure that other villagers live according to the *fomba gasy* falls on them. By presenting themselves as interpreters of the wishes of the ancestors, they raise their own group to the position of 'guardians of justice'. They also perpetuate the myth by asserting that the *andevo* do not observe the cultural norms of the Betsileo. *Tompon-tany* of noble descent are particularly vehement in expressing negative opinions of the *andevo* in the form of rhetorical monologues recited during feasts and ceremonies.

The *tompon-tany* use gossip as another means of forcing people of free descent to conform and, at the same time, to keep the *andevo* in their subordinate position. Gossip about the *andevo* usually concerns their 'misdeeds', but insinuations concerning contacts between *olona madio* and *olona maloto* also give rise to discussion within the village. Gossip has a double function. Firstly, it is a mechanism of social control within the established group, strengthening its internal cohesion. Secondly, 'talking bad' about the *andevo* serves to confirm their inferior position as 'outsiders'. Gossip then sharpens the social divisions of Marovato. On one side are the *tompon-tany olona madio* who claim social recognition as the established group. On the other side — literally as well as figuratively — are the *olona maloto* migrants of West Marovato whom they portray in scurrilous terms in their effort to identify them as 'outsiders'.

As the above case relates, marriage partners sometimes are only later identified as *andevo*. If this turns out to be the case, then a number of mechanisms are available to solve the problem. The most important mechanism is determined by the ancestors according to the *tompon-tany*. Anyone entering into marriage with an *andevo* is, and remains, polluted until the marriage is dissolved. Children who are born during these marriages are also considered 'impure', and more disastrously, can never rid themselves of the pollution because it is, contrary to the temporary pollution mentioned above, in their blood (*ra*). For the parent of free descent, this already is sufficient reason to dissolve the marriage, although there is a more forceful argument. Upon their death, the 'impure' children and *andevo* wife/husband cannot be placed in the tomb of the free descent parent. Therefore, when a man is of free descent, his *andevo* wife and children may not be buried in his family tomb. Informants told me that this means that they cannot be together as a family in the hereafter. This form of exclusion seems to be one of the most efficient because the people of free descent are able to ward off *olona maloto* from their families by appeals to the supernatural.

Tompon-tany social domination is coupled with economic control over migrants of Betsileo villages in the extreme Southern Highlands. This is ensured through dependence of newcomers upon *tompon-tany* families for land,[24] which means that the *tompon-tany* monopolise not only superior social status but also the basic means of subsistence. The inhabitants of Marovato practice both agriculture and cattle breeding. Although cows are important as status symbols, economic life in the village revolves principally around the cultivation of rice, manioc, maize and vegetables. The *tompon-tany* only cultivate one-third of their land. The rest lies fallow. They say that this land may be used in the future to replace the land that is now in use. Each year, just before the rainy season starts, villagers burn their land, a practice they refer to as *tavy*. They do this either to prepare the new agricultural season, to designate fallow land for a period of years or as a means of asserting uninterrupted 'ownership'.

In 1992, the *tompon-tany* employed no labour from outside the village. They cultivate their land themselves with the help of the migrants residing in the village. All newcomers enter into a land contract upon arrival in the village with a *tompon-tany*, who retains control of the land and holds certain rights over the newcomer. The *tompon-tany* can, for example, demand his labour during harvest time. The marginalisation of the *andevo*, however, provides *andriana* (*tompon-tany* of noble descent) with permanent workers throughout the year because *andriana* are able to demand the labour of *andevo* at any time. Often, *andevo* are called upon to do the more demeaning and dirty tasks such as cleaning cattle corrals and digging holes for foundations of *tompon-tany* houses.

As for living conditions in the *andevo* quarter, West Marovato seems materially impoverished. The huts all are of poor quality and, contrary to *tompon-tany* families, the *andevo* possess little or no cattle or farming equipment. All of these external signs point to the exclusion of the *andevo* from community life while they remain a vital part of its socio-economic dynamics.

The *tompon-tany* elite regularly referred to socio-economic relations and *fomba gasy* as a stable and timeless system. Reality was far less rigid and absolute. Socio-economic relations were constantly evolving and subject to ongoing negotiations. *Fomba gasy* was often tailored to suit the needs of the moment. Even the labels *andevo* and *andriana*[25] were recently introduced by the *tompon-tany*, although both invoke the immanent nature of the system to justify and perpetuate the inferior status of the *andevo*.

This was confirmed by the village leader *tompon-tany* Rafidy Andriana who stressed that this is how *andevo* are supposed to be treated and how the *tompon-tany* have to consolidate their position in the village. This is what his ancestors expected from him and constitutes part of *fomba gasy*. As he stated at the end of my 1992 fieldwork: 'My forefathers see to it that I follow the Malagasy customs. When I am dead myself, I will see to it that my children will also live according to the Malagasy customs.'[26]

Glossary

andevo	slave(s) or being of slave descent
andriana	being of noble descent. In Betsileo society those who reincarnate into crocodiles.
efitra	no-man's-land
fady	taboo, forbidden
fasana	tomb
fomba gasy	Malagasy customs
hova	being of noble descent in Betsileo. Betsileo *hova* do not reincarnate into crocodiles.
maloto	dirty or impure
mampidi-doza	dangerous
mpiavy	migrant(s)
olompotsy	commoner descent
olona hafa	other or different people, outsiders
olona madio	pure or clean person or people. Designation in Betsileo society for people who have 'proven' their free descent by pointing out their family tomb. They are considered to be of free descent.
olona maloto	impure or dirty person or people. Designation in Betsileo society for people who cannot demonstrate their free descent by means of a family tomb. They are considered to be of slave descent.
olona ratsy	bad people
ra	blood
razana	ancestor, dead person, corpse
tandra	bridewealth
tanin-drazana	ancestral land
tavy	slash-and-burn agriculture
tompon-tany	master(s) of the land

Notes

1 This chapter is principally based on my 1992 (seven months) field work and archival research conducted at the French Colonial Archives (*Archives d'Outre Mer*) in Aix-en-Provence. I lived and worked for two and a half years in villages in the extreme Southern Highlands.

2 To protect the privacy of the villagers, the name Marovato and the names of its inhabitants are pseudonyms. Marovato is located forty kilometres to the Southwest of Ambalavao.

3 During my field work I studied six Betsileo villages in the extreme Southern Highlands with similar socio-economic configurations as described for Marovato in this chapter (cf. Rabearimana 1997; Radriamaro 1997; Rajaoson 1997).

4 The latter date is determined by a specific event that occurred in Marovato. See page 160 of this chapter.

5 In both Merina (Bloch 1971: 106–8) and Betsileo society, possession of land and a family tomb are markers of family origin in a particular region.

6 In reality this land only became a *tanin-drazana* (ancestral land) when a *razana* was placed in the tomb. *Razana* means both 'ancestor' and 'dead person' or 'corpse' (Bloch 1971: 112). Those calling themselves *tompon-tany* say that they never replaced an ancestor from elsewhere in order to make their land ancestral, but simply waited until somebody in their family died. This is remarkable, because the common practice is that as soon as a new tomb is erected, the family will transfer at least one corpse from the old to the new tomb. This might be an indication that those calling themselves *tompon-tany* nowadays actually are of slave descent and did not have tombs.

7 The binary classification of established and outsiders comes from Elias and Scotson. In their study on the tensions and power relations between two working class districts of an English town, they conclude that those who had lived for generations in a particular area stigmatise newcomers. The established perceive migrants as outsiders to whom they ascribe all manner of stereotypical character-istics and whom they exclude as their subordinates. Elias and Scotson define this relationship between the 'old' residents of one district of the town and the 'new' residents of another as an 'established-outsiders configuration' (1985: 8–12).

8 Most slaves lost their tombs upon enslavement. Slaves were prohibited from having permanent tombs throughout the period of slavery. They were forced to bury their dead in perishable tombs (Bloch 1971: 136).

9 The zebus of the Antandroy often trample and destroy the manioc fields of the *tompon-tany*, which only serves to reinforce their bad image and leads to further animosity. In addition, local *tompon-tany* claim that Antandroy hamlets are located on their territory, which for them is unacceptable. However their fear of the 'dangerous' (*mampidi-doza*) Antandroy prevents them from taking concrete action to get them off their lands.

10 There are hills and mountains on both sides of the road (RN7) which is situated one and one-half kilometres from the Antandroy hamlets.

11 These migrants' claim to be Betsileo is accepted by the *tompon-tany* at face value, whereas their social origin within the Betsileo group is subject to a further inquiry into whether the ancestral land and family tomb of these migrants really are in the Southern Highlands.

12 Bloch (1980: 120) writes on this issue: 'Without an ancestral homeland one was a non-person.'

13 This would appear to be a general phenomenon in the extreme Southern Highlands. I personally studied six Betsileo villages with similar East–West config-urations. Kottak (1980: 137–8), who worked in Betsileo villages around the town

of Ambalavao, also refers to this. In the Highlands, people commonly know which villages are inhabited by *andevo*.

14 In 1992, Marovato had 458 inhabitants, including 292 people considered to be *tompon-tany* ('masters of the land') and 166 to be *mpiavy* ('migrants'). Of the whole population of Marovato 57 inhabitants were referred to as *andevo* ('slave' or 'slave descent').

15 Ramosa (59) assisted as an interpreter until I had sufficiently mastered Malagasy.

16 Rafidy Andriana is a *tompon-tany* claiming noble (*andriana*) descent.

17 Due to their social isolation, *andevo* cannot count on others for assistance. They therefore attempt to marry their daughters to spouses residing within proximity of the family home. Kottak (1980: 172) also refers to this issue: 'with the exception of slave descendants, postmarital residence is almost universally virilocal.' Unfortunately, he does not explain why slave descendants do not adhere to the dominant pattern.

18 The *tompon-tany* constantly reaffirm their adherence to Malagasy customs. However, the Malagasy customs invoked are not as universal and rigid as they claim. When they say *fomba gasy*, they are usually referring to their vision of social organisation and protocols within the village of Marovato.

19 When I asked Rafidy Andriana to explain this remark he said: 'I still saw you burning your food last week. You still have to learn the women things. These things of *fomba gasy* will not yet be clear to you.'

20 Ramosa is the third son of the first marriage of Rafidy Andriana.

21 Rakazy obviously had close bodily contact with Tsija and therefore, in the perception of the *tompon-tany*, had himself become 'impure'. So how could he enter Rafidy Andriana's family tomb? When I asked Rafidy Andriana about this, he said that when Rakazy would die he would be ritually cleansed by the oldest member of the former royal family in Anjoma before being buried in the tomb.

22 As a consequence, one would expect the *andevo* to marry among themselves. This, however, is not the case, because most of them deny their ascribed *andevo* status. As a villager in West Marovato explained: 'As I said, we are not *andevo*. I would never wed my children to other people here in the *maloto* part since they actually are *andevo*.'

23 One has to realise that although the *tompon-tany* claim of land is considered legitimate by the villagers, they rarely officially register their land. When asked why this is not the case, *tompon-tany* say that there is no need for it. Their tomb is supposed to be sufficient evidence that they are actually the 'masters of the land'. To my knowledge, none of the migrants objected to this principle.

24 *Andriana* ('noble descent') seems to be borrowed from the Merina.

25 'Ireo razana dia antoka ho ahy fa izao no fomba gasy. Koa raha maty koa aho dia antoka ho an'ireo zanako hiaina ny fomba gasy ihany koa.'

Bibliography

Bloch, M. (1971) *Placing the Dead: Tombs, Ancestral Villages, and Kinship Organisation in Madagascar*, London: Seminar Press.

—— (1980) 'Modes of Production and Slavery in Madagascar: Two Case Studies', in J.L. Watson (ed.), *Asian and African Systems of Slavery*, Oxford: Basil Blackwell: 100–34.

Elias, N. and Scotson, J.L. (1965) *The Established and the Outsiders: a Sociological Enquiry into Community Problems*, London: Cass.

—— (1985) *Gevestigden en de buitenstaanders: een studie van de spanningen en machtsverhoudingen tussen twee arbeidersbuurten*, Den Haag: Ruward.

Evers, S.J.T.M. (2002) *Constructing History, Culture and Inequality: The Belsileo in the Extreme Southern Highlands of Madagascar*, Reiden: Brill.

Kottak, C.P. (1980) *The Past in the Present: History, Ecology and Cultural Variation in Madagascar*, Ann Arbor, MI: University of Michigan Press.

Rabearimanana, L. (1997) 'Les descendants d'*andevo* dans la vie économique et sociale au XXe siècle: le cas de la plaine d'Ambohibary Sambaina', in *Actes du Colloque International sur l'Esclavage*, Antananarivo: Institut de Civilisations/Musée d'Art et d'Archéologie, 291–303.

Rajaoson, F. (1997) 'Séquelles et résurgences de l'esclavage en Imerina', in *Actes du Colloque International sur l'Esclavage*, Antananarivo: Institut de Civilisations/Musée d'Art et d'Archéologie, 347–57.

Randriamaro, J.R. (1997) 'L'émergence politique des *Mainty* et *Andevo* au XXe siècle', in *Actes du Colloque International sur l'Esclavage*, Antananarivo: Institut de Civilisations/Musée d'Art et d'Archéologie, 357–83.

Sick, W.D. (1984) 'Die Socioökonomische Differenzierung der Volksgruppen in Madagaskar, Kultur und Naturgeographische Hintergründe', *Paideuma* 30: 185–200.

Chapter 11

Revising the past

The heritage elite and Native peoples in North America

Laura Peers

For over a century, the heritage industry in North America was controlled by an elite group of academics, civil servants, and politically powerful citizens with a particular vision of what was important in the past and how it should be presented. This group created public historic sites which promoted the elites' view of the past and the logical progression its members saw from past to present. The vast majority of historic sites thus focused either on prosperous and powerful men of European descent, or on a nostalgic view of European pioneers and the establishment of the dominant society in North America. These narratives downplayed the contributions of indigenous and minority peoples, women, and the working class, and naturalised the power and wealth of those whose stories were highlighted.

Since the 1960s, however, social and political changes in North America have led heritage agencies to acknowledge the demands of peoples whom they formerly ignored that their historical experiences be told. Representatives of these groups have become a powerful element on the governing bodies and staffs of heritage agencies and historic sites. This paper explores one facet of a very complex phenomenon, the incorporation of First Nations/Native American (hereafter 'Native') staff and perspectives into government-funded, public heritage sites in both Canada and the United States.[1] When first opened, few historic reconstructions represented Native peoples, even at sites where, historically, Native people were numerous and played key roles. During the late 1980s and early 1990s, a number of sites chose to add Native areas and staff to their interpretive programmes and to alter the historical narratives they tell to focus on Native and cross-cultural history. This paper examines the processes and implications of these changes for elites within the heritage profession.

Fieldwork for this analysis was conducted with staff and visitors at seven reconstructed historic fur trade and mission sites in Canada and the United States since 1993. These reconstructions are located around the Great Lakes, range temporally across three centuries, and involved several different Native peoples: Sainte-Marie among the Hurons, a seventeenth-century Jesuit mission to the Huron (Wendat) people on Georgian Bay, a reconstruction operated by the Government of Ontario; Colonial Michilimackinac, an eighteenth-century nexus for Odawa, Ojibwa, Métis, and other Great Lakes peoples involved in the fur trade (operated by the Mackinac State Historic Parks Commission, a Michigan state agency); the North West Company Fur Post in Minnesota, an 1804–5 wintering post among the Ojibwa (operated by the Minnesota Historical Society); Old Fort William, the North West Company's western depot, reconstructed to 1815, which had a local Ojibwa and Métis population (operated by the Province of Ontario); and Lower Fort Garry, a Hudson's Bay Company depot and provisioning post for a culturally diverse community including Métis, Europeans, Ojibwa and northern Cree, which now interprets life in the 1850s and is operated by Heritage Canada, a federal agency. These sites are also of different sizes, with annual visitor numbers ranging from 15,000 to 120,000. Together, though, they have gone through similar processes of development in adding Native interpretation over the past two decades, and they communicate similar information about Native peoples and Native-White relations in the past.

Today, these places employ Native staff and have constructed Native dwellings to depict the historic presence and roles of Native people. Encampments consisting of one to four domestic structures appropriate to the region and period serve as a stage for interpretation (the discussion of historic facts and narratives, and the presentation of historic activities) by Native staff, who wear reproduction historic clothing (moccasins and trade cloth leggings, shirts, and skirts, trousers, or loincloth). Native interpretation has become a priority at reconstructions where the official themes now emphasise Native-White economic and political interdependence. Fur trade sites focus on the existence of intermarriage between peoples, and of widespread kinship networks between European and Native communities; mission sites discuss traditional Native religious beliefs, the struggle to choose one faith over another, and the consequences of conversion. This is a complete change in the emphases of the sites, and in the stories they tell, and in the perspectives they try to tell them from.

Issues pertaining to the control and representation of the past are not purely 'academic'; they also raise concrete issues of power affecting daily aspects of heritage management and funding, who does or does not get hired, and the course of professional careers and individual lives. These issues are also part of much larger ones for those whose histories are bound up with historic sites. In relations between indigenous peoples and nation-states, control over the representation of the past is key to either forms of control by the nation-state or to cultural survival for indigenous peoples, and a large literature has developed about the 'contested pasts' of minority groups within dominant societies (for example, Norkunas 1993; Hill 1992; Friedman 1992; Lowenthal 1990; Keesing 1989; Bodnar 1992; Connerton 1989). Within North America, First Nations and Native American groups see the process of gaining control of the representation of the past as part of a process of healing deep cultural wounds caused by colonialism, and of regaining self-determination. There are serious stakes in the changes my research has explored, and not surprisingly these are seen as sensitive issues at the institutions involved.

The assumption stated in the guidelines for this session, that 'most power elites are opaque and protected from study,' simply does not apply to the heritage tourism industry, which has come under intense scrutiny for several decades over issues of representation, voice, and authority. Museums, the art and artefact world in general, and the heritage and tourism industries have all been subject to often blistering analyses of their patterns of representation (especially of non-Western peoples), of the patterns of power which precondition such representations, and of the links between colonialism and the development of these phenomena (for example, Wallace 1981; Clifford 1991, 1988; Mackey 1995; Handler and Gable 1997; Jones 1993; Karp and Lavine 1991; Karp, Kreamer and Lavine 1992; Bruner 1993; Bruner and Kirshenblatt-Gimblett 1994). Within North America, the control exercised by the heritage industry over representations of the past has reinforced stereotypes and ethnocentric assumptions central to the control of Native peoples by the dominant society, making museums and historic sites important targets for Native people and for revisionist scholars focused on relations of power. Far from being protected from study, these institutions have been intense subjects of study.

There is even a literature on the culture of what one might call the heritage elite, the representatives of the dominant society who have controlled the heritage industry for so long, and on how change operates in and is muted by this group (Bodnar 1992; Taylor 1990; Payne and Taylor 1992; Handler and Gable 1997). Heritage agencies, whether operating on a national or federal level, or at a state or provincial level, have traditionally involved a mix of civil servants, heritage professionals and academics, and persons of wealth and influence on their governing boards and senior staff rosters. As John Bodnar notes, members of this group are 'self-conscious purveyors' of loyalty to larger political structures and existing institutions. Their careers and social positions usually depend upon the survival of the very institutions that are celebrated in commemorative activities. The boundaries of the leadership group are permeable, however, and can be crossed by rich and very influential individuals. Seldom are they crossed by factory workers, homemakers, mill hands, farmers, and others whose work and social position allow them little time and access to the organisations that shape most public commemorative events (Bodnar 1992: 15–16). This profile fits the definition of 'elites' used in Shore's introduction to this volume quite neatly: 'Elites are those who, collectively, occupy the most influential positions or roles in the governing institutions of a "community" … the leaders, rulers and decision-makers in any sector of society, or custodians of the machinery for making policy.'

Given the nature of this heritage elite, it is not surprising that the version of the past it promoted emphasised 'a common interest in social unity, the continuity of existing institutions, and loyalty to the status quo' (Bodnar 1992: 13). In particular, early public history sites in North America focused on two themes: the lives and deeds of wealthy and influential 'Founding Fathers' (such as at Monticello and colonial Williamsburg), and places and events associated with the development of the United States and Canada as distinct nations (such as at Louisbourg and Lower Fort Garry) (Norkunas 1993; Wallace 1981).

The focus on prosperous men of European descent, and their well-dressed wives and daughters, was part of a relative consensus among the heritage elite about who was important in the past. This consensus led to a uniformity among living history and historic house sites, which have been criticised for showing 'an unrepresentative sample of past Americans', focusing almost exclusively on 'the lives of middle- and upper-income Protestants' (Leon and Piatt 1989: 65). The individuals and families whose stories were highlighted were held up as the building blocks of nations, with the implication that their success stories were to be admired and emulated. The stories of their labourers, their slaves, their Native allies, or the transfer of lands from Native peoples to make nation-building possible, were simply omitted.

The bias in such narratives is clearly seen in historic sites that commemorated national development. For instance, the Canadian parks system developed many military and fur trade sites 'as examples of the advance of Euro-Canadian civilization and sovereignty across the land' (Johnstone 1994: 4). The fur trade fits perfectly into the 'nation-building' concept of historical significance as a 'necessary link between savage wilderness and civilization' and 'as the forerunner of Canadian hegemony in Western Canada', a kind of Canadian version of the 'winning of the West' (Coutts 1993: 1; see also Payne and Taylor 1992). Of the reconstructions examined here, Lower Fort Garry was interpreted for several decades more as a village of Scottish pioneers than as the economic and industrial hub of a multicultural community supported by the fur trade. Interpretation focused on middle- and upper-class characters and activities such as baking bread and having tea parties; Native people were not portrayed on site and their local presence was not interpreted (Payne and Taylor 1992; Johnstone Papers 1962).

These themes and representations were filled with power. They reinforced, naturalised and justified the attitudes, historical acts and colonial relations of power of the dominant society towards Native people (Badone 1991: 539; see also Norkunas 1993: 5–6, Lowenthal 1985: 44, Alonso 1988: 33). In this sense, historic sites acted as a type of cultural performance: they placed on display core beliefs, values and structures. They either downplayed the contributions and cultural sophistication of Native peoples, or ignored them altogether. When Native people were represented, it was as less civilised, less technologically advanced and less deserving of the continent than their colonisers, who 'naturally' came to dominate them. The social relationships evoked and displayed by historic sites were hierarchical and hegemonic.

Winds of change

James Brow notes that while control over historical representations is a 'prominent feature of hegemonic struggle in modern industrial societies', the actual attainment of complete control by the dominant society is rare (Brow 1990: 3). Officially produced representations of the past, and the ways in which they are produced, are always subject to contestation and challenge (and see Bodnar 1992: 13). Even during the early decades of Canadian heritage programmes, for instance, board members from different regions competed to commemorate events and places of significance in their own regions, and English versus French-Canadian interpretations of history often came into conflict. The enormous scale of change in historic themes interpreted at public sites over the last two decades goes far beyond this, however. The extent to which Native staff, themes and consultation with Native communities has become imperative to certain historic sites suggests a shift in the balance of power in contemporary Native–White relations, and has occurred hand-in-hand with major changes in the nature of the heritage elite.

The empowerment and civil rights movements of the 1960s and 1970s in North America had many important results. One of these was the development of skills and knowledge by Native people to deal with bureaucracy and to manipulate the media to their own ends, and it was after these experiences that Native people began to lobby successfully for inclusion within the heritage industry. As well, social and political developments of the era spurred the rise of social history within academia, and a new focus emerged on minority groups as a legitimate and important field of study. This, in turn, led to the training of a new generation of scholars, many of them young and fairly left-wing, in social history. When public history sites, spurred by widespread interest in history 'from the ground up', began growing rapidly in the early 1970s, this cohort of young social historians filled the many positions available in the field at the time. Their training and interests, combined with public interests, caused a fairly rapid refocus at many historic sites in the 1970s and 1980s from older emphases on wealthy men to the addition of women's history, Black history, and most recently Native histories. Finally, by the 1980s, these shifts were coinciding with national developments in both Canada and the USA, which embraced multiculturalism and ethnic diversity within the national framework.

These changes interacted to produce a climate in which the heritage industry shifted its emphases and the nature of its elite. By the late 1970s, women's roles in the past had become an important interpretive theme at many historic sites; throughout the 1980s, the roles of Native people had as well. By the late 1980s, representatives of minority groups were being invited to become members of advisory boards and boards of governors at both site and agency level. Finally, Native voices were beginning to be heard in the board room, and to carry considerable weight, influencing budgetary and policy decisions, and insisting on increased consultation between heritage sites and Native groups. Members of Native advisory boards were asked, on behalf of their communities, to guide policy, to assist in the correction of historical shallowness, and to note desirable and undesirable aspects of representations. Most of these advisors were and still are volunteers; Native staff and especially Native administrators are still a definite minority within the heritage profession. However, many of the non-Native administrators at sites and agencies now are those left-wing academics of the 1970s, who have risen through the ranks. They still constitute a non-Native heritage elite, but it is one that is far more likely to want to consult with Native communities, and to portray Native historical themes, than the previous generations of this institution.

The very real power that Native peoples have gained within the heritage industry also includes them among this new heritage elite. Given the very effective use of ethno-protest by Native peoples today, it would be folly for anyone administering public funds through an historic site to completely ignore Native advisors or local Native community requests. More serious than the threat of media scrums are the significant gains made by Native people toward acquiring the legal rights to co-manage their heritage resources. Budgets at some historic sites now hinge on co-management agreements with Native 'stakeholders,' as the federal Canadian jargon has it. Many heritage agencies have been mandated by government in the past decade to establish partnerships with Native peoples and procedures through which Native advisors review policy guiding the interpretation at historic sites: those advisors may be volunteers, but they must be heard before budgets are approved. Heritage (also known as Parks) Canada's current guidelines state that 'Parks will involve First Peoples in the presentation and interpretation of places, objects and historical information to which they are traditionally related' (Heritage Canada 1995: 3; see also the 'National Historic Sites Systems Plan Review,' Heritage Canada 1992). There have also been significant changes to law in both Canada and the United States which require consultation with Native communities over the management of heritage resources (NAGPRA, 1990; American Indian Religious Freedom Act, 1978; subsection 106 of the US National Historic Preservation Act, 1990, 1992, 1999; cases in the Canadian Supreme Court including Sparrow, 1990; Van der Peet, 1996; Delgamuukw, 1997: see Kennedy 1999: 6–8). The process of change in the heritage industry has snowballed, and legal decisions, agency policies, site management plans, and institutional power dynamics have swung widely toward Native peoples.

Processes of change

Implementing such changes in policies, themes, priorities, budget allocations and procedures has been a complex, difficult and slow process. Sometimes it has involved change trickling down from policy and legal decisions at the top of the heritage industry, as in federal legislation or Heritage Canada's policy documents about co-managing Native heritage resources; sometimes it has proceeded in a groundswell from the bottom up, with local impetus or staff initiative at particular sites. Despite being committed to what they see as a more balanced portrayal of the past, site and heritage agency staff face an extremely contested and mediated process of creating revised historical representations. While the character and ideals of the heritage elite have shifted, and Native people are now included to some extent within this group, there is still considerable tension between Native and non-Native people over the representation of the past. The final section of this chapter will explore these tensions within the 'new heritage elite'.

One overarching level of contestation faced by the new heritage elite is at the level of postcolonial politics. Where once board members or site historians were thought to know best what should be commemorated, local communities are now referred to as 'stakeholders' and 'partners' in heritage management, and their wishes and perspectives must be taken very seriously. In such an atmosphere, lobby groups, including Native people, which wish to focus on particular historical narratives and to have a degree of control over the representation of the past, have become forces to reckon with, so that historical representations tend to be produced in a much more collaborative and consultative (and often contested) process than before. In the case of Native advisory and lobby groups, this process is further complicated by the fact that for Native communities, control over the representation of the past is part of a larger set of goals related to self-determination, aboriginal rights, and community development, and by the fact that Native people hold a wide range of views about the past. In addition to Native groups, heritage sites receive pressures from academics, from descendants of people who lived or worked at the sites, from professional heritage organisations promoting their own views of what is important in the preservation and interpretation fields, from government officials wanting to draw on the site to promote economic development for the region or a healthy family context for a publicity photo, and many more besides. It is little wonder that one weary site director told me he did not want a 'report card' from me when I left, and that he had been the victim of quite enough lobby groups riding hobby horses.

Furthermore, while a whole set of factors has made it important to add Native staff and perspectives to these representations of the past, doing so is quite difficult, for another set of reasons.

To begin with, recruiting Native people to work at historic sites has not been easy. Native communities in general tend to be suspicious of historic sites because the sites are government-funded and have traditionally ignored their perspectives and given a European-oriented view of history. To overcome such attitudes, site administrators have taken measures to create relationships with Native communities and inform them of their changing perspectives. Native advisory boards play an important role in this process, as do special events hosted with and for Native communities. Thus, Old Fort William hosts a summer festival called 'Ojibway Keeshigan', which brings in hundreds of Native people for a pow-wow, crafts demonstrations and other heritage-oriented activities, and Lower Fort Garry has hosted a Native art show. While these events are extraneous to a historic site's primary purposes, they serve very well to establish new ties with a politicised, critical Native community and to make contacts with potential employees.

Administrators have also had to develop new methods to recruit Native people. Traditional means of advertising for jobs – in major papers or on university bulletin boards – reach only a tiny percentage of Native people, and site administrators have typically not had much knowledge about working with Native communities. One administrator responded to my suggestion that in order to find suitable Native applicants it was necessary to forge general links with Native communities by attending pow-wows, inviting elders and band council leaders for special tours of the site and so forth, by saying simply that these activities were not in his job description. (This response also demonstrates the ability of the heritage elite to stall the process of change, should they wish to.) They certainly were not part of his concept of 'hiring procedures'. Other administrators have developed special recruitment schemes that use pow-wows, cultural centres and kinship networks to advertise positions.

Once hired, Native interpreters are still a minority on staff at historic sites, and they tend to occupy seasonal rather than permanent positions. Sites in this study have between two and fifteen Native staff who constitute one-tenth to one-third of the total summer interpretive staff. Historically, the proportions were always reversed: these places were small islands of Europeans in a sea of Native people. Native interpreters are keenly aware of this patterned minimisation in the representation of their cultures and of the history depicted at their sites. They know it is historically inaccurate, and they interpret the situation as a lack of real commitment on the part of site administration. They sometimes say that because Native history is 'in' academically and politically, administrators will say that they support Native interpretation to funding agencies, government heritage departments and Native political activists in the community, but then fail to follow up by hiring Native staff or by funding the Native areas of the site sufficiently. This has become the greatest source of frustration for Native interpreters at historic sites, who feel, as Ivan Karp has expressed it, that:

> in exhibitions that celebrate cultural achievement, the very fact that the achievements of people of colour are ignored introduces implicit messages about their worth. A hierarchy of cultures is erected, in which those worth examining are separated from those that deserve to be ignored. Racial imagery and ethnocentrism can be communicated by what is not exhibited as well as by what is.
>
> (Karp 1992: 24)

At each site, interpreters asked me about the state of other Native encampments at other sites, and if the other encampments were as small as theirs.

Budget expenditure is seen by Native staff to be indicative of the site's commitment to Native issues, and of the importance and power of particular site elements. At Michilimackinac, the two Native interpreters with their few structures (at a site with about twenty summer interpreters and over a dozen large buildings) are truly frustrated by what they see as tokenism. At Old Fort William, there was a political tempest caused by the site spending $Cdn4.5 million dollars in 1992 on necessary physical repairs such as new palisading, but not a penny on the Native encampment. Armin Webber, who was then the site director, explained that there was a gap in communication between the encampment staff and his office, and he failed to notice either the gap or the encampment's needs. After complaints from visitors the following spring, Webber found money to rebuild the entire encampment and hire artisans to produce furnishings and display items the following year (Armin Webber, personal communication 1994). The incident suggests that cultural differences can contribute to such gaps, perhaps by producing suspicion or uncertainty amongst Native staff about the intentions of administrative channels and frustrations with bureaucratic process. The fact that most Native staff are still hired on seasonal rather than permanent contracts contributes to this frustration, for seasonal workers are not usually given any means of control or even input into budget decisions.

Other tensions are expressed in negatively phrased comments which indicate that there is a less than perfect fit between dominant-society institutions such as heritage agencies, and Native staff. Non-Native staff were aware that there were 'cultural differences' between them and Native staff which resulted in a rather different kind of interpretation in the Native encampments, but still tended to describe these differences in negative terms. Some non-Native staff claimed that Native interpreters did not stick to the historic themes of the site which interpreters were supposed to impart; did not work 'in character' at sites where first-person interpretation was used; had to be disciplined because they sometimes wore or used items that were not in period; and disobeyed site rules (based on provincial or state health regulations) about feeding period cooking to visitors. Native staff were also said to be difficult to deal with because they often refused to be bound by official bureaucratic structures and demanded to deal with top-level management, or demanded changes immediately rather than making proposals through ordinary channels to plan and then implement change over several seasons, in accordance with budget planning and allocation. These differences were not concentrated at any one site; a few people at each site expressed one or more of these ideas. There seems still to be a low-key but widespread perception at historic sites that Native staff do not 'fit in'.

This lack of fit was also expressed by Native staff. At one site, non-Native women have been hired every summer to portray Métis and Native wives of fur trade employees who worked within the palisades. Native staff told me that real Métis and Native people should be hired for those positions. Others felt that some non-Native staff did not know (or care) 'what history was *really* like, what *really* happened', that such staff were happy to learn and pass on a sanitised, European-oriented view of the past.

Such comments reveal significant discrepancies between Native perspectives on the past, and what the professional heritage elite have decided to add by way of Native content to historic sites. Not surprisingly, Native people often focus on the negative effects of contacts with European traders and missionaries. Their view of 'what history was *really* like, what *really* happened' includes smallpox epidemics, cultural change, dispossession, the effects of alcohol and colonisation. None of these subjects is given more than passing mention at historic sites or in official policy documents. Instead, current buzzwords are 'alliance', 'interdependence' and 'the richness of Aboriginal cultures'. While such themes certainly ring true, and are an excellent counter-balance to popular views which hold that Native people were brute savages who were of no importance in the past, they are by no means the whole picture. At the present time, the inclusion of Native themes at historic sites rests upon an overly positive view of the past in which culture contact led to happy, diverse multiculturalism (and see Castaneda 1992). This is a representation which is just as controlled, and has equally political implications, as the one which simply omitted Native people: in part, it includes Native peoples in representations of the past while also exonerating Whites from the effects of history. It also rings true with Handler and Gable's (1997) findings for colonial Williamsburg, where the revisionist programme to add African-American perspectives to historical interpretation has been softened by insistence from site management that visitors not be upset, that their perspectives not be challenged, and that the painful parts of the past be muted in the interpretive programme.

There is, however, a wide spectrum among sites in terms of the way in which revisions to historical representations and narratives are progressing. At some sites, individuals have worked especially hard to break down cross-cultural barriers – one site administrator said that he had worked hard to rid non-Native staff of what he called an 'office folklore' that held that Native people were clannish, aloof and difficult to work with – and several sites showed a remarkable sense of teamwork and mutual trust among Native and non-Native staff. There is an equal spectrum when one considers what has been the most challenging of all the changes that the incorporation of Native staff has involved, which has been the establishment of relationships between local Native communities and historic sites. These challenges are often raised initially when sites try to hire Native staff, but they are far more profound than that. Where once these sites served the dominant society by presenting a version of history that reinforced the self-image and power structures of that society, some sites are now making a conscious effort to serve Native communities as well. The processes by which such revision happens (or does not) have much to do with the specific personalities and conjuncture of events and wider politics at each site, but a comparison of two sites gives a sense of the spectrum of change.

At Michilimackinac, local White townspeople have held a pageant each year for some twenty-five years which re-enacts the capture of the fort by Native people in 1763. The pageant, which features local Whites dressed up in red coats or Halloween-style 'Indian wigs', turns the very painful conflict into a caricature, including getting the audience to laugh when someone is 'scalped' and has his wig pulled off. When the site commissioned a report from a Native American consultant on how to develop working relations with local bands and how the site might approach the representation of Native perspectives on the past, the consultant noted that:

> Some Anishinawbek stated that they will not go to any of the exhibits, facilities or activities of the MISPC (Mackinac Island State Park Commission) because of the negative attitude generated in the past and from the continued policy by MISPC in regard to the exhibits and activities, especially the re-enactment of the 1763 capture … The continuation of the re-enactment by the non-Anishinawbek community at the fort is an issue that will sustain negative tensions on the MISPC's relationship with most of the conservative element of the Anishinawbek in northern Michigan … Until something is done about this issue, the Anishinawbek believe that the MISPC is not taking their concerns seriously.
>
> (Andrews 1995: n.p.)

The site realises how offensive the pageant is to Native people, but is unwilling to broach the subject to the organisers. This position undermines both the site's verbal commitment to incorporating Native perspectives in its interpretation, and the morale of its Native staff.

In contrast to this, Armin Webber, the former director of Old Fort William, stated in an interview that he 'would like to see that people are aware that 50 per cent of the Native encampment is to serve the needs of the Native community, and 50 per cent is to serve the [site's] needs' (1994: personal communication). Webber was extremely proud of the fact that Native staff had taken ownership of the encampment and were bringing visiting friends and family to see it, and that Native people came to the Ojibwa Keeshigan festival to learn about historic cultural practices that they could not see at pow-wows or other kinds of gatherings. Webber's comment on the encampment is very powerful: it began, he says, as

> a well-researched display, just like any other place [in the fort], and we hired Natives to man the display. And the display was operated … dramatised … And [then] 3 or 4 years ago … Natives took ownership of that

encampment in a different way than had ever happened before. And they all of a sudden wanted to bring their friends out like the white people do to see the fort when the visitors are in town … and share with them their encampment, their heritage. And if that [the encampment] didn't look like it was comfy, like your home would be – do you know the difference between your home and a display? Well, that's what happened. They said, 'I don't want a display. I want [it to look like] a home.'

And that's what happened. And I stepped back and said, 'the Native development in Canada is so important right now, it [the Native community] is going through so many convulsions, we are not here to fight that trend'.

This is a real shift in intent for these places, and signals drastic changes in conceptualising and operating historic sites. Armin Webber and other administrators at these places who are encouraging such developments are not, as Handler and Gable (1997: 27) found at Williamsburg, 'interested mainly in managing an image of openness and debate rather than participating in discussions they could not control'. They are slowly – and sometimes painfully, with many false starts and misunderstandings – feeling their way into a new way of thinking about these places. Other administrators still find it easier to deal with the politics of heritage agencies and government departments than to venture far along the unfamiliar and less controllable road of creating relationships with Native communities. This is not the cookie cutter, hegemonic image of the heritage elite that this paper began with, and signals real changes within the heritage profession.

Conclusions

Native peoples have crucial stakes in the representation of the past. Control over the representation of heritage, David Lowenthal reminds us, is 'essential to autonomy and identity' (Lowenthal 1990: 302). Native American and Canadian First Nations people would add that it is essential to cultural survival and self-determination. Control over representations of the past involves issues of political power, and reflects the balance of power between the dominant society as represented by the heritage elite and minority groups within nation-states. Since at least the 1970s, the messages that are communicated at public history sites about the past have been dramatically revised as Native histories, and Native control over the representation of the past, have been added to heritage agency policies and historic sites. Such changes have reflected a parallel process of change in the composition and ideals of the heritage elite itself, as it has increasingly incorporated social historians and Native peoples committed to a vision of multiculturalism and 'balanced' history in an attempt to broaden what is shown about the past.

Figure 11.1 Keith Knecht, Odawa interpreter, with visitors at Colonial
Michilimackinac, summer 1995. Photo: Drew Davey.

This process is not complete, and has been difficult to implement. Historic
site staff and advisors still struggle with cross-cultural mistrust between Native
and non-Native staff on several levels and with budgetary and other
constraints. There is also still a great deal of control by non-Native members
of the heritage elite over the historical narratives being communicated: overly
positive messages currently in vogue ignore the negative experiences of the
past for Native people just as much as older narratives which ignored Native
people. Still, there are signs that the new heritage elite is beginning to work
with Native communities, to continue to rethink narratives about the past,
and to foster better relations between Native and non-Native people in the
present.

Edward Bruner's statement that 'to construct, produce, invent, and market
are verbs which highlight the processual, active nature of culture, history,
tradition, and heritage' reminds us that historic sites will continue to move
with the tides of scholarship, budgetary realities and contemporary
Native–White relations (Bruner 1993: 14). The politics and dynamics of
incorporating Native staff into a site, of developing relations with local bands,
and of bringing contemporary visitors together with contemporary Native
people, are tremendously important – and tremendously fluid, and often volatile.

Figure 11.2 'We are playing ourselves, the real First Nations people': Cecilia Littlewolf-Walker, interpreter, Old Fort William, summer 1994. Photo: Drew Davey.

The only certainty in this situation is that the heritage elite will continue to evolve, and to be a fruitful site for study.

Notes

1   Research for this paper was funded by the Social Sciences and Humanities Research Council of Canada and McMaster University, with additional funds for revisits from individual sites. I would like to thank staff at the sites who permitted fieldwork and assisted in many ways.

Bibliography

Alonso, Ana Maria (1988) 'The Effects of Truth: Re-presentations of the Past and the Imagining of Community', *Journal of Historical Sociology* 1: 33–57.

Andrews, W. (1995) 'Appropriate Representation, Cultural Interpretation and Exhibit Policy: A Perspective for Consulting with Native American Indian Communities in Northern Michigan', consultant's report prepared for the Mackinac Island State Park Commission.

Badone, Ellen (1991) 'Ethnography, Fiction, and the Meanings of the Past in Brittany', *American Ethnologist* 18 (3): 518–45.

Bodnar, John (1992) *Remaking America: Public Memory, Commemoration, and Patriotism in the Twentieth Century*, Princeton, NJ: Princeton University Press.

Brow, James (1990) 'Notes on Community, Hegemony, and the Uses of the Past', *Anthropological Quarterly* 63 (1): 1–6.

Bruner, Edward (1993) 'Lincoln's New Salem as a Contested Site', *Museum Anthropology* 17 (3): 14–25.

Bruner, Edward and Kirshenblatt-Gimblett, Barbara (1994) 'Maasai on the Lawn: Tourist Realism in East Africa', *Cultural Anthropology* 9 (4): 435–70.

Castaneda, Antonia (1992) 'Women of Color and the Rewriting of Western History: The Discourse, Politics, and Decolonization of History', *Pacific Historical Review* 61 (4): 501–33.

Clifford, James (1988) *The Predicament of Culture: Twentieth-Century Ethnography, Literature, and Art*, Cambridge, MA: Harvard University Press.

—— (1991) 'Four Northwest Coast Museums: Travel Reflections', in I. Karp and S. Levine (eds), *Exhibiting Culture: The Poetics and Politics of Museum Display*, Washington: Smithsonian Institution Press, 212–54.

Connerton, Paul (1989) *How Societies Remember*, Cambridge: Cambridge University Press.

Coutts, Robert (1993) *Lower Fort Garry: An Operational History, 1911–1992*, Ottawa: Parks Canada Microfiche Report Series 495.

Friedman, Jonathan (1992) 'The Past in the Future: History and the Politics of Identity', *American Anthropologist* 94 (4): 837–59.

Handler, Richard, and Gable, Eric (1997) *The New History in an Old Museum: Creating the Past at Colonial Williamsburg*, Durham, NC: Duke University Press.

Heritage (Parks) Canada (1992) 'National Historic Sites Systems Plan Review', internal document.

—— (1995) 'Parks Canada Response to Request for Update on Task Force on Museums and First Peoples', internal document.

Hill, Jonathan D. (1992) 'Contested Pasts and the Practice of Anthropology', *American Anthropologist* 94 (4): 809–15.

Johnstone, A.J.B. (1994) 'Toward a New Past: Reflections on the Interpretation of Native History Within Parks Canada', unpublished ms. 2nd draft circulated as internal report for Historical Services Branch, National Historic Sites Directorate, Parks Canada, 1995.

Johnstone Papers (1962) Hudson's Bay Company Archives, Winnipeg, E.97/53, Barbara Johnstone Papers, 'A Broad Outline of Exhibit Stories for Lower Fort Garry National History Park'.

Jones, Anna Laura (1993) 'Exploding Canons: the Anthropology of Museums', *Annual Reviews in Anthropology* 22: 201–20.

Karp, Ivan (1992) 'On Civil Society and Social Identity', in I. Karp, C. Kreamer and S. Lavine (eds), *Museums and Communities: The Politics of Public Culture*, Washington: Smithsonian Institution Press, 19–33.

Karp, Ivan and Lavine, Steven D. (eds) (1991) *Exhibiting Culture: The Poetics and Politics of Museum Display*, Washington: Smithsonian Institution Press.

Karp, Ivan, Kreamer, Christine Mullen and Lavine, Steven D. (eds) (1992) *Museums and Communities: The Politics of Public Culture*, Washington: Smithsonian Institution Press.

Keesing, Roger (1989) 'Creating the Past: Custom and Identity in the Contemporary Pacific', *The Contemporary Pacific* 1: 19–42.

Kennedy, Dorothy (1999) 'Culture and Politics in the Aboriginal Landscape: Reflections on the Identification of Culturally-Significant Places in Western North America,' unpublished ms.

Leon, Warren and Piatt, Margaret (1989) 'Living History Museums', in W. Leon and R. Rosenzweig (eds), *History Museums in the United States: A Critical Assessment*, Chicago: University of Illinois Press, 64–97.

Lowenthal, David (1985) *The Past is a Foreign Country*, New York: Cambridge University Press.

—— (1990) 'Conclusion: Archaeologists and Others', in P. Gathercole and D. Lowenthal (eds), *The Politics of the Past*, London: Unwin, 302–14.

Mackey, Eva (1995) 'Postmodernism and Cultural Politics in a Multicultural Nation: Contests over Truth in the *Into the Heart of Africa* Controversy', *Public Culture* 7: 403–31.

Norkunas, Martha K. (1993) *The Politics of Public Memory*, Albany, NY: State University of New York Press.

Payne, Michael and Taylor, C.J. (1992) 'Animated Adventures in the Skin Trade: Interpreting the Fur Trade at Historic Sites', paper presented to the Rupert's Land Research Centre Colloquium, Winnipeg.

Taylor, C.J. (1990) *Negotiating the Past: The Making of Canada's National Historic Parks and Sites*, Montreal: McGill-Queen's.

Wallace, Michael (1981) 'Visiting the Past: History Museums in the United States', *Radical History Review* 25: 63–96.

Webber, Armin (1994) former director, Old Fort William, interview.

Chapter 12

Revolution and royal style
Problems of post-socialist legitimacy in Laos

Grant Evans

The legitimacy of the Lao monarchy did not crumble from within, but was swept away by forces beyond Laos. The communists came to power in December 1975 not as a result of internal social and cultural changes, but as a result of the country being engulfed by the Vietnam War. The pressure on the tiny Royal Lao Government by larger neighbours and by the superpowers became unbearable, while the Pathet Lao (as the communist front became known) was dependent both ideologically and militarily on its North Vietnamese mentors who brought them to power and sustained them in power during the Cold War.

The following chapter looks at the ways the monarchy has remained a presence in Lao culture beyond the fall of the kingdom. Initially, what we see is a radical suppression of royal references after the revolution, but after the fall of communism globally in the early 1990s the Lao People's Democratic Republic had to selectively revive many traditional practices and rituals of the old order to shore up its nationalist legitimacy. These practices, however, bring with them unwelcome references to the former monarchy. Indeed, the importance of monarchical imagery in Buddhist and everyday rituals ensures royalty's ghostly presence. The chapter then turns to look at the 'kingdom' in exile and the paradoxical consequences this 're-traditionalization' of the communist regime has for it. The chapter highlights the need for cultural legitimacy by political elites, but also shows that culture has an autonomous logic that escapes the commands of these elites much to their consternation.

The revolution in everyday life

Among the many symbolic and ritual changes introduced into Lao life in the aftermath of the revolution none was more ubiquitous than the reform of 'elitist' language.[1] In December 1975 a decree was issued which proclaimed, among other things, that the bureaucracy would 'cease using royal language for daily record and correspondence except when necessary as in poetry or other forms of literature' (*SWB* 9/12/75). The abolition of 'royal language' saw the attempt at an egalitarian reform of the language and so honorifics, like *sadet* (prince) or *tan* (sir), were pushed aside by the universal use of *sahay* (comrade). Later, in July 1976, Phoumi Vongvichit, Deputy Prime Minister and Minister of Education, Sports and Religious Affairs, gave lectures on changes to Lao grammar and modifications in the Lao script. These linguistic shifts were most apparent among bureaucrats and in cities, but were initially often ignored by the peasants.

When reform of orthodox communism began in the 1990s, however, the ease with which Lao people reverted to an older deferential language in everyday life, and then increasingly in official speech, but still less so in print, was remarkable. As I observed in *Lao Peasants Under Socialism* (1990), many peasants ignored the language reforms anyway, and because they constitute the linguistic majority, as well as being the ones most likely to need deferential political language, they therefore constituted an enormous source of linguistic inertia.[2] Alongside the everyday reality of deferential linguistic habits within the family and village, the realities of political hierarchy, and the renewed reality of socio-economic inequality following the implementation of new market oriented economic policies in the 1990s, drew the older forms of language out of hiding and they have today swept most of the revolutionary terminology aside. For example, the more neutral appellation of *pathan*, president or vice-president, was introduced at all levels of organization, such as for the head of the Buddhist association who became *pathan song*, rather than *phra sangkarat*, and provincial heads, *chao khoueng* became *pathan khoueng*, and this reform went on right down to the village level. But today one rarely hears the term *pathan*, except when people refer to the president of the country. Similarly, at the opening of all meetings in the past one would refer to the people gathered as *banda sahay* (all comrades), whereas today it is the more respectful *banda tan* (all sirs). In the early days one would hear the more populist village style *hao* (we/I), but now it is the older form *khapachao* (I, literally, 'slave of the Buddha'), which first began to appear in speeches by Party leader Kaysone in the early 1980s. The polite response *doy*, sometimes coupled with *kanoy* (literally 'small slave'), has swept back into linguistic fashion, especially in the capital Vientiane. Nevertheless, in the absence of the monarchy, royal language has not made a full comeback in Laos, although it is encoded in rituals. Yet, through various forms of mass media Lao are exposed to Thai *rasasap* (royal language) and the higher status forms that this entails. In the main cities of Laos today one can observe widespread imitation of Thai forms of speech. Many years ago, Charles Keyes (1967: 60) observed that the ethnic Lao in the Thai northeast admired Thai elite culture because it held out the attractions of upward social mobility. Something similar has been occurring in Laos in the past decade, especially among youth.

In thinking about the apparent ease with which 'the old regime could come back', it is worth considering Paul Connerton's argument concerning 'inertia in social structures'. He argues:

Both commemorative ceremonies and bodily practices therefore contain a measure of insurance against the process of cumulative questioning entailed in all discursive practices. This is the source of their importance and persistence as mnemonic systems. Every group, then, will entrust to bodily automatisms the values and categories that they are most anxious to conserve. They will know how well the past can be kept in mind by habitual memory sedimented in the body.

(Connerton 1989: 102)

Much of what is 'sedimented in the body' among the Lao comes from religious practice. Zago writes of young boys 'who may go to the pagoda school and there learn to read and recite sacred texts. Even in home life, and in conversations, ritual practices furnish multiple occasions in which they come to understand, feel and model themselves within a Buddhist vision of existence. Later, a short period passed in the monastery deepens this experience' (1972: 44). The respect and deference paid to monks and buddhas (and kings) through the *nop*, the clasping of the palms of one's hands together in a prayerful motion, is the model of respectful behaviour and deference. This action is repeated in front of elders and other superiors, and as a general greeting, with added subtleties of height of the hands, length of time held, degree of bowing of the head, etc. For some years after the revolution this gesture was discouraged in political/state public spaces, except in the countryside, to be replaced by the more egalitarian handshake, or hugging and kissing if receiving 'comrades' – something acquired from Soviet practice. These latter practices were problematic, in that they not only blurred status, but they also entailed physical contact with strangers, which was especially disturbing in cross-sex encounters, and caused considerable psycho-physical unease – often coped with by a typically Lao burst of shy laughter. These practices were happily abandoned with the disintegration of socialism, but well before that the *nop*, with women in the lead, began to reappear in public life. Today this gesture is widespread, although not as common (nor as compulsory) as in Thailand where its practice is buttressed within the state by the fact that public servants are servants of the king. For a long time this form of salutation of teachers in Lao schools was also suppressed, but it has returned in the 1990s.

Among the many other means by which memories of an older world were reproduced were the rituals conducted by mostly female spirit mediums or *nang tiam*. Initially they were radically suppressed not only because of the communists' general hostility to 'superstitious' practices but also because the spirits they called upon were usually aristocrats from Laos's heroic past. In more recent times, however, mediums have flourished. Similarly, a crucial life-rite spirit-calling ceremony, the *baci* or *sou khouan*, was restricted in the immediate aftermath of the revolution, although it was never entirely

suppressed as it is such a fundamental ritual in Lao family life. This ritual practice too has flourished with the relaxation of communist orthodoxy.

An interesting feature of both spirit medium rituals and the *baci/sou khouan*
is their imitation of 'royal style'. According to Van Esterik (1980: 102–3) it is
'royal style which brings local ritual into a specifiable relation with royal or
court ritual. Royal style in village ritual provides a symbolic pattern for visu-
alizing and manipulating the relation between royalty and commoner.' Here
she is referring to Thailand and its intact monarchy, whereas in Laos today the
structure of the rituals can only allude to this relationship while drawing
participants into a mythical time associated with an ideal Buddhist community. Royal style is most apparent in *nang tiam* ceremonies where the women
dress as princes or lords, because while they are possessed they are princes and
lords, and are treated as such in this idealized ritual time frame. In marriage
ceremonies the bride and groom dress as a princess and a prince. This is much
more apparent in recent times, especially for grooms, who are forsaking the
austere style encouraged after 1975 and returning to formal, courtly style.
Abhay (1959: 140) records elements of the traditional banter on the arrival of
the groom's party at the bride's house. Representatives of the latter ask:
'Where does the master come from? What mountains did he come across, and
what is his wish?' To which his side replies: 'We are coming from a Palace built
of stones, where innumerable quantities of gold and silver are piling up. Every
new day brings us treasures of gold, and each new night, silver.' Of course, it is
precisely such rhetoric that the new regime objected to after 1975, but the
very structure of the ritual is making its return in recent times irresistible.
Young men about to be ordained are treated as young princes who are about
to enact the passage of renunciation of Prince Gautama. And in the ritual
sequences of all of these occasions there is a *baci*, the centrepiece of which, the
pha khouan, images Mount Meru and invokes a broader Buddhist cosmology.
For the duration of the ritual the *pha khouan* becomes the centre of the
world. Before 1975 a *baci* would begin: 'This is a very propitious day, a very
appropriate one, the day when the victorious King re-enters his Palace!'
(Abhay 1959: 130). Such explicit royal references were dropped after 1975,
but the overall royal style could not be erased. In fact, the very structure of
ritual language was shot through with royal style and has left an indelible
imprint on this most widespread of Lao rituals.

The That Luang festival held in November centred on the famous stupa in
Vientiane has become a national festival, which overshadows the 2 December
national day in the new Laos. This Buddhist festival was previously presided
over by the king, and many of the rituals surrounding this event that have
been progressively revived in the 1990s point in the direction of the absent
king. Nowhere is this more apparent than in the other key public ritual of the
Lao calendar New Year in the old royal capital Luang Prabang (officially now
held between 13 and 15 April) where the king was previously the central
ritual figure in rites of purification carried out in the city. The parading of the

famous Buddha statue, the Prabang, from the old palace to the former royal temple Vat May remains one of the central religious activities of the New Year in Luang Prabang. This holy relic, the palladium of the former kingdom, after appropriate rituals by leading members of the Buddhist sangha, is carried down the steps by museum attendants (no longer by monks, as described by Deydier 1954: 156), and placed in its palanquin. In 1996, when I last witnessed this ritual, just before the descent of the Prabang, the foreign minister, Lengsavad and the *chao khouang* of Luang Prabang lined up on the steps of the palace, dressed in traditional sampots. Previously it would have been the king who followed the Prabang to Vat May, and begun its purification. Now a high official in the LPDR fills his shoes. The Prabang is then returned to the old palace on 18 April. Just inside the grounds, a new resting place for the Prabang, begun under the old regime, is being built with its main sponsor being the Lao government and business.

Around this time of year in Luang Prabang a story has circulated every year about whether the Prabang today is real or just a copy. Rumour has it that the communist government removed the real one and placed it in a vault somewhere. I have heard this story many times. One person assured me she had

Figure 12.1 Baci Luang, or Royal Spirit calling ceremony, held by Lao Royals in exile in Paris every year at the time of Lao New Year. This attempt to ritually recreate the monarchy in exile has been slowly weakened as the communist state has re-traditionalised itself. Photo: Grant Evans.

Figure 12.2 The Thai King during his visit to Laos in 1994 arrives at the central
stupa, That Luang, in the capital city Vientiane to make offerings to
the monks there. Behind him stands the communist Prime Minister
(now President), Khamtay Siphandone. Photo: Grant Evans.

heard it from an official in the Ministry of Information and Culture in Luang
Prabang, and therefore it had to be correct! Perhaps even more astonishingly,
during an interview with me in May 1996, the vice-president of the Lao
sangha said, yes the Prabang in Luang Prabang is a fake. He claimed that in
1976 Sali Vongkhamsao, then attached to Prime Minister Kaysone's office,
went to Luang Prabang with an entourage and brought the Prabang back to
Vientiane, the seat of government. This story was obviously formed around the
assumptions of traditional cosmology that assumed that now that the communists had taken over they were the heirs of its powers.[3] Of course, I have no
way of confirming the rumour one way or another, although I believe it is
untrue. But what is important about this story from an anthropological point
of view is that it suggests that people somehow feel that the ritual since 1975
has become debased and is even 'fake', too. The fact that the person telling you
the story of the Prabang being a fake will go and pay homage to the Prabang
during the New Year ritual confirms this interpretation, showing that the

rumour reflects on the ritual as a whole rather than the object itself. It is also a comment on the collapse of the monarchy, on the pressure that Buddhism came under in the early years of the revolution, and perhaps even a comment on the illegitimacy of the Lao government. For possession of the Prabang historically has been an objectification of the legitimacy of the Lao monarchy. The idea of it being a fake therefore withdraws this legitimacy from the communist regime.[4]

Becoming a memory

King Sisavang Vatthana was forced to abdicate just before the declaration of the LPDR on 2 December 1975, and he and the former RLG prime minister, Prince Souvanna Phouma, were appointed as advisers to the new president, the 'Red Prince' Souphannouvong, who was the latter's half-brother. 'The abdication', writes Dommen, 'deprived the majority of Laos's inhabitants of their country's soul, both spiritual and temporal' (1985: 113). The abdication came as such a shock to many Lao that Pathet Lao's deputy prime minister, Phoumi Vongvichit, was compelled in late December to respond to 'rumours spread by the enemy that we had dismissed the King … Realizing that the monarchy had blocked the progress of the country, the King abdicated and turned over power to the people. He abdicated intentionally … The King is still in his palace, and is now Supreme Adviser to the President of the country. He is still enjoying his daily life as before, and his monthly salary will be sent to him as usual. The only difference is that he is no longer called King' (*SWB* 31/12/75).

In April 1976, the now ex-King was enjoined to vacate his palace in Luang Prabang. In a ceremony presided over by Phoumi Vongvichit, the palace along with its relics, including the sacred palladium, the Prabang, were 'donated' as a museum and Sisavang Vatthana moved into Hong Xieng Thong, his private residence beside the royal temple, Vat Xieng Thong. In March 1977, following *pattikan* ('reactionary') activities in the north, with whom they were alleged to have had some association, the ex-king, his wife and two sons (Vong Savang, the crown prince, and Prince Sisavang) were arrested and sent to the old revolutionary base area of Viengsai, where they apparently died of illness. Mystery still surrounds their arrest and deaths, and the regime itself has never offered an official explanation, while the whereabouts of their remains is a closely guarded secret.[5] As late as December 1996 I have overheard guides in the now palace museum telling tourists that the king is still away 'at seminar'. When challenged about the truth of this they say the king's whereabouts are a 'state secret'.

Prince Souvanna Phouma, on the other hand, continued to act as an adviser to the President until his death in January 1984, whereupon he was given a state funeral. Led by chanting Buddhist monks and Souphannouvong, his cremation took place at the That Luang pagoda, but his remains were taken to Luang Prabang, where they were interred in a family stupa at Vat That which also contains the remains of the legendary Prince Phetsarath, his older brother.

Despite the suppression of royalist references after the revolution it was the numinous figure of Prince Souphannouvong who maintained a high profile for Laos's royal past. He became a powerful symbolic figure 'precisely because, like all dominant or focal symbols, he represented a coincidence of opposites, a semantic structure in tension between opposite poles of meaning' (Turner 1974: 88–9). Almost always referred to in official pronouncements as either 'Comrade' or 'President', in everyday speech he was commonly called 'Prince Souphannouvong'. Interestingly this 'lapse' was also registered in the title of a collection of essays on him published in 1990, where in both Lao and English he was referred to as 'Prince'. The title in Lao is: 'Prince Souphannouvong: Revolutionary Leader'.[6] Unusually, the Party paper *Pasason* (30/11/95) also referred to him as 'Prince'.

For this reason, on his death on 9 January 1995, one perhaps may have expected an overflow of nostalgia for the past.[7] The state, however, maintained strict control over the funeral. Five days national mourning was declared for 'one of its best loved leaders', and his body lay in state at the National Assembly until the final high Buddhist funeral ceremony on January 15. As with Souvannaphouma there had been some speculation about whether the funeral would be held in Luang Prabang, or whether his ashes would be returned there. But, one hundred days after the cremation, led by 15 monks, Souphannouvong's family made merit for him along with President Nouhak and other party leaders, and his ashes were placed in a stupa at That Luang in Vientiane. To bury him in Luang Prabang would have re-confirmed that city's claim as royal and ritual centre.[8] Souphannouvong, however, now rests at what is today firmly established as the national shrine, That Luang. While this may seem to be the final eclipsing of the Buddhist monarchy by secular politics based in Vientiane, the shrine where he rests is a Buddhist shrine built by a Lao king. Thus this numinous figure retains his symbolic ambiguity.

But perhaps the most important royal figure in Laos today is Prince Phetsarath, who was the son of the uncle and viceroy, *ouparat*,[9] to King Sisavang Vong, and grew up with the king. He studied in France and briefly at Oxford, returning to Laos where he earned a reputation as an effective administrator. He was elevated to the position of *ouparat* in 1941. He played an important role in the Lao Issara (Free Laos) government, which seized power in Vientiane in October 1945 after the Japanese surrender. He died in late 1959. Because of his role in the Lao Issara, of which the LPRP claims to be the heir, Phetsarath is now a relatively legitimate historical royal figure under the LPDR. In recent years a cult, not unlike that surrounding King Chulalongkorn in neighbouring Thailand, has begun to form around him and so one will often come across his photo in houses, shops or temples. But Phetsarath is a popular figure not primarily because of his political role, although important legends have grown up around this, but because he is considered to have magical powers; he is *saksit*.[10] This reputation partly arose from his deep interest in astrology, about which he published a book in Thai in the 1950s. Anthropologist Joel Halpern recounts how during an expedition with Phetsarath in Luang Prabang in 1958, villagers would approach Phetsarath to carry out purification rites. He also tells stories he heard about the prince:

> One asserted that Prince Phetsarath had the power to change himself into a fish and could swim under water for long distances. It was said that bullets could not harm him. He was also reputed to have the ability to change his form, so that at a conference with the French at the time of the Free Lao Movement, he became angry with them, changed himself into a fly, and flew out the window ... People from many parts of the Kingdom often write to him requesting his picture, and some of them place it in their rice fields to keep away malevolent spirits. (Prince Boun Oum is felt by some to have similar powers.)
>
> (Halpern 1964: 124)

Stories about the prince's magical powers are still widespread. His pictures are used for protection against malevolent *phi* (spirits), and a protective amulet of him is on sale.

Almost as substitutes for Laos's 'disappeared' royalty, Thai royalty since 1990 has been playing an increasingly important, if subtle, role in Laos. Thai royals act as patrons of development projects, just as they do in Thailand, and as patrons of Buddhism, as they do in Thailand too. Ordinary Lao seem to obliquely recognize the parallel. Indeed, on walls in shops and businesses and in private homes throughout Laos, one will find calendars with pictures of Thai royalty occupying the same place that Lao royalty would have occupied in the past. In the showrooms of some retailers in Vientiane one can see proudly displayed the photo of an elite Lao family during their audience with the Thai king. Others who have met Princess Sirindhorn also proudly display photos of their encounter. Calendar pictures of the Thai king by himself or with his wife, and calendars with pictures of Princess Sirindhorn, or the crown prince of Thailand, can all be found. While these are distributed much less widely than in Thailand, their mere presence is significant because of the symbolic space they occupy, and because similar pictures of the former Lao king have been taboo. This taboo appears to apply especially to Sisavang Vatthana, and less strictly to Sisavang Vong. It was only after 1990 that people started to bring out of hiding old photos of the former kings, but much of this memorabilia had been destroyed after 1975, and is not reproduced yearly on calendars, for example, as with Thai royalty. Thus there is a diminishing supply of such reminders of the Lao royal past.

Princess Sirindhorn appears to act as the special envoy of Thai royalty to Laos. She has visited Laos every year since 1990, travelling to different parts of the country to familiarise herself with it and to hand out largesse at schools and hospitals, and of course to be received enthusiastically by the various *chao khoueng* and their wives. She has given large donations to two of the oldest royal temples in Vientiane, Vat Inpheng and Vat Ong Teu, and to temples in Luang Prabang and elsewhere in Laos. She has, in a sense, become Laos's princess.[11]

The most important occasion, however, was the visit of the Thai king and queen to Laos on 8–9 April 1994 for the opening of the Lao–Thai Friendship Bridge. It was the first visit abroad by the Thai king in twenty-seven years, a significant fact in itself. But it was also significant because the Thai king had never visited Laos when it was a kingdom. Only when the Lao king was no longer present did he visit. King Bhumibol and King Sisavang Vatthana did meet once, however, on a floating pavilion moored in the middle of the Mekong River off Nong Khai on the occasion of the inauguration of the Ngam Ngum Dam on 16 December 1968. Photos at the time show the much younger Thai king and the Lao king, both dressed in ceremonial military uniforms, shaking hands. In April 1994 the Thai king once again stood in the middle of the Mekong, this time in a pavilion erected on the new bridge, and this time with the aged communist president, Nouhak Phoumsavan. That night after a reception at the Presidential Palace in Vientiane a Lao orchestra played songs composed by the Thai king. The next morning the king paid an official visit to the national shrine, That Luang, accompanied by the president and prime minister and a large entourage. The king and queen and the princess offered flowers, incense and candles as tribute to the Lord Buddha while monks chanted their blessing. They then made offerings to the monks and presented a contribution to the president of the Buddhist Association, Venerable Vichit Singalat, for the maintenance of the stupa. After That Luang they visited an orphanage placed under the patronage of the princess during her visit in 1990, and again in 1992, and for which she had raised the equivalent of 342,000 baht and donated a further 285,000. In an audience with the king that afternoon Thai businessmen in Laos donated a further 2.5 million baht in support of this royally sponsored project, a conventional way for Thai business people to earn merit through association with the king.

Finally, a *baci*, sponsored by the president and the prime minister and their wives, was held for the royal couple and the princess at the Presidential Palace. In attendance were all the ministers, vice ministers, selected high officials and their wives. The seating arrangements only partially conformed to Thai protocol. The Lao president and prime minister and their wives sat on chairs at the same level as the Thai royal visitors underlining their equality, while before them, seated on the floor around the *pha khouan*, were the Lao high officials and their wives, acknowledging their own ritual inferiority (*VT* 11/4/94). What is striking about this occasion is the ease with which the Lao officials and their wives conformed to royal protocol, and the obvious delight they took in moving within the charmed circle of the Thai king.

One of the most important occasions in the ritual calendar of the Thai king is the *kathin* ceremony held at the end of the Buddhist lent. In October 1995 the Thai king extended his yearly sponsorship of the *sangha* to Laos. General Siri Thivaphanh from the Ministry of Foreign Affairs in Thailand, on behalf of the king, offered one set of monk requisites and donations of 510,000 baht to Vat That Luang Neua in Vientiane for the renovation the temple and the promotion of Buddhism. What was most interesting about this occasion was that joining in the merit-making were President Nouhak, Prime Minister Khamtay and Foreign Minister Somsavath. The offerings were made again in 1996 and thereafter and it was as if the Thai king had become a proxy for Lao royalty.

The kingdom in exile

Although King Sisavang Vatthana was encouraged by some people to flee into exile he refused, apparently saying that he preferred to die on Lao soil. The crown prince also stayed, as did the king's second son, Prince Sisavang. His two daughters and his last son, Sauryavong, slipped across the Mekong in December into exile, along with other members of the aristocracy, many of whom had held important positions in the RLG. Of those who remained behind, the men were rounded up and sent off to long years in the 're-education' camps.

The RLG remnants attempted to form a government in exile and an armed resistance to the communist regime, and all swore allegiance to the deposed king. But they were factionalized and weak, and their supporters were either confined in refugee camps or already scattered around the world. Only the remnants of the Hmong soldiers formerly commanded by General Van Pao, who also remained loyal to the king, provided serious military opposition to the new regime. They were, however, ferociously crushed in campaigns over 1977 by Vietnamese and Pathet Lao troops. From then on armed resistance was sporadic, and the Lao in exile were more of an ideological threat to the new regime than an armed one.

Because of their long-standing connections with France, most of the former Lao elite and aristocrats found exile there. With their country under what they believed was virtually foreign occupation (because of Vietnamese communist influence in the Pathet Lao regime) they saw one of their major tasks being a cultural one – to preserve 'traditional' Laos. One of the Lao Women's Association's main tasks was to organize traditional Lao dances and to train the young in such cultural skills as well as to offer classes in Lao language and history. As one of these children who grew to maturity in France has subsequently documented, social occasions are crucial public demonstrations of former status:

> In the cultural and social parties, men and women are excessively elegant which often has little to do with their actual standard of living. Men wear ties and brand-name suits, while women display traditional dresses in

shimmering silk. Dresses costing from US$150 to US$800 are not unusual in a Lao refugee woman's wardrobe: appearance-conscious, she rarely wears the same dress in the same season and thus participates in an illusory, glittering world. There is a hierarchy in the parties that must be respected. The Samakhom's parties are attended by former personalities, the *'phou nyai'*, whereas others attract a younger set. And when one belongs to the elite, one cannot escape from some parties or marriage celebrations. The way tables and tables of honour are organised in these events show the social stratification that existed in Laos before 1975, and this is re-enacted in France, for an evening or a meeting.

(Sisombat-Souvannavong 1999)

Weddings are also crucial occasions for demonstrating status and adherence to custom, especially royal weddings.

The key ritual event of the year for those in exile is the Baci Louang, or Grand Baci, held every New Year at a time dictated by the traditional Lao calendar. This spirit calling ceremony, a ritual of integration, was a high point of the year under the RLG when key ministers and individuals from around the country would gather at the palace in Luang Prabang. Today it is held in a large hall in the suburbs of Paris and is organized by the Fa Ngum Association.[12] Guests are issued invitations, for which there is considerable competition, and Lao exiles from overseas also attend this temporary re-creation of the kingdom in exile. Since 1984, after the exile community conceded that the king and the crown prince were dead, the government in exile declared Prince Sauryavong as regent. In 1981 the seventeen-year-old eldest son of the crown prince, Soulivong, and his younger brother had escaped across the Mekong and made their way to France, and this young man, as pretender to the throne, took his place at the centre of this ritual. Only the women attend this ceremony in traditional dress, except for the regent and the crown prince who wear the traditional gentleman's dress, the *sampot*. An aristocratic inner circle, plus former members of the elite, kneel around the regent and his wife, the regent's elder sister princess Savivan, and the crown prince who sit elevated on chairs, while former ritual officiants from the palace lead the ritual and invoke the former glory of the kingdom in their prayers. The majority of the people watch this from their tables around the hall. It is followed by a dinner, a display of traditional Lao dancing, including ethnic minority dances,[13] and then a dance for all.

Culturally conservative in its desire to preserve things 'as they were' and to preserve a pool of counter-memory to the new regime, these exiles have also been challenged by the changes that have taken place in Laos with the global collapse of communism and the attempts by the LPDR to cloak itself in tradition. The latter has had the effect of highlighting the theatricality of these exile ritual performances. Now both the exiles and the LPDR compete for ritual authenticity, but it is an uneven battle given the regime's possession of all the key sacred spaces in the form of temples, stupas and even the palace itself. Furthermore, as the years pass, the exile's children have been fundamentally shaped by their host culture and can be accused of not being 'authentic' heirs of Lao 'national culture'. Since the relaxation of political controls in Laos some of the latter have returned to see the fabled land of which they may have only childhood memories, and many find it surprisingly alien.

For some years the Lao in exile have realized that their hope of a political reversal of the LPDR is a mirage, but they have been buoyed up by their sense of cultural authenticity. But as the LPDR reaches its twenty-fifth year in power even the younger leaders during their initial exile are approaching retirement age and their thoughts are turning to the prospect of dying in a foreign land. Some are quietly returning to Laos to die and be cremated there.

Conclusion

The state-sponsored 'revival of tradition' in Laos today by a post-socialist government in search of legitimacy raises important theoretical questions concerning the nature of change and continuity in Lao culture.

A great deal of popular religious ideology based on Buddhism, and a great deal of ritual practice in Laos today, presumes a 'galactic polity' (Tambiah 1976) with a king at the center. Thus the return to 'tradition' in Laos by the LPRP is not without its problems because the whole structure of 'Lao tradition', its rituals in particular, revolve around certain principles which are continually pointing in the direction of a monarch who is no longer there and who cannot be mentioned. Overthrow of the *sakdina*, 'feudal', system has been the central raison d'être of the regime up to now, therefore any suggestion of a royal revival would naturally pose the question: 'why the revolution?'[14] For this reason all questions relating to the monarchy remain extremely sensitive. When asked about the fate of the old king by a BBC journalist at a press conference during the regime's twentieth anniversary, the foreign minister, Somsavath Lengsavad, was visibly unnerved and angry.[15] The government, however, attempts to fill this absence by stepping into the king's shoes – structurally that is – on ritual occasions, such as with the foreign minister himself when the Prabang was brought out of the palace during the New Year celebrations in 1996. This cultural structure which now evokes both a sense of absence and of presence also combines with an awareness that such rituals do not have the same grandeur as before. Yet, it is also a structural space able to be filled by Thai royalty from a distance, at least in the imagination.

Having deserted communism and having failed to create potent rituals or symbolic centres of their own, the LPRP leaders have spontaneously gravitated towards older sacred centres of the cultural order. In doing this they have been responding to a deeper cultural programme, and in this regard it is important to understand that these leaders (or the majority of them) were brought up to be culturally Lao, imbibing Buddhist ideas from their infancy, and learning to act and speak like Lao. Indeed, with the reforms one cannot help but feel that everyone is more comfortable, and as I remarked when discussing bacis for visiting royals, the new Lao elite responded smoothly and joyfully to the protocol. In all this one senses a growing congruence between power and legitimacy. Geertz has argued for 'the inherent sacredness of central authority' (1985: 33), no matter whether that authority is a king or a party president. He argues that sacred centres 'are essentially concentrated loci of serious acts; they consist in the point or points in a society where its leading ideas come together with its leading institutions to create an arena in which the events that most vitally affect its members' lives take place. It is involvement … with such arenas and with the momentous events that occur in them that confers charisma. It is a sign, not of popular appeal or inventive craziness, but of being near the heart of things' (1985: 14). No doubt this 'inherent sacredness' of power partly helps explain the formation of political cults with semi-divine leaders. But the 'sacredness' of secular leaders is always fragile as their 'majesty' is so clearly made and not born or inherent in the order of things. But a further problem for the communist state was that there was a permanent hiatus between the leading ideas of the culture and the leading institutions of the new regime, which ensured that no coherent and potent 'loci of serious acts' emerged.

For those in exile the opposite problem emerged as the communist regime re-integrated the leading political institutions with the sacred centres of old and were able to draw on the power of these centres and the palladia of power to re-legitimize themselves. This had the effect of weakening the legitimacy of the exiles' claim to be the true guardians of traditional Lao culture. Furthermore, the revival of tradition in Laos has further bolstered the legitimacy of the LPDR internationally, and so unlike the situation in Cambodia, where King Sihanouk retained his place as a legitimate leader thus enabling a comeback, there is no equivalent figure among the Lao exiles. The exiles appear to sense their weakness too, and have been making conciliatory overtures to the LPDR regime.

Trying to grasp the full cultural and social implications of the destruction of the monarchy by the Lao communists is not easy. That it has been a dramatic instance of cultural discontinuity is indisputable. That its loss has culturally enfeebled the country is certainly arguable. Thus one might suggest that with their reversion to a manifestly incomplete 'tradition', the Lao will have greater difficulty differentiating themselves from the Thai. This problem was not as stark while the LPDR remained communist because then a line was drawn sharply in political terms on both sides of the border, and to some extent Vientiane's strong alliance with Hanoi suggested a shift in cultural orientation away from Thailand. The 'bamboo curtain', however, has lifted and now the cultural boundary between the two countries has blurred.

'Leach,' writes Ohnuki-Tierney (1990: 3), 'has repeatedly reminded his colleagues that they cannot think of a culture in the same sense as they think of a society, which is a bounded political unit. Culture, in contrast to society, is never bounded.' In the Thai–Lao case this is most apparent with reference to Buddhism, whose sacred topography as defined by pilgrims does not conform to political topography (Keyes 1975). The opening of the Thai–Lao border once again to Buddhist pilgrims has revived the cultural bonds between the two countries. Lao make pilgrimages to Wat Doi Suthep in Chiang Mai or to the Emerald Buddha in Bangkok, and they once again participate in the long-established rituals of Lao Buddhism associated with Phra That Phanom in the Thai northeast. Meanwhile Thai make pilgrimages to That Inghang, or That Luang, or to the former royal temples of Luang Prabang. In the modern world it has been kings as 'high priests' who have symbolically mediated between the sacred topography of Buddhism and the political topography charted by the state. In this way, modern monarchs have served to anchor their subjects' allegiance to the nation-state despite cultural blurring. The disappearance of the Lao monarch, however, has also led to a blurring of the symbolism of the Thai monarchy in Laos. Hence all over Laos we find images of Thai royalty where once we would have found images of Lao royalty, and it suggests that at least in some respects the Lao have been drawn into the orbit of the Thai realm.

Lao nationalists of all stripes will sometimes complain about the interest taken by ordinary Lao in the rituals and quotidian activities of the Thai royal family, sensitive as they are to the country's loss of similarly potent symbols. For example, during the Thai King's birthday celebrations in December 1998, Thai television was saturated with coverage of the event, and Lao followed it closely. Yet, the extravagance of the event was a cause for comment, at least among some of the young Lao with whom I watched some of this coverage. For them the protocol was 'over the top'. But as Michael Billig's examination of conversations about royalty in the UK points out, an ideology like that of royalty (or nationalism) 'provides the interesting and contrary topics for debate and argumentation' (1990: 78). These young Lao were implicitly asserting one of Laos's claims to distinctiveness compared with the Thai. They generally assert greater simplicity in their practices, and therefore greater authenticity, whether it be in Buddhism or other rituals (interestingly, this is a claim also made by Lao aristocrats about the Lao monarchy). Nevertheless, how royalty should conduct itself was an important issue, and as Billig observes 'the effects of ideology might be gauged by what is *not* a matter for interesting discussion' (1990: 78).

Notes

1   For a detailed discussion of such changes after the revolution see Evans (1998).
2   Paradoxically, however, as the communist reforms of language unevenly penetrated the countryside so the rural areas in the late 1990s have become a source of 'archaic' communist rhetoric. It is among rural cadres that one is now most likely to hear the use of 'comrade'.
3   For good measure, during this same interview he also claimed that the Emerald Buddha on display in Bangkok is also a fake. The real object is kept in an

antechamber to the Thai king's bedroom. To add to such Emerald Buddha stories, in the south of Laos I came across one story which claimed that the real Emerald Buddha is hidden at the old Khmer temple of Vat Phu, the former ritual centre of the Champassak royal line. That one can so easily collect such stories on the recent wanderings of major Buddhist palladia points to a profound sense of ambivalence about the loss of royal centres of power in Laos.

4 S.J. Tambiah (1984: 241) writes on 'the possession of palladia and regalia, which are enduring sedimentations or objectifications of power and virtue. Possession of them is a guarantee of legitimacy. But these sedimentations of virtue and power will remain with the possessor for as long as he is virtuous and deserving. They cannot be removed from their locations against their consent; and their travels are evidence of their changing hands and their passage from one deserving ruler to another. For us, anthropologists and historians, the travels of a Buddha statue, such as those of the Sinhala Buddha (or the Emerald Buddha Jewel) [or the Prabang] provide us with a chain or 'genealogy' of kingdoms and polities that these statues have legitimated ...' It is of interest to note that all of the Lao I know who have visited Bangkok have gone to see the Emerald Buddha Jewel in the Thai king's palace. It is a point of fascination partly because they know it was once housed in Vat Phra Keo in Vientiane. Given its fame, and given its association with Laos's much bigger neighbour, some people have expressed surprise that it is so small and appear to wonder, 'how can something so small be so powerful?' Some have said it is more beautiful than the Prabang, which I have interpreted as being a statement of the relative powers of the two palladia.

5 During a visit to France in December 1989, the General Secretary of the communist party, Kaysone Phomvihane, finally confirmed that the king had died of malaria in 1984, but no other details were provided. For a dogged attempt to trace the final days of the king and his family see Kremmer (1997).

6 The English title is *Autobiography of Prince Souphannouvong*, published by the Committee for Social Sciences, Vientiane, 1990. However, the book is not autobiographical.

7 In fact after 1975 it is not at all clear how popular Souphannouvong was. Many people associated with the RLG saw him as having betrayed their trust and his own royal heritage.

8 Souvanna Phouma's ashes were taken to Luang Prabang and placed in a stupa at Vat That. This stupa also contains the remains of his older brother, the legendary Prince Phetsrath, and some assumed that Souphannouvong's ashes may have been destined for this stupa too. But Vat That in Luang Prabang was historically connected with the 'Vang Na', the Front Palace, compared with Vat That Luang in Luang Prabang, historically connected with the 'Vang Luang', the Main Palace, and the remains of King Sisavangvong rest there in a large stupa. Souvanna Phouma, despite his titular status under the LPDR, was part of the old regime, and not as symbolically potent as his half-brother, and therefore there was less political need to control the disposal of his remains.

9 The *ouparat*, often translated as the 'second king', played a key administrative role in the traditional political structure.

10 *Saksit* is usually translated as 'holy', 'sacred', or 'powerful' in dictionaries, and it most often combines all of these meanings.

11 For a discussion see Keyes (2000).

12 Fa Ngum was the first king of a united Lao kingdom in the fourteenth century. The office-holders in this association are mainly those with aristocratic titles or links.

13 Dances by ethnic minorities are a key ritual activity in the LPDR as well for demonstrating 'minority solidarity'. The similarity in form is striking.

14 It should be said that resistance to a revival would also be based on the fact that the revolution has been a source of rapid upward social mobility for many of its cadres, and has given them a solid material interest in the regime's maintenance.

15 One could interpret this anger as a continuing sign of guilt among the leaders of the new regime. As Walzer has argued in *Regicide and Revolution* (1974: 1), subjects of the king believed in his sacredness and inviolability: 'The murderers of kings presumably do not share these feelings and beliefs, though we may doubt that they escape them entirely.' Walzer argues that the intense debate about whether to execute the king or not after the French Revolution finally came down on the side of public execution because, 'Public regicide is an absolutely decisive way of breaking with the myths of the old regime, and it is for this reason, the founding act of the new' (1974: 5). This decisive public act of symbolic disenchantment never occurred in Laos, hence the older symbolism remained potent, and this is reflected in the guilty secretiveness with which the new regime has surrounded information about the fate of the old king.

Bibliography

SWB: BBC Summary of World Broadcasts: Far East.

VT: *Vientiane Times*, Ministry Information and Culture, LPDR.

Abhay, Thao Nhouy (1959) 'The That Luang Festivities', in René Berval (ed.), *Kingdom of Laos: The Land of the Million Elephants and the White Parasol*, Saigon: France-Asie.

Billig, Michael (1990) 'Collective Memory, Ideology and the British Royal Family', in David Middleton and Derek Edwards (eds), *Collective Remembering*, London: Sage Publications.

Connerton, Paul (1989) *How Societies Remember*, Cambridge: Cambridge University Press.

Deydier, Henri (1954) *Lokapala: Génies, totems et sorciers du Nord Laos*, Paris: Libraire Plon.

Dommen, Arthur J. (1985) *Laos: The Keystone to Indochina*, Boulder, CO: Westview Press.

Evans, Grant (1990) *Lao Peasants Under Socialism*, New Haven, CT and London: Yale University Press.

—— (1998) *The Politics of Ritual and Remembrance: Laos Since 1975*, Chiang Mai/University of Hawaii Press: Silkworm Books.

Geertz, Clifford (1985) 'Centers, Kings, and Charisma: Reflections on the Symbolics of Power', in Sean Wilentz (ed.), *Rites of Power: Symbolism, Ritual and Politics Since the Middle Ages*, Philadelphia: University of Pennsylvania Press.

Halpern, Joel M. (1964) *Government, Politics, and Social Structure in Laos: A Study of Tradition and Innovation*, Monograph Series No. 4, Southeast Asia Studies, Yale University.

Keyes, Charles (1967) *Isan: Regionalism in Northeastern Thailand*, Cornell Thailand Project, Interim Reports Series, Number 10.

—— (1975) 'Buddhist Pilgrimage Centres and the Twelve-Year Cycle: Northern Thai Moral Orders in Time and Space', *History of Religions* 15: 71–89.

—— (2000) 'A Princess in a People's Republic: A New Phase in the Construction of the Lao Nation', in Andrew Turton (ed.), *Civility and Savagery: Social Identity in Tai States*, London: Curzon Press.

Kremmer, Christopher (1997) *Stalking the Elephant Kings: In Search of Laos*, Chiang Mai: Silkworm Books.

Ohnuki-Tierney, Emiko (1990) 'Introduction: The Historicization of Anthropology', in Emiko Ohnuki-Tierney (ed.), *Culture Through Time: Anthropological Approaches*, Stanford, CA: Stanford University Press.

Reynolds, Frank (1978) 'The Holy Emerald Jewel: Some Aspects of Buddhist Symbolism and Political Legitimation in Thailand and Laos', in Bardwell L. Smith (ed.), *Religion and Legitimation of Power in Thailand, Laos and Burma*, Singapore: Anima Books.

Sisombat-Souvannavong, Si-ambhaivan (1999) 'Elites in Exile: The Emergence of a Transnational Lao Culture,' in Grant Evans (ed.), *Laos: Culture and Society*, Chiang Mai: Silkworm Books.

Tambiah, S.J. (1976) *World Conqueror and World Renouncer*, Cambridge: Cambridge University Press.

—— (1984) *The Buddhist Saints of the Forest and the Cult of Amulets*, Cambridge: Cambridge University Press.

Turner, Victor (1974) *Dramas, Fields, and Metaphors: Symbolic Action in Human Society*, Ithaca, NY and London: Cornell University Press.

Van Esterik, Penelope (1980) 'Royal Style in a Village Context', *Contributions to Asian Studies* 15.

Walzer, Michael (1974) *Regicide and Revolution: Speeches at the Trial of Louis XVI*, London: Cambridge University Press.

Zago, Marcel (1972) *Rites et Ceremonies en Milieu Bouddhiste Lao*, Documenta Missionala 6, Universita Gregoriana, Editrice, Roma.

Part III

Elites, professionals and networks

Chapter 13

How far can you go?

English Catholic elites and the erosion of ethnic boundaries

John Eade

The relevance of English Catholics for wider debates about elites

Except for Mary Douglas (1966, 1970/73), anthropologists have shown scant interest in Britain's largest ethnic minority, preferring to concentrate on rural communities and 'black and Asian' urban minorities.[1] Anthropological research has usually looked beyond the world of church institutions and parish life towards religious and secular pilgrimage as well as 'new age' and other cults.[2] The Catholic presence in England and other parts of the United Kingdom has been left to historians and sociologists, despite the ethnic and racial boundaries that have long served to distinguish Catholics as a distinctive minority. Consequently, any contemporary discussion of English Catholic elites for an anthropological audience has to rely on research undertaken by those operating beyond anthropological boundaries and cannot proceed far from suggesting the avenues which future anthropological research might pursue. Since one of the best ways to study elites anthropologically is to focus on how they reproduce themselves over time, I will develop in this chapter an ethnographic case study of Catholic educational changes during the late nineteenth century. Using Giddens's definition of elites as consisting of those 'at the head of a specific social organisation which has an internal authority structure' (1973: 120), I will explore the ways in which highly educated Catholics have looked beyond their community's leaders and institutions towards mainstream elites. While the Catholic educational system has survived into the new millennium, Catholic elites now provide only one among numerous avenues for ambitious English Catholics entering middle-class occupations.

From ascription to choice: the decline of a 'Fortress Church'

During the nineteenth century and the first half of the twentieth century the vast majority of Catholics in the country came from the urban Irish working class. The ethnic boundary between Catholics and outsiders was defined by a mingling of social, cultural and political forces where an ecclesiastical elite, with strong ties to Continental Europe, claimed to represent a united community to powerful outsiders. The scattering of Catholic aristocratic families maintained an ambiguous position within this ethnic minority (memorably envisioned through *Brideshead Revisited* written by Evelyn Waugh, a middle-class convert, and published in 1945). The separate system of Catholic schools, inaugurated by the Poor Schools Committee from 1850, provided primary education for working-class, Irish settlers in the inner city areas of London, Birmingham, Liverpool and Glasgow — a system closely tied to the ecclesiastical structure of diocese and parish. The pre-war religious elite was partly recruited through this educational system that led to seminaries provided by particular dioceses across Britain or those based in the heartland of Catholic Europe (Italy, Spain, Portugal). The educational training of the religious elite encouraged a sense of ethnic distinctiveness where social and cultural associations with the 'home country' (Ireland) blended with the 'Roman' influences of Catholic Europe. These associations and influences narrowed the gulf between the religious elite and the mass of 'ordinary' Catholics.

A number of private, boarding Catholic schools had also been established on the British public school model before 1939. They attempted to provide a Catholic context for the education of the minute landed elite and a larger number of middle class children from urban homes. Elite Catholics were still attracted by the most prestigious mainstream public schools. Yet they were vulnerable to appeals insisting on 'their duty' to send their sons away to Ampleforth, Beaumont, Downside and Stonyhurst and their daughters to the Sacred Heart school at Roehampton or St Mary's Ascot, for example. Yet for parents wanting their children to meet the 'right kinds of people' in non-Catholic elite circles, the Catholic boarding schools provided a far more limited range of contacts than the mainstream public schools.

The pre-Second World War system of Catholic education was considered by the religious elite as the bastion of the community's distinctiveness — however disastrous to the sensibilities of its pupils! Consequently, Catholic opinion was mobilised in defence of that system when the financial implications of the 1944 Education Act were fully appreciated (see Hornsby-Smith 1987). During the 1950s the state responded to pressure from Catholic as well as Anglican leaders by gradually increasing its grant to 'the voluntary sector'. The rapid expansion of Catholic and Anglican schools and colleges during the 1960s and 1970s was made possible through state support rising from 50 per cent to 85 per cent of the total costs incurred (Hornsby-Smith 1987: 161). A 'new middle class' emerged which moved through higher education[3] into professional occupations where their religious affiliation had become more a matter of personal conviction than public significance.

Since the end of the Second World War increasing social pluralism among English Catholics has been accompanied by the rapid decline of anti-Catholic prejudice. While the weakening of separatism between Catholics and others may have been most apparent in the suburbs, even in inner city areas such as London's East End, where working-class Irish settlers had long encountered a range of social exclusions, anti-Catholic feeling had clearly waned by the early 1980s. Some of the principal causes appear to be (a) social and cultural assimilation into mainstream society associated with (b) the decline of inner city, Irish working-class communities, and (c) the movement of Catholics into the suburbs as educational mobility encouraged the rapid expansion of Catholic middle-class families.

The dissolution of a 'distinctive Catholic sub-culture' was accompanied by a shift in the nature of Catholic belonging to the Church. No longer was being a Catholic a part of one's intrinsic identity, an indication of ancestry and membership of an identifiably distinct religio-ethnic community, something normally ascribed. Now Catholics were invited to make a positive choice and affirm the calling to participate fully in the work of the whole 'People of God' (Hornsby-Smith 1991: 9).

The reforms initiated by the Second Vatican Council during the 1960s played a prime role in encouraging this transformation. The Council, held in Rome between 1962 and 1964, was called by Pope John XXIII and was attended by members of the religious elite from around the world. A series of conciliar pronouncements sought to introduce fresh understandings of the Church's temporal mission, which was expressed at the level of ritual practice in a demystified new liturgy and the weakening of traditional markers between Catholics and others (see Douglas 1970/73; Hornsby-Smith 1991). A sense of community was to be shaped by people's active involvement in the affairs of the Church not just locally but globally. 'Belonging' was defined not in terms of ethnicity but 'voluntary religious commitment' (Hornsby-Smith 1991: 9). The combination of social mobility through educational achievement and the religious reforms of the 1960s and 1970s drastically weakened the social and cultural boundaries sustaining the 'Fortress Church'. Religious and social pluralism eroded the ties of ethnicity and class as definitions of Catholic community identity were increasingly left to individual choice and private practice.

The post-Second Vatican Council middle class was educated at British universities where university chaplaincies and parish churches catered for the rapidly expanding numbers of Catholics produced by the Catholic grammar and public schools, as well as those coming from the state sector. These university graduates swelled the ranks of an already long-established Catholic middle class[4] as they entered senior positions in the traditional professions (law, medicine and education), central and local government, the banking and financial sector based around the City of London, and the rapidly expanding realms of the media (television, journalism, advertising) and high technology. They contributed to a wider process of social and economic change taking place during the last three decades of the twentieth century which has been described by sociologists in terms of deindustrialisation, globalisation, the expansion of the private service sector, the emergence of a new service class and the privatisation of state welfare provision (see, for example, Lash and Urry 1994; Amin 1994; Waters 1995).

The changes described by Mike Hornsby-Smith and his colleagues have led the journalist Peter Stanford, in his book *Cardinal Hume and the Changing Face of English Catholicism* (1999) to present English Catholics as a model of assimilation and a source of inspiration for more recent 'black and Asian' settlers:

> The successful integration of Catholics into the mainstream of English society and the Establishment after centuries of persecution and hostility is a story of tolerance to inspire an age when religious and ethnic intolerance is at the heart of so many world disputes. Old prejudices can die. And for other more recent arrivals on the English scene – Muslims, Sikhs, Afro-Caribbeans – who today experience a lack of understanding and discrimination, the example of how the nation has grown to embrace Catholicism is a hopeful one.
>
> (Stanford 1999: 199)

Yet this popular interpretation of secularisation and assimilation has not gone unchallenged. Mary Hickman has pointed to the continuing importance of Irish Catholic community ties and identities in working class, inner city localities across Liverpool and London (Hickman 1990, 1995, 1999). Social class, region and generation are potent forces shaping and sustaining a 'religio-ethnic' identity, which is expressed by second-generation pupils in the local schools. Movement from these working class neighbourhoods into suburban middle class areas has enabled those of Irish descent to choose between:

> secularization, convergence with English Catholicism or retaining a collective-expressive basis to the meaning of their Catholicism. The stronger the Irish identity, the more likely that the first or the third path will be chosen. For those who are secularized their critique of the Church is not necessarily based on the Church's teaching on moral issues (this form of critique is encompassed within English Catholicism), but is possibly also based on a critique of the role of the Church in relation to the Irish community: for example, criticisms of the lack of teaching about Ireland and/or the Church's silence about Northern Ireland.
>
> (Hickman 1999: 198)

It could also be argued that Catholics have benefited from, and may have contributed to, a shift in racial and ethnic differentiation where new exclusions are forged through distinctions between a white majority and 'black and Asian' minorities (see Paul 1997). The new outsiders are negatively defined through constructions of skin colour difference and 'alien' religions, especially

Islam. The old religious distinctions and prejudices[5] between Catholics and non-Catholics may survive but they do not prevent alliances being forged between 'white' residents in opposition to 'black and Asian' citizens (see, for example, Cohen *et al.* 1994; Back 1996). These racialised boundaries may also be producing new lines of division between 'white' and 'black and Asian' Catholics.

Competing Catholic elites and the limits to competition

This expanding middle class sought to take advantage of the reforms accompanying the Second Vatican Council and its aftermath. The greater involvement of lay people in the liturgy was paralleled by formal moves towards increasing lay involvement in decision-making at parish and diocesan levels. During the late 1970s this process of consultation resulted in the 1980 National Pastoral Congress attended 'mainly by lay people but included 42 bishops, 255 clergy, 150 religious men and women and 36 ecumenical observers' (Hornsby-Smith 1987: 37). At this high point of deliberation across diocesan boundaries a lay 'power elite' emerged. This new elite was 'overwhelmingly progressive in its religious ideology and committed to action alternatives in the reforming spirit of the Second Vatican Council' (Hornsby-Smith 1987: 152).

Outside the National Pastoral Congress the influence of the members of this progressive lay elite was mediated through a number of Catholic voluntary organisations whose networks ranged across the nation and, in some cases, the globe. These organisations include the Catholic Institute for International Relations, Catholic Association for Overseas Development, Catholic Association for Racial Justice, Pax Christi, the Justice and Peace Commission. However, the limits of the influence wielded by this power elite when opposed by the Catholic religious hierarchy became clear soon after the Congress had ended. Its members' progressive views on such controversial issues as Catholic teaching on 'marriage, sexuality and contraception', the ordination of women, poverty and war (Hornsby-Smith 1987: 38) alarmed conservative (clerical and lay) groups within the Church hierarchy. Resistance was launched by 'the "established elites" of parish clergy and traditionalist core groups in parishes and organisations', while a more passive form of resistance was encountered from 'the mass of passive, uninvolved nominal Catholics' (Hornsby-Smith 1987: 152).

The election of Pope John-Paul II in 1978 strengthened further the position of those who wished to rein in progressive Catholic lay elites across the globe. The National Pastoral Congress did not result in formal consultation between clerical and lay delegates across diocesan boundaries. The ecclesiastical hierarchy successfully defended their long-established claim to represent the 'community' to the outside world. Lay elite members were forced to exercise their influence through the existing diocesan and parish structures or the voluntary organisations representing specific issues (justice and peace, anti-racism, aid to Third World countries). By the late 1980s the conflict between traditional and progressive leaders remained latent as different networks were formed within separate sectors of the institutional structure. Some progressives resolved this latent conflict by seeking fresh pastures – 'where traditional elites have retained a dominant position, progressives have either been driven to the periphery of the Church or have sought to achieve their goals through secular channels' (Hornsby-Smith 1987: 156).

The growing heterogeneity of the English Catholic lay elite was part of a more general process where the boundaries between highly educated Catholics and non-Catholics rapidly weakened. Catholic religious leaders still fought to maintain their elite status through their pronouncements on a range of moral issues. Some lay Catholics continued to lead the wide range of Catholic voluntary organisations that claimed to represent the Catholic community both across the nation and globally. However, many other highly educated Catholics took scant interest in what others defined as 'Catholic concerns'. Their lifestyles revealed the impress of changing class dynamics and a minimal or residual boundary between themselves as Catholics and others. This process has sharpened the gulf between these middle class Catholics and the surviving pockets of working class Irish Catholic residents in urban 'inner cities' (see Hickman and Boyce in Hornsby-Smith (1999).

The struggle for power between different Catholic elites and the weak-ening boundaries between many middle-class Catholics, who ignored these struggles, and non-Catholics coincided with a decline in the numbers of priests, those in religious orders, and regular attenders of weekly services. Yet this evidence of decline was offset in certain urban localities, especially in London, by the growing numbers of workers and refugees from Catholic-majority countries, such as Poland, Colombia and the Philippines, and greater lay participation in liturgy and administration as power was devolved at the parish level. These developments have helped to soften the blow dealt by the religious elite when it brushed aside the threat to its leadership posed by lay rivals. Rather than directly challenge the religious elite's hegemony many lay leaders have chosen to work within existing Church institutions and develop new forms of religious expression, such as the Renew move-ment, within particular parishes and dioceses (see Hornsby-Smith 1999). This strategy has been encouraged by the pragmatic, 'centrist' policies adopted by Cardinal Hume and continued by his successor, Cormac Murphy-O'Connor.

Murphy-O'Connor was bishop of the Arundel and Brighton diocese, where the Renew movement had been highly active and had attempted to build on the liturgical reforms inspired by the Second Vatican Council. While his ancestry was obviously Irish, he came from a middle-class family rather than the Irish urban working class. When the issue of Irish ancestry was raised by journalists after his election he rejected the narrow confines of the nation and Irish nationalism in particular:

> I come from an Irish family which was very proud to be here. My father was never [an Irish] nationalist and he had no interest in Irish politics. When we were evacuated to Cork at the beginning of the war and I spent two terms in a school there, I was always known as the English boy, so when people ask me whether I am Irish or British I don't answer. I feel a wider context than narrow nationalism.
>
> (*The Guardian* 1 May 2000: 8)

His father's career as a doctor may have helped pay for Murphy-O'Connor's education at a private Catholic secondary school. The future archbishop then moved through the Church's educational system, attending the English College and Gregorian University in Rome. After only one year as a parish priest in Southampton he returned to Rome as Rector of the English College in 1971 and, six years later, was elected Bishop of Arundel and Brighton. His international and ecumenical links were strengthened through such elite positions as chair of the Bishop's Committee for Europe 1978–83, co-chair of the Second Anglican-Roman Catholic International Commission in 1983 and chair of the Bishops' Department for Mission and Unity 1994 (*Who's Who in Catholic Life* 1997). His election to the most senior position within the English Catholic religious elite may well have benefited from the support of the country's foremost old aristocratic family, the Fitzalan-Howards and the Duke of Norfolk in particular, whose ancestral seat overlooks Arundel's Catholic cathedral (see *The Guardian* 2000).

Murphy-O'Connor's rejection of 'narrow nationalism' appears to confirm the decline of the 'fortress church' and the religious elite's refusal to get drawn into communal conflict in Northern Ireland. English and Scottish Catholics are decreasingly seen as alien, and such public figures as Cherie Blair (Booth), Anne Widdecombe, Chris Patten, Charles Kennedy, Michael Martin, Keith Vaz, the Duchess of Kent, Lord Longford, Lord Rees-Mogg and Germaine Greer are not necessarily associated with a Catholic community. English Catholics have become more diverse and this diversity has been encouraged by greater diversification of responsibilities across the structure of parishes and dioceses. Definitions of what is irreducibly Catholic have narrowed and when Catholic leaders have defended what they see as vital Catholic interests they have sought to build an alliance with non-Catholic groups or with the 'national interest'. To understand how this process has developed I will first draw on my experience of working in a Catholic higher education institution during the last three decades and attending mass at a local parish, and then consider what Catholic educational interests were publicly defended during the 1990s.

Roehampton and Putney: educational change and middle-class parishioners

The institution where I teach reflects faithfully the changes described above. I arrived at Roehampton in 1973 to introduce social anthropology at the Digby Stuart teacher training college. The college had been founded by the Sacred Heart religious sisters and had moved to Roehampton from Bayswater in 1946, replacing the private boarding school whose students during the 1930s included Mary Douglas[6] (see O'Leary 1992; Fardon 1999). Digby Stuart has remained a centre for Catholic teacher training but its role has widened as general undergraduate degrees have expanded and a partnership developed, from 1975, with three other local teacher-training colleges. The Roehampton Institute of Higher Education – now the University of Surrey Roehampton (USR) – brought together colleges grounded in Catholic, Anglican, Methodist and non-denominational traditions. These traditions have become more attenuated as students were taught together regardless of religious confession and allocated to a particular college by subject interest, while staff were recruited with little or no regard for their ideological commitment. Those working in the areas of sociology, social policy and anthropology, for example, are now based in Southlands College, a Methodist foundation but recently rebuilt in the grounds of Digby Stuart College. Some Catholic insignia still survive through the occasional statue, crucifix and place name, while the chapel provides a focus for religious expression. Although they may shock some non-Catholic newcomers, these insignia and sites reflect the minimalism of contemporary Catholic college life.

Yet these outward symbols of Catholic identity remain important for the justification of a Catholic presence within the federal structure of the Roehampton colleges and now the federated university – just as religious and/or ancestral symbols and sites are significant for the other colleges. Members of Catholic religious and lay elites are appointed to the Digby Stuart governing body and the college Principal must negotiate the continuing preoccupation among religious and lay elites with moral issues. (During the 1980s, for example, considerable stir was caused by a parent who wrote to the *Daily Telegraph* deploring the request to the governors to allow the introduction of a condom machine in the student union.) Close links with religious and lay elites are maintained through its Catholic teacher training role, the continuing recruitment of Catholic students from London and the Home Counties, the round of activities arranged by the chaplain and assistant chaplain (one male, one female), the recent revival of making a pilgrimage to Lourdes, and extensive social networks.

The changes in college life and teaching reflected the wider religious and educational changes which I outlined in the previous section of this chapter. The weakening institutional and social boundaries between Catholics and others prepared the ground for the appointment of a Sacred Heart sister as the USR's new rector in 1999. She had attended a Catholic grammar school, before studying at Digby Stuart and King's College London. She then taught at the Sacred Heart boarding school at Woldingham and another Sacred Heart college near Newcastle, as well as a Ugandan mission school, before returning to Digby Stuart where she eventually became college principal. Her life as a religious sister is kept separate from her official role, where she works with other members of a national educational elite as one of very few female heads of a higher educational institution. To some of my non-Catholic colleagues, who have a dated image of Catholic religious orders, she does not 'look like a nun at all'.

Like many other higher educational institutions across the nation the new rector and her colleagues were minimally involved in the everyday lives of local residents. The Roehampton site adjoined an extensive council estate built by the Greater London Council as a post-war residential centre for working class families from other areas of the metropolis. The tall blocks, dilapidated shopping area and tough pubs appeared to confirm the estate's reputation for high levels of deprivation and social dislocation.[7] Roehampton 'village' boasted an old-established Catholic church, but over the years there has been little scope or desire for mixing between students and local working-class residents. Students living in the college's residential accommodation can easily avail themselves of the chapel and chaplaincy if they so desire. For 'practising Catholics', who are day students, the choice is largely between college chapel and their home church somewhere in London or the Home Counties. The teaching staff largely commute from various suburban neighbourhoods beyond the council estate.

So differences of social class and some minimal college resources sustain the boundary between Catholic students and local residents in Roehampton. The more middle-class parishes towards Putney and Richmond are far more attractive to staff and students who wanted to get involved in local parish activities. The Putney parish church, for example, is an aesthetically pleasing, brick-built church that complements the imposing arts-and-crafts houses with extensive back gardens surrounding it. It attracts working-class Catholics from the local council estate and privately rented sector but its middle class membership has considerably increased over the last twenty years. Council properties have been sold to owner-occupiers while privately rented houses for multiple occupants have been converted for middle-class families. Perhaps not surprisingly, the vast majority of the middle and working-class worshippers are white; approximately ten per cent of the regular attenders hailed from the Caribbean, Africa, South Asia and the Pacific Rim. The large numbers of cars parked during the three masses on Sundays do not attract the same kinds of hostility that greet the building of mosques in other parts of London (see Eade 1996; Dwyer 2000). No church bells invite worshippers and proclaim the Catholic presence in this middle-class neighbourhood, while religious and community activities are contained within the church, the priests' house, hall and large back garden.

As elsewhere in London, the competition for places at the parish primary school is intense. The competition became even more intense after the publication of the 1999 performance tables where the school came top of the list of local schools. According to one disgruntled, regular mass-attending parent, 'local' children were being eased out by middle-class newcomers. Whatever the truth of this claim, priority was clearly being given to siblings. Of the twenty-two pupils entering the school in 2000, only two were non-siblings; one was the daughter of an American-German professional couple while the other's father was a naval officer, who had bitterly – and successfully – complained when his daughter failed initially to gain a place. English and other British middle-class Catholics vied with North American and continental European professionals who were spending several years in corporate offices and private business ventures across central London. In this highly competitive market the parish priest plays a key role, since applications have to be supported by his letter of commendation.

For these ambitious parents, keeping their children within the local Catholic educational system becomes much more problematic at secondary level. Several Catholic comprehensive schools are available within and across the borough boundaries, but the attraction of private schooling is strengthened by growing concerns about performance, as well as by all the other middle-class misgivings concerning urban comprehensive schooling. Many of those who had been taught at Catholic grammar and comprehensive schools are now pondering the feasibility of encouraging their children to compete for places at local non-Catholic, single-sex private schools – for instance, Putney High, Wimbledon High, Tiffin's Girls School, Kingston and St Paul's (for girls), King's College School (Wimbledon), Tiffin's, Kingston Grammar and St Paul's (for boys) – or of sending them to boarding schools (Catholic and non-Catholic) outside London.

The parish's burgeoning fortunes were also expressed through the opening of another mass centre in an Anglican church near its southern boundary and the appointment of the senior parish priest, born in Ireland, as a canon of the Catholic Southwark Cathedral. During visits to the cathedral, the centre of diocesan authority, he could meet a former chaplain of Digby Stuart College, who is an expert on canon law and heavily involved in the adjudication of applications for marriage annulments. The parish priest tries to balance the different class interests and religious tastes of his changing congregation through a discreet negotiation of Catholic prescriptions with the individual desires of his parishioners.

I have emphasised the forces of class expressed through educational competition and mobility. The nuances of class are also revealed in the subtle distinctions of status differentiation – accent, clothing, type of housing, car, newspaper readership and other forms of consumption. The Catholic bishops' attempt to take a lead in certain areas of life, especially defending a distinctive Catholic educational system at primary and secondary level and certain moral imperatives concerning pre-marital sex, childbirth, genetics and euthanasia, for example. Yet for Putney's ambitious middle-class parents the religious elite's emphasis on Catholic education as a vehicle for community identity and cohesion appears to be less important than enhancing their children's chances of educational achievement. Confident in their own professional abilities and intellectual capacity, these parents listen to the pronouncements of priests and bishops with respect but also appear to draw their own conclusions commensurate with their lifestyle. On their way into and out of church they navigate their way past the pamphlets, stalls and collecting boxes of different pressure groups (the Society for the Protection of the Unborn Child, the Confraternity of the Knights of Columba, the Catholic Association for Overseas Development, for example). They may agree or disagree with the aims of these organisations, but any tensions remain beneath the surface of formal worship and the informal mixing over teas and coffees in the parish hall after the two morning masses. These are the kinds of English Catholics who, if they wanted to enter elites, would look beyond the world of Catholic elite groups to mainstream professional organisations. In these secular organisations they can use their cultural capital to achieve their ambitions. They can use their social networks and professional skills to satisfy their desire to be leaders within organisations where their Catholic identities are peripheral or irrelevant to the internal authority structure of these institutions.

Catholic elites and the Catholic educational system

Education plays a key role in shaping and sustaining the class boundaries which we can see on the ground in Roehampton and Putney. Digby Stuart College, the Roehampton estate and Putney parish illustrate the various ways in which these boundaries operate. It is not surprising, therefore, that when members of Catholic religious and lay elites decide to put their head above the parapet it is the future of the Catholic educational system which provides their battle ground. Yet, as the changes taking place at Digby Stuart College indicate, it is on the future of the primary and secondary schools, rather than the higher educational sector, that they have taken their stand.

We have already seen that the 1944 Education Act set the scene for the post-Second World War expansion of Catholic schools under the dual system of Church-State partnership established at the beginning of the twentieth century. When the Conservative government decided to alter the arrangements through the 1988 Education Reform Act and changes introduced by a Catholic-educated John Patten in 1992, Cardinal Hume took the lead in challenging these alterations. As Peter Stanford (1999) points out in his discussion of the saga, on which this summary relies, Catholic schools appeared to exemplify the very kind of principles which Margaret Thatcher's administration were trying to encourage:

> In return for a bit of leeway, many turn in substantially better results than their secular counterparts ... And market forces, freedom to choose, those buzz-words of the Thatcherite reforming zeal of the 1980s, vindicated Catholic schools. A large number of neighbourhood Catholic comprehensives are over-subscribed at the expense of their secular counterparts, often by parents who are not of the faith but who admire the end results of the Catholic system. For many such colleges have a reputation for firm discipline and a sceptical approach to some of the more avant-garde education techniques.
>
> (Stanford 1999: 121–2)

Competition for places raised once again the thorny question of how to define and maintain the distinctive Catholic ethos of these schools. The reforms introduced by the Conservative administration were seen by Cardinal Hume as threatening the historic mission of the Church to produce 'rounded human beings' through its 'mechanistic', utilitarian approach towards education. The government's emphasis on learning skills transferable into the job market, the introduction of City Technology Colleges and a National Curriculum and, even more importantly, the opting-out of schools from the state sector led Cardinal Hume to present himself as the defender not only of the Catholic ethos but also of the values underpinning the post-1944 national educational system in general.

In the dispute over opting-out, which focused on the attempt by Cardinal Vaughan School to free itself from the control of the Westminster Diocesan Educational Service, what was so significant was the defiance by the school's governors, staff and parents of Cardinal Hume's policy. Despite the Cardinal's threat to defy the law and go to prison rather than agree to the opting out, he was forced to back down. The school joined the London Oratory (where, amid much publicity, Cherie Blair's son was to attend), as a grant-maintained school directly funded by the state. Despite the Cardinal's dire warnings, supported by the bishop's conference, about the threat to Catholic school ethos, the Catholic and national community generally, and to educational opportunity across the nation, some Catholic schools decided to opt out with the blessing of one of the Cardinal's senior colleagues, the Archbishop of Birmingham. Further dissension among Catholic elite ranks was publicly expressed when Charles Moore, the editor of the *Daily Telegraph*, who was educated at Ampleforth where Hume had been Abbot, championed the principle of parental choice. Stanford defends the Cardinal on the grounds that he was not opposed to parental choice but to the possibility that such choice might lead to the creation of 'popular schools who will be able to choose between children, and the impetus of the system will drive a wedge between successful and unsuccessful schools' (Stanford 1999: 144).

What is interesting about this dispute for my purposes is the way in which the leader of a religious elite – Cardinal Hume – sought to build an alliance between Catholic and other interests in the name of a national community. He presented the issue of opting out as part of a government strategy undermining the values informing good educational practice, both within Catholic and non-Catholic schools. He sought to forge an alliance between interest groups which had been sidelined by the Conservative introduction of such quangos as the School Curriculum and Assessment Council, the Funding Agency for Schools and the Teacher Training Agency. Support came from Anglican religious leaders as well as local education authorities. Anglican and Catholic leaders found common ground in defending church schools not only against central government but also their secular opponents such as the General Secretary of the National Secular Society, who argued that:

> The very concept of pupils being selected with reference to their parents' belief is abhorrent in a secular society in the 21st century. Instead of opening more church schools we should be concentrating on improving mainstream schools open to all pupils.
>
> (*The Guardian* 17 April 2000: 15)

After the 1997 general election, rather than simply defending the existing cohort of schools, Catholic and other religious leaders began to see the possibilities of expansion as the new government considered handing over 'failing' local authority schools. Religious elites had already combined to pressurise the government over 'poverty, housing, unemployment, even inner-city blight' (Pyke 1997: 664). Now they could develop Cardinal Hume's attempt to place education within the context of the Church's social teaching about Christian moral responsibility for the welfare of their neighbours. In a recent report by the English and Welsh bishops' committee for community relations, Bishop Konstant, chairman of the Department for Catholic Education and Formation, argued that:

> If schools in the poorer areas of the country are not able to offer pupils an education similar to that which is offered in more affluent areas, then we will inevitably pass on the legacy of a divided society to the next generation ... The nature and scale of these problems which many of these schools face are almost unknown in more affluent areas ... It is imperative that as a society we do not leave them alone in [their] struggle.
>
> (Pyke 1997: 664)

Conclusion

The evidence outlined in this chapter is highly derivative and anecdotal but, even with this limited ethnographic foundation, certain suggestions can be formulated for a general discussion of the relationship between elites and their potential recruits.

I have focused on two types of Catholic elite – religious and secular – and their tangential relationship to (a) staff and students at Digby Stuart College and (b) middle-class parishioners who still choose, for various reasons, to attend a particular church in London's south-west suburb. During the period under discussion – the last three decades of the twentieth century – the college has been intimately involved in a wide range of changes affecting not only English Catholics but also mainstream society. Whereas previously staff and students may have focused on entering Catholic religious and lay elites, they have become aware of wider opportunities beyond the ethnic-religious boundary. The fading away of the 'Fortress Church', described by Hornsby-Smith and his colleagues, has been expressed locally in the strengthening links with non-Catholics through the federation of the four colleges and closer ties with the University of Surrey at Guildford. Even if some Catholic religious leaders may have liked Catholic colleges to remain separate during the last quarter of the twentieth century, they were forced by political and economic developments to acknowledge the breakdown of boundaries at the level of higher education. Students who wanted to teach in Catholic schools were still required to gain a certificate during their training, but the relatively closed system of Catholic teacher training colleges faded away, encouraging students and staff to look beyond such traditional avenues of Catholic employment as education and religious vocations. This process strengthened the diversity of interests and convictions among those entering Catholic lay elite positions during the last quarter of the twentieth century. It also encouraged the ambitious to look beyond the limited world of Catholic elites. If these products of the higher educational system still believed *and* belonged (see Davie 1994), they were likely to be highly sceptical of religious elite pronouncements and willing to construct their own 'pick and mix' set of beliefs about this world and an afterworld.[8] Secular elite organisations provided them with an arena and authority structure where they could use their cultural capital much more effectively. They could pursue their professional ambitions and, if they so chose, remain 'practising' Catholics through compartmentalising their different social roles.

Yet the religious elite was determined to draw a line at the level of secondary and primary schools. Attempts to define the Catholic ethos of educational institutions – a quest which was abandoned at Digby Stuart College during the 1980s – were sustained through a political and ideological struggle between religious leaders and central government. Here Catholic social teaching underpinned the attempt by Cardinal Hume to prevent a Catholic secondary school from taking advantage of Conservative government legislation and opting out. He sought to construct an alliance extending beyond his religious and lay elite supporters to local education authorities and other defenders of the 'national community'. After the 1997 general election other Catholic religious leaders reconstructed this alliance to take advantage of the possibility that the new government might hand over 'failing' local authority schools to the Church of England and other religious institutions. The Catholic religious elite tried to protect the dual, church–state system by forging links with other religious elites under the banner of social concern and the national interest.

This process of political and ideological reconstruction attempted to build bridges between religious elites (Catholic and non-Catholic), suburban middle-class Catholics and, in the inner city areas, the remnants of working-class Irish communities and the new global migrants from Eastern Europe, Latin America, Africa and Asia. Yet my observations of the 'pick and mix' religiosity and educational aspirations of middle class practising Catholics in Putney suggest that this process may have been more attractive to religious elites than to these suburban residents. Although, in principle, they may have approved of elite pronouncements concerning social justice and equality, in practice they were not prepared to send their children to schools (Catholic or non-Catholic) with poor league table standings. In answer to the question – how far can you go? – it appears that some English Catholic middle-class parishioners have moved far beyond the scope of what the religious elite approves. Catholic schools still provide the foundation for the reproduction of religious and lay Catholic elites but ambitious professionals are more likely to seek access to mainstream elites whose internal authority structures confirm their professional knowledge and expertise. Once they have moved away from their Catholic schools into higher education and their occupational careers, the role of representing their community to a wider world through Catholic elite groups holds little charm. As 'black and Asian' leaders contemplate the possibility of joining such venerable elite institutions as the House of Lords on the basis of their ethnicity, they might consider this journey taken by these professional Catholics and its implications for the future of their communities.

Acknowledgements

This chapter would never have appeared but for the encouragement and invaluable suggestions from Cris Shore. I am also very grateful to Caroline Egan-Strang, John and Liz Hall, Mike Hornsby-Smith, Fr Michael Hayes, Garry Marvin, Bernie Porter, Fr Richard Quinlan and Matt Wood for their comments and support.

Notes

1   See, for example, Shaw (1988); Werbner (1990, 1996); Ballard (1994); Rapport (1994); Cohen (1996); Eade (1989, 1996); McLoughlin (1996); Nye (1996).
2   See Eade and Sallnow (1991), Reader and Walter (1993), Coleman (1998) and Heelas (1996). A recent exception to this rule is provided by Jenkins (1999).

3   Those attending university could make use of the Catholic chaplaincies established specifically for Catholic students as well as local parishes, of course. Many members of this new middle class also emerged from the expanding Catholic teacher training colleges, as we will see later on.

4   The role played by middle-class Catholics before the Second Vatican Council can easily be forgotten in the discussion of the Irish working class in Britain's cities and the minute landed gentry.

5   A report by *The Guardian*'s religious affairs correspondent claimed that the Director of the Catholic Association for Racial Justice had accused the Church of racial discrimination (16 October 2000). The Director was quoted as saying: 'It is ironic that the Catholic Church calls itself universal when it is driving black people away by its attitudes.'

6   She returned to Roehampton in 1999 to receive an honorary doctorate.

7   This landscape typifies the north-western part of the estate. The south-eastern section has become more middle class as newcomers have bought accommodation in the low-rise apartment blocks and terraced housing.

8   Davie argues that generalisations about Britain becoming an increasingly secularised society are based on a narrow range of data. Emphasis on attendance rates at church services, for example, ignores the much larger proportion of people who retain religious beliefs but do not wish to express them through formal religion – believing but not belonging. The middle class parishioners I am describing could be described as belonging but not believing. A more complex situation of 'pick and mix' appears to exist.

Bibliography

Amin, A. (1994) *Post-Fordism: A Reader*, Oxford: Blackwell.

Back, L. (1996) *New Ethnicities and Urban Culture: Racisms and Multiculture in Young Lives*, London: UCL Press.

Ballard, R. (ed.) (1994) *Desh Pardesh: The South Asian Presence in Britain*, London: Hurst.

Baumann, G. (1998) *Contesting Culture: Discourses of Identity in Multi-Ethnic London*, Cambridge: Cambridge University Press.

Boyce, F. (1999) 'Catholicism in Liverpool's Docklands: 1950s–1990s', in M. Hornsby-Smith (ed.), *Catholics in England 1950–2000: Historical and Sociological Perspectives*, London and New York: Cassell, 46–66.

Bruce, S. (1995) *Religion in Modern Britain*, Oxford: Oxford University Press.

Cohen, A. (1996) *Symbolising Boundaries: Identity and Diversity in British Cultures*, Manchester: Manchester University Press.

Cohen, P. (1996) 'All White on the Night? Narratives of Nativism on the Isle of Dogs', in T. Butler and M. Rustin (eds), *Rising in the East: The Regeneration of East London*, London: Lawrence and Wishart, 170–96.

Cohen, P., Qurechi, T. and Toon, I. (1994) *Island Stories – 'Race', Ethnicity and Imagined Community on the Isle of Dogs*, New Ethnicities Unit, University of East London.

Coleman, S. (1998) 'Performing Pilgrimage: Walsingham and the Ritual Construction of Irony', in F. Hughes-Freeland (ed.), *Ritual, Performance, Media*, London: Routledge, 46–65.

Davie, G. (1994) *Religion in Britain since 1945*, Oxford and Cambridge, MA: Blackwell.

—— (2000) 'Religion in Modern Britain: Changing Sociological Assumptions', *Sociology* 34 (1): 113–28.

Douglas, M. (1966) *Purity and Danger: An Analysis of Concepts of Pollution and Taboo*, London: Routledge & Kegan Paul.

—— (1973) *Natural Symbols*, Harmondsworth: Pelican Books.

Dwyer, C. (2000) 'Contested Spaces: Mosque Building and the Cultural Politics of Multiculturalism', unpublished paper presented at the 'New Landscapes of Religion in the West' conference, School of Geography, University of Oxford, 27–29 September 2000.

Eade, J. (1989) *The Politics of Community: The Bangladeshi Community in East London*, Aldershot: Ashgate.

—— (1996) 'Nationalism, Community and the Islamization of Space in London', in B. Metcalf (ed.), *Making Muslim Space in North America and Europe*, Berkeley, CA and Los Angeles: University of California Press, 217–33.

Eade, J. and Sallnow, M. (1991) *Contesting the Sacred: The Anthropology of Christian Pilgrimage*, London and New York: Routledge.

Fardon, R. (1999) *Mary Douglas: An Intellectual Biography*, London and New York: Routledge.

Gardner, K. (1998) 'Identity, Age and Masculinity amongst Bengali Elders in East London', in A. Kershen (ed.), *A Question of Identity*, Aldershot: Ashgate, 160–78.

Giddens, A. (1973) *The Class Structure of the Advanced Societies*, London: Hutchinson.

Hall, S. (1992) 'New Ethnicities', in J. Donald and A. Rattansi (eds), *'Race', Culture and Difference*, London: Sage, 252–9.

Heelas, P. (1996) *The New Age Movement: The Celebration of the Self and the Sacralization of Modernity*, Oxford: Blackwell.

Hickman, M. (1990) 'A Study of the Incorporation of the Irish in Britain with Special Reference to Catholic State Education: Involving a Comparison of the Attitudes of Pupils and Teachers in Selected Catholic Schools in London and Liverpool', unpublished PhD thesis.

—— (1995) *Religion, Class and Identity: The State, the Catholic Church and the Education of the Irish in Britain*, Aldershot: Avebury.

—— (1999) *The Religio-Ethnic Identities of Teenagers of Irish Descent*, in M. Hornsby-Smith (ed.), *Catholics in England 1950–2000: Historical and Sociological Perspectives*, London and New York: Cassell, 182–98.

Hornsby-Smith, M. (1987) *Catholic Education: The Unobtrusive Partner*, London: Sheed and Ward.

—— (1987) *Roman Catholics in England: Studies in Social Structure since the Second World War*, Cambridge: Cambridge University Press.

—— (1991) *Roman Catholic Beliefs in England: Customary Catholicism and Transformations of Religious Authority*, Cambridge: Cambridge University Press.

—— (ed.) (1999) *Catholics in England 1950–2000: Historical and Sociological Perspectives*, London and New York: Cassell.

Jenkins, T. (1999) *Religion in English Everyday Life*, Oxford and New York: Berghahn Books.

Lash, S. and Urry, J. (1994) *Economies of Signs and Space*, London: Sage.

McLoughlin, S. (1996) 'In the Name of the Umma: Globalisation, "Race" Relations and Muslim Identity Politics in Bradford', in W.A.R. Shadid and P.S. van Koningsveld (eds), *Political Participation and Identities of Muslims in Non-Muslim States*, Kampen, The Netherlands.

Nye, M. (1996) *A Place for Our Gods: The Construction of an Edinburgh Hindu Temple Community*, London: Curzon.

O'Leary, A. (1992) *Living Tradition: The Chronicle of a School, Roehampton-Woldingham 1842–1992*, published by Woldingham School.

Paul, K. (1997) *Whitewashing Britain: Race and Citizenship in the Postwar Era*, Ithaca, NY and London: Cornell University Press.

Pyke, N. (1997) 'The Churches Recover Their Voice', *The Tablet* 78: 662–4.

Rapport, N. (1994) *The Prose and the Passion*, Manchester: Manchester University Press.

Reader, I. and Walter, T. (eds) (1993) *Pilgrimage in Popular Culture*, Basingstoke: Macmillan.

Ryan, D. (199) *The Catholic Parish: Institutional Discipline, Tribal Identity and Religious Development in the English Church*, London: Sheed and Ward.

Shaw, A. (1988) *A Pakistani Community in Britain*, Oxford and New York: Blackwell.

Stanford, P. (1999) *Cardinal Hume and the Changing Face of English Catholicism*, London: Geoffrey Chapman.

Waters, M. (1995) *Globalization*, London and New York: Routledge.

Werbner, P. (1990) *The Migration Process: Capital, Gifts and Offerings among British Pakistanis*, Oxford: Berg.

—- (1996) 'Stamping the Earth with the Name of Allah: Zikr and the Sacralizing of Space among British Muslims', in B. Metcalf (ed.), *Making Muslim Space in North America and Europe*, Berkeley, CA and Los Angeles: University of California Press, 167–85.

Who's Who in Catholic Life, Manchester: Gabriel Communications.

Chapter 14

Pre-symptomatic networks

Tracking experts across medical science and the new genetics

Monica Konrad

The precedent: ANT and French networks

Actor-network theory (ANT) argues that the application and cultural legitimisation of innovative technologies in contemporary Western society depends upon aligning and *translating* a diverse range of human and non-human actors into stable socio-technical networks (Callon 1987). Various social theorists claim that these networks emerge through new social practices and forms of state regulation whereby 'heterogeneous engineers', as network builders, form alliances and mobilise different social, technical and economic resources (Callon 1986; Callon *et al.* 1986; Latour 1993; Law 1991; Law and Hassard 1999).

Describing nineteenth-century public health initiatives in France, Bruno Latour has written an ethnographic sampler as to how such networks come into social existence. He has remarked somewhat provocatively that 'each network makes a whole world for itself, a world whose inside is nothing but the internal secretions of those who elaborate it' (Latour 1988: 171). Pasteurism is one example, he has contended, of a ramifying social network linking the formerly unconnected worlds of French laboratory science with those of the contemporaneous hygiene and health education movements. Cast widely afield to enlist the support of many hygienists, the extensional dispersal of Louis Pasteur's medical 'net' could be read as the story of elite cultures in the making. But it is also something more than just a group of science experts commanding strategic positions of power or 'centers of calculation' (Latour 1999: 55) in post-revolutionary French society. The 'internal secretions' to which Latour refers had as much to do with the physical substance of the bacilli cultures laid out before the laboratory scientist, as with the way health professionals from disparate fields (biologists, surgeons, sanitary engineers, medical and military doctors) were recruited and brought together as 'allies' to create new social knowledge.[1] Public recognition of the cultural significance of bacteriology and the invention of anthrax was about making links, and in terms of the analytical power of ANT, these links are about the way relations between humans, non-humans, organic and non-organic entities can be studied as *associations*.

Networks and bioinformatics

This chapter on British biomedical and other experts is less about strategic alliance formation and 'posthuman' life forms than about how networks themselves may offer a *method* of study for anthropological research. Given that the recent turn to multi-sited ethnography questions not only many previous assumptions about the nature of territorially bounded regions for anthropological analysis, but partakes also in a fundamental reconfiguration of space itself (Augé 1998), Latour's claim that theoretical anthropology is statically fixed and unable to study networks seems unnecessarily harsh (1993: 114–16). The claim is one that also seems to overlook the centrality of cultural translation for the anthropological project. Since knowledge may acquire cultural value in certain societies precisely because its circulation is restricted (Harrison 1995), and does not always travel well, to paraphrase Clifford (1997), limited access to strategic sites for the field worker is equally likely to be bound up with the more endemic, and possibly covert, political force of systemic social inequality and marginalisation. I suggest here that a focus on networks as a method of tracking the creation of social value over time may yield helpful insights for social anthropology in general, including an anthropology of elite cultures and other institution-based work concerned with problems of researcher access. In this way, the potentially radical deterritorialisation of a multi-sited ethnographic agenda presents not just new acts of spatial engagement for the fieldworker, but expressly political ones too.

The network analogy is applied here to question how certain developments in genetic science and medicine have led to the identification of a new classificatory category of 'pre-symptomatic' populations. I consider some of the 'expert' methods for pre-empting such 'anticipated' persons, given that these populations are transformed into persons, and corporeal value, at risk not just of developing an hereditary illness in later life, but of experiencing in the meantime – pre-symptomatically – the effects of social exclusion. However, instead of taking as its object of study a specific group of elites as a bounded and internally cohesive formation, the chapter 'tracks' some of the spatial and temporal associations of 'bioinformatics' in contemporary biomedical Britain. It asks how these informational associations constitute intersecting pathways – or networks – of 'expert' power and knowledge.

Bioinformatics conventionally refers to the use of large-scale information processing systems to manage datasets derived from the sequencing of genetic information and protein structure DNA libraries within genome research. Bioinformatics analysts attempt to integrate and model processes of life at the cellular level through the development of new computer science and information technology techniques; work that is sponsored in large part by the biological research initiatives of the Human Genome Project.[2] However, the term 'bioinfomatics' can be applied more broadly to include a diverse range of technocrat-specialists responsible for regulating the provision of genetics-related information in the biomedical field, and it is this more generic sense of bio-information with which this paper is concerned. It is not possible to trace here all the network paths of such multiple interests: how scientists, molecular biologists, health practitioners and bio-administrators encompass different domains of expertise with intersecting interests (public policy and ethics, philosophy and human rights, law and insurance, drug development, marketing and patenting claims). However, a few key organisational 'land-marks' within this geography of biotechnology and bioinformatics in the UK can be signposted, most notably the recently established Human Genetics Commission (HGC). Part of the UK government's Department of Health, its remit is extensive but with loosely defined terms of reference such as conducting reviews of scientific progress at the frontiers of human genetics and investigating ways to build public confidence in, and understanding of, the new genetic technologies. Other statutory and non-statutory bodies such as The Nuffield Council on Bioethics, the Human Fertilisation and Embryology Authority (HFEA), and the Advisory Group on Scientific Advances in Genetics (AGSAG) represent powerful institutional forces feeding into the national regulatory and advisory framework for genetics overseen by the HGC.[3] Formal and informal cross-committee links often characterise the memberships of these bodies,[4] whose representation includes an ostensibly diverse but negligible mix of scientific/medical/ academic experts and 'lay' experience or skills. Though changes are apace in the field of science communication policy (see House of Lords 2000), still too often the token consumer, patient or medical charity worker is seen to sit alongside his 'expert' counterparts, as though knowledge systems are discretely embodied yet capable of synthesis for a common 'consensus'.

In the following sections, two separate but interconnected 'elite cultures' are tracked in order to show how processes of standardisation and objectifica-tion emerge as certain pathways of power and how '[networks] become operationalised as manipulable or usable artefacts in people's pursuit of inter-ests and their construction of relationships' (Strathern 1996: 521). In the first example, I consider how human genetics is linked to systems of accounting and to the British insurance industry. The second example connects up molecular biology to theoretical homologies and the analytic and technical tool of sequencing databases as divisions of labour and skill. Both examples are relevant to a discussion of the ways that different knowledge experts admin-ister, and therefore help shape and classify, the worlds (and networks) of the 'pre-symptomatic'. For my methodology I insert myself into the network by locating the gap, or more precisely, the *interval* of social time between medical diagnosis and prognosis. I start by asking what kinds of relations would come into being were one to transpose the delayed 'return' of (Maussian) gift exchange to the bioinformatics networks of medicine and health. Here the gift as provisional trope serves political ends, since I am interested to track how knowledge gets lost as social value in such space. The same trope also enables my positing a retroflected question relevant to the relational power of pre-symptomatic networks. What forms of value would be invoked were one to speculate that the very ideal of *cure* in Western biomedicine is structured according to the same dimensions of gift-giving that delineate the classical anthropological model of reciprocity and delayed exchange between dependent (patient–practitioner) 'partners'?

Between diagnosis and prognosis

In anthropological discourse, the notion of gift exchange as exemplary of relations of dependence rests implicitly on the value of reciprocity as a measure of balance, equivalence and mutuality, with more or less equivalent returns of gifts and counter-gifts restoring a sense of proportion between actors. Though things exchanged may be concretely different, they are presumed equal in value in the sense that a balanced reciprocity represents equality through the *matching* series of reciprocal prestations. In Western biomedical practice, the patient is somebody who occupies ideally, within the health care system *in toto*, the structural positioning of the intended *recipient* of a diagnosis.[5] One only need consider the cases of those persons who evade diagnosis and never quite become acknowledged as authentic 'patients' (Kleinman 1995; cf. Young 1981) for verification of this claim. Confirmation of illness through diagnosis happens also to take place as a professional pledge by physicians that medical assistance is offered as human beneficence: in the West this has been the ancient Oath of Hippocrates to which all medical initiates must swear 'foremost not to harm', or *primum non nocere* (Sinclair 1997).

However, what the diagnosed patient 'gives back' over time to the medical system itself is the *process* of having become a subject whose personal details have been amassed cumulatively throughout the course of the individual's 'medical' career. To receive care, the patient knows she will have to be complicit in 'giving up' information about herself. Whether or not a fee-paying 'private' patient, an implicit wager – the pact of cure – exists between patient and practitioner that is dependent on each party *matching* the other's expectations.

The extraction of human and non-human substance from living and dead organisms for the development of new medicinal products, the emergence of bioprospecting, and the increase in the number of licensed international patent agreements to pharmaceutical companies, all de-stabilise this implicit biomedical homology between gift and cure. New post-surgical genetic testing techniques to 'open up' the body for microscopic diagnostic inspection means that a new order of predictive knowledge as 'microkinship' is created about the patient and kin, and the likelihood of becoming ill in the future (Konrad 1999b).

Genetic testing is currently available for those few hereditary diseases whose genes so far have been successfully isolated and mapped such as breast cancer, ovarian cancer, cystic fibrosis and Huntington's Disease. The latter, a chronic degenerative autosomal condition, was the first neuropsychiatric disorder for which predictive genetic tests became available in the early 1990s. Classified a so-called 'late-onset' illness, carriers develop symptoms of the disease only in adult life. For those who choose to find out whether or not they are carriers, one type of uncertainty is traded for another since no accurate prognosis can be given as to what the time of 'onset' for any particular individual will be (Wexler 1979; Burgess and Hayden 1996).

On the one hand, this emergence of the category of the pre-symptom, and with it the labelling of persons and relatives as 'pre-symptomatic', returns to an earlier preoccupation with statistics and measurement and the control of populations as particular sciences of the state (Foucault 1990). On the other, this modern epidemiology of foreknowledge is thoroughly post-industrial and global: it effects simultaneous change in real embodied time. In other words, the aetiological progression of disease once formerly detectable by the gap of time between diagnosis and prognosis collapses *everywhere* due to the duplicity of these new systems of corporeal surveillance in not having founded themselves upon the offer of an available, if not always effective, therapy.[6] In cases of late-onset and chronic degenerative illnesses, such as Huntington's, this rescission of cure as beneficent 'gift' may be experienced as a particularly acute violation of *primum non nocere*. My fieldwork with members of such families has considered how some persons with a positive carrier diagnosis get enchained irreversibly within processes of knowledge revelation that in retrospect many say they would rather not have been party to (Konrad 1999a).

Finding that certain of one's biological kin are caught similarly within this biomedical 'net', the pre-symptomatic person may as well look to alternative knowledge sources to fathom still other pathways for making matches out of 'like' kinds of returns. Although the equivalence thesis in anthropology epitomises relations of imagined equality, the ideal of matching also denotes relations of force, power, domination and difference. Chris Gregory (1982) once put this in terms of 'tennis-balls-on-a-string'. The original owner or producer of a thing could, as it were, 'pull' this thing back to herself by 'jerking' the strings to which relationships were symbolically attached, and crucially, the relationships within which the donor was implicated. This description suggests not only how claims over things previously given may seem to have an imperative of inalienability worked into them (Weiner 1992), but in addition, how such returns to the donor require some degree of coercion, intention and projection to make them effective. In networks made from diverse associations, reciprocal gift giving functions as more than a benign levelling mechanism; it is also a material and symbolic conduit through which personal power passes, creating values and relations of ranking, hierarchisation and social difference between exchange partners. As evinced by Boas's early account of the ostentatious destruction of potlatching Amerindians, the gift structure itself has always been one complicated by conflict, competitiveness and agonistic desire (Beidelman 1989).[7]

Whilst medical experts are not known to pile up their social capital in observable heaps for others to see, preferring instead the confidential machinery of a tidy anonymity, the agonistics of the bioinformatics network is nonetheless increasingly caught up by the productions of more and more technological expertise. The power of scientists to keep on creating and manipulating organic and non-organic entities as various reconfigured part-to-whole organisms and relations is one reason why, as Strathern suggests (1996), we might wish to 'cut' the network. After all, medico-administrative experts depend for at least some of their regulatory power on complex acts of imagination, anticipation and projection in which *ex vivo* body parts must be kept still as cryopreserved suspended life-forms. On the one hand, bodily parts as samples stand in synecdochally for the 'whole' person, present only *in absentia*. On the other, techno-medicrats are those who mediate the person through practices of matching bodies by bringing together the closest approximation of different partible samples (cf Strathern 1991). In these contexts, equivalence as value creation has the effect of dissolving the place of the boundary (Strathern 1996: 523) since an array of bodily parts is produced whose features get broken down into digitised displays and fractions of wholes (as data mining and profiling techniques, for example). Synecdochic persons thus become a complex of statistics mobilised for comparison, juxtaposition and manipulation across electronically interlinked storage and retrieval database systems. The network through its 'heterogenous engineers' thereby cuts and resumes its alliances by recourse to a growing repository of sub-cellular possibilities from which to identify or re-assess the (genetical) status of 'somebody' at some later date, whether for medical purposes or forensic science (Huber 1991; Jones 1993).

To rework the model of medical beneficence as 'gift' and Western assumptions of the 'cure' as forms of (equivalent) delayed exchange, I would suggest that predictive genetic testing technology comprises forms of clinical capital that flow into networks as (mis)appropriated time. Biotechnocratic experts are key and publicly unaccountable players in these temporal appropriations, during which they too may suffer adverse effects. The following sections consider some of the ways that the experts who comprise these diverse and interdependent cultures marshal such appropriations. Attention is paid to how the value of 'matching' persons in these spaces comes to be restructured as regulatory flows of time through the *loss* of information.[8]

Underwriters and actuarial science

Insurance in most Western societies is an ideology whose rationale is clearly predictive and future-governed. It is also an explicit practice of valuing and measuring the self in terms of monetary value. Many Euro-Americans enter into legal contracts with life companies in the expectation monetary recompense can be determined against unforeseen material damage to person or thing. Insurance in these societies is also a knowledge-based industry, and like biomedicine it is dependent upon the surrender of personal information that is assessed by specialists against a comparative frame. In exchange for information, one 'receives' a premium, though how risk is thought to be conceived as something *shared* between pre-defined groups of persons is the outcome of a *process* of calculation (see Caplan 2000). Yet at the same time insurance is also a practice whose knowledge basis is founded very obviously on uncertainty. Whilst nobody may be able to insure against entirely predictable loss, there is still in the West the folk belief that it is possible to investigate and make a science out of the probability of death. *Primum non nocere* meets *uberrima fides*.[9]

Underwriters constitute just one of the forking pathways of the diverse and ramifying medico-administrative network of the new bioinformatics. They are included in this paper since many seem to have become increasingly wary not just about the basis of their own claims to specialist knowledge, but how indeed to express and make known such uncertainty in the face of the impending clinical applications of genome research. Even more confusingly perhaps, some seem to talk a language that looks as though it has come straight from a social science discourse! Underwriting philosophy remains a practice informed principally by the key notions of 'mutuality' and 'solidarity'. In the case of the former, underwriters are wont to talk of how their practice is an essential aid to determining 'equivalence of value' (Association of British Insurers 1997a: 21). Mutuality may be thought of as an imaginary pseudo-kinship, an anonymously encompassed virtual system of relatedness in which the 'pooling of similar risks and the achievement of broad equity between persons of similar circumstances' produce the entity of an insured risk pool (Association of British Insurers 1997a). Like-configured 'pooled' persons share between themselves 'equivalence of value' between cost and benefit, a notion that derives from the idea of equivalence between risk and premium where value is held to inhere in the entity of a single, nondivisible person.

In 1997, the Human Genetics Advisory Commission (HGAC) set up an Insurance Group to investigate the Association of British Insurers' (ABI) statement on the use of genetic tests.[10] The aim was to develop the Commission's view on the implications of genetic testing for life insurance[11] and to provide 'independent advice' to Health and Industry Ministers. Prior to issuing a consultation document, the Commission informed the public (in a narrowly circulated press release) that it had met a number of experts 'in the field' and that the consultation period was devised with the aim of learning more about how the insurance industry operates in such cases. Response was invited from insurance companies, professional bodies and individual experts on the issue of the implications of genetic testing for life insurance. When the Commission issued its report at the end of the year, a two-year moratorium was recommended on asking clients seeking insurance products for their genetic test results (Human Genetics Advisory Commission 1997).

The HGAC consultation paper raised a number of questions for consideration, many of which turned on the problem of how different kinds of experts could translate and interpret each other's findings: the problem was precisely one of entering and traversing different professional 'worlds'. 'What is the relationship between the knowledge the genetic test can reveal and the information that insurers obtain?' 'What is the relationship between confidentiality and security of personal information and the openness and feedback of underwriting decisions?' 'What is the impact of genetic testing on the insurance industry and its method of administering actuarial justice?'

These questions proved difficult for the Commission to broach, partly because most of the experts consulted – senior underwriters, insurance ombudsmen, the chief medical officers attached to insurance companies and the ABI's own genetic advisors – were themselves not sure how genetic testing could be used as a method for evaluating predictions about life expectancy. The consultation gave rise to a general sense of confusion concerning the impact of genetic testing on the insurance industry, especially the extent to which predictive genetic test results would help the profession to refine the actuarial basis on which premiums would be decided, and in particular, policies with 'preferred life' terms avoided (Human Genetics Advisory Commission 1997: 27–8, 40–4).

And yet since the consultation exercise and despite the moratorium, the organisational ethics of the British insurance industry has remained one vindicated through the key concept and discourse of mutuality: the principles of actuarial justice in this sense have remained firmly intact. The relationship of genes and clinical genetics to actuarial knowledge may not be one that is able to be appended to material and physically present bodies, but this does not prevent the industry from imagining how these connections could and would be objectively embodied as standardised calculations.[12] We could say that the population to be worked on here is a critical bio-mass of numbers and statistics, a complex accounting of assessed risks made up from pools of persons that have been drawn together by relative degrees of 'mutuality' or 'solidarity' (ABI 1997a and b). In the case of the former (where purchase of insurance is optional rather than mandatory), such estimations of 'kinship' depend on the capacity to move or exchange persons between different pools of relatedness as flows of perceived risk. Particular premiums (by which should be understood notional measurements that underscore imaginary assessments of so-called 'risks') get attached to particular persons within the space and time of flows of imputed equivalence.

This system of objectivised measurement is a type of informational 'literacy' that goes by the philosophy of underwriting.[13] Actuaries are professional risk takers by name, but they are also master designers of nets and slippage and of all that which is allowed to pass through space invisibly – as well as quite seamlessly, without explicit accountability. As informational experts, actuaries are able to write *under* the ledger, to craft creatively for their actuarial net undeclared passageways and escape holes through which compound figures and percentages get directed, and people – by the way – are quietly transferred across these boundaries – most, however, without their even knowing they have crossed such borders.[14]

To explain how creative shifts in numbers and persons (between pools) could materialise as the knowledge claims of these actuarial experts, the British insurance industry has arrived at the nostalgic and evolutionarily loaded terms of 'cherry picking' and 'adverse selection'. In a (kinship) system of adverse selection, a collectivity of standard risk persons is overloaded with the inclusion of 'high-risk' individuals. This leads the former to exit the pool thereby driving up costs for those persons remaining. Low risk persons react to what they perceive to be too high premiums for their circumstances by 'migrating'.

Related to this is 'cherry picking', a euphemism for the eugenic-inspired practice of attributing 'preferred' lives to persons. It refers to the process whereby actuaries selectively identify a subgroup of persons within the standard group with a lower risk than the average (person) of the pool, these latter are then offered lower premiums and migrate from the standard pool to join the preferred pool with cheaper premiums. The effect of such flows of persons is to increase the average risk in the standard pool, therefore raising the premium as the cross-subsidies from the lower risk category are no longer present as counterbalancing measure (HGAC 1997: 3.19).

The symbolic violence committed here is arguably the bland, anodyne language of 'discretion' and 'perceived risk'. Information officers will explain their decisions (if called to do so through adjudication tribunals, for example) by recourse to statements such as: 'Insurers exercise discretion in setting premiums, which are based on an individual's perceived risk at the time of purchase'. Apparently equivalence of value is so elastic (cf. Gregory's tennis balls) that it can even extend to a belief in the authenticity of 'fair selection'[15] as a means to describe this normative reassessment of persons and their future claims.

Scientists and 'dry', 'wet' and not so wet labs

The experts framing this next example figure as scientists. More precisely, they are molecular biologists for whom certain (mis)appropriations of knowledge and persons take place throughout the course of professional relationships. Here, a different negotiation of border knowledge constructed from a different production of value and different mobilisations of persons comes into play. In the sense that scientists working in the same laboratory are self-present to one another through ongoing negotiations of spatial boundaries, these experts do not materialise as value simply because quotas and pieces of paper have been shuffled around.[16] Like the previous case from insurance and the actuarial profession, what matters is how information *escapes* across boundaries: boundaries of knowledge formation that are permeable and that network builders keep having to maintain in place as contested claims over what counts as skill, expertise and disciplinary speciality.

One of the ways that data-base technologies for human genomic sequencing have affected the division of labour between scientists is most apparent in the case of DNA homology searches. These entail an increasing separation of roles between computational theoretical biology and laboratory molecular biology. As mentioned earlier, databases are the computerised version of publications of sequence information – besides storing informa-tion, sequence databases enable scientists a faster, more streamlined method than manual analysis for accessing and interpreting information used in their experiments.[17]

In the UK, parts of Western Europe and North America, scientists have developed a language of accountability in accordance with a work ethic built upon the difference between 'dry' and 'wet' working environments. 'Dry' labs refer to computational theoretical laboratories: in these spaces scientists conduct 'pure' basic research constructing theoretical relationships by means of computer search and match procedures. A key activity in these labs is the production of genetic linkage 'maps' – calculations that are not based on phys-ical distance between certain gene 'markers' but as statistical frequencies of recombinations between chromosome pairs. For molecular biologists, these (not yet charted) maps provide a starting point for what is referred to as 'walking down' the relevant chromosome to physically locate a gene of interest, whereas the precise location of a gene on a chromosome is desig-nated by actual 'physical maps': these vary according to resolution, something in turn dependent on techniques of production.[18] 'Wet' labs, by contrast, are staffed by applied biologists who run an endless series of biochemical experi-ments to try out the previously formulated hypotheses of the dry labs' homologous sequence relationships.

Whilst the work methods of the former are relatively quick compared to the mechanical and often painstaking precision of biochemical experiments in 'wet' space, these temporally determined differences do not get incorporated according to how flows of information pass invisibly as unacknowledged social value between the different labs and their staff. Since computational theoretical biologists use the sequences submitted by molecular biologists and biochemists, they are often viewed as 'feeding off' the extensive work prac-tices of the 'wet' lab technicians and researchers. At issue is the problem of collaboration as (temporalised) exchange and what counts as 'original' insofar as it is not clear amongst these experts themselves which group of scientists should be credited with constructing homologous relationships and making a successful gene match upon making a 'hit'.[19]

Issues concerning claims to ownership of knowledge as the mobilisation of informational flows also instruct various national and international efforts at collaborative science as, for instance, when researchers withhold or delay submitting their sequences to public (shared) on-line data bases for commercial reasons.[20] When scientists talk about the threat of being scooped by other researchers who might later find matches to their sequences and publish articles based on these (rather than their own matches), experimentation for the good of 'common man' (Grobstein 1990) looks more like an impoverished project for the social engineering of scientists and their own individual research careers.[21] These temporal strategies of delaying or withholding information are not symptomatic of the problem of access to the means of production, but of the problem of exclusive access to and manipulation of the *technical* relations of production. It is access to, and the manipulation of, these relations that will later determine personal fame and funding allocations and ultimately, within the worlds of agonistic science, which discipline and which type of expertise can survive the rest as distinguished sub-speciality. In other words, which network is most durable. Such internal competitiveness, though not explicitly systematised, is a fundamental feature of the way institutions at times tend to think about how they think (Douglas 1987). Yet not stoking the flames of a fraternal 'science war' among scientists *themselves* also gives a different inflection to recent social and feminist critiques of science as the objective production of unitary knowledge (Galison and Stump 1996, Harding 1998, Rose 1994).[22] The same reservation also questions the extent to which networks can indeed remain durable enough over time to establish themselves as an 'heterogeneity of alliances' (Latour 1988).

Changes in the division of labour, as well as symbolic prestige and repute, are bound up also in these networks with a broader infrastructural reorganisation of biology as technological expertise or a set of skills for servicing other sciences. This, in part, has to do with the claim – resisted by biologists – that biology is becoming less its own science and more dependent on tools and techniques from mathematics, statistics, information and computer science (cf. Clarke and Fujimura 1992). However, organisational wrangles within many of these institutional settings turn on the desire to transform molecular biology from an experimental science into a theoretical one, and this is why the computerised databases of sequencing technologies are becoming such a prized tool in the 'dry' labs. The new genetic technology 'assists' then not only the sub-fertile to procreative capacity, it helps biologists to continue to reproduce themselves into persons that matter: into experts armed with a set of supposedly unique and distinctive skills and techniques that cannot be 'serviced off' as a disciplinary sub-speciality.

And yet partly to allay professional disquiet amongst physicists of a new ascendancy of biologics and biologists in British science, the increased expenditure allocated by the government to the latter is rationalised in terms that celebrate the multidisciplinary (read financially flourishing) dimension of the UK genome project research base.[23] At a recent House of Commons Science and Technology meeting in November 1998 the Director General of Research Councils emphasised the broad extent of the contributory knowledge base: chemistry, physics, computing, the biomedical sciences were all significant players in the process of wealth, enterprise and knowledge production. 'Science is the absolute bedrock of our economic performance', remarked British Prime Minister Tony Blair just a little earlier ('It's all in the genes', *The Guardian*, 3 November 1998, 23).[24] The belief, of course, works equally well the other way round. Economics governs science. Indeed, economics *is* science, as the earlier example of 'cherry picking' showed. What, then, are we to make of our Western systems of scaling knowledge, upon which the original project of social anthropology was itself based, when science and capital have become so commensurate, so inextricably interconnected, that they can interchange with one another without seeming to make any difference?

The paradox of the local offers here perhaps a salutary reminder. Some of the greatest intensities of power are invested in persons who appear to be doing nothing at all, or else who seem barely visible to others because they manage what looks like the seemingly mundane or routine. Consider the manual work of DNA sequencing undertaken by graduate and undergraduate students that many describe as 'tedious'. Make a single slip, though, mix up the genetic substance of cytosine for guanine – a 'C' for a 'G' – and the dry labs will not get their homologies. Or what about the nurse or genetic counsellor in a genetics unit drawing up a patient's medical family history as a diagnostic tool of clinical genetics. These deceptively innocuous kinship charts, a standard feature of a patient assessment, are much more than any given array of circles and triangles. These particular paper lines of transmission will be used by the biomedical expert to interpret whose medical past makes them most eligible for further genetic investigation based around the deployment of such loaded concepts as 'risk', 'affected offspring', 'viability', 'mutation', 'defective genes' or 'carrier status' (Konrad 1999a; Ettorre 1999). I would agree then with Laura Nader (1969: 292) that the method of studying 'up' ought not to become any kind of totalising or exclusive strategy in its own right, but that it be integrated within traditional study-down approaches. However, this is not to say that 'studying up' cannot be further 'worked up', nor indeed that the very dichotomies of 'up' and 'down' cannot themselves be revised.

Working up 'studying up'

Perhaps one of the immediate problems for a project intent on the anthropological study of elite cultures concerns the very terms of reference that may be used to describe the relations of power the 'indignant' anthropologist (Nader 1969) seeks to expose. I would like to turn now to consider briefly some of the structuring conditions of production within social anthropology itself that make certain knowledge claims appear less visible than other forms of knowledge. How is it that knowledge recedes and vanishes within the anthropological corpus itself? How can we see social anthropology's own disciplinary network as a spatial topology bound up with questions of procedure, and the framing devices the discipline has developed through the professionalisation of the 'distinctive other' tradition?

My starting point is the continual awkwardness of the home-focused anthropologist to have to invoke as strange and 'other' the seemingly commonplace world that the researcher habitually traverses and knows as simultaneously alien and mundane (Clifford 1997; Amit 2000). In this sense, Nader's project may be recombined with a certain kind of 'anthropology of trouble', to borrow a phrase from Rappaport (1993), yet in what sense is it possible for sources of indignation (the stimulus behind Nader's points about the rearticulation of anthropological research methods) to get worked back into the conceptual schema of 'reinventing complexity' (Hymes 1969)?

Following Nader, I suggest two key problems may be identified: first, the privileging of non-Western fieldwork, and second, the privileging of the method of participant observation.

In the pre-symptomatic networks I have been describing, participation by the field worker is necessarily a selective, carefully planned activity, and sometimes the full implications of this engagement may not even be apparent until some time later, for instance, through the writing up and dissemination of research reports. Anthropologists in the future can and should make significant contributions to many of the social responsibility, advocacy, citizenship, science awareness education movements that are currently forming around national agendas in Britain (and elsewhere) to promote greater accountability of science activity and better communication between scientists and non-scientists. Building on previous anthropological work on processes of dispute settlement and conflict arbitration, there is certainly a case to be made for the future 'studying up' of complaints processes and adjudication systems in the area of the social regulatory systems of these new life technologies. Intensive studies of cases of adjudication and repeal tribunals in health insurance and processes of medical litigation would all be relevant. Much applied work urgently needs to be done in the area of tracking and exposing how such systems define 'malpractice', what problems are allowed to constitute 'grievance', and in turn relaying such findings to public policy health forums, as well as contributing further to theoretical scholarship in the anthropology of law, medicine and science.[25]

Public consultations are also a fertile ground for implementing a praxis-based, action–orientated strategy for studying up, including possibly collective team-based action. Consultations may take the form of citizens' juries, 'consensus conferences' or 'science parliaments' where groups of professional and lay experts meet in specially convened 'assemblies' to debate and discuss sensitive and topical issues in medicine and science. Held typically over a period of three days or slightly longer, the aim at the end of a session is to 'report back' findings or cast votes with a view to influencing the future formulation of policy. In the UK these events are usually co-organised by consumer groups, government agencies and policy think tanks such as the Institute for Public Policy Research and Demos, and may involve marketing agencies for the targeting, selection and recruitment of members of the public.[26] Anthropologists also need to find ways of sitting in on ethics committees and actively shaping the very terms of reference by which scientists and others draw up future policy agenda. Finding ways of sharing their experiences of working on such committees and talking to academic and non-anthropological colleagues about how cross-disciplinary relations can be fostered without loss of professional face would also be enormously constructive work.

However, doing this kind of reflexive work requires that the anthropologist expand, refine and revise her understanding of 'participatory' engagement to take account of how, in many of these institutional settings, whilst there may not always be anything concrete 'to see', the anthropologist's traditional role is more than likely reversed from one of domination to one of a relation of dependency and supplication (upon one's host institution, on teams of clinical professionals or groups of scientists, for example). There are many issues arising from such dependency, for instance questions about the nature of knowledge co-production and collaboration, ethics, funding and fieldwork integrity, and questions of intellectual compromise and the presentation of identity well before and beyond 'the field'.

There is also a further issue to do with language. For much of this kind of applied work, having an ear for the unsaid depends on more than just subtle attention to and command of the spoken word. Nader has suggested that 'contributions penetrating enough to be theoretically significant are most likely to come from study of the cultural circumstances of which one has the most and most rapidly available background knowledge, namely, one's own' (1969: 32). Yet one's 'own' cultural circumstances may also present certain difficulties for generating theory. Even familiarity with knowledge 'at home' may be difficult to acquire as the attempt to 'translate' the specialist language of molecular genetics between different conceptual frameworks has shown (Konrad 2000). Turning to one frequently visited source of support, the third edition of the *Shorter Oxford English Dictionary* (1980) contains a vocabulary of about 163,000 words. Let us suppose (generously) that an adult native English-speaker is at best only familiar and fully competent with less than a quarter of these entries and all their various idiomatic applications. When *another* language can be claimed after just months or even several years' field exposure as one of the principal media for the construction of politically consequential knowledge claims, what do such aspirations hide in terms of the theoretical processes of modelling anthropological knowledge? Should we not ask more directly, after Hymes (1969: 31), what manner of objectification may be committed in the 'hit and run' tactics of some field workers, many of whom may be working under sometimes impossible financial and time constraints in order to preserve their own professional livelihood as academic 'experts'?

Networks, elite cultures and the wider relevance of pre-symptomatic worlds

If anthropology stopped privileging the method of participant observation in order to focus on systems and relations of power that cannot *always* expect to be seen, could the discipline reinvent itself as a conceptual language divested of units of scaling, relativity and degrees of measurement? And what would be the implications for the anthropological study of elites? I have attempted to show how network tracking allows the fieldworker to draw creatively upon multiple sources of knowledge generation in different and related fields. Further, by playing off divergent knowledge claims between different kinds of 'experts', the fundamentally deterritorial practices of multi-sited ethnography (Marcus 1998) become not just modified acts of spatial engagement, but expressly political ones too.

For example, by reflecting and commenting on previous media stories in their own terms and 'expert' language, pre-symptomatic families from my research have become involved in the active assemblage of their own 'mediafile' of 'factfiction'. Samples of 'expert' reportage from newspaper cuttings and other visual sources can be given 'back' to research subjects for critical comment and discussion, enabling the co-construction by participants of their own documentary materials. Through our joint explorations we have found out that within this 'net' we are all of us – scientists and clinicians included – *already* the embodiment of pre-symptomatic lives, but that only some of us to date have an heightened awareness about the lived uncertainties of genetic testing technologies.

In conclusion, the possibility to critique and expose the ethnocentrism of expert 'versus' lay distinctions would seem to be one of the key analytic and conceptual merits offered by an anthropological study of 'elite cultures'. By network-tracking how all manner of expertise is encompassed within the rubric of 'lay' knowledge, studying 'up' becomes something that is not simply an unidirectional activity on the part of the sole ethnographer, but hopefully an opportunity for productive cross-collaborations through heterogeneous space.

Acknowledgements

This paper is based on the one-year ESRC-funded project 'Culture, Kinship and Ethics in the Context of the New Reproductive and Genetic Technologies' granted to the author. The support of the ESRC is gratefully acknowledged (R000222290). For all their expertise, I especially thank the Huntington's families who participated in this research. Alastair Kent and associates of the Genetic Interest Group, David King and members of Human Genetics Alert, and the networks intersecting around the UK Science Policy Support Group have also channelled much valuable information. Bethlee Jones and Peter Engstrom from the Association of British Insurers have offered ongoing help and advice with enquiries. I am grateful too for the insights of Chris Smith, Actuarial Analyst, and Paul Cooper, Principal Underwriter, from Swiss Re for their presentations at the one-day seminar of the UK Forum for Genetics and Insurance held at the Royal Society, London, in 1999. The views expressed in this paper are those of the author and do not necessarily represent those of the ABI or any other non-governmental or statutory body or other organisation. I would also like to thank Cris Shore for helpful comments on an earlier version of this paper.

Notes

1   How experts in institutional settings collaborate and make strategic allies is a theme running through much of the recent critical, historiographic and ethnographic study of Western 'science-in-action', notably the pioneering laboratory studies of Latour and Woolgar (1986), Shapin (1988), Knorr-Cetina (1999) and Rabinow (1999). See also Traweek (1991), Dubinskas (1988) and Czarniawska (1997) on other organisational and 'high-technology' settings.

2   Electronic search tools such as the Nix, Blast, Glue and Rhyme programs have been developed at dedicated bioinformatics centres such as the European Molecular Biology Laboratory (EMBL) in Heidelberg, Germany, and the European Bioinformatics Institute (EBI) affiliated to the Sanger Centre, the genome campus at Hinxton Hall, south of Cambridge, UK. These enterprises are founded upon the belief that a DNA sample is a coded sequence of letters (e.g. AGG ATC GTC GAC). Geneticists hold that the 'informational' content of DNA signified by the substance of adenine (A), cytosine (C), guanine (G), and thymine (T) can be 'read' as 'the book of life'. It is beyond the scope of this paper to consider the discursive politics of according such primacy of informational value to the substance of the human genetic 'code'. Konrad (2000) sets out an anthropological critique of ethnogenetics and its re-translation in non-informational idiom.

3   The list of advisory bodies is by no means inclusive. Other key agents deal with regulatory policy on the safety of medicines and xenotransplantation regulation, for example. See Office of Science and Technology (OST) 1999.

4   Committee sub-groups may be composed of joint memberships such as the ACGT/HFEA working group consultation and report on Preimplantation Genetic Diagnosis, or else organisations may have multi-executive funding and accountability. The AGSAG, for instance, has a joint secretariat with the Department of Health (DH) and Medical Research Council (MRC).

5   The reader will appreciate that reference to structured positioning(s) within a system does not necessarily implicate a structuralist analysis. See point on the 'disunity of science' in note 22 below.

6   Certain parallels may be drawn with certain experiences of persons living with HIV and AIDS. See for example Davies (1997).

7   A sceptic would say that the heavily gendered medical discourse of altruism, reflected in assumptions about the self-sacrificing good-will of the 'prototypical'

ova donor, for example, illustrates how health professionals and others are only too happy to misappropriate the gift analogy to their own limited ends (see Konrad 1998).

8   See anthropological critiques of the equivalence thesis of value by Foster (1995), Appadurai (1986) and Jamieson (1999).

9   'Along with uncertainty, the other guiding principle that allows the industry to operate is that of *uberrima fides* (utmost good faith): the belief that each side should disclose all the relevant information available' (The Royal Society and the Actuarial Profession 1997: 3).

10 The ABI is the main institutional body representing the interests of the insurance industry in the UK. It represents some 440 companies, accounting for over 95 per cent of insurance businesses. Its operation is supported by a number of contributory organisational channels including the Continuous Mortality Investigation Bureau and the Institute of Actuaries.

11 The ABI defines a genetic test as 'an examination of the chromosome, DNA or RNA to find out if there is an otherwise undetectable disease related genotype, which may indicate an increased chance of that individual developing a specific disease in the future' (Association of British Insurers 1997a: 2).

12 Based on consideration of the detailed submission from the ABI, the Genetics and Insurance Committee (GAIC), a non-statutory Advisory Committee with a UK-wide remit, announces its decision in October 2000 that the reliability and relevance of the genetic test for Huntington's Disease is sufficient for insurance companies to use when assessing applications for life insurance. See James Meek 'Insurers to take on government over gene tests', *The Guardian*, 13 October.

13 Cf. accounts of embodied quantifying, for example, Watson (1990). See also Power (1995).

14 'Proposers have little knowledge of the terms offered to others with similar profiles, of the actuarial risk which their own profile represents, or of the factors insurers have used in setting premiums. They do not have the evidence to judge whether the terms they have been offered are fair or reasonable; nor do they have the evidence to judge whether the terms they have been offered discriminate unacceptably in other ways' (Human Genetics Advisory Commission 1997: 16).

15 See ABI Code of Practice (1997a: 22), paragraph 23.

16 On the cultural significance of physical space in laboratory settings and critical discussions of science and spatial topology, see Latour and Woolgar (1986); Mol and Law (1994); Lynch (1991).

17 Examples of the kinds of analyses scientists perform using the database system include mapping of restriction enzyme sites and the translation and location of potential protein-coding regions. One of the most common uses of sequence databases is for inter- and intrasequence homology searches. Homology in this context is a theoretical construct that refers to two similar DNA sequences assumed to be linked in evolutionary terms to a common ancestor.

18 For instance, pieces of human DNA, cut into sizes of varying length, are cloned into the genomes of bacteriophage or other 'vectors' that can be kept in culture, and 'ordered' or arranged in linear sequences by means of experiment and statistical algorithms run on computer software packages.

19 However, these homologies are theoretical in more than just their abstraction. The 'science' of matching DNA samples in applied settings (for example between suspects in criminal cases as evidence for conviction) can be inexact and less foolproof than scientists are usually willing to acknowledge. Also, the design decisions about these databases shape what can be most readily compared to what else, and determine therefore the kinds of uses that can be made of the raw 'original' data; for instance, what precisely counts as natural and of how much nature to exclude

from theoretical formulae. In other words, design decisions, which at point of practice are rendered invisible, keep informing the very kinds of ideas and constructs of human nature, and indeed species, that can be sustained by such theoretical work (Downey 1998).

20 Public research effort represented by the transnational Human Genome Project on the one hand, and private sequencing competition on the other, converges around debates on property rights on the human genome and patent applications. This has been brought to a head in the United States by the 'shot-gun' sequencing approach of bio-industrialist Craig Venter who in 1998 established a joint venture between the Institute for Genomics Research (TIGR) and Celera Genomics to pick the 'crown jewels' of the human genome (Lehmann and Lorch 1999: 7). Venter's aim has been the identification of those genes that have the most commercial potential for further drug and pharmaceutical development.

21 On aspects of the politics of science research, funding and the implications for career pathways, see Latour and Woolgar (1986) and Knorr-Cetina (1999).

22 Alan Sokal's inflammatory famous 'hoax' essay originally published in *Social Text* has since been reprinted in the extended critique by A. Sokal and J. Bricmont (1997) *Intellectual Impostures*, London: Profile Books. For social science commentary on the 'science wars', see *Social Text* 46/47, Volume 14, Nos 1–2 (special issue 'Science Wars'). Critical perspectives on the 'disunity of science' have so far discussed knowledge as epistemological practice. Claims relating to the epistemological 'disunity of science' may be seen as self-organising in other contexts in which knowledge is not synonymous with a goal-driven end pursuit, but is part of a broader (auto) generative system.

23 The UK government's science budget from 1998–99 to 2001–02 prioritises genome research with increased allocations of £90 million to a total of £334 million to the Medical Research Council and £50 million to £208 million to the Biotechnology and Biological Sciences Research Council (Office of Science and Technology 1998).

24 Compare with the strategic elitism of other nation states to promote themselves as powerful global actors in and brokers of cultural policy formation, for example Japan (Traweek 1992) and the European Union (Shore 1993). In the manner of a network's natural expansiveness, strategic (national) elitism can also make appeals to the 'private' concerns of individual welfare. Philippe Busquin, EU Commissioner for Science Research responsible for preliminary discussions of Framework 6 with the European Parliament, recently justified increased science research expenditure thus: 'European citizens need scientific knowledge to avoid getting lost in their own lives, just as Europe's scientific expertise needs a higher level of acceptance' (Martin Ince 1999 'Spreading the EU science net', *The Times Higher Educational Supplement*, 17 December, 24–5).

25 For example, questions of ethics and problems relating to confidentiality and kinship may be approached through further critical investigative research on the way such notions as 'disability' and 'personhood' are culturally appropriated by different interest and user groups as legal and political strategy (see for example Mulkay 1997; Rapp 1991; Weir 1996).

26 See for example the ABI Citizens' Jury and its deliberation over a four-day period in November 1997 on the following questions: 'Should insurance companies continue to have access to the results of genetic tests? What responsibilities do the insurance industry and government have for meeting the insurance needs of citizens?' See also the Citizens' Jury conducted in 1998 by the Welsh Institute for Health and Social Care, University of Glamorgan which sat to consider: 'What conditions should be fulfilled before genetic testing for susceptibility to common diseases becomes widely available on the NHS?'. Since 1987, the Danish Board of

Technology has run a series of 'consensus conferences' on subjects such as human molecular genetics, food irradiation and childlessness. Lay panel reports have been presented to the Danish Parliament, and in several cases these reports have influenced the course of public debate and policy making. On the Danish experience, as well as biotechnology and science promotion in the Nordic countries, see Miettinen (1999).

Bibliography

Amit, Vered (ed.) (2000) *Reconstructing the Field*, London: Routledge.

Appadurai, Arjun (1986) 'Introduction: Commodities and the Politics of Value', in A. Appadurai (ed.), *The Social Life of Things: Commodities in Cultural Perspective*, Cambridge: Cambridge University Press.

Association of British Insurers (1997a) *Genetic Testing. ABI Code of Practice*, London: ABI.

—— (1997b) *Policy Statement on Life Insurance and Genetics* (Industry Briefing), London: ABI.

Augé, Marc (1998) *A Sense for the Other: The Timeliness and Relevance of Anthropology*, trans. A. Jacobs, Stanford, CA: Stanford University Press.

Beidelman, Thomas (1989) 'Agonistic Exchange: Homeric Reciprocity and the Heritage of Simmel and Mauss', *Cultural Anthropology*, 4 (3): 227–59.

Burgess, M. and Hayden, M. (1996) 'Patients' Rights to Laboratory Data: Trinucleotide Repeat Length in Huntington's Disease', *American Journal of Medical Genetics* 62: 6–9.

Callon, Michel (1986) 'Some Elements of a Sociology of Translation: Domestification of the Scallops and Fishermen of St. Brieuc Bay', in J. Law (ed.), *Power, Action, Belief: A New Sociology of Knowledge?*, London: Routledge and Kegan Paul, 196–233.

—— (1987) 'Society in the Making: The Study of Technology as a Tool for Sociological Analysis', in W.E. Bijker, T.P. Hughes and T.J. Pinch (eds), *The Social Construction of Technological Systems*, Cambridge, MA: MIT Press.

Callon, Michel, Law, John and Rip, Arie (eds) (1986) *Mapping the Dynamics of Science and Technology: Sociology of Science in the Real World*, London: Macmillan.

Caplan, P. (ed.) (2000) *Risk Revisited*, London: Pluto Press.

Clarke, Adele and Fujimura, Joan (eds) (1992) *The Right Tools for the Job*, Princeton, NJ: Princeton University Press.

Clifford (1997) 'Spatial Practices', in A. Gupta and J. Ferguson (eds), *Anthropological Locations: Boundaries and Grounds of a Field Science*, Berkeley, CA: University of California Press, 185–222.

Czarniawska, Barbara (1997) *Narrating the Organisation: Dramas of Institutional Identity*, Chicago: University of Chicago Press.

Davies, M. (1997) 'Shattered Assumptions: Time and the Experience of Long-Term HIV Positivity', *Social Science and Medicine* 44: 561–71.

Douglas, Mary (1987) *How Institutions Think*, London: Routledge and Kegan Paul.

Downey, Gary Lee (1998) *The Machine in Me*, New York: Routledge.

Dubinskas, Frank A. (1988) *Making Time: Ethnographies of High-Technology Organisations*, Philadelphia: Temple University Press.

Ettorre, Elisabeth (1999) 'Experts as "Storytellers" in Reproductive Genetics: Exploring Key Issues', in P. Conrad and J. Gabe (eds), *Sociological Perspectives in the New Genetics*, Oxford: Blackwell, 35–57.

Foster, Robert (1995) 'Value Without Equivalence: Exchange and Replacement in a Melanesian Society', *Man*, n.s. 25: 54–69.

Foucault, Michel (1990) 'Right of Death and Power over Life', *The History of Sexuality*, vol. 1, London: Penguin.

Galison, Peter and Stump, David (1996) *The Disunity of Science: Boundaries, Contexts and Power*, Stanford, CA: Stanford University Press.

Gregory, Christopher (1982) 'Alienating the Inalienable', *Man*, n.s. 17 (2): 340–45.

Grobstein, Clifford (1990) 'Genetic Manipulation and Experimentation', in D.R. Bromham, M.E. Dalton and J.C. Jackson (eds), *Philosophical Ethics in Reproductive Medicine*, Manchester: Manchester University Press, 15–30.

Harding, Sandra (1998) *Is Science Multicultural? Postcolonialism, Feminisms, and Epistemologies*, Bloomington, Indiana University Press.

Harrison, Simon (1995) 'Anthropological Perspectives on the Management of Knowledge', *Anthropology Today* 11 (5): 10–14.

House of Lords (2000) Select Committee on Science and Technology, *Science and Society* (Third Report), London: HMSO.

Huber, Peter W. (1991) *Galileo's Revenge: Junk Science in the Courtroom*, New York: Basic Books.

Human Genetics Advisory Commission (1997) *The Implications of Genetic Testing for Insurance*, London: HGAC.

Hymes, Dell (1969) 'The Use of Anthropology: Critical, Political, Personal', in D. Hymes (ed.), *Reinventing Anthropology*, New York: Vintage.

Jamieson, Mark (1999) 'The Place of Counterfeits in Regimes of Value: An Anthropological Approach', *Journal of the Royal Anthropological Institute* 5 (1): 1–11.

Jones, Carol A. (1993) *Expert Witnesses: Science, Medicine and the Practice of Law*, Oxford: Oxford University Press.

Kleinman, Arthur (1995) 'Pain and Resistance: The Delegitimation and Relegitimation of Local Moral Worlds', in A. Kleinman, *Writing at the Margin. Discourse Between Anthropology and Medicine*, Berkeley, CA: University of California Press, 120–46.

Knorr-Cetina, Karin (1999) *Epistemic Cultures. How the Sciences Make Knowledge*, Cambridge, MA: Harvard University Press.

Konrad, Monica (1998) 'Ova Donation and Symbols of Substance: Some Variations on the Theme of Sex, Gender and the Partible Person, *Journal of the Royal Anthropological Institute* 4: 643–67.

—— (1999a) 'Foretelling Fore-Knowledge: Medical Histories and Huntington's Disease', paper presented to the Medical Anthropology Section of the Royal Anthropological Institute/British Sociological Association Autobiography Study Group at *Narrative, Illness and the Body* Conference, University of Bristol, 20 March.

—— (1999b) 'Technogenesis: The Beginnings of Microkinship', paper presented to *Kinship and Temporality* Conference, Goldsmiths College, 16–18 December.

—— (2000) 'Remodelling Anthropos?: Posthumanism and Life Science Cultures', paper presented to Anthropology Department, University of Manchester, 27 March.

Latour, Bruno (1988) *The Pasteurization of France*, trans. A. Sheridan and J. Law, Cambridge, MA: Harvard University Press.

—— (1993) *We Have Never Been Modern*, trans. C. Porter, London: Harvester Wheatsheaf.

—— (1999) *Pandora's Hope: Essays on the Reality of Science Studies*, Cambridge, MA: Harvard University Press.

Latour, Bruno and Steve Woolgar (1986)[1979] *Laboratory Life: The Construction of Scientific Facts*, Princeton, NJ: Princeton University Press.

Law, John (ed.) (1991) *A Sociology of Monsters: Essays on Power, Technology and Domination*, London: Routledge.

Law, John and Hassard, John (eds) (1999) *Actor Network Theory and After*, Oxford: Blackwell/The Sociological Review.

Lehmann, Volker and Lorch, Antje (1999) 'The Race for the Human Genome', *Biotechnology and Development Monitor* 40: 6–9.

Lynch, Michael (1991) 'Laboratory Space and the Technological Complex: An Investigation of Topical Contextures', *Science in Context* 41: 81–109.

Marcus, George (1998) *Ethnography through Thick and Thin*, Princeton, NJ: Princeton University Press.

Mauss, Marcel (1990)[1925] *The Gift*, trans. W.D. Halls, London: Routledge.

Miettinen, Reijo (ed.) (1999) *Biotechnology and Public Understanding of Science. Proceedings of the UK-Nordic Co-operative Seminar Helsinki*, 25–27 October 1998, Helsinki: Edita.

Mol, Annemarie and Law, John (1994) 'Regions, Networks and Fluids: Anaemia and Social Topology', *Social Studies of Science* 24: 641–71.

Mulkay, Michael (1997) *The Embryo Research Debate: Science and the Politics of Reproduction*, Cambridge: Cambridge University Press.

Nader, Laura (1969) 'Up the Anthropologist – Perspectives Gained from Studying Up', in D. Hymes (ed.), *Reinventing Anthropology*, New York: Vintage, 248–311.

Office of Science and Technology (1998) *Science Funding 1998–2002*, London: OST.

Office of Science and Technology (1999) *The Advisory and Regulatory Framework for Biotechnology: Report from the Government's Review*, London: OST.

Power, M. (ed.) (1995) *Accounting and Science: National Inquiry and Commercial Reason*, Cambridge: Cambridge University Press.

Rabinow, Paul (1999) *French DNA: Trouble in Purgatory*, Chicago and London: University of Chicago Press.

Rapp, Rayna (1991) 'Moral Pioneers', in M. di Leonardo (ed.), *Gender at the Crossroads of Knowledge: Feminist Anthropology in the Postmodern Era*, Berkeley, CA: University of California Press.

Rappaport, Roy (1993) 'Distinguished Lecture in General Anthropology: The Anthropology of Trouble', *American Anthropologist* 95 (2): 295–303.

Rose, Hilary (1994) *Love, Power and Knowledge. Towards a Feminist Transformation of the Sciences*, Cambridge: Polity Press.

Royal Society and the Actuarial Profession (1997) *Human Genetics – Uncertainties and the Financial Implications Ahead*, Chesham: Prestige Press (UK) Ltd.

Shapin, Steven (1988) 'The House of Experiment in Seventeenth-Century England', *Isis* 79: 373–404.

Shore, Cris (1993) 'Inventing the "People's Europe": Critical Perspectives on EU Cultural Policy', *Man* n.s. 28 (4): 779–800.

Sinclair, Simon (1997) *Making Doctors: An Institutional Apprenticeship*, Oxford: Berg.

Strathern, Marilyn (1991) *Partial Connections*, Association for Social Anthropology in Oceania special publication 3, Savage, MD: Rowman & Littlefield.

—— (1996) 'Cutting the Network', *Journal of the Royal Anthropological Institute*, n.s. 2: 517–35.

Traweek, Sharon (1992) 'Border Crossings: Narrative Strategies in Science Studies and among Physicists in Tsukuba Science City', in A. Pickering (ed.), *Science as Practice and Culture*, Chicago: University of Chicago Press, 429–65.

Watson, Helen (1990) 'Investigating the Social Foundations of Mathematics: Natural Number in Culturally Diverse Forms of Life', *Social Studies of Science* 29: 283–312.

Weiner, Annette (1992) *Inalienable Possessions. The Paradox of Keeping-While-Giving*, Berkeley, CA and Los Angeles: University of California Press.

Weir, Lorna (1996) 'Recent Developments in the Government of Pregnancy', *Economy and Society* 25: 372–92.

Wexler, Nancy S. (1979) 'Genetic "Russian Roulette": The Experience of Being at Risk for Huntington's Disease: Harbinger of the New Genetics', in S. Kessler (ed.), *Genetic Counselling*, New York: Academic Press, 199–220.

Young, Allan (1981) 'When Rational Men Fall Sick: An Inquiry into Some Assumptions Made by Anthropologists', *Culture, Medicine and Psychiatry* 19: 1–38.

Chapter 15

Anthropologists: lions and/or foxes

An afterword

Ronald Frankenberg

Elite is a term (both of pride and abuse: equivalents/opposites like Durkheim's sacred and profane) within so-called natural language. It is also a conceptual term of art for scholars in political science and its anthropological offshoots. The excitement of this book derives from the partially resolved tensions of its multivocality, of its ambivalent claims. The papers have a clear unity, over and above this, which arises first from the surprisingly still-surviving shared outlook of the social organisation style of even those ASA participants who still recognise culture as a concept rather than as a way of life. Second its shape derives from the dual nature of textual production and the words that constitute its raw material. The unity of the book's argument lies not only in its study of very diverse elites in widely scattered areas but also in its very method of using a concept of elite as a productive device. The writers have used this to produce a series of texts and, above all, leave us with a number of useful questions to seek to answer and elaborate elsewhere. This method, a kind of thought experiment, is at once highly rational and totally unrealistic or perhaps non-real: a heuristic device of pretending to accept in advance the existence of elites as grounded entities. It is an approach as classical in anthropology as it is in theoretical natural science and other analytical (rather than descriptive) scholarship and, of course, in the practice of daily life. Evans-Pritchard (1940), after all, took seriously the Nuer's acting as if lineages existed and analysed their social reality as if they did. In this way he demonstrated the extent to which their desired realities were produced or destroyed by this belief. Lineage proved less useful (a masterpiece of understatement) in analysing New Guinea highlanders (Barnes 1962). Similarly the concept of blood relationship, which its inhabitants use to organise family reality in a Northern British town, is adopted and used by Jeanette Edwards (1999). It could, perhaps, be used in the same way in parts of 'traditional' Hackney or respectable New York but not on the wilder shores of bohemian Islington or The Village. When Pareto (Bellamy 1987: ch. 2; Bottomore 1964) early in the century introduced elite theory as a method of analysis in order to understand and to change rationalities and irrationalities in Italian society, he first used the concept in this kind of way with a very broad series of criteria marking different elites. Later as he moved towards both understanding and providing an ideological basis for fascism, he essentialised them into just two circulating types derived from Machiavelli: Lions who ruled by force and Foxes who ruled by cunning. Despite this unfortunate beginning, partly rehabilitated by C. Wright Mills (1956) in the US and Bottomore (1964) in Britain, elites as a concept remain a useful way of organising our understanding of the production of hierarchy, differential power, status and cultural display in many social areas where such processes exist. What anthropologists (like some but not all other social scientists) are always studying are the processes of production of social outcomes. One cannot choose one's theoretical device for this until one has identified which of them seem to be crucial to those whose reality one seeks to understand. Medical diagnosis, for example, relies crucially on how the patient chooses to answer the question 'What *seems* to be the matter?' which in turn depends on the mutually shared understanding of the parties on what a doctor/patient culture might be expected to be able to produce (Mol 1998, 2000; Konrad, Chapter 14 in this volume). Anthropological analysis again entirely depends on the practitioners' sharing of reality with those practised upon. This can only be discovered by the anthropologists' bringing their view of reality as close as possible (even if only temporarily) to that of the people they are studying. Many conventional sociologists practising outsider, rear-view mirror analyses (as McLuhan informally used to call them) do not aspire to this and physicians and nurses are least effective in dealing with patients' personal suffering (but not necessarily, bodily disease) since their rigorous training in avoiding involvement is unfortunately inappropriately successful (Good 1994: ch. 3).

Is it perhaps possible that all anthropology is what has come to be called autoanthropology? Was it only Sir James Frazer who never left home? It is true, in one sense, as Cris Shore argues in his introduction, that British social anthropologists have a natural (by which as usual is meant a cultural) propensity towards elite analysis since they themselves seem to constitute an elite or at least once did, and that radical US culturalists urged them to study up (i.e. those whom *they*, but see Hart, this volume, perceive to be elite) rather than down. The book may therefore be an achievement not just in the analysis of the other but a belated and unsuccessful form of judo-like self-defense! Peers are us! As one who in the 1960s frequented the seminars and conferences of both sociology and anthropology, I was conscious at the time and wrote about (Frankenberg 1990) the sometimes non-natal, sometimes dynastic, hyphenated names, Oxbridge College venues and hacking jackets of the latter and the monosyllabic monikers, denim clothes and Liverpool, Nottingham, Leicester student blocks of the former. Only LSE liminally (not marginally) straddled both worlds, patronised, and was frequented by, both, but usually only for day trips. Some who now share anthropologists' interest in popular culture, at home perhaps rather than abroad, seek to avoid the stigma of elitism by avowing cultural studies, inadvertently

giving their enemies in government and broadsheet press the weapons they need
to counter the counterculture.

I suspected then, however, and still believe that those anthropologists, at
least in their professional capacity, were the poor of the metropolitan elite
studying the elite of the colonial (and soon to be postcolonial) poor. Like
Church of England evangelists and missionaries at home and abroad they
frequented the very poor and (at least in the African ethnography with which
I am most familiar) by colonial standards, the very rich. The assertion, for
example, that class did not exist in Africa was based partly on a consumption
view of class (Frankenberg 1978); the aristocratic elites of African kingdoms,
unlike Indian princes, were no better off than the common people apparently,
seen from the viewpoint of the certainly richer whites. Anthropologists
replaced what Radcliffe-Brown (Gluckman 1965: 2) called the 'If I were a
horse' methodology of the intellectualists in their armchairs (described by
Evans-Pritchard 1933) with the 'If they were my tribe' attitude immortalised
in Barbara Pym's novels (1980: 88, 1955: 66) when custom and practice
unearthed and analysed by one colleague in 'their tribe' were critiqued and re-
analysed on the principle of 'If a New Guinea Highlander was a Nuer' but also
often in terms of 'If an "X" chief was an "X" commoner'. What they needed
and still need to do is to study those not marginalised, but liminal, those in the
middle: those who face both ways and might be hypothesised as helping to
produce both the lower boundary of those above and the upper boundary of
those beneath. And it may be here that the nature of text and the concept of
elite becomes most pertinent. It is also not only in colonial times that the elite
may live geographically elsewhere: absent landlords of local power and culture.
Some of the 'natives' moreover may have seen even the resident colonial elite
above them as more unitary than it was in reality. Many, as the system moved
towards its transformation, recognised and made use of the literally marked
differences among the whites (see Gluckman 1942). In immediate post-
independence Zambia, when customs of interpersonal deference were in a
melting pot of liminality, a public works department employee told me with
approval that, unlike the recently departed governor, when the new vice president was on tour even PWD officers and their wives were officially presented.
It had made a difficulty for his wife, he went on to explain, because it had
meant shaking hands with a black man. She had solved the problem, not by
withdrawing from the situation but by wearing a bandage and explaining that
she had cut her hand, significantly while cutting bread. She simultaneously
through complex body symbolism claimed her new elite status while asserting
and maintaining the domestic and public consciousness of the old.

The apparent, but at the same time justifiable, inconsistency of the use of
the term elite in this book and elsewhere also arises from the fact that like
anthropology, organisation, society, and indeed a book in the hands, eyes and
mind of a reader, an elite is, both in its emic and its etic guise, at once both
ongoing process and aspired-to thing. The members of elites are forced to

perceive themselves as entities in order to seek, as the detailed subject matter of the book demonstrates throughout, to maintain themselves through cultural and physical practices. Their victories, like charismatic status, have to be continually replayed to remain as victories. Hostile non-members of elites, as is again frequently demonstrated in the volume, are forced to see their enemies as members of entities in order to mobilise potential, personal and behavioural allies against other individuals and groups. In both cases they identify movement towards (and potential movement away from) as always-already achieved although it remains an aspiration towards a hoped for virtual reality; an imagined or imaged used-to-be that one must strive to restore and reclaim. Weber (1948) pointed out, using what he regarded as a largely fraudulent German aristocracy, Swiss bourgeois and the First Families of Virginia as examples, the more elites (status groups in his term) are threatened, the more assertive their display of status honour becomes. As Victor Turner (1974: ch. 1) might have said had Walter Benjamin (1973) already become fashionable in his day: 'Structure is process looked back on in tranquility or would be if tranquility were ever possible'. Anthropologists are normally obliged by their version of grounded theory and their fieldwork approach to endure and to work with the complexity of meaning of the subject's and the subjects' discourse in a way that sociologists, historians and others may choose, but are not compelled, to do.

An historical monograph or paper, for example, analyses or describes an event or geographical location at a particular time in general terms or in terms of a particular interest as, for example, law, politics or surgery. My own special interest in anthropological matters medical means that I may refer to texts by historians on the plague in fourteenth-century Venice, seventeenth-century Britain, nineteenth-century China and twentieth-century India and the USA. In each case I am looking for specific answers to questions that I define about how difference is produced in the experienced sociocultural and personal reality of (endemic, epidemic or individual) disease. I assume that outbreaks of plague in different places and times are sufficiently similar to make fruitful comparisons of the social causes, cultural realities and economic outcomes. I can pose questions about the texts that are nearly always different from the questions posed by the original authors in their production. I might even, guided by general works on plagues in history, produce an anthology, as conference collection or a course outline, juxtaposing diverse accounts in divers places and seeking to produce, to the anathema of respectable scholarly historians focused on primary sources, a theory of incidence, prevalence, even causation and consequences of plague and epidemics in general. Indeed, at the first of the two conferences (one in the USA, one in the UK, but including African scholars as well as those from Australia and other parts of Europe and the Americas) which, in Washington DC in 1972, laid the foundations of medical anthropology as a discipline, the very first speaker was the historian William H. McNeill who gave a preview of his later book *Plagues and Peoples*

(1976) which did just that. Such an activity involved for him treating his historian colleagues as primary sources; both elevating them by accepting their accounts as sufficiently reliable and demeaning them by rejecting or ignoring their conventional particularising theories in favour of his own generalising ones.

Shortly afterwards I was deeply shocked, in my youthful innocence, at one of the earlier conferences on the then burgeoning but still budding discipline of African history to hear scholars, to me irreverently, discussing the reliability of the writings of the already late Max Gluckman as primary sources for the historiography of Southern Africa. He, although white and Jewish, was after all an inhabitant of both Zululand and Barotseland in crucial periods of their history. My explosive intervention outlining the elegance and intellectual power of his theories of law and kingship, and his influence on British sociology and anthropology, was listened to politely and such examples as I gave from the master's unpublished works noted lest I, one day, might also become a useful primary source on the history of anthropology. Indeed, in the corridors and bars, competing claims for the final resting place of Gluckman's papers on Barotseland were being asserted by historians of Africa against those of his anthropological followers. (The results seem to have been an equitable draw?)

Many of the studies in this volume have produced and presented relevant, topical and specific information, fashionably useful (in Research Council and policy terms) to those concerned, whether as part of global or of local elites, with bringing about beneficial change. They may provide immediate offensive ammunition for those concerned with the overthrow of those above them or defensive shields for those defending established elite positions, food for the foxes and the lions amongst each. The ethnographic present is relevant to the prospective future. At the same time, as well as when, in the more distant future, the particularities are no longer present, they can also be described as 'merely' academic, that is, like those as of the classical academies, of truly lasting significance, and not just as primary sources to be weighed critically by future historians. We now know more than Marx about late nineteenth-century political economies and more than Freud about early twentieth-century psychic structures, and we have some knowledge of what they were wrong about. Their answers were, like ours are also sure to be, often wrong and have therefore become uninteresting. The questions they asked however were by definition neither true nor false but meaningful and capable of development, food for the foxes. So may it be with us!

Bibliography

Barnes, J.A. (1962) 'African Models in the New Guinea Highlands', *Man* 62: 5–9.

Bellamy, Richard (1987) *Modern Italian Social Theory*, Oxford: Polity Press.

Benjamin, Walter (1973[1940]) 'Theses on the Philosophy of History', in Hannah Arendt (ed.), *Illuminations*, London: Collins/Fontana.

Bottomore, T.B. (1964) *Elites and Society*, London: Watts.

Edwards, Jeanette (1999) *Born and Bred*, Oxford: Oxford University Press.

Evans-Pritchard, E.E. (1933) 'The Intellectualist (English) Interpretation of Magic', *Bulletin of the Faculty of Arts*, Cairo, Egyptian University, II: 1–21.

—— (1940) *The Nuer*, Oxford: Clarendon Press.

Frankenberg, Ronald (1963) 'Participant Observers', *New Society* 7 March, reprinted in Frankenberg (1990: 194–99).

—— (1978) 'The Barotse Social Formation: A Case Study', in John Clammer (ed.), *The New Economic Anthropology*, London: Macmillan, 31–60.

—— (1990[1957]) *Village on the Border*, Prospect Heights, IL: Waveland Press.

Gluckman, Max (1958[1940, 1942]) *Analysis of a Social Situation in Modern Zululand*, Rhodes Livingstone Paper No. 28, Manchester and Lusaka: Manchester University Press.

—— (1965) *Politics, Law and Ritual in Tribal Society*, Oxford: Basil Blackwell.

Good, Byron (1994) *Medicine, Rationality and Experience: An Anthropological Perspective*, Cambridge: Cambridge University Press.

McNeill, W.H. (1976) *Plagues and Peoples*, Oxford: Blackwell.

Mills, C. Wright (1956) *The Power Elite*, Oxford: Oxford University Press.

Mol, Annemarie (1998) '"Missing Links", Making Links: On the Performance of Some Atheroscleroses', in Marc Berg and Annemarie Mol (eds), *Differences in Medicine: Unraveling Practices, Techniques and Bodies*, Durham, NC and London: Duke University Press, 145–65.

—— (2000) 'Pathology and the Clinic: An Ethnographic Presentation of Two Atheroscleroses', in Margaret Lock, Allan Young and Alberto Cambrosio (eds), *Living and Working with the New Medical Technologies: Intersections of Inquiry*, Cambridge: Cambridge University Press, 82–102.

Pym, Barbara (1980[1952]) *Excellent Women*, Harmondsworth: Penguin Books.

—— (1955) *Less Than Angels*, London: Jonathan Cape.

Turner, Victor (1974) *Dramas, Fields and Metaphors: Symbolic Action in Human Society*, Durham, NC and London: Duke University Press.

Weber, Max (1948) 'Class, Status and Party', in H.H. Gerth and C. Wright Mills (ed. and trans.), *From Max Weber: Essays in Sociology*, London: Routledge and Kegan Paul, 180–85.

Index